CHINESE HERITAGE COOKING

FROM MY

AMERICAN KITCHEN

CHINESE HERITAGE COOKING

FROM MY

AMERICAN KITCHEN

DISCOVER AUTHENTIC FLAVORS
WITH VIBRANT, MODERN RECIPES

SHIRLEY CHUNG

CHEF AND OWNER OF MS. CHI CAFÉ

PAGE STREET
PUBLISHING CO.

First published in 2018 by
Page Street Publishing Co.
27 Congress Street, Suite 105
Salem, MA 01970
www.pagestreetpublishing.com

Distributed by Macmillan, sales in Canada by The Canadian Manda Group.

22 21 20 19 18 1 2 3 4 5

ISBN-13: 978-1-62414-677-0
ISBN-10: 1-62414-677-5

Library of Congress Control Number: 2018948765

Cover and book design by Laura Gallant for Page Street Publishing Co.
Photography by Albert Law

Printed and bound in the United States

Page Street Publishing protects our planet by donating to nonprofits like The Trustees, which focuses on local land conservation.

This book is dedicated to my grandma Silvia Siyi Liang, who introduced the world to me through food and culture. It's also dedicated to Jimmy Lee, who constantly pushes me to be better; you are my rock, my foundation.

CONTENTS

FOREWORD

From the moment I first met Shirley Chung through her work on *Top Chef*, I knew she was going to leave a mark on the food industry in a big way. As we got to know each other, I realized that her being born and raised in a supersized city like Beijing, China, must have prepared her in many ways to succeed in the restaurant world of America as an immigrant and a woman. Sure, immigrants and women have and continue to be the backbone of the food service world, but in the world of fine dining, the hierarchies are patriarchal. By working her way up the ladder, proving and reproving herself, and putting up with the slings and arrows of daily restaurant life, her skills were quickly mastered. Her talent for leadership and cooking became clearly defined, grown and honed to a razor's edge. She was part of the opening team at Thomas Keller's Bouchon, Mario Batali's chef de cuisine at Carnevino and the chef at José Andrés' China Poblano in Las Vegas, to name a few. Bravo gave her a shot in *Top Chef*'s season 11 and again in season 14, and a star was born. With her infectious smile, quick wit and unselfish spirit she became a fan favorite. The post-TV years have been filled with ups and downs, some restaurant projects abated, a new dumpling restaurant called Ms. Chi Café opened and now this book. So she's a TV chef, right? Dead wrong.

Chefs in America today, if they have the talent, are invariably sucked up by the modern media machine, packaged and presented. Many are emperors with no clothes, many others are some of the most serious, bright and earnest culinarians in our country. Those characteristics don't make for great TV in the competition genre, where challenges often don't showcase the best aspects of what it means to be a chef, a true leader, inspiring and dedicated to the craft of making and sharing great food. Shirley Chung is a great cook—a superb chef, in fact—who happens to have been on TV, and this book is all the proof you need if you haven't been able to meet her or taste her food.

Shirley found her voice, her style and her point of view on TV because it forced her to have an internal reckoning. "What do you want to say as a chef?" is the question I always ask when mentoring young cooks with giant-sized aspirations. Shirley's upbringing in China, her move to America as a teenager, her short-lived career in the tech world and her many years of cooking in some great restaurants forced her to answer that question in front of a global audience. Soulful Chinese heritage cuisine, shot through the prism of American modernist cookery, is her niche. Rather than seeking to be the authoritative voice speaking for all eight major regions of Chinese cooking, she chose her own path, guided by her own experience, a vital decision that should be a signpost for all cooks to follow. The results of that choice are in your hands.

In this book Shirley makes the case, brilliantly, of when to be honest and authentic and when to simply make great food that's relevant to our way of eating and celebrating in America today. Her simple attitude about when to wok and when not to, along with her master class on noodles, are testaments to both sides of the equation. Woks aren't a necessity; there are many ways to achieve the effects of wok cookery without a slavish reliance on them. Noodles, well, that's a different story. Two of her recipes sum it up best for me. First, her Tiger Tiger Sauce (page 152). I had the same reaction that she did when I tasted my first version of this dipping sauce in south-eastern China over twenty years ago. The crunch and piquancy of the pickled radish swimming in a soy-based, herb-spiked puddle of flavor reminded me of regional salsas I had eaten in Mexico, more philosophically than flavor wise, but achieving the same effect. The perfect companion for many foods, this sauce can be served with anything. Beholden not to tradition, but to the exacting demands of flavor and texture and the ultimate litmus test: Does it taste good? And does it work for the way we eat today? It sure does. Make a big batch and keep it on hand in the fridge. I use it on day one for dipping boiled dumplings and on day four as a marinade for meat before grilling. It's brilliant.

As is her Grilled Asparagus with Fried Eggs (page 85). Asparagus with black bean sauce is a Chinese classic, and the sauce itself has become a bedrock of Chinese American cookery. The simple, salty-sweet sauce, a flavor bomb that acts as an accelerant to the explosion of flavor from the year's first asparagus, the umami of the fermented beans . . . everyone loves this dish. In fact, a version of it was the very first solid food my son ever ate. The addition of a fried egg, which to some might feel clichéd, is a superb choice. The crispy-edged whites and the runny yolk are a perfect platform for the sweet vegetal asparagus and a superb foil for the accessible funk of the black bean sauce. There is a real statement being made here by these and all the other recipes in the book.

Chinese American food is as valid and historically relevant a cuisine as any other. Yup, I said that. Let it sink in. Like Tex Mex, or a handful of other hybridized cuisines with a lengthy history and even more important legacy, it stands on its own. Thanks to 160 plus years of Chinese immigration to America, the 1882 law that halted immigration after the first wave and the rampant racism that created it, Chinese Americans settled into tight-knit communities and used entrepreneurship to establish business links within those communities and in the surrounding neighborhoods and cities. Creating laundries and restaurants were primary avenues of upward mobility, and foods were tweaked and developed for American palates, from Egg Foo Yong to Chop Suey, from Egg Rolls to Sweet & Sour Chicken. These were the vehicles for acceptance into an American society that inhales other people's cultures from around the world first and foremost on the end of a fork. For generations, Americans ate Chinese food almost universally designed not for subsequent waves of immigrants (that would come later) and not representative of true regional Chinese cooking that would explode after Nixon's Chinese sojourn in the early '70s, but for people who looked like me.

This is not food to be ignored. It's food to be celebrated and enjoyed. To treat it any other way would be to ignore the history, both good and bad, of the immigrant experience in America. As importantly, it would cast aside a whole world of flavors and dishes that are delicious and universally beloved. Even worse, it would invalidate the lives and loves of chefs and people like Shirley Chung, a brilliant and caring cook, a true culinarian who represents everything I love about this country and our pursuit to make the invisible known, to take the hidden and make it seen.

—Andrew Zimmern

Chef, TV Personality, Director, Producer and Author

INTRODUCTION

I am Chinese American. I was born in Beijing, and my family migrated back to the United States when I was in high school. I say migrated back because for five generations, the Chung family have been Chinese Americans from California. In 1900, my great-grandfather came to Southern California from Canton, China, because of the better life he heard existed in the "golden mountain." Later on he married my great-grandmother, who was the first Chinese girl ever born in Ventura. He sent his youngest son, my grandfather, back to China to study medicine. My grandfather then met my grandmother while at Beijing University. And that marked the beginning of my grandpa and grandma's thirty years of circular migration between China and the United States.

When I was born, my grandpa went back to California by himself due to a toxic political environment in China. My family was forced to be silent and told everyone, including me, that my grandfather had passed away before I was born.

I had the best childhood growing up in Beijing. While working for the Red Cross China as their foreign ambassador, my grandma believed in introducing me to world culture through food. Every time she came back from traveling, she would bring a local snack with a story. I learned to ask for "stinky feet" (cheese) if she was going to Switzerland and "chocolate bubbles" (Coca-Cola) if she traveled to the United States. When I was three, my favorite foods were ice cream, spaghetti and chocolate, and I would ask for them in English.

Grandma also brought me to the government's national banquets. I was never embarrassed about asking for the last piece of abalone, and I was always in awe of the beautifully carved vegetables and intricate plating of traditional, fancy Chinese cuisine. My grandma planted the seed for my love of food and food history: everything I ate had a story.

It's safe to say, I didn't grow up as a traditional Chinese. In my life, Western food and traditional Chinese food always exist side by side. Because grandma opened my palate at a young age, I became extremely picky about the quality of my meals. I was not happy with the way my nanny cooked, so I started to cook lunch for myself when I was eight years old. That very soon escalated to a big gathering of my schoolmates at my house after school, where I cooked them fried rice and noodle soup for fun.

Then I fell in love with Chinese literature, and the vivid paragraphs about food interested me the most. I remember I read that the best water to brew spring new harvest tea is the snow water you collect from the snow that lands on cherry blossoms. So I rushed out at the first sign of snow, climbed the cherry tree and sat on the tree branches waiting to collect water for tea. And the first essay I ever won an award for in school was about how I snuck behind my mom's back and went to the night market to feast on street foods with my best friend.

After my grandma passed away, my father's political career ended all of a sudden because he openly supported the Tiananmen Square student protest. Then he told me, for my future, for freedom of choice, we were moving back to the United States to be reunited with my grandpa, who was alive and well, still practicing medicine in Sonoma, California. And we have four generations of Chung relatives who all live in Los Angeles. I am a child of an American citizen, so I became an American.

Moving to a foreign country during high school was not the most fun time, and I found comfort in cooking. Food Network and PBS cooking shows taught me how to use American ingredients and also helped me learn English vocabulary. I started to cook dinner for my parents every day using the new techniques I learned, but with familiar Chinese flavors. After graduating from college, I started to work in the Silicon Valley, but the cooking bug never left me. I was able to go to the best restaurants in the Bay Area for dinner, and then come back and try to re-create the dishes at home for my friends. I had a dinner party every weekend, and my friends started to request that I cook them their birthday dinners.

The high-tech market crashed after a few crazy years, and I was at a startup that was about to run out of money. I had just started getting serious with my future hubby, Jimmy. He told me I should think about what I really love to do, because he was sick of listening to me complain about my boring high-tech career. I knew my love and passion was food. I had been exploring the world through eating since the age of three, but I had never considered cooking as a career because my family and everyone around me expected me to become a doctor, an engineer or a business woman.

I went to tour California Culinary Academy in San Francisco. From the moment I stepped into the building, I was intoxicated by the aroma of baking bread and pastry that permeated the air, the sound of chopping and slicing, the quiet "dances" performed by the students and chefs in the kitchen. The hair on the back of my neck stood up. My stomach sank. My heart was beating out of my chest. I felt love, and I knew I had found my calling.

Restaurant life is hard. My first paying job was working in Bouchon for Thomas Keller. I woke up at 2:30 a.m. every day so I could drive 2 hours from Fremont to Yountville and arrive before 5:00 a.m. to work as prep cook. My first project was to correctly re-ice fish shelves. I would maneuver fifty pounds (23 kg) of ice, fish and fish water by myself in the cold wine country mornings, happily humming "I am the champion" to push myself to work harder. Before this job, I was such a princess that I had never washed dishes at home, and I had spent all of my salary on shoes and a sports car. At twenty-eight years old, making less money than my first job in the United States as a barista, wearing ugly kitchen clogs, I had never been more fulfilled and happy.

Fast-forward to ten years later, I had an amazing culinary career in Las Vegas. I opened seven new restaurants for world-renowned chefs, and I cooked classic French, Italian, Mexican and Chinese cuisine. I was really good at translating my bosses' creative visions, and I built a little reputation for myself as the best shadow chef on the Las Vegas strip. I became an executive chef that restaurant groups headhunted. Coming back to California was always on my mind. Then, in 2013, as Jimmy and I were thinking about packing up and moving back, I was cast to compete on *Top Chef*.

I found my voice on *Top Chef*. When you are competing under so much pressure and limited time, there is no thinking; it's all reacting. What came natural to me the most was to use whatever technique the time called for, but to always cook with Chinese flavors. I was actually always a little intimidated by traditional Chinese cuisine because I have so much knowledge and know so much of its history. The more I learned, the more I felt like I didn't know enough. I didn't know which of the eight regions of Chinese cuisine I should focus on.

But, at the same time, I didn't want to give up all the techniques and the skill set I had accumulated over the years and fully dive into traditional Chinese cooking. Chinese people are good at integrating with other cultures through food. There is Korean-Chinese cuisine, Indo-Chinese and so many more—all use local ingredients and cooking techniques, but still make a version of Chinese cuisine that's authentic to the area. I realized I had become who I am as a chef. Deep Chinese culture is embedded in my blood. Chinese American, or American Chinese cuisine, is the food of my heritage.

I am so happy to share my heritage with you in this cookbook. I can't wait to show you how to cook soulful Chinese food, no matter where you live, without Chinese cookware and tools. I will teach you about how I marry traditional flavors with local seasonal ingredients, and how untraditional ingredients, such as butter, enhance an old recipe. Most importantly, thank you for letting me take you through my journey as a Chinese American chef.

PSSSST!

Let Me Give You Some Tips on Regional Chinese Ingredients

We don't have to use a wok to stir-fry, and we can use local vegetables and meats to produce delicious Chinese food. The secret is to use the correct sauces and condiments. We are cooking Chinese cuisine, so we will use Chinese soy sauce, chili paste and vinegars.

Did you know there are many different types of soy sauce? They vary based on how and when they were harvested and brewed. Each one has its own unique texture and flavor, and each one has its own purpose. I have about nine different types of soy sauce in my kitchen, but the three I use the most often are light, regular and dark soy.

Light soy is the saltiest out of all the soy sauces. Light means light in body, not light on sodium. It's best used for stir-fry vegetables, seasoning fish and when you want to use soy without the dark color. Regular soy sauce is the most balanced out of them all. It's harvested from the middle of the barrels. I like to use aged soy sauce. It's aged for more than three years in the barrel. It has an almost sweet taste to it, but because it's still so savory, it's the best all-around soy sauce. If I can only have one soy sauce in my kitchen, this is it. The final one is dark soy. It's darkest in color, but lowest in sodium. It has a molasses flavor to it, and it's best used for braising meats and for anything you want to give a deep amber color to.

The most popular cooking wine from China is called Shaoxing wine. It's light-gold in color, and warm and savory in taste. It's similar to a very dry vermouth, and it's a crucial ingredient in Chinese cuisine for cooking seafood and meat. It kills the gaminess of any protein. You can also warm it up and drink it with preserved sweet plums and rock sugar.

There are two types of black vinegar in China. The first one is Chinese Worcestershire sauce and we use it mostly for dipping. This is a new vinegar for us, and only started to be produced after British concession brought Worcestershire to Shanghai. It's not as potent as the regular American Worcestershire, so if you want to substitute, just dilute it with a little water. Chinkiang (Zhenjiang) vinegar is a traditional black vinegar from southern China; it is also called fragrance vinegar. It tastes like an earthy balsamic vinegar. It's my favorite vinegar to cook with, and it's the base of the original sweet-and-sour sauce.

Cantonese, Hong Kong–style cooking uses oyster sauce as one of the main seasoning sauces. Most of the old-school Chinese American restaurants are opened by Cantonese, so most stir-fries use it as a base for dishes such as beef and broccoli and cashew chicken.

Doubanjiang, fermented broad bean chili paste, is the base of famous Mapo Tofu (page 132) and Sichuan-style cooking. We also use it in many stir-fries and we use it to spice up many northern-style dishes. There are two types of fermented bean paste we use a lot in Beijing cooking. The famous Beijing duck sauce is made with sweet fermented bean paste, and if you combine it with soy bean paste, you will make my favorite Zhajiang Mian noodle sauce (page 61). We use bean paste in place of soy sauce a lot in northern China. So, now you are wondering why restaurants use hoisin sauce as duck sauce. It's because before all the fermented bean paste products were approved for import into the United States, only sauces from Hong Kong were allowed to come in to America. Hoisin sauce is sweeter than the fermented bean paste, but close enough to be substituted.

Beijing people also love sesame paste. The bottle I have in the picture is from an old shop that has thousands of years of history as the producer of sauces for the Emperor's kitchen. But make sure you read the labels—there are versions that have peanut butter mixed in. It's extra tasty, but be careful with allergies.

Now you have the basic building blocks of traditional Chinese flavors. I will continue to share a few unique ingredients with you in the recipes. You can find all these ingredients in Asian markets, or order them online. We can get pretty much everything at our fingertips nowadays. Armed with these flavors, let's go cook some Chinese food!

TO WOK OR NOT TO WOK?

用？或不用炒锅？

Meat Dishes from My Chinese American Kitchen

When it comes to Chinese cooking, one of the first things you're taught is to buy a wok. Well, the eagerness to learn how to cook Chinese dishes ends right there for many people because a wok is intimidating to use! In a traditional Chinese kitchen, a wok is an all-in-one cooking vessel. We use it to stir-fry, boil noodles, smoke chickens, char vegetables, deep-fry eggrolls—a wok is all you need.

When I came to the United States, the first apartment my family lived in only had an electric stove. It was very hard to use a traditional wok on the flat surface because of its round bottom. I soon discovered and began using cast-iron pans, the oven and the grill! I realized there are so many other kinds of pots, pans and tools to use. To cook Chinese food, you don't really need to use a wok.

A lot of wok cooking is about high-heat, fast cooking. The hot surface can instantly sear anything. The caramelization it creates at that moment even has a name: it's called "wok chi," wok's aroma, wok's energy. To create wok chi, you cook the meat or veggie to the perfect caramelized stage, with a little bit of char. The slight smokiness instantly adds a touch of savory flavor to anything. In my kitchen, I often create this "magical touch" by using a cast-iron pan over high heat, hard sear or grill over an open flame; the nice grill marks are just like wok chi!

So . . . to wok? Or not to wok? It's totally up to you! Use whatever is comfortable for you. In fact, none of the meat dishes in this chapter need to cook in a wok. We will be grilling, braising and sautéing. I will give you tips on heat control and timing. Very soon, you will be able to show off to your friends how you can cook Chinese food with anything. No wok? No problem!

GRILLED SKIRT STEAK WITH BROCCOLINI

Broccoli beef is one of the best known Chinese American dishes. This simple dish is very hard to execute perfectly because it requires extensive wok skill. I use a grill to make my version of broccoli beef, and I created the nice, charred "wok chi" flavor by giving the steaks nice grill marks. Broccolini is a closer cousin to Chinese broccoli, gai lan, than regular broccoli. It also grills a lot better. You might not want to go back to regular broccoli after you taste it!

SERVES 4

2 lb (900 g) skirt steak

Steak Marinade

1 bunch green onions

2 oz (56 g) ginger

2 oz (56 g) garlic

3 tbsp (45 ml) oyster sauce

2 tbsp (30 ml) soy sauce

2 tbsp (30 ml) canola oil

2 red onions

1 lb (450 g) broccolini

2 tbsp (30 ml) sesame oil

Kosher salt, to taste

1½ tbsp (11 g) ground black pepper, plus more to taste

Crunchy sea salt, to finish

PRO TIP: Serve this dish with the Black Pepper Sauce on page 163. Black pepper steak!!

Pat the skirt steak dry with paper towels. In a blender, combine the green onions, ginger, garlic, oyster sauce, soy sauce and cooking oil. Blend until smooth. Pour this mixture into a shallow bowl and rub it all over the steak. Allow to marinate for 1 hour.

Meanwhile, clean and peel the red onions. Slicing against the grain, cut them into 1-inch (2.5-cm) rings. Clean the broccolini and put them into a large bowl with the onions. Dress them with sesame oil, season with salt and pepper to taste and set aside.

Preheat the grill on high heat. After the steak is marinated, wipe off the marinade. Season the steak with all 1½ tablespoons (11 g) of black pepper on both sides, and salt to taste. It is very important to grill the steak over high heat so there is a nice char and a quick sear, just like cooking in a wok. Skirt steak is very thin, so it cooks really fast; each side will only take 90 seconds to 2 minutes for medium rare, which I think is the best temperature to enjoy this cut of steak.

Meanwhile, on the other side of the grill, char the red onions, about 2 minutes on each side. When both sides are charred, but the onions are still raw, place these into a salad bowl and cover with plastic wrap. The carry-over heat will create steam to finish cooking them. Lightly grill the broccolini for 1 quick minute, so they are still green and crunchy.

Allow the skirt steak to rest for a couple minutes before slicing. Set the steak on top of the red onion rings and the grilled broccolini. Finish with sea salt on the steak.

PRO TIP: To cook a thin piece of protein, give it a harder sear on one side. Cook until it's almost done on that side only. Then give it "a light kiss" by quickly cooking the other side for no more than 30 seconds. This way you will have a well-seared, caramelized crispy side with a lightly cooked tender side. This cooking technique works well on all meats and seafood.

SOY-GLAZED OXTAIL

In Chinese culture, we believe in eating everything from nose to tail—nothing goes to waste. I happen to love to cook and eat oxtail. I find it more flavorful than any other cut of beef, and it's the best cut for braising dishes. The rich and sweet soy glaze, balanced with a touch of heat from the dry and fresh chili peppers, all slowly cook into the oxtail, and pieces of meat fall off the bone and melt into the sauce. I always cook extra rice when I have this dish for dinner. Oh, the sauce makes the plain rice so good! You can always substitute chuck roast or short rib for oxtail in this recipe.

SERVES 4

2 lb (900 g) oxtail

2 oz (56 g) fresh ginger

2 oz (56 g) garlic

2 oz (56 g) green onions

1 cup (240 ml) aged soy sauce

2 cups (480 ml) Shaoxing wine

½ cup (120 ml) water

½ cup (120 ml) mirin wine

1 tsp black pepper

2 oz (56 g) rock sugar (can substitute raw sugar)

4 dried arbol chilies

2 star anise

1 stick cinnamon

2 tbsp (30 ml) oyster sauce

½ cup (120 ml) maltose (can substitute with agave syrup or corn syrup)

2 fresh Fresno chili peppers

3 leaves Napa cabbage

3 sprigs cilantro, for garnish

Clean the oxtail and trim off the extra fat, leaving a thin layer of fat surrounding the meat. Smash the ginger and garlic on the cutting board with the back of a chef's knife and roughly chop. Smashing the garlic and ginger will release their oils. Cut the green onions into 4 sections.

Combine the oxtail, ginger, garlic, green onions, aged soy sauce, Shaoxing wine, water, mirin, black pepper, rock sugar, arbol chilies, star anise and cinnamon in a braising pot. Cook over medium heat. When it starts to simmer, skim the protein bubbles. Reduce the heat to low, cover the pot with a lid and simmer for 3 hours until the oxtail is tender. Allow the oxtail to cool down to 140°F (60°C) in the braising liquid, about 1 hour. When it comes to finishing up braising meat, always let the protein cool in the braising liquid at the end. This extra step will ensure the meat will stay moist.

Strain the oxtail, discarding the aromatics, and save all the braising liquid. Reduce this liquid to one-third—be patient, this should take about 10 minutes—and skim the fat floating on top. Add the oyster sauce and maltose to the reduction, and cook until the sauce coats the back of a spoon, about 3 minutes, and is glossy from the maltose. Slice the Fresno chilies, keeping the seeds for spice if desired. Slice the Napa cabbage into 1-inch (2.5-cm)-wide pieces.

Add the oxtail to the reduction and bring back to heat. Add the Fresno chilies and Napa cabbage, and cook for 2 minutes, making sure the Napa cabbage is still crunchy. Plate up and serve, garnishing with the cilantro sprigs.

FIVE-SPICE SEARED DUCK BREAST

The most famous Beijing dish is whole roasted Peking duck. When people find out I grew up in Beijing, they always ask if I know how to make it. Well, I do! But that's a three-day prepping and cooking process, plus it requires specialty tools and a duck oven. For this seared duck breast, it will only take 15 minutes to create a really impressive result. We only need to make sure we give all the love and patience needed to slowly render the duck fat from the skin, which creates an almost puffed chicharrón-like crispy skin. The kumquat mustard can be made ahead of time, and it stores well. My mom has a kumquat tree in her garden in California. After we harvest them each spring, we make kumquat mustard and preserve the kumquats to last for months. If you don't have kumquats, oranges will work fine to give that sweet citrusy flavor. This vividly colorful dish appears often on our Sunday dinner table in the spring.

SERVES 4

Duck

2 (8-oz [224-g] each) duck breasts with skin

½ tsp Chinese five-spice powder

1 tsp kosher salt, or more to taste

Pepper, to taste

Kumquat Mustard

½ lb (225 g) kumquats or oranges

1 tbsp (15 ml) canola oil

1 tbsp (7 g) minced onion

1 tbsp (7 g) minced ginger

1½ cups (360 ml) Pinot Grigio

1½ cups (338 g) sugar

1 tbsp (6 g) whole mustard seeds

1 tbsp (6 g) dried mustard powder

2 tbsp (30 ml) white wine vinegar

½ tsp kosher salt

½ tbsp (7 g) unsalted butter

Sugar Snap Peas

Salt, as needed

¼ lb (113 g) sugar snap peas

To prepare the duck breasts, lightly score the skin with diamond cuts. Rub with the five-spice, and then season with the salt and pepper. Set aside.

For the kumquat mustard, slice the kumquats into ¼-inch (6-mm)-thick rings. In a saucepan, add the oil, then the onion and ginger. Sweat them over medium heat until you can smell the aroma in the air and the onions are turning translucent, about 2 minutes. Add the wine, sugar, mustard seeds, dried mustard and vinegar, then stir and mix well. When everything melts together, add the sliced kumquat and simmer for 15 minutes. Season with the kosher salt, and add the butter at the end to finish.

Meanwhile, preheat the oven to 325°F (170°C, or gas mark 3). In a dry, ovenproof sauté pan heated over medium heat, put the duck breast skin-side down. The duck skin has plenty of fat; we don't need to add cooking oil here.

Once you hear a little sizzling sound from the duck skin, lower the heat to medium-low. Render the fat over medium-low heat for 5 minutes. When the skin is light gold, baste the meat with the duck fat in the pan, then place the pan in the oven for 7 minutes. Make sure the duck breasts are skin-side down when you place them in the oven. When done, allow the meat to rest for 2 minutes. The duck will be medium at this point. If you would like your duck to be more cooked, you can leave it in the oven for 2 minutes longer.

While the duck is in the oven, bring a saucepot of water to a boil. When the water is at a rapid boil, add salt; it should taste like sea water. Blanch the sugar snap peas in the boiling salt water for 30 seconds, and they are ready!

To plate, slice the duck breasts and spoon a generous amount of kumquat mustard on the plate. Place the sliced duck, skin-side up, on top of the mustard, and add the sugar snap peas around the plate.

Black
The
Unwrap the
10 FL OZ
NET WT.

PANFRIED PORK CUTLET WITH BLACK VINEGAR

This modern Chinese dish was created around the beginning of the 1900s in German concessions near Tian Jing seaport. Obviously, the inspiration was schnitzel. We even created a Chinese version of Worcestershire sauce and call it Chinese black vinegar. I like to use dry instant potatoes as a crust instead of bread crumbs; it forms a lighter and fluffier coating texture.

SERVES 4

4 (6-oz [168-g] each) boneless pork chops

2 eggs

Salt and pepper, to taste

¼ cup (60 ml) water

1 tsp Chinese five-spice powder

1 cup (126 g) cornstarch

1 cup (100 g) instant mashed potatoes mix

½ cup (120 ml) canola oil, divided

2 tbsp (28 g) unsalted butter, divided

½ cup (120 ml) Chinese black vinegar

First, wet the cutting board with a clean, damp towel, and lay down 1 large piece of plastic wrap over it. The damp surface will keep the plastic secured to the cutting board. Place 1 pork chop on the plastic, and cover with another piece of plastic wrap. Using a meat mallet, evenly beat the pork chop a couple times to gently break down the muscles. Repeat this process for all the pork chops.

Next, prepare the egg wash, coating starch and instant potato crust to fry the pork chops. In a mixing bowl, beat the eggs well and add 1 pinch of salt, the water and Chinese five-spice. Pour the egg wash into a shallow container. Pour the cornstarch onto a similar size plate, and pour the instant potato mix onto a third plate. Line them up in order: starch, egg wash, potato crust. Season the pork chops with salt and pepper.

To bread the cutlets, first dip one in the starch, making sure to cover all surfaces of the pork chop. Shake of the excess. Next, dip it into the egg wash, allowing the excess to drip off. Last, dip the pork chop into the instant potato mix, making sure to completely coat. Repeat with the remaining pork chops.

Preheat a cast-iron pan over medium heat for 3 minutes. Add ¼ cup (60 ml) of oil. When the oil is hot, panfry 2 pork chops at a time. Fry each side of the pork chop for 2 minutes. When they are golden brown, add 1 tablespoon (14 g) of butter into the pan and baste the pork chops with the brown butter. Remove to a plate, then repeat to cook the other 2 pork chops, using the remaining ¼ cup (60 ml) of oil and finishing with 1 tablespoon (14 g) of butter.

After the pork chops are done, rest them for 1 minute, and slice them. Serve with Chinese black vinegar as a dipping sauce.

RED-BRAISED PORK BELLY

This is a classic Chinese dish that is made in every region of China, and everyone's grandma has her own version. My mom is from the northeast part of China; it takes over three days on a train to get there from Beijing. We only visited grandma once every two years, during Chinese New Year vacation. Every time we visited, grandma would kill a pig for the celebration. Grandma always saved the best part of the pig—the belly—for me, the little city girl. After years of eating this dish, I came up with my own version. Pork belly is slow simmered in caramelized soy sauce and warm spices. The layers of fat are rendered into the braising liquid and create this rich gelatinous sauce. Mom said, "It tastes like home." I hope my lao lao grandma would be proud.

SERVES 4

2 lb (900 g) skin-on pork belly

3 oz (84 g) ginger

2 oz (56 g) garlic

3 green onions

4 tbsp (60 ml) canola oil

½ cup (112 g) sugar

1 cup (240 ml) Shaoxing wine

1 cup (240 ml) soy sauce

2 tbsp (30 ml) fish sauce

3 star anise

1 stick cinnamon

1 cup (240 ml) water

2 tbsp (30 ml) maltose (can substitute with agave nectar or corn syrup)

Dice the pork belly into 2-inch (5-cm) squares. Smash the ginger and garlic on the cutting board with the back of a chef's knife and roughly chop. Smashing the garlic and ginger will release their oils. Cut the green onions into 4 sections.

Take out a 12-inch (30-cm) Dutch oven or a heavy-duty braising pot. If you have a clay pot, that's even better! Preheat the pot over high heat and when the pot is hot, pour the canola oil in the pot. Add the ginger, garlic and green onions, and when the aroma comes out, about 30 seconds, add the diced pork belly. Mix well and when the oil comes back to heat, add the sugar into the pot. This process is called "red coloring" in Chinese cooking. At this point with the sugar in the pot, you need to stir rapidly as the sugar will start to bubble and caramelize when it meets the hot oil. Allow the sugar to turn into a dark amber caramel; this takes about 2 minutes. Immediately deglaze the pot with the Shaoxing wine, and drop the heat to medium. Using a spatula, scrape off all the tasty little bits on the bottom of the pot. Add the soy sauce, fish sauce, star anise and cinnamon into the pot, and stir well. Slowly add the water into the pot to barely cover the pork; it may be a little more or less than 1 cup (240 ml). Bring this to a simmer, cover with a lid and drop the heat to low.

Slowly simmer the pork belly over low heat for 2 hours. Remove the lid and let the sauce reduce to a glaze consistency, nicely coating the pork belly. This will take about 10 minutes. Finish with the maltose to add shine and a little more sweetness.

SWEET-AND-SOUR BABY BACK RIBS

Sweet-and-sour baby back ribs have always been my go-to dish for dinner parties. It's easy to share and eat, and this dish will taste great hot or cold. This is no red sweet-and-sour sauce like you see in every Chinese American restaurant. My version is made with Chinkiang black vinegar. The flavor is more earthy and less sweet, and the color of the sauce is more of a dark amber-maroon.

SERVES 4

1 side baby back pork ribs (about 3 lb [1.4 kg])

2 oz (56 g) ginger

2 green onions

4 qt (3.8 L) water

½ cup (120 ml) Chinkiang vinegar

2 tbsp (30 ml) distilled white vinegar

¼ cup (60 ml) soy sauce

¼ tsp ground black pepper

½ cup (100 g) sugar

3 tbsp (45 ml) maltose

1 tsp sesame oil

1 tbsp (9 g) toasted white sesame seeds

Pat dry the baby back ribs with paper towels. On a cutting board with a chef's knife, divide the ribs into 3 even pieces by slicing the ribs along the bones. Slice the ginger into ⅛-inch (3-mm)-thick slices, and cut the green onions into 2-inch (5-cm) pieces. Combine the baby back ribs, ginger, green onions and water in a 12-inch (30-cm) pot. Place the pot over medium heat; the liquid should be barely covering the ribs. When the water comes to a boil, turn down the heat to low and simmer the ribs for 20 minutes. While the ribs are simmering, use a small skimmer to remove the impurities from the surface of the liquid. By keeping the cooking liquid free of floating proteins, we will produce a nice and shiny final sauce.

After 20 minutes of simmering the ribs, remove the pot from the heat and let the ribs rest in the liquid for 10 minutes. It is always good to allow braised meat to cool down in the cooking liquid so the meat doesn't dry out. Remove the ribs out of the liquid and set aside.

Strain the cooking liquid into a 12-inch (30-cm) sauté pan. Cook over high heat to reduce the liquid to one-third of its original volume. It will take about 10 minutes to reduce. Add the Chinkiang vinegar, distilled white vinegar, soy sauce, black pepper and sugar. Continue cooking to make a glaze. As the glaze reduces, portion the ribs into single ribs. Add the maltose to the glaze and once completely melted, add the portioned ribs into the pan as well. Simmer over low heat for 10 minutes. The glaze in the pan will continue to reduce and become a shiny layer coating the ribs. Remove from the heat and finish with the sesame oil. Sprinkle sesame seeds all over, and they're ready to eat!

BEIJING-SPICED LAMB CHOPS

Growing up in Beijing, lamb has always been my favorite red meat. I used to sneak off to the night market with my besties after school for grilled, spicy lamb skewers. I can never get enough of the intoxicating smells of spices and lamb drippings hitting the fire. This Beijing-spiced lamb chop became a signature dish in my restaurants, and I will have it on the menu for many years to come.

SERVES 4

Beijing Spice Rub

3 tbsp (18 g) cumin seed

3 tbsp (18 g) coriander seeds

3 tbsp (21 g) Sichuan peppercorns

1 tbsp (6 g) chili flakes

Lamb

2 (16-oz [450-g] each) rack of lamb

Salt

2 tbsp (30 ml) canola oil

2 tbsp (28 g) butter

2 sprigs thyme

Sesame Sauce

½ cup (100 g) tahini sesame paste

2 tsp (10 ml) rice vinegar

1 tsp soy sauce

½ tbsp (8 ml) warm water

Salt

Roasted Shallots

12 whole shallots

1 sprig thyme

Olive oil

Salt and pepper, to taste

Finishing Salt

4 tbsp (36 g) sesame seeds

4 tbsp (59 g) Maldon coarse sea salt

Toast each spice in a small sauté pan over high heat for about 2 minutes. When you can smell the spices in the air, they are ready. Grind them separately into powders with a spice or coffee grinder. Then sieve the spice powders, and combine them together to make Beijing spice rub.

Clean the racks of lamb, keeping the fat caps on. Season generously with spice rub, and store them in the refrigerator overnight.

Combine the tahini paste, rice vinegar, soy sauce, warm water and 1 teaspoon of the spice mix in a bowl. Stir and adjust the seasoning with salt.

Clean and peel the shallots. Put them in a mixing bowl, and toss them with the thyme and olive oil. Season with salt and pepper. Roast them in a 400°F (200°C, or gas mark 6) oven for about 15 minutes; the shallots should be tender. After removing the shallots from the oven, cover the roasting pan with plastic, and hold them warm in their own juice.

Heat up a small sauté pan over high heat. Put the sesame seeds and coarse sea salt in the pan, and toss the pan to mix these 2 ingredients together while toasting, about 2 minutes.

Before cooking the lamb, let the racks come to room temperature, about 10 minutes. Preheat the oven to 375°F (190°C, or gas mark 5). Season the lamb with salt. Preheat a large cast-iron pan over medium heat. Add the canola oil, and place the 2 racks of lamb in a large 12-inch (30-cm) skillet, fat cap down. Slowly roast and render the fat cap first. When they are golden brown, flip the lamb to the other side, and sear all sides until golden, about 2 to 3 minutes.

When the lamb racks are finished searing, put the butter and thyme in the pan. Baste the lamb with the brown butter. Drain the extra fat and oil from the cast-iron pan. Leave the racks of lamb in the pan with the fat cap on top and bone on the bottom. Put this pan of lamb in the oven on the middle rack, and finish cooking for 10 minutes. When the internal temperature reaches 130°F (55°C), the lamb will be about medium. Rest the lamb racks for 5 minutes, then slice and plate.

To plate, spread the sesame sauce on the bottom, arrange the lamb chops with the shallots and garnish with finishing salt on top.

RICE WINE–BRAISED LAMB SHANK

My dad's favorite dish, cooked by me: Chinese flavor with an Italian cooking technique. We mince aromatic vegetables and cook them with lamb shanks to contribute to the maximum flavor. Also, when all the bits of vegetables are slow cooked for a long time, they melt into the sauce—oh, so, so good.

SERVES 4

4 (10-oz [280-g] each) lamb shanks
Salt and pepper, to taste
2 tbsp (16 g) cornstarch
1 onion
2 oz (56 g) ginger
1 head garlic
1 carrot
3 ribs celery
2 green onions
4 tbsp (60 ml) canola oil
1 stick cinnamon
2 star anise
⅛ tsp chili flakes
3 cups (720 ml) Shaoxing wine
4 tbsp (60 ml) oyster sauce
1 tbsp (15 ml) honey
2 tbsp (30 ml) soy sauce

Clean the lamb shanks and pat them dry with paper towels. Season with salt and pepper, and dust them with cornstarch all over in a thin layer. The cornstarch will help to brown the shanks when searing and help to thicken the sauce. Set the shanks aside.

Using a food processor or by hand, mince the onion, ginger, garlic, carrot, celery and green onions separately. The density of the veggies is different, and it's important to chop them separately in the food processor.

Preheat a large cast-iron sauté pan over high heat. Add canola oil and put 2 shanks in, searing them until all sides are golden brown, about 2 minutes on each side. Remove the shanks from the pan, and repeat with the remaining 2 shanks. Place all 4 shanks into a roasting pan, and set aside.

After browning the lamb shanks, pour out the remaining grease from the pan, but save all the bits. The professional chefs call these flavor bits "fond." Using the same pan, turn down the heat. Toast the cinnamon, star anise and chili flakes over medium heat for about 2 minutes. Add the minced vegetables, and then sweat until the aroma of the vegetables fills the kitchen, about 1 minute.

Deglaze the pan with the Shaoxing wine, and cook off the alcohol for 1 minute. Add the oyster sauce, honey and soy sauce into the pan. Use a spatula to scrape the bottom of the pan, so all the fond will melt into the cooking liquid. Bring this liquid to a boil and pour everything over the shanks. Cover the roasting pan with a piece of parchment paper first, followed by foil.

Preheat the oven to 325°F (170°C, or gas mark 3). Place the roasting pan in the middle rack, and braise the lamb shanks in the oven for 2½ hours until fork tender.

LABOR DAY CHICKEN WINGS

Because I am a chef, I normally work on most weekends and holidays. There are two holidays I always get to stay home and celebrate with my family. One is Labor Day, the other one is Thanksgiving. Naturally, on Labor Day I will be the one that's grilling and cooking. These chicken wings are easy to make, and they taste great grilled or baked. The sweetness from the honey and soy will help the wings caramelize in the oven, and create all the yummy charred and crispy bits. The heat from the hot sauce is subtle, but makes you want to keep eating it. This is my go-to, easy recipe for wings. You can't just eat one!

SERVES 4

2 lbs (900 g) party chicken wings
4 tbsp (60 ml) soy sauce
6 tbsp (90 ml) honey
4 tbsp (60 ml) sambal chili sauce
4 tbsp (60 ml) hoisin sauce
2 tbsp (30 ml) ketchup
1 tbsp (7 g) minced ginger
2 tbsp (18 g) minced garlic

Clean and dry the chicken wings before marinating. Combine the soy sauce, honey, sambal, hoisin, ketchup, ginger and garlic in a mixing bowl, and mix well. Pour the marinade over the chicken wings, making sure all the wings are evenly coated. I like to marinate the wings overnight in the refrigerator. If you don't have that much time, this marinade tastes great after just a couple of hours.

Preheat the oven to 400°F (200°C, or gas mark 6). Place the wings on a sheet pan in an even layer, making sure to give them a little space in between. Bake the wings for 15 minutes. You don't even need to turn them. The sugar in the marinade will caramelize in the oven and create a little crust on the outside of the wings.

WHOLE ROASTED CORNISH HEN WITH SCALLION VINAIGRETTE

If you ever attended a traditional Chinese banquet, I am very sure you have eaten the "deep fried whole chicken." Chicken in Chinese sounds like "plentiful savings." It's a staple dish for all celebrations. I like to roast whole Cornish hens instead, and I always brine my hens to help them stay moist. This scallion vinaigrette is a classic sauce that's often paired with whole chicken. I like changes, but I also appreciate classics.

SERVES 4

Brining Liquid

2 oz (56 g) ginger

1 head garlic

1 cup (248 g) kosher salt

2 tbsp (30 ml) honey

4 qt (3.8 L) water

Cornish Hens

4 Cornish hens

Salt and pepper, to taste

6 tbsp (90 ml) canola oil, divided

4 cloves garlic, skin on

Scallion Vinaigrette

1 tbsp (9 g) minced garlic

2 tbsp (30 ml) canola oil

¼ cup (60 ml) soy sauce

¼ cup (60 ml) chicken stock

2 tbsp (30 ml) rice vinegar

4 tbsp (24 g) chopped scallions (green onions)

1 tsp sesame oil

Garnish

Thinly sliced scallions (green onions), green parts only

To make the brining liquid, in a medium-size stock pot, combine the ginger, garlic, salt, honey and water. Bring it to a boil over high heat, then cool it down completely. Clean and pat dry the Cornish hens and place into 2-gallon (8-L)-size ziplock bags, 2 hens in each bag. Pour the cooled brining liquid into each bag so the hens are fully submerged. Refrigerate for about 2 hours (no more than 3 hours or your hens will become too salty).

After the hens finish brining, remove them from the bags and dry them with paper towels. Next, tie the legs of each hen together with butcher's twine and tuck in the wings to the back. Season with salt and pepper.

Place 2 large cast-iron skillets over high heat, and preheat the oven to 425°F (220°C, or gas mark 7). When the skillets are hot, put 3 tablespoons (45 ml) of canola oil in each. Place 2 hens in each skillet, back-side down and breasts up. Smash the garlic cloves, leaving the skins on, and place 2 cloves into each skillet. Once you smell the garlic aroma in the air, start basting the hens with the garlic oil in the skillet.

After all the hens are basted, place them on the center rack in the oven and roast for 25 minutes. Check the hens by sticking a meat thermometer into the thigh of the hens near the bone. Once the internal temperature reaches 160°F (71°C), the hens are done. Remove the hens from the oven and rest on a cooking rack for 5 minutes.

While the hens are resting, we are going to make the scallion vinaigrette. Heat up a small saucepan over medium heat. Sweat the minced garlic with the oil until the garlic is translucent. Add the soy sauce, chicken stock and rice vinegar. When it comes to a simmer, turn off the heat. Add the scallions and sesame oil, and the dressing is finished.

Garnish the hens with scallions, and serve the vinaigrette on the side for dipping.

TYPE: BD-ML03N-OS
APOLIS - GLOBAL CITIZEN
ISSUE: MARKET BAG
BANGLADE
BD-LAT23

BEIJING GIRL IN CALIFORNIA

住在加州的北京女孩儿

Salads and Chilled Dishes

When I first arrived in Northern California for high school, I used to spend hours in the supermarket after school, walking up and down the aisles checking out different packaged foods and learning English. But I always lingered in the produce section wondering, "How is there a beautiful tomato in the middle of January side by side with Napa cabbage, a winter vegetable, and there is also summer squash on the shelf?" After I became a professional chef and cooked around the United States, I realized California is blessed with only two seasons: spring and summer! So many different types of fruit and vegetables grow year-round here, and farmers' markets are always filled with vibrant colors. I guess this is the reason Californians love salads!

Traditional Chinese cuisine doesn't have a lot of cold dishes because the Chinese like to eat warm things. Hey, we even ask for warm water at restaurants instead of ice water. I have included my take on a couple of classic dishes—Drunken Shrimp (page 43) and Jasmine Tea Eggs (page 55)—that are traditionally served warm, but I think they taste even better cold. Now that I have spent most of my life on the West coast, enjoying California produce, I have become an expert at making and eating salads, too! Sorry, no Chinese chicken salad here, but I think you will love my Crab Salad Lettuce Wraps with Ginger Dressing (page 40)!

CRAB SALAD LETTUCE WRAPS WITH GINGER DRESSING

Autumn is when the river crab season starts in Beijing. Families all rush to the nearby seafood market, pick out the fattest crabs, steam them and eat them with gingery vinegar. In traditional holistic Chinese medicine, they believe crabmeat is very cold to the human body, and ginger is very warm. By eating them together, you create a balanced environment in your body, and you will be less likely to get a stomachache from eating too much crab. After we moved to California, Dungeness crab became a year-round treat. I still always pair crab with ginger, and I never get a stomachache from eating crab on California rolls: creamy avocado with sweet crab meat is a combo that's proven to be delicious. This refreshing crab lettuce wrap is a fun change to the typical chicken lettuce cup.

SERVES 4

Crab Salad

8 oz (227g) Dungeness crab meat (or blue crab meat)

2 medium-size Fuji apples

1 large avocado

2 ribs celery

Ginger Dressing

4 tbsp (60 ml) mayo

2 tsp (5 g) finely minced ginger

2 tbsp (30 ml) fresh orange juice

½ tbsp (8 ml) lemon juice

Salt and pepper, to taste

1 tbsp (3 g) minced chives

To Serve

1 head butter lettuce

Place the crabmeat in a salad mixing bowl and make sure there are no shells in the meat. With the skin on, dice the apples into 1-inch (2.5-cm) cubes. Dice the avocado into 1-inch (2.5-cm) cubes. Dice the celery into ⅛-inch (3-mm) cubes, and add all diced vegetables to the crab meat.

For the dressing, in a small mixing bowl, combine the mayo, minced ginger, orange juice and lemon juice together. Mix well, and adjust the seasoning with salt and pepper.

Fold the mayo-based dressing into the crab mixture. Mix well, making sure everything is evenly coated, but try to keep the crabmeat as whole as possible. Adjust the seasoning with salt and pepper, and finish the salad with minced chives.

Clean the butter lettuce, separate the leaves and use the leaves as a wrap for the crabmeat salad.

DRUNKEN SHRIMP

The first time I ever had drunken shrimp was in Shanghai. It was a big bowl of LIVE baby shrimp, jumping and swimming in this tasty boozy sauce. I loved the sauce, but I was traumatized that I needed to bite into live baby shrimp. So, I created this easy peel-and-eat recipe that everyone can enjoy! Traditionally this dish is served warm; I don't know about you, but I like my cocktail cold! Think of this dish as an old-fashioned classic, with some shrimp hanging out.

SERVES 4

16 pieces 21/25 size head-on whole white shrimp (substitute headless shell-on shrimp)

Drunk Sauce

1 tbsp (15 ml) canola oil

1 tbsp (7 g) minced ginger

1 star anise

1 cup (240 ml) brandy

½ cup (120 ml) sweet vermouth

1 tbsp (15 ml) honey

⅛ tsp ground black pepper

¼ tsp kosher salt

1 tsp sesame oil

¼ cup (60 ml) shrimp poaching liquid

Garnish

3 tbsp (9 g) chopped green onions

½ orange for zest

Remove the shrimp veins by using a pair of scissors to cut open the shell on the back of the shrimp. After cutting open all the shrimp backs, use a shrimp devein tool or a toothpick to remove all the veins. Set the shrimp aside.

In a small saucepot, heat up the canola oil over medium heat. When the oil is hot, sweat the minced ginger in the pot. When the aroma releases into the air, add the star anise into the pot. Deglaze the saucepot with brandy and sweet vermouth, and simmer for 30 seconds. Add the honey, black pepper and salt and cook for 1 minute. Turn off the heat and add the sesame oil. Set aside to finish with the shrimp poaching liquid after the shrimp are cooked.

Use a medium-size stock pot, about 8-quart (7.6-L) size or larger. Fill the pot a little over half full with water, bring it to a boil and season with salt. Put the clean shrimp in the boiling salt water, and turn the heat down. Your cooking liquid should be simmering, not rapidly boiling at this point.

Cook the shrimp for about 3 minutes until fully cooked. Pour ¼ cup (60 ml) of the cooking liquid into the brandy sauce, stir and mix well. Place all the shrimp onto a large deep plate. While still hot from cooking, pour the brandy sauce over them, cover the plate and place it in the refrigerator to cool down. While the shrimp are cooling down, they will absorb the brandy into their meat and get "drunk" in the brandy sauce.

After the shrimp are nice and cool, sprinkle with green onions and the orange zest to serve. Peel and eat the shrimp. If you are brave enough to suck the heads of the shrimp, the cocktail of brandy mixed with sweet shrimp juice is the best savory cocktail you can ask for.

GLASS NOODLES SALAD

This is the ultimate summer lunch dish. Mung bean vermicelli glass noodles are full of protein and gluten-free. They're healthy, but satisfying to eat—the perfect fix to curb noodle cravings without guilt. Break up the avocado and toss everything together when you eat. The creaminess from the avocado coats the noodles, becoming another sauce, and with other crunchy vegetables inside, you won't get bored eating this bowl. This is also a perfect dish to make for a dinner party. It's vivid in color, sits very well and can be made a few hours before you serve it!

SERVES 4

Noodles

2 (2-oz [28-g]) packs dry mung bean vermicelli noodles

4 qt (3.8 L) hot water

Dressing

1 tbsp (9 g) minced garlic

5 tbsp (75 ml) rice vinegar

2 tbsp (30 ml) soy sauce

1½ tbsp (23 ml) agave nectar

1 tsp sambal chili sauce

2 tsp (10 g) Dijon mustard

5 tbsp (75 ml) canola oil

1 tsp sesame oil

Vegetables

4 oz (112 g) Napa cabbage leaves

6 radishes

1 large avocado

1 oz (28 g) bean sprouts

1 cup (50 g) cilantro leaves

1 tbsp (9 g) toasted sesame seeds

Place the mung bean noodles in a large bowl that will fit more than 4 quarts (3.8 L) of liquid. Pour the hot water over the noodles and stir, making sure the noodles are fully submerged. The glass noodles will rehydrate and cook in the hot water. Drain the noodles after 5 minutes of soaking; the noodles should be translucent and soft. Run the hot noodles under cold water until they are cold. Set aside.

Combine the garlic, rice vinegar, soy sauce, agave nectar, sambal chili and Dijon mustard in a mixing bowl. Slowly drizzle the canola oil into the mixture while stirring. After the dressing is emulsified together, finish with the sesame oil.

Slice the Napa cabbage leaves against the grain into ¼-inch (1-cm)-thick strips. Slice the radishes with a mandolin into thin rounds. Cut the avocado into halves and slice them thin.

To plate, mix the glass noodles, Napa cabbage and bean sprouts in a large salad bowl. Dress with the dressing, but reserve 2 tablespoons (30 ml). Lay the sliced avocado halves, radishes and cilantro leaves on top of the noodle salad. Drizzle the reserved dressing over the avocado and radishes, and sprinkle sesame seeds all over.

LITTLE GEM SALAD (OR CHINESE CAESAR SALAD)

Okay, let's be honest, Caesar salad must be the best-known salad in the world. It's one of my favorite salads, and I always make it for staff meals in my restaurants. One of the key ingredients for the dressing is anchovy paste, which I didn't always have, but I always have fish sauce in my kitchen. I use lime juice instead of lemon and, because of the salted eggs, I added a little sweetness to balance with the savoriness. And the bread crumbs! They add so much texture and toasty flavor! Slowly, this version of Caesar salad has become the one everyone always asks for.

SERVES 4

Lime Dressing

¼ cup (60 ml) lime juice

1 tsp minced garlic

1 tbsp (15 ml) fish sauce

½ tbsp (7 ml) agave nectar

1 tsp Dijon mustard

¼ cup (60 ml) canola oil

½ tsp kosher salt

Herb Bread Crumbs

½ cup (62 g) bread crumbs

½ tsp sesame oil

3 tbsp (9 g) chopped chives

1 tbsp (3 g) chopped cilantro stems

1 lime for zest

For Salad

4 heads little gem lettuce (can sub 2 heads romaine lettuce)

Salt and pepper, to taste

2 cooked salt-cured duck eggs (can sub for 2 tea eggs [page 55] or 2 hard-boiled eggs)

Combine the lime juice, garlic, fish sauce, agave, Dijon, canola oil and salt in a mixing bowl. Whisk well. This dressing has fresh juice, so it will last for 3 days in the refrigerator.

Heat up a small sauté pan over medium heat. Put all of the bread crumbs in the warm pan, toss with the sesame oil and continue to toss and cook until the bread crumbs are hot. Make sure you don't overtoast them; the bread crumbs should not turn brown. After about 30 seconds of cooking, remove the pan from the heat and mix in the chives and cilantro stems. Use a microplane to zest the lime into the pan, toss and mix well. Let the herbed bread crumbs cool down before using.

Wash and dry the little gem lettuce and separate the leaves. In a large salad bowl, place all the cleaned lettuce leaves in the middle of the bowl. Season with salt and black pepper, drizzle the lime dressing on the walls of the bowl and gently fold the dressing onto the leaves, making sure all the leaves are evenly dressed with the lime dressing. Peel the cooked salt-cured duck eggs. If you can't find cured eggs, you can always use hard-boiled eggs, or substitute with tea eggs (page 55); just remember to add a little extra salt and pepper.

On a large serving plate, put one layer of the dressed lettuce on the bottom of the plate. Sprinkle on a layer of the bread crumbs, and use a microplane to zest some salted egg on top. Repeat each step to build this salad into 3 layers.

PRO TIP: Salt-cured duck eggs are duck eggs that are preserved in salt. Raw duck eggs are buried in salt for up to 2 months. The whole egg becomes salty and will last for a long time without refrigeration. Chinese like to eat them with porridge or rice as a side dish, or cook with them to add natural saltiness to a dish. You can find them in any Asian market; all Asian cultures have a version of salt-cured egg.

RADISH SALAD WITH CITRUS

This recipe is for my fellow radish-lovers! This simple salad showcases different types of radishes, playing with the subtle texture and flavor differences. Growing up in Beijing, we ate watermelon radishes in the summer like they were fruit, sprinkling with some salt and biting them like an apple. This simple pleasure of showcasing radish, just as it is, is what I want to embrace.

SERVES 4

2 medium-size watermelon radishes

1 (16-oz [450-g]) daikon radish

1 bunch common red radishes, about 5 to 6

2 oranges

Citrus Dressing

¼ cup (60 ml) rice vinegar

2 tbsp (30 ml) fresh orange juice

3 tbsp (38 g) sugar

1 tsp kosher salt

1 tsp sesame oil

1 tsp toasted sesame seeds

Salt and pepper, to taste

2 tbsp (6 g) chopped chives

Wash all of the radishes. Peel the skin off of the watermelon radishes and daikon radish. We will need to slice the larger-size radishes into very thin strands. You can use the teeth attachment of a mandoline slicer, or slice the radishes into thin discs and then slice them into thin strands. Slice the small radishes into thin rounds. Combine all the radishes in a large salad mixing bowl.

Remove the peel and outer membrane from the oranges with a paring knife, exposing the juicy flesh. Now you have 2 "peeled" orange balls in front of you. Use a small paring knife to cut between the connecting membranes with a v-shaped cut, harvesting the segments of the orange. It is best to segment the oranges over a bowl, so all the juice will drip into it and you can use the juice for the dressing.

In a small bowl, mix the rice vinegar, orange juice, sugar, salt and sesame oil together, making sure the sugar is completely dissolved. Add the toasted sesame seeds.

Dress the bowl of radishes with the citrus dressing, and season with salt and pepper. Toss in the orange segments, and garnish the whole salad with chopped chives.

1985年荣获中国
镇江
ZHENJIANG

BABY ARUGULA SALAD WITH BLACK VINEGAR DRESSING

The Chinese have a love for bitter vegetables just like the Italians. But traditional Chinese cuisine hardly has any salads; they prefer their vegetables cooked. I had wild baby arugula cooked before, but truly fell in love with it when I ate it raw in Italian cuisine. Chinkiang vinegar is one of my most-used vinegars. I always describe it as an "earthier version of balsamic vinegar." It's only natural for me to marry two of my favorite cuisines and create this salad.

SERVES 4

Mushrooms

6 king oyster mushrooms, divided

Salt and black pepper, to taste

2 tbsp (30 ml) canola oil

1 tbsp (14 g) unsalted butter

1 clove garlic

1 sprig thyme

Pickled Red Onion

1 cup (240 ml) rice vinegar

¼ cup (25 g) sugar

1 tsp kosher salt

1 star anise

½ tsp chili flakes

½ tsp Sichuan peppercorn

1 red onion

Black Vinegar Dressing

1 cup (240 ml) Chinkiang black vinegar

1 tbsp (15 ml) honey

1 tsp Dijon mustard

½ tbsp (8 ml) soy sauce

½ cup (120 ml) canola oil

1 tsp sesame oil

4 oz (112 g) wild rocket arugula

To prepare the king oyster mushrooms, slice 4 mushrooms in half lengthwise and score the cut sides with a shallow diamond crosshatch pattern. Season them with salt and black pepper. In a hot sauté pan, add the oil. When hot, add the butter. When the butter starts to brown, put the mushrooms in flat-side down. Add the garlic and thyme, and baste the mushrooms with the hot oil-butter from the pan. Roast them until golden brown on the flat-side, about 2 minutes, and lightly seared and tender on the other side. You can keep them warm by leaving them next to the stove.

Meanwhile, cut the remaining 2 raw mushrooms lengthwise. Using the thinnest setting on a mandoline, slice the mushroom into paper thin ribbons.

To make the pickled red onion, combine the rice vinegar, sugar, salt, star anise, chili flakes and Sichuan peppercorn in a pot, and bring to a boil. Slice the red onion with the grain into ¼-inch (6-mm)-thick slices. Place in the hot pickling liquid, remove it from the heat and allow it to cool. You can keep them in the fridge for up to 2 weeks.

To make the black vinegar dressing, combine the Chinkiang black vinegar, honey, Dijon and soy sauce together, and drizzle in the canola oil while mixing. Add the sesame oil at the end. It's okay if the dressing does not fully emulsify.

To plate, toss the arugula, sliced raw mushrooms and pickled red onion with dressing. It will take about ½ cup (120 ml) of dressing for all the salad. Garnish with warm roasted mushrooms around the plate.

PRO TIP: You can use white wine vinegar instead of rice vinegar to pickle the red onion.

WARM POTATO SALAD WITH SICHUAN PEPPERCORN DRESSING

In northern China, potatoes are a staple vegetable. But the southerners will tell you only leafy greens are vegetables; potato is a starch, not a vegetable! This argument has been going on for hundreds of years and will continue till the end of the world. The most unique preparation from northern China is to cut the potato into matchsticks and stir-fry it, always finished with vinegar at the end. I like to use red skin or Yukon gold potatoes for this salad. This is a great dish to make ahead of time and serve at room temperature. The texture of the potato in this dish is crunchy, not starchy, and the flavor is bright. I prefer this version of potato salad!

SERVES 4

2 medium-size red skin potatoes

3 inner ribs celery with leaves

¼ cup (36 g) roasted peanuts

2 tbsp (30 ml) canola oil

½ tsp Sichuan peppercorns

⅛ tsp chili flakes

1 tbsp (15 ml) Chinkiang black vinegar

½ tbsp (8 ml) rice vinegar

¼ tsp kosher salt

Slice the potatoes on a mandolin into ¼-inch (6-mm) rounds and then cut them into matchsticks. Soak them in a large container of cold water. This process helps remove extra starch from the potatoes. Meanwhile, thinly slice the celery ribs against the grain about ¼ inch (6 mm) thick. Pick the young celery leaves and soak them in ice water. Chop the roasted peanuts and set aside.

Place a wok or skillet over high heat with the canola oil. While the wok and oil heat up, drain the sliced potatoes and pat them dry with paper towels. When the wok is smoking hot, add the Sichuan peppercorns and chili flakes to make the wok fragrant. After about 30 seconds, when the aroma of the spices fills the kitchen, put the potatoes in right away. Start stirring and rocking the wok so the potatoes won't stick. Cook over high heat for about 2 minutes. The potatoes should be cooked through, but still crunchy, not falling apart. Deglaze the wok with the black vinegar and rice vinegar, and season with kosher salt. Take the wok off the heat, and then toss in the sliced celery. Garnish the plate with celery leaves and chopped peanuts.

茉莉花茶
中华人民共和国产品

JASMINE TEA EGGS

Tea eggs are the easiest breakfast. They are boiled eggs that are soaked in soy and tea. It's a tasty break from plain hard-boiled eggs. A lot of Chinese families will have a jar in the fridge, so the kids always have something healthy to snack on. I like to make my tea eggs with jasmine tea; it is floral and pairs perfectly with the warm spices.

SERVES 4 TO 12

1 dozen large eggs

2 slices of ginger

3 star anise

1 stick cinnamon

2 bay leaves

2 tbsp (4 g) loose jasmine tea leaves

1 tsp Sichuan peppercorn

3 tbsp (30 ml) soy sauce

4 tsp (20 ml) dark soy sauce

1 tsp sugar

2 tsp (12 g) kosher salt

2 tsp (10 ml) Shaoxing wine

7 cups (1.7 L) water (enough to submerge all the eggs), plus 4 qt (3.8 L) for boiling

Remove the eggs from the refrigerator and allow them to come to room temperature for a few minutes so they are not super cold.

Prepare the tea egg marinade by putting the ginger, star anise, cinnamon, bay leaves, jasmine tea, Sichuan peppercorn, soy sauces, sugar, salt, Shaoxing wine and 7 cups (1.7 L) of water into a medium pot. Bring the mixture to a boil, and turn the heat down to a simmer. Cover and simmer for 10 minutes. Turn off the heat, remove the lid and let it cool completely.

Bring another pot of water, about 4 quarts (3.8 L) of water, to a boil for the eggs. Once the water is boiling, gently and quickly lower the eggs into the boiling water using a large spoon. It's very important to not crack the eggs in the pot.

Let the eggs cook in the boiling water for 7 minutes. Make sure to use a timer because the eggs can overcook within seconds. Make an ice bath to cool down the eggs by filling a large bowl with ice and water. Once the timer goes off, turn off the heat, quickly scoop out the eggs and transfer to the ice bath. Allow them to sit in the ice bath until they are completely cool to the touch.

Once the eggs are cooled, lightly crack the egg shells. The goal here is to make enough cracks to allow the flavor of the marinade to seep into the egg. I like to use a small spoon to tap the eggs, but be careful: if you tap or crack too hard, you might crack open the egg since the egg yolk is still very soft.

Soak the cracked eggs in the tea marinade for 24 hours in the refrigerator, making sure all the eggs are completely submerged in the liquid. After 24 hours, they're ready! You can also soak them longer for a stronger flavor. These tea eggs last for 3 to 4 days in the refrigerator.

JUST DOUGH IT

只认面食

Better Than Mama's Noodles, Dumplings and Pancakes

As a kid growing up in northern China, we started our dumpling folding "career" early. Pretty much all of us have perfected at least one task by the age of six—either rolling out the wrappers, or folding the dumplings. Homemade pancakes called Bing (page 77) and hand-cut noodles are staples on our dinner tables. In northern China, we also eat less rice than the southern Chinese do, but we will always have something made out of dough with every meal.

With a lifetime of training, and my love and passion for eating noodles and pasta, I became quite an expert on everything made of flour dough. Not only will I share techniques and tips on how to make noodles, crepes, bings and dumplings, I will also show you the best dipping sauces and pairings that go with them. I always have the most "likes" on my social media when I post my dumplings and scallion pancakes. Many of you requested recipes, and now your wish is granted. Many recipes were learned from my mom, and made better by me. But shhhh . . . don't tell her, because no matter what, mom is the best.

SCALLION PANCAKES WITH HAZELNUT PESTO

Scallion pancakes have been around for thousands of years, but they are like the result of a pizza and a croissant having a baby—the pancake is savory and round, but filled with layers. Traditionally the flaky and tender layers are created with lard. I make it with canola oil, and it's a lot less greasy. Instead of dipping into chili oil and vinegar, spread your pancake with this hazelnut pesto and pair it with some thinly sliced prosciutto. Way better!

SERVES 4

Scallion Pancakes

2 cups (240 g) all-purpose flour

2½ tsp (15 g) kosher salt, divided

½ cup (120 ml) boiling hot water

½ cup (120 ml) cold water

5 scallions (green onions)

½ tsp Chinese five-spice powder

10 tbsp (150 ml) canola oil

Hazelnut Pesto

½ cup (75 g) toasted hazelnuts

2 cups (40 g) Italian parsley leaves

1 tbsp (9 g) minced garlic

½ cup (120 ml) extra-virgin olive oil

Juice from ½ lemon

2 tsp (12 g) kosher salt

½ tsp ground black pepper

To make the pancakes, add the flour and ½ teaspoon of salt to a large mixing bowl, and pour the boiling hot water all over the flour. Use a fork or chopsticks to stir and mix so all the flour is damp from the hot water. As soon as all the hot water is absorbed, pour cold water all over the dough and knead the dough with your hands. When the dough is formed and there aren't any visible dry flour lumps (be careful not to overknead it), cover the dough with plastic wrap and rest it for a minimum of 30 minutes.

Clean the scallions and finely mince them, making sure there aren't any chunky pieces. Put the minced scallions, 2 teaspoons (12 g) of salt and the five-spice into a heat-safe bowl. Heat up the canola oil in a small pot. When the oil is smoking, pour the hot oil onto the minced scallions. Let it cool down before using.

Divide the well-rested dough into 4 equal balls. Roll out 1 ball on a well-oiled, flat surface as thin as possible into a large circle, about 12 inches (30 cm) in diameter. Use a pastry brush and slotted spoon to spread the oiled scallions onto the pancake. Leave a little rim. Roll up the dough tightly into a long rope, then pinch both ends lightly and roll up this "log" into a cylinder. Repeat and roll the other 3 balls. Cover them with plastic wrap, and rest them for 15 minutes before cooking.

Heat up a 12-inch (30-cm) nonstick skillet over medium heat. Press the stuffed dough flat and roll it out to a thin pancake about ¼ inch (6 mm) thick. Lay it flat in the skillet and start cooking it without adding oil. Cook one side for 1 minute, then flip to the other side and cook for 1 more minute. Repeat this a couple more times. When the pancake starts to puff up a little in the middle and both sides are golden and crispy, the pancake is ready.

For the pesto, combine the hazelnuts, parsley, garlic and extra-virgin olive oil in a vegetable chopper. Pulse them together and keep it a little chunky. Finish with the lemon juice, salt and pepper.

Cut the pancakes into quarters and dip in the hazelnut pesto!

ZHAJIANG MIAN

How many of you have a picture from your childhood of you eating a plate of spaghetti with red sauce smeared all over your face? Well, zhajiang mian to a Beijing kid is the equivalent of that spaghetti. Whether it's one of your favorite Chinese dishes, or you've never tried it before, this is a must-make recipe. This earthy and savory pork belly sauce with noodles, garnished with crunchy vegetables, is as traditional as the forbidden city. I don't really want to mess with perfection, so this is my grandma's recipe. My mom doesn't even know how to make it, and now you have part of my family heirloom.

SERVES 4

Pork Belly Sauce

1 lb (450 g) skin-on pork belly

1 star anise

1 tbsp (7 g) minced ginger

1 tbsp (9 g) minced garlic

1 cup (240 ml) sweet fermented bean paste (tian mian jiang)

¼ cup (60 ml) fermented soy bean paste (huang jiang)

2 tbsp (6 g) chopped green onions

Hand-Cut Noodles

4 cups (480 g) all-purpose flour

1 cup (240 ml) water

1 tsp kosher salt

Toppings

2 cups (200 g) sliced Napa cabbage strips

1 cup (150 g) sliced cucumber strips

1 cup (100 g) watermelon radish strips

To make the sauce, first we need to prep the pork belly. Have your local butcher grind the pork belly through a ½-inch (1.2-cm) hole on the grinding plate. Otherwise, chop and dice the pork belly yourself at home into minced pieces that are similar to coarse ground pork.

Heat up a medium-size cast-iron pan over medium heat. When the pan is hot, add the ground pork belly, and start to render the pork fat and brown the meat. Let the ground pork start to turn golden brown and the pork fat start to render out; this will take about 6 to 7 minutes. Add the star anise, ginger and garlic to the pan. Stir-fry everything for a couple of minutes. Next add the sweet fermented bean paste and the soybean paste to the pan, and mix well. When the sauce comes to a simmer, drop the heat to low. Simmer the sauce for 30 minutes, stirring often so it won't burn on the bottom. After the sauce is done, add the green onions at the end. If you find the sauce is too greasy at this point, you can cool it down and skim off the pork fat on top. I love fat, so I mix it into my noodles.

While the sauce is cooking, make the hand-cut noodles. Combine the flour, water and salt in a mixer or a heavy bottom bowl. Knead the dough until smooth, and then rest for 30 minutes. After the dough is well rested, separate it into 4 equal-sized balls and roll them out into large circular sheets with a rolling pin to about ⅛ inch (2 mm) thick. Fold the sheets onto themselves, forming them into a rectangular shape, and then cut them into ¼-inch (6-mm)-wide noodles.

To cook the noodles, boil a big pot of water over high heat. Drop the fresh noodles into the boiling water and as soon as the noodles float to the surface, they are done. This will take less than 1 minute. Use the remaining boiling water to blanch the sliced Napa cabbage. Cook for 1 minute, then drain and it's ready to serve.

To plate the zhajiang mian, put the noodles in a big bowl. Place 3 tablespoons (45 ml) of sauce in the middle and surround with cucumber strips, watermelon radish strips and Napa cabbage. Mix them all together when eating.

JIAOZI WITH CHICKEN FILLING

According to Chinese legend, jiaozi was invented thousands of years ago by an Emperor's doctor during a cold winter. That winter was so cold, lots of poor peoples' ears were falling off and many of them were getting sick. So, the doctor begged the Emperor to give him some flour, and then he went around collecting mutton trims from the rich families. The doctor made jiaozi dumplings folded in an ear shape and filled with mutton and herbal medicines, and then he fed the poor of the whole city. Jiaozi became a staple dish to make when guests come to visit, during the Chinese New Year celebration, when kids go back to visit mom . . . The Chinese show their love through these dumplings. Lots of people get intimidated by folding dumplings—don't be. They don't have to be perfect: just seal them with filling inside, or use a dumpling folder. Don't miss out on this deliciousness!

SERVES 4

Jiaozi Wrapper

4 cups (480 g) all-purpose flour

1¼ cups (300 ml) water

1 tsp salt

Chicken Filling

1 lb (450 g) ground chicken

4 tbsp (60 ml) oyster sauce

4 tbsp (60 ml) soy sauce

4 tbsp (60 ml) chicken stock

1 large egg

1 tbsp (15 ml) sesame oil

2 tbsp (14 g) minced ginger

½ cup (50 g) minced green onions

For Serving

Black vinegar

Chili oil

Tools to Help You

Dough mixer

Pasta roller

3-inch (8-cm) cookie cutter

Dumpling folder

Jiaozi Wrapper

Combine the flour, water and salt in a mixer. Knead until it forms a smooth dough, and rest it for 30 minutes. In my house, after the dough has rested, I will portion it into bottle cap–size balls (about 7 grams each), then individually roll them out into small rounds with a rolling pin to make wrappers. Alternatively, you can run the dough through a pasta roller. Roll them to #4 thickness, then use a 3-inch (8-cm) cookie cutter to cut out round wrappers.

Chicken Filling

Put the ground chicken in a medium-size mixing bowl. Combine the oyster sauce, soy sauce and chicken stock together in a cup. Slowly pour this liquid into the ground chicken while stirring, until all the liquid absorbs into the meat. Next add the egg and sesame oil, and mix well. After all the seasoning is mixed into the chicken, add the ginger and green onions, and mix well. It's ready for folding.

Dumplings

Using a dumpling folder, if you'd like, take 1 wrapper and 1 tablespoon (15 g) of chicken filling per dumpling. Place the filling in the middle of the wrapper, close the edges and make them into an ear shape (half-moon shape). After all the jiaozi are folded, boil water in a large pot. Add the jiaozi in when the water is boiling. When the water returns to a boil, add ½ cup (120 ml) of cold water, and bring back to a boil. When all the jiaozi are floating on top of the water, they are done. Enjoy them hot with some black vinegar and chili oil.

WONTON SOUP

Hong Kong–style wontons have thin wrappers filled with shrimp and pork, and they are normally served with a clear broth. They are light and fluffy, and in Cantonese they're called "swallow a cloud." Northern-style wontons have a thicker wrapper, very little filling and are served with hearty vegetables, dry nori seaweed and lots of toppings. I like to take the best of both: Hong Kong–style wontons and a northern-style soup filled with California vegetables . . . Ha, it's like me! One hundred percent Chinese American.

SERVES 4

For the Wontons

¼ lb (113 g) ground pork

¾ lb (338 g) chopped medium shrimp

3 tbsp (45 ml) oyster sauce

1 tbsp (15 ml) Shaoxing wine

2 tbsp (30 ml) soy sauce

1 tbsp (15 ml) sesame oil

2 tbsp (14 g) minced ginger

2 tbsp (6 g) minced green onions

1 large egg (for egg wash)

1 (75-piece) pack Hong Kong–style wonton wrappers (they are thinner and yellow in color)

For the Soup

6 cups (1.4 L) chicken stock

2 tbsp (30 ml) light soy sauce

1 cup (110 g) sugar snap peas

1 bunch pea tendrils

1 tbsp (15 ml) sesame oil

2 radishes, sliced thin

4 sheets nori seaweed, cut into strips

1 handful cilantro leaves

In a large bowl, combine the ground pork, shrimp, oyster sauce, Shaoxing wine and soy sauce, and stir together. Then add the sesame oil, ginger and green onions into the bowl and mix well. Crack the egg into a small bowl, and whisk it with 2 tablespoons (30 ml) of water to make the egg wash. Put 1 tablespoon (about 9 g) of the filling in the middle of the wonton wrapper, then dab some egg wash on the rim of the wrapper. Fold it in half into a triangular shape. Seal the edges well, then pinch the 2 side points together to form a wonton.

Boil a big pot of water over high heat, and drop the wontons into the boiling water. When the water comes back to a boil, add 1 cup (240 ml) of cold water. The wontons are ready when the water returns to a boil again and all the wontons are floating on top.

While the water is boiling, heat up the chicken stock over medium heat in a soup pot. Season the stock with the soy sauce. When the stock comes to a boil, add the sugar snap peas and pea tendrils and cook for just 30 seconds. Finish with the sesame oil.

To serve, put 6 to 8 cooked wontons in a large soup bowl. Add 1 cup (240 ml) of soup with peas, and top with sliced radish, nori strips and cilantro.

EGG PANCAKES WITH VEGETABLES

I hated cooked carrots growing up and refused to eat them. My mom was a doctor, and though she might not be the best cook, she always made sure I never missed out on any nutrition. She would shred carrots and cook them with my favorite breakfast crepes, so I couldn't pick them out. I still dislike cooked carrots, so I include additional vegetables with this pancake. They are crispy on the outside and tender inside, with crunches from the fresh veggies, and the carrots to add some sweetness. I won't pick them out this time for sure. These pancakes are great as breakfast, and they also make the best side dish.

MAKES 4 LARGE PANCAKES

Pancake Batter

2 large eggs

1 cup (120 g) all-purpose flour

1 cup (240 ml) milk

1 tbsp (15 ml) canola oil, plus more for cooking

1 tsp sesame oil

1 tbsp (18 g) kosher salt

½ tsp ground black pepper

Vegetable Mix

1 cup (50 g) shredded carrots

1 cup (150 g) shredded zucchini

½ cup (24 g) chopped garlic chives

1 cup (150 g) sliced onion

½ cup (50 g) chopped green onions

Crack and whisk the 2 eggs into a large mixing bowl. Add the flour, milk, canola oil, sesame oil, salt and pepper to the eggs. Mix until everything forms a smooth batter. Add all of the vegetable mix ingredients into the pancake batter, and mix well.

Heat up 2 tablespoons (30 ml) of canola oil in a 10-inch (25-cm) nonstick skillet over medium heat. When the oil is warm, add 1¼ cups (300 ml) of pancake mix into the skillet, and spread it into an even layer that almost fills the whole pan. Cook on one side for about 2 minutes. When the edge starts to turn golden brown, flip to the other side, and cook until golden brown. Repeat the steps to make a total of 4 large pancakes. Cut the pancakes into wedges and enjoy.

TOMATO EGG WITH MISSHAPEN NOODLES

Sheets of misshaped noodles are the best vessels to soak up sauces. Here they're paired with a stir-fried tomato-and-egg sauce, which is the staple summer dish of Beijing. Remember to make this dish at the peak of summer, when heirloom tomatoes are at their best. When the tomatoes are really ripe, don't overcook them—just sauté briefly, and keep them chunky.

SERVES 4

Noodle Sheets

Basic Noodle Dough (page 74) or use store-bought wonton wrappers cut in half into large triangles

Egg Mix

5 large eggs

1 tbsp (15 ml) Shaoxing wine

1 tbsp (15 ml) light soy sauce

1 tsp sesame oil

¼ tsp ground white pepper

2 tbsp (30 ml) canola oil

Tomato

1 tbsp (15 ml) canola oil

1 tbsp (7 g) minced ginger

2 tbsp (18 g) minced garlic

2 lbs (900 g) heirloom tomatoes (sub hothouse tomatoes on the vine)

¼ cup (60 ml) Shaoxing wine

1 tbsp (15 ml) light soy sauce

¼ cup (60 ml) chicken stock

2 tbsp (30 ml) ketchup

1 tsp sesame oil

3 tbsp (9 g) chopped green onions

Salt, to taste

For the misshaped noodles, use a pasta machine or a rolling pin to roll the dough to ⅛ inch (3 mm), #5 on the pasta roller. Cut the noodle sheets into large triangular shapes.

Whisk the eggs, Shaoxing wine, light soy, sesame oil and pepper together with a fork, trying not to whisk too much air into it. Heat up 2 tablespoons (30 ml) of canola in a large skillet or wok over medium heat. When you see the first sign of smoke from the oil, add the egg mix into the wok, moving the wok and your spatula in a circular motion so the bottom of the egg is coagulated and the top is still runny. Note: This is fast. It will take about 10 seconds. Remove the soft-cooked eggs right away, and set them aside.

In the same wok, heat up 1 tablespoon (15 ml) of canola oil over medium heat. Add the ginger, garlic and tomatoes into the wok. Stir-fry until the tomatoes become soft and juice starts to come out, about 1 minute or so. Add the Shaoxing wine into the wok and allow the alcohol to cook off for 30 seconds. Next add the light soy, chicken stock and ketchup into the wok, and mix well. When the tomato mixture comes back to a simmer, add the sesame oil, green onions, salt and the soft-cooked eggs in the wok and stir. The tomato-egg sauce is done.

Meanwhile, bring a large pot of water to a boil over high heat. Cook the noodles in boiling water. As soon as they are floating on top of the water, they are ready. Add them into the tomato-egg sauce. Cook for 30 seconds, and it's ready to plate.

CHEESEBURGER POT STICKERS

This whimsical creation came from a *Top Chef* brunch challenge on creativity. I won the challenge by marrying the beloved American comfort food cheeseburgers with the Chinese classic dumpling pot stickers. I love to see people's faces when they bite into the pot stickers and cheese oozes out! Cheese might leak out when you are cooking the dumplings. Don't worry, they will crisp up in the pan, like the burnt cheese ends on a lasagna, and everyone will fight for it.

MAKES ABOUT 40 POT STICKERS

1 lb (450 g) Comté cheese (sub Gruyère or Swiss cheese)

1 lb (450 g) lean ground chuck beef

¼ lb (113 g) shredded cheddar cheese

½ cup (75 g) chopped red onion

2 tbsp (30 ml) Worcestershire sauce

1 tbsp (18 g) kosher salt

½ tbsp (4 g) ground black pepper

1 tbsp (15 ml) canola oil, plus more for cooking the potstickers

Pot Sticker Wrappers (page 78), or you can use store-bought

Thousand Island dressing, for serving (optional)

Dice the Comté cheese into 40 cubes. In a large bowl, mix the ground beef, cheddar cheese, red onion and Worcestershire sauce together, and season with salt and black pepper. Finish with canola oil, and mix well.

Put 1 tablespoon (9 g) of beef filling and 1 cube Comté cheese in the middle of a pot sticker wrapper, and fold the pot sticker. Repeat to make all the pot stickers.

After all the pot stickers are folded, heat up 2 tablespoons (30 ml) of canola oil in a 12-inch (30-cm) nonstick skillet over medium heat. When the pan is hot, line up 20 pot stickers flat-side down in the pan. Add ¼ cup (60 ml) of water and cover it with a lid. Drop the heat to low. Cook for 4 minutes and remove the lid. The top of the pot stickers will have cooked from the steam. Turn up the heat to medium and allow the bottoms of the pot stickers to crisp up, about 1 minute. When they are golden on the bottom, the pot stickers are done. Repeat the steps and make another batch of 20 pot stickers. Eat them straight, or dip them into Thousand Island dressing, so they taste like California-style burgers!

EGG CREPES

I am pretty sure you have been reading in this book about how much I love eggs, both cooking them and eating them. These thin crepes stuffed with soft scrambled eggs are like eating a cloud—you can never stop at eating just one. You can take out the spiciness in this dish by only using hoisin sauce as the spread.

MAKES ABOUT 8 TO 10 CREPES

Crepes

2 large eggs

1¼ cups (300 ml) milk

1 cup (120 g) all-purpose flour

1 tsp kosher salt

1 tbsp canola oil plus ½ tbsp (23 ml), divided

1 tsp sesame oil

½ tsp ground black pepper

4 tsp (12 g) toasted sesame seeds

Soft Scrambled Eggs

2 tbsp (30 ml) canola oil

4 large eggs

1 tbsp (15 ml) light soy sauce

4 tbsp (12 g) minced green onions

Spread Sauce

6 tbsp (60 ml) hoisin sauce

½ tbsp (8 ml) Doubanjiang (fermented bean chili paste)

To make the crepes, combine the eggs, milk, flour, salt, 1 tablespoon (15 ml) canola oil and sesame oil together, mix well and season with black pepper. Heat up ½ tablespoon (8 ml) of canola oil in a 12-inch (30-cm) nonstick skillet over low heat. Pour ¼ cup (60 ml) of batter into the skillet and swirl around to evenly spread the batter. Sprinkle ½ teaspoon of the toasted sesame seeds all over the crepe, and cook until it sets. Then flip to the other side to finish cooking.

For the eggs, heat up the canola oil in a large skillet over medium heat. Crack the eggs and add the light soy and green onions into a bowl. Don't whisk air into it, just break the yolk and stir everything together. Pour the egg mixture into the hot skillet and quickly stir with a heat-resistant rubber spatula. When the bottom of the egg is coagulated and the top is still runny, take it off the heat. Stir the eggs, and they're ready to eat.

Mix the hoisin and Doubanjiang together. Spread 1 thin layer of sauce on a crepe, fill it with soft scrambled eggs, roll it up and enjoy.

BASIC NOODLE DOUGH

This lean noodle dough recipe is good for both hand rolling and a pasta machine. You can increase the water by 25 milliliters to make softer noodles for hand rolling and hand cutting.

SERVES 4

4 cups (480 g) all-purpose flour
1 cup (240 ml) water
1 tsp kosher salt

Combine the flour, water and salt together, and knead the dough until smooth. Separate the dough into 4 even portions. Let rest for 30 minutes before you roll them out. You can use a pasta machine or rolling pin to roll the dough, and then cut the noodles.

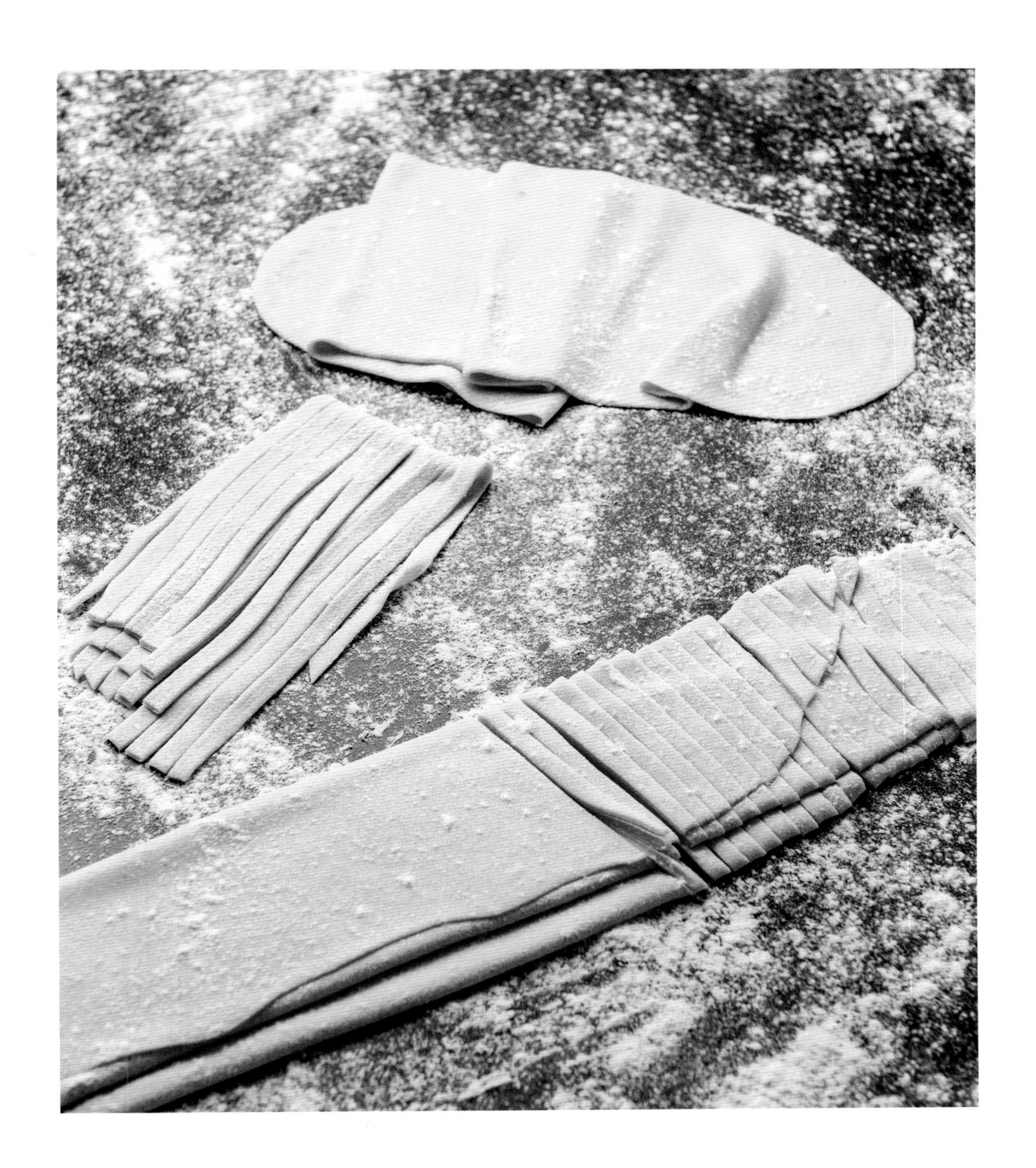

BASIC CHINESE PANCAKES (BING)

Every culture has their version of flat bread. Bing is very similar to a flour tortilla, and traditionally it is made with lard for tenderness. One of the keys to making a soft and chewy bing is to use hot water to kill the gluten first, then finish the dough with cold water. Also, remember, the longer you rest the dough, the more tender the bing will be. Rest it overnight in the refrigerator if you have time. This is an all-around side starch that's great with braised meat, stir-fried veggies or even scrambled eggs!

MAKES 6 PANCAKES

2 cups (240 g) all-purpose flour

1 tsp kosher salt

½ cup (120 ml) boiling hot water

½ cup (120 ml) cold water

2 tbsp (26 g) lard (sub canola oil [30 ml])

Put the flour and salt into a mixing bowl. Pour boiling water over the flour, and stir with a fork. When all the boiling water has absorbed into the dough, add the cold water and lard. Knead the dough and when it's formed, but not 100 percent smooth, cover it with plastic wrap and let rest for at least 30 minutes at room temperature. After the dough is fully rested, portion it into 6 balls and roll them out on an oiled surface into thin rounds, about ¼ inch (6 mm) thick and 9 inches (23 cm) in diameter.

Heat up a large nonstick skillet over medium heat. When the skillet is hot, lay a pancake in the pan and cook for 1 minute. Flip it over and cook for 1 minute. When the middle of the pancake bubbles up, flip to the other side and cook for 10 seconds. The pancake is done. Repeat for the remaining pancakes.

POT STICKER WRAPPERS

The trick to making a soft-but-chewy pot sticker wrapper is to use warm water instead of cold water to form the dough. Adding warm water to flour will denature the protein and prevent too much gluten from forming. Wrappers made of warm water are tender and flexible. I promise you, you will never want to buy pot sticker wrappers ever again.

MAKES ABOUT 40 WRAPPERS

4 cups (480 g) all-purpose flour
1¼ cups (300 ml) warm water
1 tsp salt

Combine the flour, warm water and salt in a mixer. Mix until the dough is smooth. Wrap it with plastic, and let it rest for 30 minutes. Using a pasta machine, roll the dough to #4 thickness and cut circles with a 3¼-inch (8.2-cm) cookie cutter.

If you feel like hand rolling the wrappers like we do in northern China, you can portion the dough into 10 gram balls, flatten them, then roll them out individually in a circular motion.

SOUTHERN CHINA ROOTS

我的南方人的根儿

Seasonal Vegetables and Rice Dishes

A little interesting fact before we start this chapter of seasonal vegetables and rice dishes. Wheat, corn and medium-grain (sushi) rice are the main grains grown in northern China. So, northerners eat a lot of dough as the main source of starch. We love our noodles, buns and pancakes. Jasmine rice is the main grain grown in southern China, so southerners will have rice with pretty much every meal.

Northern China is a lot colder, and it's hard to grow vegetables year-round, so northerners eat a lot more red meat. Southern China is pretty warm year-round, and their diet is very similar to California and the Mediterranean: light and fresh, with plenty of fruits and vegetables. I am a hybrid of North and South: my mom is from the northeast, and my dad's family is Cantonese. I grew up eating the best of both regions.

The Chinese truly love to eat and cook a lot of vegetables, but most restaurants just stir-fry them with a lot of oil. All the green vegetables start to taste the same after a while, and they are always a side dish. I really want to show you vegetables can be the star of the table, too! And you can do it by using a cooking technique you are already familiar with and a bright Chinese sauce.

Rice and vegetables are a big part of Chinese cuisine. Our traditional diet is not protein-driven, and it's all about balance. A typical dinner table will have one protein dish, two vegetable dishes, one starch (rice or noodle) and one soup. After this chapter, I hope you will be able to create your own complete Chinese dinner at home.

WHOLE ROASTED CAULIFLOWER WITH GARLIC CHIVE SAUCE

My love for cauliflower started long before the "healthy superfood" trend. When I feel like eating clean and having more vegetables, but don't feel like chewing through greens . . . my go-to is cauliflower. It's hearty and filling, and the added smokiness from grilling it makes the cauliflower extra savory. In this recipe, I pair grilled cauliflower with a garlicky and herbaceous sauce. Trust me, after you eat this hearty and flavorful dish, your body won't crave meat afterwards.

SERVES 4

Garlic Chive Sauce

2 tbsp (30 ml) canola oil

1 tbsp (9 g) chopped garlic

1 tbsp (7 g) chopped ginger

1 lb (450 g) garlic chives, cut into 1-inch (2.5-cm) pieces

1 serrano pepper, chopped with the seeds left in

1 tbsp (15 ml) soy sauce

Salt, to taste

2 tbsp (30 ml) lemon juice

Grilled Cauliflower

2 small cauliflower, halved carefully to keep florets attached

Black pepper

2 tbsp (12 g) Crispy Fried Garlic (page 164)

2 tbsp (6 g) chopped chives

Fill a large pot with 8 quarts (7.6 L) of water. Bring to a boil over high heat. Preheat the grill on high heat.

Meanwhile, to make the garlic chive sauce, heat a large sauté pan over high heat and add the oil in when the pan is hot. When the oil is smoking, add the garlic, ginger, garlic chives and serrano pepper. Stir-fry for 1 minute. The garlic chives should be completely cooked with a tiny bit of char. Season with soy sauce and salt, and remove the pan from the heat. In a blender, blend everything until smooth. Add the lemon juice after the green purée is formed, and adjust the seasoning with salt at the end.

After finishing the garlic chive sauce, the pot of water should be boiling. Add salt to the water; it should taste like sea water. Cook the cauliflower in the boiling water for about 4 minutes; it needs to be tender but not falling apart. Remove the cooked cauliflower from the hot water, pat dry with paper towels and season with black pepper. Place the cauliflower flat-side down on the hot grill. When the sides are charred, they are ready.

Place the cauliflower on a serving plate, spoon a generous amount of sauce over each piece and top them off with crispy garlic and chopped chives. Eat this cauliflower like a steak! It's bold in flavor and meaty in texture.

GRILLED ASPARAGUS WITH FRIED EGGS

I believe everything tastes better with an egg on top, especially vegetables. Asparagus and egg yolk are meant to be together always. Asparagus with black bean sauce is a common dish in Chinese American restaurants, and I make it way better by putting crispy fried eggs on top.

SERVES 4

Asparagus

1 lb (450 g) medium-size asparagus

2 tbsp (30 ml) canola oil

Salt and pepper, to taste

Black Bean Sauce

2 tbsp (30 ml) canola oil

1 tbsp (9 g) minced garlic

1 tsp chili flakes

2 tbsp (30 ml) black bean sauce

1 tbsp (15 ml) light soy sauce

2 tbsp (30 ml) water

1 orange, zested and juiced (zest reserved for serving)

Fried Eggs

4 tbsp (60 ml) canola oil

2 large eggs

Salt and pepper, to taste

Preheat the grill on high heat. Clean the asparagus, and cut off the tough ends, but keep them whole. Place the asparagus in a large bowl, dress with the canola oil and season with salt and pepper.

To make the sauce, in a 9-inch (23-cm) sauté pan, heat up the canola oil over medium heat. Add the garlic and chili flakes, and cook for 1 minute. Add the black bean sauce, light soy sauce and water to the pan, followed by a splash of fresh orange juice. When it comes to a simmer, cook for 30 seconds and the sauce is ready.

Grill the asparagus for about 3 minutes, until cooked but still a little crunchy.

For the eggs, heat a cast-iron pan over high heat for 2 minutes and then add the canola oil. When the oil is smoking hot, crack the eggs into the pan. The egg whites will immediately bubble up and become golden and crispy. Fry for 30 seconds until they become crispy sunny-side up eggs. Season with salt and pepper.

Place the black bean sauce down on a large plate and lay the grilled asparagus on top. Put both eggs on the asparagus, and finish the dish with some freshly grated orange zest.

DANCING EGGPLANT

One of the well-known Chinese eggplant dishes is called "fish fragrant eggplant," a.k.a. "spicy garlic eggplant." There is no fish in the traditional version; it is called that because the spicy, tangy garlic sauce is a classic sauce for braised fish. So I made this "fish fragrant eggplant" true to its name by adding bonito fish flakes on top. Not only will it look stunning visually, but the bonito flakes will also add umami to the eggplant. You can find bonito flakes in your supermarket's Asian section or at Asian markets, or just get them online.

SERVES 4

1½ lb (675 g) Japanese eggplant

3 tbsp (45 ml) rice oil (or substitute canola oil)

1 tbsp (9 g) minced garlic

1 tbsp (15 ml) black bean sauce

1 tbsp (15 ml) Doubanjiang chili paste

2 tbsp (30 ml) Shaoxing wine

3 tbsp (45 ml) soy sauce

1 tbsp (12.5 g) sugar

1 tbsp (15 ml) rice vinegar

½ cup (120 ml) chicken stock

½ tbsp (4 g) cornstarch

1 tbsp (15 ml) room temperature water

Garnish

2 tbsp (12 g) chopped green onions

1 handful bonito flakes

Clean and cut the Japanese eggplant into 2-inch (5-cm)-thick pieces. In a large sauté pan, heat the rice oil over high heat. After about 45 seconds, when the oil is smoking, add the eggplant and toss the pan really quickly so the pieces are all coated with oil. Add the garlic, stir and mix well. When you can smell the garlic in the air, add the black bean sauce and Doubanjiang chili paste. Stir well and then add the Shaoxing wine, soy sauce, sugar and rice vinegar. When everything is mixed well in the pan, add the chicken stock and cover the pan with a lid. Turn the heat down to low and simmer the eggplant for 6 minutes, until it is tender.

In a small bowl, mix the cornstarch with the water to form a slurry. When the eggplant is tender, add the slurry into the cooking liquid. You will see the sauce thicken right away. Stir and let the thickened sauce come to a simmer. The eggplant is ready.

Plate the eggplant in a shallow bowl, garnish with the green onions and place the bonito flakes on top. The heat from the eggplant will make the bonito flakes move, just like they're dancing.

KALE MIXED RICE WITH SMOKED TROUT ROE

As northerners in China, we usually eat noodles and buns a lot more than we eat rice. When I was young, I had a nanny from Shanghai, and because of her, I had rice for lunch a lot more often than before. I was way more excited about eating day-old rice than freshly made rice. That's because she would cut everything into tiny little bits and slowly sauté it. Green bok choy, smoky ham and savory dry shrimp all melting together, with just a little bit of chicken stock. The cold and crumbly rice came back to life in front of me, each grain absorbing the liquid and becoming plump and shiny. She told me, "This is called Shanghai mix rice." Here is my own California version of the mix rice, using kale and other local ingredients. I hope you will start to look forward to day-old rice just like little me.

SERVES 4

1 lb (450 g) kale

3 tbsp (45 ml) canola oil

2 tbsp (18 g) minced garlic

1 tbsp (7 g) minced ginger

½ cup (75 g) finely diced onion

1 tbsp (15 ml) light soy sauce

½ cup (120 ml) chicken stock

2 pinches white pepper

4 cups (744 g) cold steamed rice

1 tsp kosher salt

Garnish

2 tsp (6 g) toasted sesame seeds

2 tbsp (28 g) smoked trout roe

2 tbsp (12 g) Crispy Shallots (page 164)

Clean and cut the kale into ½-inch (1.2-cm)-thick strips. In an 8-quart (7.5-L) pot, add the canola oil and turn the heat to medium. When the oil is warm, add the garlic, ginger and onion, and sauté for 1 minute. When the onion turns translucent, add the kale. Sauté for 2 minutes; the kale should start to wilt. Next, add the light soy sauce and chicken stock to the pot. Turn the heat down to low, and let it simmer for 2 minutes. Season the kale with the white pepper.

Add all of the rice into the pot and slowly stir. Incorporate the kale and stock into the rice. It's ready when the rice is hot, all the liquid has been absorbed into the grains and the kale is tender but not falling apart. Season with the kosher salt.

Top off the rice with toasted sesame seeds, smoked trout roe and crispy shallots.

MILK-BRAISED NAPA CABBAGE

Napa cabbage used to be the only vegetable you could get during Beijing winters. Families would buy up to 100 pounds (45 kg) at the beginning of the winter, stack them in the yard, cover them with thick comforters and eat them for the whole winter. So, my love for Napa cabbage is by default. I am constantly looking for different ways to cook it. I read about this imperial style of braising with milk in Chinese novels, and because I am very familiar with this technique in French cooking, I re-created this dish. Now you can eat like a Chinese Emperor at home! Using milk to braise this humble vegetable brings out the sweetness of the cabbage. The texture is velvety and creamy, and it feels luxurious. The addition of cured ham and goji berries to balance the sweet and salty is very common in forbidden city cooking.

SERVES 4

1 Napa cabbage

½ oz (14 g) ginger

5 cloves garlic

1 oz (28 g) Virginia ham, sliced (can substitute Serrano ham)

2 tbsp (30 ml) canola oil

½ cup (120 ml) chicken stock

1 cup (240 ml) whole milk

1 tbsp (7 g) goji berries

1 tsp sea salt

1 pinch white pepper

Wash and clean the Napa cabbage. Remove the outside leaves, and set them aside for something else; we are only using the tender hearts for this dish. Split the hearts into quarters lengthwise, making sure the leaves are still attached to the root. Peel the skin off the ginger and thinly slice. Peel the garlic and keep the cloves whole. Slice the ham.

In a large sauté pan, heat up the oil over medium heat. Sauté the garlic and ginger for about 30 seconds. When the garlic turns golden brown on all sides, add the sliced ham. Once the aroma of ham and garlic fills the kitchen, about 1 minute, add the chicken stock and the Napa cabbage hearts into the pan and cover with a lid. Simmer for 5 minutes. Next add the milk and goji berries, and season with salt and pepper. Cover again and allow to braise for 1 more minute. It's ready to plate.

SUMMER CORN AND JALAPEÑO

Corn is one of my favorite vegetables in summertime! When the season starts in the early summer, when corn is so sweet and tender, I only want to grill or steam it and eat it off the cob. As summer gets warmer and warmer, corn starts to get a little starchy and firmer. I like to take the kernels off the cob, and stir-fry them with something spicy. This recipe is enough for four people to share, but watch out, you might not want to share with anyone!

SERVES 4

6 ears fresh summer corn

2 tbsp (30 ml) canola oil

1 tbsp (14 g) unsalted butter

½ onion, diced small

1 tsp minced ginger

1 tbsp (15 ml) soy sauce

1 tbsp (15 ml) oyster sauce

1 chopped jalapeño pepper

½ tsp ground black pepper

1 tsp rice vinegar

4 tbsp (24 g) Crispy Shallots (page 164)

Peel and clean the corn, making sure to remove all the corn silk. Cut the corn kernels off the cob. Heat a large skillet over high heat. Add the canola oil, followed immediately by the butter. Canola oil has a higher smoke point. Adding butter after the oil helps to stabilize the butter so it won't burn so quickly. When you see the butter start to brown, add the corn kernels, onion and ginger, and stir-fry for 2 minutes. Sometimes the corn kernels will pop out of the pan. This is a good sign that means your corn is cooking and roasting properly.

When the corn is a little caramelized on the outside and the roasted corn aroma is released, about 2 minutes, add the soy sauce, oyster sauce, jalapeño and black pepper, and cook for 30 seconds. Take the skillet off the heat, then add the rice vinegar and toss well. Finish the plate with crispy shallots on top.

PRO TIP: Brown butter and soy sauce is one of the best combinations of flavor! This is a Chinese American creation. Try it with poultry or hearty veggie dishes!

BACON FRIED RICE

The first dish I ever made for myself, at age seven, was ham fried rice. I first had it in a fancy Russian restaurant in Beijing. I thought fried rice was not Chinese food but Western food. When making it myself, I made sure the rice was plated on a plate instead of in a bowl, and I ate it with a spoon and fork. Later in life I found out fried rice is really a Chinese dish, but it never stopped me from adding nontraditional ingredients into it. Who wants to eat the common egg fried rice when you can have bacon? Bacon makes everything better, right?

SERVES 4

½ lb (225 g) chopped bacon

1 tbsp (7 g) minced ginger

1 tbsp (9 g) minced garlic

1 medium-size onion, diced small

3 large eggs

1 tbsp (15 ml) canola oil

1 cup (125 g) medium-diced asparagus

1 qt (774 g) cold steamed rice

2 tbsp (30 ml) soy sauce

¼ cup (24 g) chopped green onions

½ tsp ground black pepper

In a wok, or a very big cast-iron pan, render the fat from the bacon over medium heat. When the bacon is cooked but not yet crispy, remove all of the bacon from the pan. Strain the bacon drippings into a container, but leave about 2 tablespoons (30 ml) of bacon fat in the pan.

Sweat the ginger, garlic and onion in the wok until they become translucent and aromatic, about 1 minute.

Crack the eggs into a small bowl, and stir them to break the yolk. Pour the eggs into the wok and quickly stir to cook. While the eggs are still shiny and a little runny, push them to the side of the wok. Add the canola oil into the center of the wok and add the asparagus, quickly stir-frying in the oil for 10 seconds. Then push it next to the eggs.

Turn the heat to high, and add all of the steamed rice into the pan, breaking up the rice lumps with a wooden spoon or metal spatula. Once the rice becomes loose, start mixing and folding the eggs and asparagus into it. When everything in the pan is well mixed, drizzle soy sauce all over, and continue to stir and fry the rice. Last, add the cooked bacon and chopped green onions and season with black pepper. You shouldn't need extra salt because the bacon should provide enough salt. Mix everything together and cook for another 30 seconds, then plate and serve.

PRO TIP: The key to making a delicious fried rice is to be patient when you are toasting the rice in the pan. Let it caramelize a little to bring out the nuttiness of the rice.

BOK CHOY WITH CRISPY GARLIC

If superior stock-braised bok choy had a younger ABC (American-born Chinese) sister, it would be this dish! Braised bok choy is such a Chinese banquet staple, it appears at all weddings, birthdays, funerals. . . . All of us ate a lot of it growing up. It's very heavily starched and cooked with a lot of oil. My version is the opposite: very light, cooked with minimal oil and seasoned with crispy garlic and lemon zest to ensure it's packed with vibrant flavor!

SERVES 4

1 lb (450 g) baby bok choy
1 tbsp (15 ml) canola oil
1 tbsp (7 g) sliced ginger
¼ cup (60 ml) Shaoxing wine
1 tbsp (15 ml) light soy sauce
½ cup (120 ml) chicken stock
⅛ tsp ground white pepper
½ tsp kosher salt
1 tbsp (15 ml) water
½ tbsp (4 g) cornstarch

Garnish

3 tbsp (18 g) Crispy Fried Garlic (page 164)
Zest from 1 lemon

Wash and clean the bok choy, removing any yellow leaves but keeping the bok choy whole. Heat up a wok or an 8-quart (7.6-L) pot over medium heat. When it's hot, add the canola oil. Sauté the ginger in the hot oil for 30 seconds, until the ginger starts to brown on the edges. Deglaze the pot with the Shaoxing wine and light soy sauce. Let it simmer for a few seconds to cook off the alcohol, then add the chicken stock, white pepper and salt.

Pick up all the bok choy with both of your hands, holding onto the leaves, and carefully lower the stems into the pot. Cook only the stems for 1 minute. Be careful not to burn yourself. It's important to cook whole bok choy like this because the stems and leaves cook at different speeds; we need to give the stems a head start. After the stems change to a darker colored green, lay the whole bok choy into the pot. Cover with a lid, and let it simmer for 1 minute. Meanwhile, mix the water and cornstarch to make a slurry, and when the minute is up, add it into the cooking liquid and stir well. The liquid will slightly thicken.

Plate the bok choy and pour all the sauce over them. Finish with crispy garlic and fresh lemon zest on top.

JASMINE RICE

It's not easy to make perfect rice. My mom still has trouble cooking rice in a rice cooker. Here is a step-by-step method with a pro tip at the end. I've got you covered.

SERVES 4

2 cups (370 g) jasmine rice
2¼ cups (540 ml) water
1 tsp canola oil

Using a fine-mesh strainer, rinse the rice under running water. While rinsing, massage and rub the rice between your hands. You will see the water draining from it is opaque white. Repeat this for 2 minutes until you see the water becoming clearer. This means you have successfully removed the extra starch from the rice which will produce a fluffier steamed rice.

Make sure you have drained out all the water from the rice. Put the cleaned rice into a 4-quart (3.8-L) pot. Fill the pot with the water, and add the oil. Cook the rice over high heat. When it comes to a boil, turn down the heat to low. Stir the rice and cover the pot with a lid. Allow it to simmer for 20 minutes, and then turn off the heat and let it rest for 5 more minutes. Open the lid and use a fork to fluff the rice.

PRO TIP: Just like cooking any grains and beans, if you soak them before cooking, you will have a better, more evenly cooked result. After you add the rice and water in the pot, let it soak for 30 minutes before you start cooking. It will still take the same amount of time to cook the rice.

STEAMED BROWN RICE

I had brown rice for the first time when I was in culinary school. I refused to try it before because I used to "hate" everything that was labeled as the "healthier version." When I wanted to eat rice, I only ate white rice. After I tried brown rice for the first time, I regretted not eating it sooner. It's nutty, has more flavor and the bran on the outside gives it a chewier bite which I really like! I like to soak my brown rice before I cook it. This way it will cook up evenly and you won't have that layer of dry crust that everyone tries to avoid.

SERVES 4

2 cups (380 g) brown rice
3½ cups (840 ml) water
1 tsp canola oil

Using a fine-mesh strainer, rinse the rice under running water. Stir the rice, and wash it for about 1 minute. Drain the rice well.

Put the washed rice, water and oil into a 4-quart (3.8-L) pot, and allow the rice to soak for 30 minutes. When ready to cook, place over high heat. When the rice comes to a boil, turn down the heat to low, stir and cover the pot with a lid. Allow it to simmer for 30 minutes, then turn off the heat. Keep the rice covered, and let it rest for 10 minutes before fluffing the rice with a fork.

THE FISH MASTA

海鲜教主

Everyone Can Cook Fish and Shellfish

When I was a cook, I always got assigned to the fish station. Maybe this was because my chefs thought all Asians are good at cooking seafood because we eat more seafood than anybody? And you can always find live fish, crab and lobster in Asian markets. I was crowned the "Fish Masta." I can look at a piece of fish and know if this fish is cooked to medium rare or medium. I can tell you if the seared scallops are overcooked just by smelling them.

Okay, did I tell you that I didn't eat fish until I started culinary school? The reason I became very good at cooking fish is because I needed to make them taste as perfect as possible, so I would choose to eat them instead of meat. Now I am teaching you all my secrets and tricks: how to sear perfect scallops, achieve crispy-skinned fish and cook salmon without oil! Plus, I'll show you all the yummy sauces to go with them. You just entered level one of becoming the next Fish Masta.

SEARED SCALLOPS WITH SPICY BLACK BEAN SAUCE

Scallops are the ocean's sweet jewels for us. They are easy to clean, and they cook fast. And they're super meaty with all lean proteins. But when you overcook them, they become this rubbery, fishy hockey puck. Scallops should only cook to medium. Many people tell me they disliked scallops until they tasted this dish. This black bean sauce is spicy and earthy, and it really brings out the sweetness from the scallops and the corn. I use rice oil, because it has a high smoke point. It will give the scallops a beautiful sear. If you can't find rice oil, grapeseed oil and avocado oil are just as great! Stay away from olive oil if you want to cook anything at high temperature; the smoke point is too low, and your food will burn before you get a good sear.

SERVES 4

Spicy Black Bean Sauce

1 tbsp (15 ml) canola oil

1 tbsp (9 g) minced garlic

1 tbsp (15 ml) Doubanjiang chili paste

¼ cup (60 ml) black bean sauce

3 tbsp (45 ml) freshly squeezed orange juice

½ orange for zest

Scallops

12 scallops (size U20/10)

Salt and white pepper, to taste

3 tbsp (45 ml) rice oil

1 tbsp (7 g) minced ginger

½ tbsp (5 g) minced garlic

¼ cup (38 g) chopped onion

3 cups (495 g) corn kernels

2 tbsp (30 ml) soy sauce

½ tbsp (8 ml) rice vinegar

1 tbsp (3 g) chopped chives

2 tbsp (12 g) Crispy Fried Garlic (page 164)

To make the spicy black bean sauce, heat up the oil in a small sauté pan over medium heat. When the oil is hot, add the garlic and immediately drop the heat to low. Sweat the garlic for 15 seconds, then add the Doubanjiang chili paste and black bean sauce. Continue to slowly sauté for 2 minutes. The sauce is almost ready for the next step when you smell the chili paste and black bean sauce. The sauce will become shiny and thicken. Add the orange juice and mix well. If the sauce is a little thick, add 1 tablespoon (15 ml) of water until you get to a spoon-coating consistency. Finish with fresh orange zest.

Pat dry all of the scallops, and season with salt and white pepper on all sides. Heat up the rice oil in a large cast-iron skillet over high heat. When the oil is smoking, quickly lay all the scallops in the pan, and remember to give them space in between. Baste the scallops with hot oil from the skillet, and do not flip or move the scallops. Let them get a really good sear. When the sides of the scallops are golden brown, flip them and quickly cook the other side for about 3 seconds. I like to call this step "let the hot oil kiss the other side." The scallops are finished cooking and they should be medium doneness at this point. From start to finish your cooking time should be around 4 minutes total.

Remove all of the cooked scallops and drain out some oil, leaving about 1 tablespoon (15 ml) of oil in the pan. Adjust the heat to medium. In the same cast-iron pan, add the ginger, garlic and onion. Sauté them and scrape the little bits of fond (the little bits of yummy goodness that make a flavorful sauce or soup) at the same time. When the onion is translucent, add the corn. Sauté for 2 minutes. Season with soy sauce and rice vinegar at the end. Toss in the chives after removing the skillet from the heat, and the corn is ready.

To plate, place all of the corn on a large plate. Lay the seared scallops on top, and put ½ teaspoon of spicy black bean sauce on each scallop. Season to taste, and finish with crispy garlic on top.

SEA BASS WITH SWEET-AND-SOUR SAUCE

Did you know the famous sweet-and-sour sauce was originally paired with fish from a region near Shanghai? Instead of batter frying the whole fish, I re-created a healthier version that's seared with crispy skin for texture. Now that you mastered the sweet-and-sour sauce, try to resist the urge to put sweet-and-sour on everything, okay?

SERVES 4

Sweet-and-Sour Sauce

½ tbsp (4 g) minced ginger

½ cup (120 ml) orange juice

1 cup (240 ml) plum sauce (sub apricot jelly)

2 tbsp (30 ml) ketchup

½ tsp kosher salt

Sea Bass

4 (6-oz [168-g] each) skin-on sea bass fillets

Salt and pepper, to taste

6 tbsp (90 ml) canola oil, divided

Vegetables

2 tbsp (30 ml) canola oil

1 cup (150 g) sliced onion

1 cup (225 g) sliced celery

½ cup (50 g) rehydrated sliced wood ear mushrooms (sub shiitake mushrooms)

1 cup (100 g) sliced green onions (white part only)

1 red jalapeño pepper, sliced

Salt, to taste

To make the sweet-and-sour sauce, combine the ginger, orange juice, plum sauce and ketchup in a small saucepot. Cook over low heat. After the sauce comes to a simmer, season with salt and it's ready to use. This sweet-and-sour sauce tastes great both warm or at room temperature.

Pat dry the sea bass fillets and use a sharp paring knife to slice the skin of the fish 3 times. Make sure your cuts are shallow, and be careful not to cut into the flesh of the fish. By scoring the fish skin, the fish will stay flat and not curl up when you sear the skin. Season the sea bass with salt and pepper on both sides, and be ready to cook them.

We are going to cook 2 fillets at a time so the skin of the fish will be crispy. If you try to cook too many fillets at the same time, it creates too much steam during cooking and the skin of the fish will become soggy. Heat up 3 tablespoons (45 ml) of canola oil in a large skillet over medium-high heat. Slide 2 sea bass fillets skin-side down into the skillet. When the fish hits the hot oil, the flesh will immediately tense up and the center of the fillet will rise. The fillets look like they "form into a fist." Hold back the urge to push them down right away. The sea bass fillets will slowly relax in about 30 seconds.

While waiting, baste the fish with hot oil from the pan. After they are coated with hot oil, use a spatula or the spoon you were basting with to push down the fillets gently, making sure all the skin touches hot oil. Continue to cook the fish on the skin side for about 3 minutes, basting hot oil all over the fillets while searing. After the skin is golden brown and crispy, flip the fish to cook on the flesh side for 30 seconds and they are ready. Repeat and cook 2 more fillets.

To make the vegetables, heat up the canola oil in a large sauté pan over high heat. Add the onion and stir-fry until slightly charred, about 30 seconds. Add the celery, wood ear mushrooms, green onions and jalapeño, and quickly stir-fry for 30 seconds. Season with salt to taste. Make sure all the vegetables are still crunchy, not overcooked.

To plate, place the vegetables on the bottom. Lay the sea bass skin-side up with sweet-and-sour sauce on the side.

KING SALMON IN A BAG

Cooking in a bag in a bath of temperature-controlled water has a fancy French name, "sous vide." Professional chefs have been using this technique for years, and now there are many sous vide machines built for home use. But you can also easily achieve controlled water temperature with a thermometer. I like to cook salmon this way, because it barely uses any oil and cooks to temperature consistently every time without worry. The herbaceous celery with black vinegar helps to cut the richness of salmon. I always like to pair something acidic with a fatty fish like salmon.

SERVES 4

Salmon

1 tsp sesame oil

4 (6-oz [168-g] each) sashimi-grade salmon portions

Salt and pepper, to taste

Celery

1½ cups (338 g) sliced celery (sliced against the grain)

1 tsp sesame oil

Salt and pepper, to taste

1 lemon for zest

Garnish

½ cup (120 ml) black vinegar

1 cup (20 g) young celery leaves

4 tbsp (56 g) salmon roe (optional)

Heat up 8 quarts (7.6 L) of water in a 12-quart (11.4-L) or larger stock pot to 125°F (52°C). If you have a sous vide circulator or an induction burner, set the temperature to 125°F (52°C) and hold. If you don't have one, all you need to do is keep a thermometer in the pot and control the water temperature by turning the heat up and down.

Rub the sesame oil all over the salmon, and season them with salt and pepper. Place them flat into a gallon-size ziplock bag.

Toss the celery with sesame oil, and season with salt, pepper and fresh lemon zest. Put the celery into another gallon-size ziplock bag, and try to push extra air out of the bag, then seal it. Using clips, secure the opening side of both ziplock bags to the rim of the pot, making sure the fish and celery are fully submerged in the water. Cook for 20 minutes.

Place the barely cooked celery slices on the plate and lay the salmon portions over them. Finish with black vinegar and celery leaves all around, and place salmon roe on top (if desired).

STEAMED CLAMS AND GARLIC

I love cooking shellfish at home. They normally take the least amount of time to prepare, but always deliver maximum flavor! This simple steamed clam dish is warm and garlicky, and tastes like the best version of the ocean—and it only takes 2 minutes to cook! Remember when you are cooking any shellfish, the moment they open their shells, they are ready to eat. Don't overcook them; they will turn to rubber bands in seconds.

SERVES 4

1 tbsp (15 ml) canola oil

1 tbsp (9 g) minced garlic

1 cup (48 g) garlic chives, cut into 1-inch (2.5-cm) pieces

2 lbs (900 g) small- to medium-size clams

1 cup (240 ml) Shaoxing wine

1 tbsp (14 g) unsalted butter

Salt, to taste

2 tbsp (12 g) Crispy Fried Garlic (for garnish, page 164)

Heat up the oil in a 6-quart (5.7-L) saucepot over medium heat. When the oil is hot, add the garlic and garlic chives. When the garlic starts to turn golden, add the clams to the pot and stir. Pour Shaoxing wine in and cover the pot with a lid.

Check after about 90 seconds; all of the clams should have opened up. Add the butter to the broth, then season to taste with salt. Plate the clams and all the broth in a shallow bowl. Garnish with plenty of crispy garlic on top.

PRO TIP: Soak the clams in clean, cold water for 20 minutes before cooking so they will spit out the sand. After soaking, clean the outside shell under running water. This way you won't have sand in your clams.

SHRIMP AND PEAS

Growing up in China, every year during springtime we would eat freshly harvested dragon well tea stir-fry with freshwater shrimp. The grassy fresh note of dragon well tea paired with sweet shrimp announced the arrival of spring! In the United States, spring marks the start of fresh English pea season. English peas lightly stir-fried with shrimp bring out the natural sweetness from both the peas and the shrimp. This dish tastes like a plate of ocean candy, and it is sure to make you happy.

SERVES 4

1 lb (450 g) peeled and deveined raw medium-size shrimp

1 tsp sesame oil

1 tbsp (8 g) cornstarch

¼ tsp ground white pepper

1 cup (85 g) sugar snap peas

2 tbsp (30 ml) canola oil

1 tbsp (7 g) minced ginger

½ cup (113 g) shucked English peas

4 tbsp (60 ml) Shaoxing wine

1 tbsp (15 ml) light soy sauce

Salt, to taste

1 lemon for zest

Rinse and clean the shrimp under running water, then pat dry. In a mixing bowl, toss the shrimp with the sesame oil, cornstarch and white pepper. Massage the cornstarch onto the shrimp so they are evenly coated. Clean the sugar snap peas, snip off the stringy ends and slice them into thirds.

Heat up the canola oil in a wok or large skillet over medium heat. Add the ginger into the oil. When the ginger starts to brown, about 30 seconds, add the shrimp and start to stir-fry. When the shrimp start to curl up and turn pink, about 1 minute in, add both types of peas and continue to stir-fry for 1 minute. Add the Shaoxing wine and soy sauce to the wok, cook for 10 seconds and add salt to taste.

Plate the shrimp. Add fresh lemon zest all over, and it's ready to serve.

ENVELOPE SOLE WITH XO CHILI SAUCE

Cooking in parchment paper is consistent and easy. Once you master the cooking time, your dish will come out perfect every single time. When you bake the parchment envelope in the oven, the paper traps all the steam inside, so your fish will not dry out, and you can bake many portions at the same time! And who doesn't like to open a "gift" at the dinner table? Both Chinese and French cuisine like to cook fennel with a white fish for its liquorish flavor. I also like to use the crunchy wood ear mushroom to contrast with the flaky fish. Finally, the XO Chili Sauce (page 155) is not overly spicy for a delicate fish, but it adds the perfect heat and savoriness.

SERVES 4

2 tbsp (30 ml) canola oil

1 fennel, cut in quarters

Salt and pepper, to taste

4 (6-oz [168-g]) sole fillets

4 tsp (20 ml) sesame oil

4 rehydrated wood ear mushrooms

2 tbsp (30 ml) XO Chili Sauce (page 155)

4 tsp (19 g) unsalted butter

4 tbsp (60 ml) Shaoxing wine, divided

Preheat the oven to 450°F (230°C, or gas mark 8).

Heat up the canola oil in a medium pan over high heat. Sear and roast the fennel quarters until all sides are golden brown, about 2 minutes on each side. Season with salt and pepper to taste.

Pat the sole fillets dry, rub each fillet with 1 teaspoon of sesame oil and season with salt and pepper. Fold 4 pieces of 15 x 10–inch (38 x 25–cm) parchment paper into thirds the long way. Place 1 sole fillet in the middle with 1 quarter of the roasted fennel and 1 wood ear mushroom next to it. Spread ½ tablespoon (8 ml) of XO sauce on the sole fillet and place 1 teaspoon of butter next to it.

Pick up the 2 sides along the creases to form a "roof" over the fish, then fold the "roof" down into ½-inch (1.2-cm)-thick folds. Fold them 3 to 4 times, until the "roof" is lying almost flat. Pick up 1 open side of the envelope and fold with ½-inch (1.2-cm) creases to close. Pour 1 tablespoon (15 ml) of Shaoxing wine into each envelope from the other open end, then close it by folding it with ½-inch (1.2-cm) creases. Repeat to wrap all portions.

Place the envelopes on a large rimmed baking sheet, and roast them in the middle rack of the oven for 8 minutes. Be careful; the steam inside the packets will expand the envelopes. Slit the tops with a knife and gently open them to serve.

SINGAPORE-STYLE CHILI PRAWNS

I married a Singaporean, and Jimmy and I bonded over food before we started to date. I spent a good amount of time trailing his mom and learning how to cook Singaporean food. Chili crab is their national dish. It's mud crab cooked in sweet and spicy tomato sauce then finished with egg ribbons. I perfected the sauce over the years, and it pairs well with most seafood. I even won a *Top Chef* challenge making chili crawfish. The secret ingredient for the sauce is ketchup!

SERVES 4

Singapore Sweet Chili Sauce

3 tbsp (45 ml) canola oil
1 tbsp (7 g) minced ginger
1 tbsp (9 g) minced garlic
2 tbsp (12 g) minced green onions
1 tbsp (5 g) minced lemongrass
2 tsp (10 ml) black bean sauce
1 tbsp (30 ml) sambal chili paste
1 tbsp (15 ml) soy sauce
1 cup (240 ml) tomato sauce
2 tbsp (30 ml) ketchup
1 tsp kosher salt
2 tbsp (25 g) sugar
½ cup (120 ml) chicken stock
1 tbsp (8 g) cornstarch
2 tbsp (30 ml) water

Prawns

12 head-on jumbo prawns
3 tbsp (45 ml) canola oil
1 tbsp (7 g) minced ginger
1 tbsp (9 g) minced garlic

To Finish

2 eggs
Bread or rice, for serving (optional)

To make the Singapore sweet chili sauce, heat up the canola oil in a wok or sauté pan over medium heat. When the oil is hot, add the ginger, garlic, green onions and lemongrass to the pan. Slowly stir-fry for about 3 minutes, until the aroma fills the kitchen, and all the aromatics start to brown. Add the black bean sauce, sambal chili paste, soy sauce, tomato sauce, ketchup, salt and sugar. Stir well. When everything melts together, add the chicken stock. In a small bowl, mix the cornstarch and water to create a slurry. When the sauce comes to a simmer, add the slurry and stir well. Set the sauce aside for the next step.

Clean the prawns by slitting open the back of the shell and removing the vein. This will also help the prawns to absorb the sauce. Heat up the canola oil in a large skillet. When the oil is smoking, lay the prawns in the pan. When one side is cooked and the color changes to red, flip the prawns to the other side—about 1 minute each side. Next add the ginger and garlic into the pan. When both sides of the prawns are seared, but the prawns are still rare inside, add the Singapore chili sauce and drop the heat to low. Simmer the prawns for 2 minutes.

Meanwhile, crack the eggs into a small bowl. Break the yolks, and mix with a fork. Slowly pour the egg into the sauce to form ribbons. Let the egg coagulate for 10 seconds, then swirl the pan and fold the egg ribbons into the sauce. The egg will thicken the sauce and look like egg drops.

This dish is all about the sauce! Sop it up with bread or eat over rice. And don't be afraid of being messy when you eat them—prawn heads are the best vessel to slurp up the sauce!

BOWL OF HUGS

一碗碗的拥抱

Soups, Congees and Comfort Foods

People always say, food is the key to someone's heart. This is especially true for Chinese culture. We are very reserved when it comes to expressing our feelings. Our parents hardly ever tell us they love us, or give us hugs, and they show us they love us by asking us to come home to have mom's dumplings. Or they drop off soup when they hear we are not feeling well. Nothing can compare to the feeling of hot and hearty broth rolling down into your stomach: you start to feel warm and fuzzy right after a sip, and you can feel the sickness sliding away from you at that very moment.

Here is a chapter full of stick-to-your-ribs comfort foods, from Steamed Egg Custard (page 124) to spicy Mapo Tofu (page 132). Each and every one of them is close to my heart; each one of them has warmed my soul. Take this hug from me, and spread the love. Xoxo

MEAT-AND-BONE HERBAL TEA SOUP

My great-grandpa came to the United States as an herbalist in 1900. He was the only Chinese doctor that was serving the railroad workers, and he made a name for himself in the southern California community. I heard about this meat-and-bone broth soup from my grandpa and grandaunts; it was their breakfast growing up. The heavy use of whole garlic and angelica root prevented them from getting colds, and they all grew up healthy. Although this is a classic soup from southern China, no one in my family knew how to make it after my great-grandma passed away. I re-created the soup. This is for you, great-grandpa!

SERVES 6 TO 8

2 lb (900 g) pork neck bone
2 lb (900 g) pork sparerib
½ cup (120 ml) canola oil
4 whole heads garlic
¼ cup (40 g) black peppercorns
¼ cup (40 g) white peppercorns
3 star anise
3 tbsp (18 g) whole cumin seeds
2 oz (56 g) dry Angelica root
1 stick cinnamon
2 tbsp (30 ml) soy sauce
2 tbsp (30 ml) dark soy sauce
4 dry shiitake mushrooms
2 tbsp (14 g) goji berries
Salt, to taste

To ensure a clear broth for the soup, we are going to blanch the pork bones first. Add the pork neck bone and spareribs to an 8- to 10-quart (7.6- to 9.5-L) stockpot, fill it with water and cook over medium heat. When the water starts to bubble but not quite boil, turn off the heat and let it rest for 10 minutes. You will see blood start to coagulate at the ends of the bones: discard the cooking liquid. Wipe off the blood from the ends of the bones and place all the bones into a new large stockpot to make the soup. Fill the pot with new water to barely cover the bones.

Heat the oil in a medium-size sauté pan over medium heat. Fry the whole garlic in the oil until golden. Put the black peppercorn, white peppercorn, star anise and cumin seeds into a soup spice pouch, place it into the soup pot and then add the fried garlic, Angelica root, cinnamon, soy sauce, dark soy and dry shiitake mushrooms. Simmer the soup over low heat for 3 hours. Add the goji berries during the last 5 minutes of cooking, and salt to taste. Enjoy the soup with pork bones and goji berries.

CHINESE SHRIMP AND GRITS

When I had shrimp and grits in New Orleans for the first time, I was shocked by how similar it tasted to the corn congee I had when I was young in Beijing. Northern China grows a lot of corn, so cornmeal is part of our everyday diet. To see that a dish I grew up with is also a staple comfort food in the United States blows my mind. Food does connect the world. My shrimp and grits started as a classic Chinese garlic shrimp recipe, but now I like to finish it with butter.

SERVES 4

Chinese Grits (Corn Congee)

2 tbsp (30 ml) canola oil

1 tbsp (7 g) minced ginger

1 tbsp (3 g) chopped green onions

2 qt (1.9 L) water

1½ cups (240 g) fine grain corn grits, or polenta

1 tsp kosher salt

1 tsp sugar

Garlic Shrimp

16 medium raw shrimp, peeled and deveined

1 tbsp (15 ml) Shaoxing wine

1 tbsp (15 ml) light soy sauce

½ tbsp (4 g) cornstarch

4 tbsp (60 ml) canola oil

2 tbsp (18 g) minced garlic

3 tbsp (9 g) chopped garlic chives

2 tbsp (30 ml) soy sauce

1 tbsp (15 ml) water

½ tbsp (7 g) butter

4 tbsp (24 g) Crispy Fried Garlic (page 164)

For the grits, heat the canola oil in a 6- to 8-quart (5.7- to 7.6-L) pot over medium heat. When the oil is warm, add the ginger and green onions, stir and cook for 30 seconds. Add the water and bring it to boil. As soon as it starts to bubble, add the grits and whisk well. Turn the heat to low and constantly stir the grits while it slowly simmers. Usually grits take about 45 minutes to cook. Always check the instructions on the package as the cooking time may vary. Season with the salt and sugar at the end.

To make the shrimp, toss them with the Shaoxing wine, light soy and cornstarch, massaging them so they are completely coated.

Heat up the canola oil in a large skillet over high heat. When the oil starts to smoke, add the shrimp and garlic and stir-fry for 3 minutes. When the shrimp are cooked and have turned opaque and curl up, add the garlic chives, soy sauce and water and toss for 10 seconds. Take the skillet off the heat, and finish with the butter.

To serve, spoon grits into each bowl, place some shrimp on top and cover with crispy garlic.

STEAMED EGG CUSTARD WITH MINCED PORK

My mom was a doctor, so she never really spent too much time cooking. When I was not feeling well, she would make steamed egg custard to go with medicines. It's warm and silky, and it feels like mom is hugging me from inside. For me, this is the ultimate comfort food. This version is made with ground pork, but day-old roasted chicken, tofu or other proteins will all work just as perfectly.

SERVES 4

Custard

½ cup (115 g) ground pork

½ tbsp (8 ml) soy sauce

¼ tsp Chinese five-spice powder

1 tsp minced ginger

2 large eggs

1 cup (240 ml) chicken stock

1 tsp sweet mirin cooking wine

1 tsp light soy sauce

¼ tsp fish sauce

1 pinch ground white pepper

To Finish

1 green onion

1½ tbsp (23 ml) soy sauce

1 tsp sesame oil

Tools

1 (10-qt [10-L]) soup pot

Steamer

1 large shallow bowl that fits in the steamer, with a lid

In a small bowl, combine the ground pork, soy sauce, five-spice and ginger. Mix well, and set it aside to marinate while you whisk the eggs.

In a medium-size mixing bowl, combine the eggs, chicken stock, mirin, light soy sauce and fish sauce, and whisk with a fork. Season with white pepper. Make sure the mixture is smooth and pale yellow with minimal air bubbles. Use a fork instead of a whisk so less air whips into the egg mixture.

To set up the steamer, fill the 10-quart (10-L) pot half full of water and cook on high heat. When the water is rapidly boiling, set the steamer on top of the pot and get ready to steam the custard.

Chop up the green onion into little circles for garnish.

Spread a thin layer of the ground pork evenly on the bottom of a large shallow bowl. Pour the egg mixture over it. Place the bowl in the steamer and cover with a lid. Steam on high heat for about 7 to 8 minutes. The egg custard should be fully set in the middle, silky and smooth. If there are a lot of tiny holes in the custard, this means it is overcooked.

Drizzle soy sauce and sesame oil all over the surface of the custard, and sprinkle the chopped green onions on top.

BROKEN RICE CONGEE WITH PUMPKIN

It takes a long time to slowly simmer rice congee, a porridge that's mainly made of rice. By slowly cooking the rice, the starch is released into the liquid, and it will become a big pot of creamy goodness without adding any dairy. I wish I could have congee more often, but it just takes too long. I first started to break the rice before making the congee on *Top Chef* during a Quick Fire Challenge. Within 20 minutes of cooking time, I was able to make a creamy congee and won that challenge. I have been using this method to cook congee ever since!

SERVES 4

1½ cups (292 g) Calrose medium-grain rice

2 qt + 1 cup (2.13 L) water

1 tbsp (7 g) minced ginger

2 tbsp (28 g) unsalted butter

2 cups (232 g) large diced peeled pumpkin

1 star anise

1 pinch ground cloves

2 tbsp (25 g) dark brown sugar

Salt, to taste

1 tbsp (9 g) toasted sesame seeds

Using a blender, blend the dry rice on high speed for 5 seconds. All of the grains should be broken, and some should have become powder. Boil the water with ginger in a 6- to 8-quart (5.7- to 7.6-L) pot over high heat. When the ginger water comes to a rapid boil, add the rice and stir like crazy. When it comes back to a boil, turn down the heat to low. Simmer it about 15 minutes, stirring often with a heat-resistant rubber spatula.

While the congee is cooking, cook the pumpkin. Heat up the butter in a large sauté pan over medium heat. Let the butter brown in the pan, then add the pumpkin. Add the star anise, cloves and brown sugar, and cook until tender. Season with salt to taste.

To plate, pour 2 cups (460 g) of congee on the bottom of a bowl. Add roasted pumpkin on top, and garnish with sesame seeds.

CLAMS AND HAM CONGEE

The Chinese believe that rice has healing powers. When you have a cold, you eat hot congee to sweat it out. When you have a stomachache, you eat a bowl of warm congee to soothe it. The first food we had when we were babies was most likely congee instead of baby cereals. This is what I like to fill my belly with at night to help me sleep. In this recipe, we will be making congee the traditional way, slowly simmered for a long time. If you are short on time, you can always use my broken rice shortcut (page 127).

SERVES 4

1½ cups (292 g) Calrose medium-grain rice

2 tbsp (30 ml) canola oil

1 tbsp (7 g) minced ginger

1 tbsp (9 g) minced garlic

2 tbsp (6 g) minced green onions

2 qt + 1 cup (2.13 L) water

3 oz (84 g) Virginia-style cured ham (can sub Serrano ham), chopped

1 lb (450 g) cleaned Manila clams

1 tsp sesame oil

¼ tsp white pepper

Salt, to taste

Put the rice in a fine-mesh strainer, run it under water and wash and rinse the rice for 1 minute.

Heat the oil in an 8-quart (7.6-L) pot over medium heat. When the oil is warm, add the ginger, garlic and green onions to the pot, and cook them for about 1 minute. Add the water and bring it to a low boil. Next, add the rice and stir well. Turn the heat to low, and add the ham. Simmer for 40 minutes, making sure you are stirring often and scraping the bottom of the congee with a wooden spoon or heat-resistant spatula.

When the congee is thick and creamy, it is done. Add the clams to the congee, cover it with a lid and steam the clams for 2 minutes. When the clams all open, add the sesame oil, white pepper and salt to taste.

SPINACH EGG DROP SOUP

When I was growing up in Beijing, my grandma was very particular about family dinners. We had to have one vegetable, one meat and one fish dish, with a side of starch and a soup to complete the meal. Everyone sat at the dinner table sharing our days with one another; even little me got to have a voice among the adults. This simple soup represents one of our family's values. I hope this will warm your heart as much as it does mine.

SERVES 4

1 tbsp (15 ml) canola oil

1 tbsp (7 g) chopped ginger

1 tbsp (3 g) chopped green onions

2 qt (1.9 L) chicken stock (sub vegetable stock for vegetarian version)

1 cup (248 g) diced soft tofu

½ oz (14 g) dry seaweed

1 tbsp (15 ml) light soy sauce

1 tbsp (8 g) cornstarch

2 tbsp (30 ml) water

4 cups (120 g) baby spinach leaves

2 large eggs

1 tsp sesame oil

Heat up the oil in a 4-quart (3.8-L) soup pot over medium heat. Add the ginger and green onions, sweat them for 30 seconds and add the chicken stock. When the soup base is simmering, add the tofu, seaweed and light soy sauce. Stir well. To make the slurry, combine the cornstarch and water in a small bowl, mix well and add to the soup. Stir well. When the soup has thickened from the slurry, add the spinach.

Crack the eggs in a small bowl. Break the yolks and mix with the egg whites using a fork; do not whisk air into the eggs. Float the egg mixture on top of the soup, and gently stir and fold to create ribbons of egg in the soup. As soon as the egg ribbons are formed, remove the soup from the heat and finish with sesame oil.

MAPO TOFU

Legend says, Mapo tofu was invented by Grandma Chen hundreds of years ago in Chengdu, a city in the Sichuan province of China. This soft, spicy, custard-like tofu dish became the most known tofu dish in the world. The Japanese version is a little on the sweeter side. The Korean version uses less numbing Sichuan peppercorn with more heat from chili peppers. Here is my version of the recipe: I am trying to stay true to the original Grandma Chen version, using ground beef and preserved radish (zha cai, salt-cured radish) instead of ground pork. The heat is from Doubanjiang (fermented, spicy, broad bean chili paste). Be careful with the Sichuan peppercorns; they can be an overpowering, numbing, yet fun ingredient. Use it sparingly. This is a bowl of hugs that can sometimes slap you back with spice.

SERVES 4

2 tbsp (30 ml) canola oil

½ tbsp (4 g) Sichuan peppercorns

4 oz (112 g) ground beef

1 tbsp (7 g) minced ginger

2 tbsp (18 g) minced garlic

3 tbsp (38 g) preserved radish (zha cai), minced

3 tbsp (45 ml) Doubanjiang (use less to make less spicy)

1 tbsp (15 ml) Shaoxing wine

¼ cup (60 ml) chicken stock

1 (18-oz [504-g]) box silken tofu, diced into large bite-size pieces

2 tbsp (6 g) chopped green onions

Cooked rice, for serving

Heat up the canola oil in a large skillet or a wok over high heat. When the oil is smoking hot, add the Sichuan peppercorns. You will smell the floral, spicy scent right away. Stir-fry for 5 seconds, and add the ground beef. Stir-fry and brown the beef in the skillet, about 3 minutes, then add the ginger, garlic and preserved radish to the skillet.

When the aromas start to release into the air, about 1 minute, add the Doubanjiang and Shaoxing wine and stir well, then add the chicken stock; you will have a spicy beef ragú in the skillet. Lower the heat, and let it simmer for 3 minutes so all the flavors melt together. Add the tofu into the skillet; simmer for 5 minutes, and be gentle when you stir, so the silken tofu will stay intact. After 5 minutes, add the green onions into the tofu, gently mix well and serve it when it's piping hot with a big bowl of rice.

PRO TIP: Cooking uses all of your senses. Don't just rely on a timer. Cook with your nose, using your sense of smell, watch with your eyes, listen to the food sizzle, taste as you are cooking and touch the ingredients with your hands. The estimated time is meant to help you, but you can use your own senses to determine when a dish is done.

Best wishes for the New Year
HAPPY WEDDING

DOUBLE HAPPINESS

庆双喜

Larger Dishes for Holidays and Celebrations

Holidays, birthdays, weddings, funerals, promotions, retirements—we celebrate all these important life moments through a table full of food. And every single gathering will need a star dish that has special meaning to the event, accompanied by a series of smaller dishes and a starch.

In Chinese culture, being whole and complete is considered lucky and the way of life, so celebration dishes often involve cooking a whole animal. Steamed whole fish is a staple at every single feast; whole chicken is a must for Chinese New Year. In this chapter you will learn how easy it is to soy-poach a whole chicken (page 139), roast a whole lobster without a wok (page 140) and how to eat Hot Pot (page 148) with a group of friends.

I will decode the hidden meaning behind each dish. Read this chapter like your navigation assistant for Chinese American culture.

WHOLE STEAMED RED SNAPPER

Steamed whole fish is the staple of any Chinese celebration feast. Fish symbolize prosperity, luck and opportunities in our culture. My version is extra exciting, with bean sprouts tossed in and Doubanjiang to add texture and spice. The aged soy sauce brings in more umami, and the final pour of hot oil over the steamed fish will push the aroma to overdrive. You want to source the freshest fish to steam. Make sure the gills are bright red, the eyeballs are clear and the flesh bounces back when you press it. If a whole fish freaks you out a little bit, you can always steam a fish fillet; just drop the cooking time to 4 to 5 minutes. Don't worry, prosperity won't run away from you. Decode the special meaning behind this dish: Bean sprouts represent growth, and fish represents prosperity and wealth. Eat this dish, and you will grow your wealth.

SERVES 6

1½ lb (675 g) whole red snapper, cleaned, scaled and gutted

Salt and white pepper, to taste

1 oz (28 g) bean sprouts

1 tsp Doubanjiang chili paste

1 tbsp (15 ml) Shaoxing wine

2 thinly sliced green onions, divided

1 tsp sesame oil

1 tbsp (7 g) thinly sliced ginger

1 red Fresno chili, thinly sliced, seeds removed

4 tbsp (60 ml) aged soy sauce (I like Wan Ja Shan brand)

4 tbsp (60 ml) canola oil

Tools

Stainless steel or bamboo steamer that is big enough to fit the whole fish

A large plate that fits in the steamer and holds the fish

Fill the bottom of the steamer with water and start boiling the water. Score the fish 3 times on each side for even cooking. Rub the inside and the outside of snapper with salt and pepper, and set aside.

In a small mixing bowl, toss the bean sprouts with the Doubanjiang, Shaoxing wine, 1 pinch of sliced green onions and the sesame oil, and season to taste with salt. Stuff the snapper with the seasoned bean sprouts. Place a few slices of ginger on the flesh of the fish, and place the fish on a plate for steaming. Steam the stuffed whole snapper over high heat in the steamer for 8 minutes.

Meanwhile, toss the sliced Fresno chili pepper and the rest of the green onions together. Heat up the soy sauce in a small saucepan, simmer for 1 minute and turn of the heat. This cooked soy sauce is part of the sauce for the steamed fish.

When the fish is finished steaming, take it out of the steamer and place on a serving dish. Drizzle the soy sauce all over the fish, and place an even layer of green onions and Fresno chili on the steamed fish. In a small sauté pan, heat up the cooking oil until smoking hot and then pour the hot oil over the green onions on the fish. You can smell the caramelized soy sauce and onion aroma.

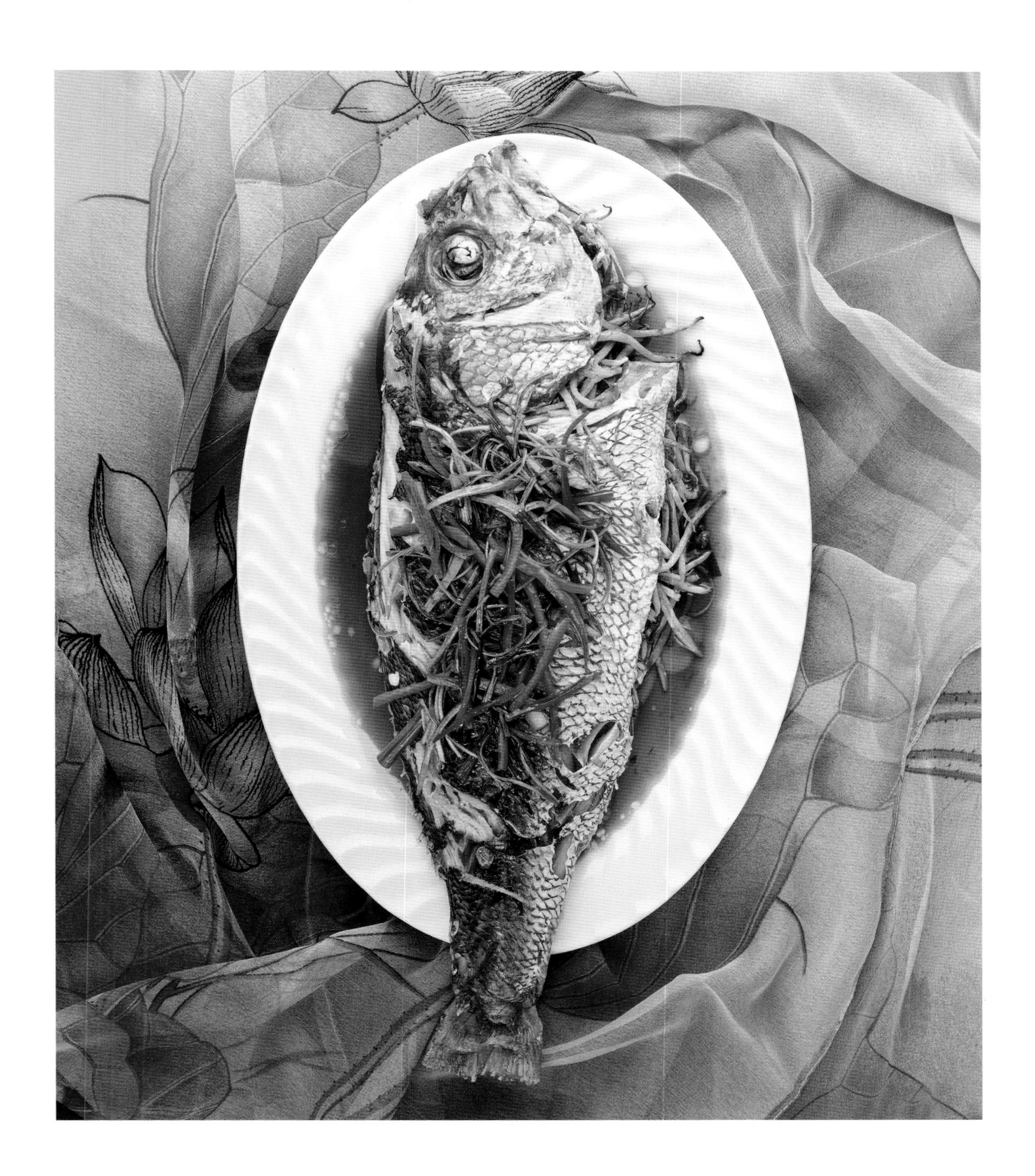

SOY-POACHED WHOLE CHICKEN

One of the first hawkers who got a Michelin star in the world is Hawker Chan in Singapore. He sells traditional, Chinese-style, soy sauce chicken. I am not guaranteeing you will get a Michelin star when you follow my recipe, but I can tell you it's life-changingly easy to make and delicious. Make sure you save this poaching liquid for the next few times you make this dish. It will only get better and better after each use. Mine sits in my freezer, and I have been using it over and over again for 2 years now.

SERVES 4

3 star anise

1 stick cinnamon

1 tsp cloves

1 tsp chili flakes

1 tbsp (8 g) Sichuan peppercorns

2 tbsp (30 ml) canola oil

4 oz (112 g) ginger, smashed and roughly chopped

6 green onions cut in 2-inch (5-cm) pieces

1 head of garlic (break up the cloves, but don't peel them)

½ cup (112 g) sugar

2 cups (480 ml) Shaoxing wine

2 cups (480 ml) soy sauce

2 tbsp (30 ml) dark soy sauce

3 qt (2.8 L) chicken stock

1 tbsp (18 g) kosher salt

1 (2½-lb [1.1-kg]) whole chicken

Tie all of the spices into a cheesecloth sachet. Heat up the canola oil over high heat in a medium-size stock pot. The pot needs to be able to fit a whole chicken; an 8-quart (7.6-L) pot should work. When the oil is smoking hot, add the ginger, green onions and garlic to the pot. Stir-fry for 30 seconds, and when you can smell the aroma from them in the air, push everything to the outer sides of the pot. Add the sugar into the middle of the pot and let it caramelize. Stir the sugar as it cooks. When it turns into a dark amber color, about 3 minutes, push and stir the ginger, scallions and garlic into the caramel.

Next add the Shaoxing wine to the pot. Turn the heat down to medium, and stir and scrape the bottom of the pot so all the little bits melt. Add the soy sauce and dark soy into the pot. When it comes back to a simmer, add the chicken stock and drop the spice sachet into the liquid. Season with salt, and turn the heat down to low to simmer for 30 minutes.

Pat the chicken dry inside and outside with paper towels, and turn the heat of the poaching liquid to high. When the poaching liquid comes to a boil, put the whole chicken into the pot and turn the heat down to low again. Cover the pot with parchment paper that's set directly on top of the liquid so the body of the chicken is fully submerged. Cover with a lid.

Simmer the chicken for 20 minutes. Check and stir the pot every 10 minutes to make sure the chicken is poaching evenly. After the time is up, turn off the heat, and leave the chicken to continue soaking in the liquid for 15 minutes. To make sure the chicken is fully cooked, you can poke a thermometer into the thickest part of a chicken thigh; the internal temperature needs to reach at least 160°F (71°C).

After the chicken is cooked, cut it up and pour a little soy liquid over it, and it's ready to serve! Strain the poaching liquid, freeze it and use it again next time. You will be able to use this liquid for a few times before you need to add more chicken stock to it.

STORM SHELTER–STYLE BAKED LOBSTER

Hong Kong has a famous street that serves the best seafood in town called "under the bridge." One of the most popular preparations is called fishermen's storm shelter–style stir-fried seafood, fried in tons of crispy garlic. I find baking lobster in the high-temperature oven, dry roasting it, can mimic the wok stir-fried flavor. Cover the lobster with crispy garlic, and it will help you shelter the storm.

SERVES 4

1 (1½-lb [675-g]) Maine lobster (or any lobster)

Storm Shelter Sauce

2 tbsp (30 ml) canola oil

2 tbsp (14 g) minced ginger

3 tbsp (27 g) minced garlic

3 tbsp (9 g) minced green onions

1 tsp chili flakes

1 tbsp (15 ml) fermented black beans (can sub black bean sauce)

½ cup (120 ml) Shaoxing wine

½ cup (120 ml) vegetable stock

1 tbsp (13 g) sugar

1 tsp kosher salt

¼ tsp ground white pepper

½ cup (48 g) Crispy Fried Garlic (page 164)

Preheat the oven to 425°F (220°C, or gas mark 7). Rinse the lobster under running water to clean it, then split the lobster in half from head to tail. The trick to easily cut the lobster in half is to locate a "cross" mark on the back of the lobster head. After you find the mark, stab the tip of a chef's knife into the center of the "cross," and use the blade to cut straight down to the tail and split it. Then turn around starting from the same point, and split the head of the lobster. Crack the claws with the back of a knife for easier cooking.

For the storm shelter sauce, heat up the canola oil in a medium-size skillet over medium heat. Add the ginger, garlic and green onions, and stir-fry for 2 minutes until they start to turn brown. Add the chili flakes and fermented black beans. Stir, then add the Shaoxing wine and cook off the alcohol for 1 minute. Next add the vegetable stock. After the sauce comes to a simmer, add the sugar, salt and white pepper. Simmer for 30 seconds, and the sauce is ready.

Place the lobster halves in an ovenproof pan, shell-side down, and spoon the sauce over the lobster to completely cover it. Pour the remaining sauce into the pan so that the lobster is sitting in the sauce. Bake for 15 minutes. Cover the lobster with crispy garlic, and bake for 2 more minutes. The lobster is ready.

CARAMEL CHICKEN WITH CHESTNUTS

Chestnuts roasting on an open fire . . . The holidays are here, and I love and hate chestnuts! When I was young, I liked to help out in the kitchen with grandma. She always made me peel raw chestnuts in the winter for her to braise chicken, and it was NOT fun. I feel blessed that I found peeled chestnuts in the United States; you will be able to cook this dish painlessly. The savory aroma of chicken, chestnuts and shiitake mushrooms simmering together is the perfect holiday melody.

SERVES 4 TO 6

2 tbsp (16 g) cornstarch

1 (2½-lb [1.1-kg]) whole chicken, cut into chunks

6 dry shiitake mushrooms

2 tbsp (30 ml) canola oil

2 thumb-size pieces of whole ginger

1 head garlic, peeled

3 shallots, cut in half

¼ cup (56 g) sugar

1 cup (240 ml) Shaoxing wine

¼ cup (60 ml) soy sauce

1 tbsp (15 ml) dark soy sauce

1 star anise

½ cup (120 ml) chicken stock

12 peeled chestnuts

Salt, to taste

Sprinkle the cornstarch over the chunks of chicken and massage them together. Soak the dry shiitake mushrooms in water for 1 hour to rehydrate them.

Heat the canola oil in a Dutch oven over medium heat. Add the ginger, garlic and shallots, and sauté them for 1 minute. Push all of the vegetables to the side and add the sugar to the middle of the pot. Allow the sugar to caramelize to a dark amber color, about 3 minutes, then add the chicken into the pot and stir-fry quickly for about 1 minute. Add the Shaoxing wine, and stir and scrape the pot to get all the caramel to melt into the liquid. Cook off the alcohol for 1 minute, then add the soy sauce, dark soy and star anise to the pot. When it comes to a simmer, turn down the heat to low, and add the chicken stock. Skim the surface of the braising liquid by removing the floating protein gunk, and then add the shiitake mushrooms and chestnuts. Cover the pot with a lid and simmer for 25 minutes. Adjust seasoning with salt before serving.

MOLASSES-GLAZED PORK SHANK

This is a very rich dish. Gelatin from the pork skin melts into the sauce from long hours of braising. The meat becomes silken under the protection of the fat, and savoy cabbage added at the end will sop up all the succulent sauces. . . . Indulge, and bury your face in this pork heaven—this is a celebration dish after all.

SERVES 6 TO 8

2 (2-lb [907-g]) skin-on pork shanks

2 tbsp (30 ml) canola oil

2 oz (56 g) ginger, smashed and chopped

2 green onions, cut in pieces

1 cup (240 ml) Shaoxing wine

3 tbsp (45 ml) oyster sauce

¼ cup (60 ml) molasses

½ tsp Chinese five-spice powder

½ tsp chili flakes

¼ cup (60 ml) soy sauce

2 tbsp (30 ml) dark soy sauce

½ cup (120 ml) chicken stock

½ head savoy cabbage, cut into 4 wedges

2 tbsp (30 ml) Chinkiang vinegar

1 tbsp (15 ml) sesame oil

Put the pork shanks in a medium-size pot, fill with water to barely cover the shanks and cook over medium heat for about 7 minutes. When the water is simmering, turn off the heat and let the shanks rest in the hot water while you start working on the braising liquid.

Heat up the canola oil in a Dutch oven over medium heat. When the oil is hot, add the ginger and green onions into the pot. When they start to turn golden, about 2 minuntes, deglaze the pot with the Shaoxing wine. Next add the oyster sauce, molasses, five-spice, chili flakes, soy sauce and dark soy into the pot.

When the liquid comes to a simmer, take the pork shanks out of the hot water, pat dry and add them into the Dutch oven. Cook and turn the shanks for 5 minutes, until the shanks take on an amber color. Add the chicken stock into the pot, and cover the pot with a lid. Turn the heat down to low and simmer for 3½ hours, stirring and checking on the shanks in between. After 3½ hours, the shanks should be fork tender. Add the savoy cabbage into the pot, cover with the lid and cook for 10 minutes. Turn off the heat, and add the Chinkiang vinegar and sesame oil to finish the dish.

THANKSGIVING WILD RICE STUFFING WITH ROASTED PUMPKIN

The holiday season is one of the busiest times for restaurants and professional chefs. So the chef team always rotates taking one holiday off per year. I always chose Thanksgiving, so my sous chef can spend Christmas with his family. I host a Thanksgiving feast just about every year, and that became the event both sides of our family members look forward to the most. The Chinese are not into eating turkey that much; we usually serve whole chicken or duck for Thanksgiving with stuffing made out of rice instead of bread. This wild rice stuffing is slow cooked with pumpkin and Chinese sausage. It's soft and creamy, finished with crispy shallots and garlic on top, just like traditional stuffing's crusty top. You can even switch out the Chinese sausage to turkey sausage. I hope you will enjoy this Thanksgiving addition.

SERVES 6 TO 8

2 tbsp (30 ml) canola oil

1 tbsp (7 g) minced ginger

1 tbsp (9 g) minced garlic

2 tbsp (6 g) minced green onions

2 cups (275 g) chopped Chinese sausage (can sub turkey sausage)

2 cups (232 g) diced pumpkin

2 cups (370 g) wild red rice

1 tbsp (15 ml) soy sauce

2 tbsp (30 ml) oyster sauce

4 cups (960 ml) chicken stock

2 tbsp (14 g) goji berries

1 cup (225 g) diced celery

1 tbsp (15 ml) sesame oil

Salt and pepper, to taste

Topping

2 tbsp (12 g) Crispy Fried Garlic (page 164)

3 tbsp (18 g) Crispy Shallots (page 164)

1 tbsp (3 g) chopped green onions

Heat the canola oil in a large deep skillet over medium heat. Add the ginger, garlic and green onions, and stir-fry until you can smell the aroma, about 2 minutes, then add the Chinese sausage and stir-fry until they start to turn golden, about 2 minutes.

Add the diced pumpkin and rice next. Season with the soy sauce and oyster sauce, and add all the chicken stock into the pan. Stir well. Cover the skillet, turn the heat to low and simmer the rice for about 35 minutes. After the rice is cooked, add the goji berries and celery. Stir and make sure all the liquid is absorbed into the rice stuffing.

Finish with the sesame oil, and adjust the seasoning with salt and pepper. Sprinkle with crispy garlic, crispy shallots and green onions right before serving.

HOT POT

Hot pot, shabu shabu, fondue! These three dishes all involve cooking meat and vegetables table-side in a pot of liquid. It's fun and very easy to serve a group of people. There are many different styles of hot pot in China. Sichuan hot pot is filled with spicy chili, Sichuan peppercorn and beef fat. Taiwanese-style hot pot is also so spicy that I can breathe fire after I eat it. Here I list a traditional Beijing-style hot pot. We want to taste the flavor of the meats, so the broth is clear, and we only use sesame sauce as a dipping base. Once you've mastered the skill, you can make any broth and pair it with your favorite dipping sauce!

SERVES 4 TO 6 PEOPLE

Soup Base

2 qt (1.9 L) chicken stock

2 thumb-size pieces of ginger, smashed and chopped

2 green onions, cut into 2-inch (5-cm) pieces

3 dry shiitake mushrooms

1 tbsp (7 g) goji berries

1 tbsp (18 g) kosher salt

Dipping Sauce

Beijing Sesame Sauce (page 160)

½ cup (50 g) chopped green onions

½ cup (25 g) chopped cilantro

Feast

1 lb (450 g) thinly sliced lamb shoulder

1 lb (450 g) thinly sliced rib eye steak

½ lb (225 g) silken tofu

½ head Napa cabbage

3 cups (90 g) spinach leaves

1 bunch glass noodles

Tools

6- to 8-quart (5.7- to 7.6-L) soup pot

1 induction burner or a hot plate

Combine the chicken stock, ginger, green onions, mushrooms, goji berries and salt in a medium 6- to 8-quart (5.7- to 7.6-L) soup pot and simmer for 20 minutes on an induction burner. The soup base is ready to use.

Customize your dipping sauce by using Beijing sesame sauce as a base and adding chopped green onions and cilantro to your liking.

How to Eat Hot Pot

When the soup base is boiling, pick up 1 slice of meat with chopsticks and dip it in the hot pot to cook for a few seconds. You can see the meat is cooking; don't overcook it. Then dip the cooked meat into the sauce and enjoy!

We normally start with meat first. After we are halfway done, we start to add tofu and vegetables. We always cook and eat the glass noodles at the end when the soup base has become meaty and full of complex flavor. Enjoy the glass noodles with a bowl of the soup to finish the meal.

THEY CALL ME FIRECRACKER

他们叫我小炮仗

Hot Sauces and Condiments

A big part of Chinese cuisine is built on sauces and condiments. There are a lot of dishes that are just simply steamed or boiled, but when they are paired with an exciting sauce and a textured condiment, they are transformed from simple to spectacular in the blink of an eye.

My love of spicy food was revealed on national TV. Everyone was shocked to hear that to help me stay awake when I was cooking, I used to take a bite of a very spicy pepper—Serrano or habanero—instead of drinking coffee. So, recipes for hot sauce and spicy condiments take up a good part of this chapter. A lot of these sauces are really good to keep in your fridge. Imagine when you've just ordered some fried chicken to go, and then you dip them in the Sweet-and-Sour Sauce (page 156) you already have—all of a sudden you are eating sweet-and-sour chicken. Or add Black Pepper Sauce (page 163) to your grilled steak instead of butter. Or even add some Crispy Fried Garlic (page 164) on top of your cup 'o noodle to jazz it up. They called me firecracker on TV, and I've embraced the nickname. I hope this chapter will add some fireworks to your everyday eating.

TIGER TIGER SAUCE

I like to call this dipping sauce "Chinese salsa." Originally a version of this sauce was a breakfast condiment from the southwest part of China. When I first tasted it a few years ago, all the texture and freshness of this dipping sauce reminded me of "pico de gallo," fresh Mexican salsa. This sauce combines fresh herbs with crunchy preserved radish and spicy chili pepper—it will add some fireworks to anything you eat it with! I like to put this over my dumplings, grilled chicken and steamed vegetables. This is a simple, healthy sauce that pretty much goes with everything!

MAKES 1 CUP (240 ML)

¼ cup (13 g) minced cilantro

¼ cup (50 g) minced preserved radish (zha cai)

¼ cup (25 g) minced green onions

1 tbsp (9 g) minced garlic

1 Thai chili, minced

1 tbsp (15 ml) rice vinegar

¼ cup (60 ml) soy sauce

1 tbsp (15 ml) sesame oil

1 tbsp (15 ml) canola oil

Combine all the ingredients in a bowl. Mix well, and it's ready to serve!

This sauce can be kept in the refrigerator up to 3 days.

XO CHILI SAUCE

What is XO sauce? It is a very special chili sauce made with dry scallops, dry shrimp and cured ham from Hong Kong. It "borrowed" XO from cognac to represent that it's made of premium products. It's very pricy. I normally dehydrate scallop trimmings myself for XO sauce to cut the cost. This version is made of dry shrimp. It's a lot easier to find in the markets, and you can even find them in the Hispanic section of regular supermarkets. This chili sauce is packed with umami from the dry shrimp and savoriness from the ham. It's spicy, but not very hot, and I like to finish it with fresh orange zest instead of the traditional aged mandarin peels to add a touch of fresh sweetness. This is a versatile sauce for seafood, noodles and stir-fried vegetables. I love to pair this with seared scallops!

MAKES 1 CUP (240 ML)

½ cup (120 ml) canola oil

½ cup (24 g) minced shallots

¼ cup (36 g) minced garlic

2 tbsp (14 g) minced ginger

2 tbsp (19 g) minced Virginia ham (can sub Serrano ham)

3 tbsp (36 g) minced dry shrimp

1 tsp chili flakes

1 Fresno red chili or green jalapeño pepper, minced

2 tsp (12 g) kosher salt

Zest of 1 orange

Heat up the canola oil in a cast-iron skillet or a wok over medium heat. When the oil is hot, add the shallots to the pan and sauté until golden, about 2 minutes. You need to be super patient to make this sauce. Our goal is to slowly dehydrate everything by sautéing the ingredients in the oil step by step. The shallots have the highest water content, and it's important to sauté them first to cook out all the liquid. After the shallots turn golden, add the garlic, ginger and ham into the pan and continue to sauté until everything turns golden, at least 5 minutes. Add the dry shrimp, chili flakes and Fresno chili at the end, sauté for 3 more minutes and season with the salt.

Place the sauce into a blender, and pulse it for a couple of seconds. The sauce should have a little texture and not be completely smooth. After the sauce is blended, finish with the orange zest. This is an oil-based sauce, and when made properly, all the ingredients are dehydrated and it can be kept in the refrigerator for a really long time.

SWEET-AND-SOUR SAUCE

This red sauce is the signature of Chinese American cuisine. Everyone loves sweet-and-sour on anything. I don't think I need to say much about it. Here is my version of this beloved sauce.

MAKES 2 CUPS (480 ML)

½ cup (120 ml) orange juice

1 cup (240 ml) plum sauce (sub apricot jelly)

4 tbsp (60 ml) ketchup

2 tbsp (30 ml) honey

¼ cup (60 ml) lemon juice

½ tsp kosher salt

Heat up the orange juice in a small saucepot over medium heat. When it comes to a boil, add the plum sauce, ketchup and honey, and whisk to mix well.

When the sauce comes to a boil, remove the pot off the heat. Add the lemon juice and salt. When the sauce cools down, it's ready to use. Keep it in your fridge for up to 1 week.

DIPPING SOY SAUCE

Call me crazy, but I can taste if soy sauce has never been cooked. There is a slight metallic flavor that only goes away by cooking it. Most Chinese soy sauces are for cooking, and a good Chinese cook won't give you dipping soy from a bottle. Here is my recipe for a well-rounded dipping soy sauce.

MAKES ABOUT 1¾ CUPS (420 ML)

1 green onion, cut into 1-inch (2.5-cm) pieces

¼ cup (60 ml) canola oil

¼ cup (60 ml) Shaoxing wine

1 cup (240 ml) soy sauce

¼ cup (60 ml) water

¼ tsp sugar

In a 2-quart (1.9-L) saucepan, combine the green onion and canola oil together. Cook over medium heat. When the oil and green onion start sizzling, and the green onion starts to turn into a shade of yellow and you can smell it in the air, about 2 minutes, deglaze the pot with the Shaoxing wine, followed by the soy sauce, water and sugar. When the sauce comes to a simmer, remove it off the heat and strain it into a container.

This can be stored in the refrigerator for several weeks.

CHILI SAUCE (MY FRIENDS CALL IT "SHIR-RACHA")

This is a hot sauce that is inspired by the popular Sriracha chili sauce. My version is so good that my friends jokingly renamed it. This sauce is spicy and garlicky with a hint of sweet. If you like spicy food, this sauce is great with everything!

MAKES 1 CUP (240 ML)

2 tbsp (30 ml) canola oil

¼ cup (34 g) minced garlic

¼ cup (38 g) chopped onion

2 tbsp (14 g) minced ginger

½ cup (45 g) chopped Fresno red chili or green jalapeño pepper

⅛ tsp cayenne pepper

1 tbsp (13 g) sugar

2 tbsp (30 ml) ketchup

3 tbsp (45 ml) rice vinegar

1 tsp kosher salt

Heat up the canola oil in a medium sauté pan over medium heat. When the oil is hot, add the garlic, onion and ginger. Stir-fry until the onion becomes translucent, about 2 minutes, then add the red chili or green jalapeño and cayenne pepper. Cook for 2 minutes. Add the sugar, ketchup and rice vinegar, and season with salt. Simmer the sauce for 1 minute. Put the sauce into a blender and blend until smooth.

Keep it in the fridge in an airtight container for up to 2 weeks.

BEIJING SESAME SAUCE

Beijing people love sesame sauce. It's great with cold noodles and as salad dressing in the summertime. It's also the only dipping sauce for lamb hot pots in the wintertime. Many people prefer to add peanut butter to the sesame sauce, but I like the toasty, slight bitterness that pure sesame paste has.

MAKES 1 PINT (½ L)

1 cup (224 g) sesame paste
¾ cup (180 ml) water
2 tbsp (30 ml) soy sauce
½ tbsp (5 g) minced garlic
4 tbsp (60 ml) canola oil
1 tbsp (8 g) Sichuan peppercorns
2 tbsp (30 ml) rice vinegar
Salt, to taste

In a heavy-bottom mixing bowl, combine the sesame paste and water, stirring in one direction and slowly emulsifying the paste and water. If you have a heavy-duty blender, you can also blend this mixture until smooth.

Place the soy sauce and minced garlic in a soup bowl. Heat up the canola oil in a small sauté pan over high heat and when the oil is smoking, place the Sichuan peppercorns into the hot oil. Be careful of the oil popping; don't get burned. After about 30 seconds, when the aroma of the Sichuan peppercorns fills the air, remove the pan from the heat and immediately pour this Sichuan peppercorn–infused hot oil through a small strainer into the soy sauce bowl. The hot oil will flash cook the garlic soy sauce.

Pour this soy sauce–hot oil mixture into the sesame sauce, add the vinegar and mix well. Adjust the seasoning with salt to your liking.

You can keep this in the refrigerator for up to 1 week.

BLACK PEPPER SAUCE

This is the perfect sauce for meats! It's a big bold sauce. Savory and peppery, it's best paired with a nicely charred grilled steak, but also really good with roast chicken and even fried tofu. This is the sauce that can transform anything from plain to exciting.

MAKES 1 CUP (240 ML)

2 tbsp (30 ml) canola oil

½ tbsp (4 g) minced ginger

½ tbsp (5 g) minced garlic

¼ cup (60 ml) Shaoxing wine

¼ cup (60 ml) oyster sauce

¼ cup (60 ml) soy sauce

1 tbsp (7 g) coarse ground black pepper

¼ cup (60 ml) chicken stock

1 tsp cornstarch

2 tbsp (30 ml) water

Heat up the canola oil in a small saucepot over medium heat. When the oil is hot, add the ginger and garlic, and stir-fry them for 1 minute. When the garlic and ginger start to turn golden, add the Shaoxing wine and cook off the alcohol for 2 minutes. Next add the oyster sauce, soy sauce, black pepper and chicken stock.

Mix the cornstarch with the water in a small bowl to make a slurry. When the sauce comes back to simmer, add the slurry. Let the sauce simmer for 2 minutes, and the black pepper sauce is done.

Keep this in the fridge for up to 1 week.

CRISPY SHALLOTS

You can buy crispy shallots in many Asian supermarkets. They are really yummy, and they make a great topper for soups, braised meats or just as a snack. But the homemade version is so much better and even more addictive! It's really easy to make, just remember the magical number: 280°F (138°C). This is the temperature to fry shallots, and also the temperature to fry a lot of other vegetable chips.

MAKES 2 CUPS (260 G)

6 shallots

¼ cup (32 g) cornstarch

2 tsp (12 g) kosher salt

2 qt (1.9 L) canola oil

Use a mandoline slicer to slice the shallots into thin rings—about ⅛ inch (3 mm) thick. Place all the sliced shallots in a large mixing bowl, sprinkle the cornstarch and salt over them, and toss them together. Use both hands to toss and separate the shallots to make sure they are evenly coated with cornstarch. Heat up the canola oil in a 6-quart (5.7-L) soup pot over medium heat and place a heat-resistant thermometer in it. When the oil temperature reaches 280°F (138°C), add a small handful of shallot rings into the oil. Fry the shallots till golden brown, about 2 minutes, remove from the oil and spread over some paper towels to cool. Repeat 4 times to finish frying all the shallots. Save the oil for cooking; this shallot oil is delicious for stir-frying. The crispy shallots can be kept in an airtight container for up to 1 week.

CRISPY FRIED GARLIC

Chinese cuisine plays with a lot of different textures and contrasts. Any dish that's soft and tender most of the time will have a garnish that's crispy or nutty. Crispy garlic is something I always have plenty of in my kitchen. Try a spoonful of it over soup noodles, salad or seafood—these crunchy little bits will make you so happy!

MAKES 1 CUP (150 G)

4 qt (3.8 L) water

2 qt (1.9 L) canola oil

2 tbsp (34 g) salt

2 cups (272 g) minced garlic

Boil the water in a 6-quart (5.7-L) soup pot. Heat up the oil to 325°F (170°C) in another 6-quart (5.7-L) soup pot over medium heat. When the water is boiling, season the water with the salt, and then add the minced garlic. Boil for 1 minute, then strain and remove the garlic. Put the cooked garlic in the middle of a large cheesecloth or cloth napkin. Squeeze as much water out of the minced garlic as possible.

When the pot of oil reaches 325°F (170°C), add the garlic and fry till golden. This will take less than 1 minute. Be careful not to overcook them. They will continue to cook after they are removed from the hot oil, so it's important to pull them out when only golden. They will turn brown and crispy after they cool. Spread the garlic bits over paper towels to cool them down. Store them in an airtight container for up to 1 week.

Ball

PICKLED CAULIFLOWER IN SICHUAN SPICE

This simple pickling liquid can be the base for any vegetable. I especially like to pickle cauliflower for the hearty texture. The floral note of Sichuan peppercorn makes it unique.

MAKES ABOUT 4 QUARTS (3.8 L)

2 qt (1.9 L) distilled vinegar

1 pt (473 ml) water

2 cups (450 g) sugar

3 tbsp (54 g) kosher salt

2 oz (56 g) ginger

4 star anise

2 tsp (4 g) chili flakes

2 tsp (6 g) Sichuan peppercorns

1 tbsp (9 g) white peppercorns

1 head cauliflower

To make the pickling liquid, combine the vinegar, water, sugar, kosher salt, ginger, star anise, chili flakes, Sichuan peppercorns and white peppercorn in a 4-quart (3.8-L) saucepan. Bring them to a boil.

While cooking the pickling liquid, cut the cauliflower into bite-size florets, about 1 inch (2.5 cm) in diameter. I also love cauliflower stems, so don't throw them away. Slice them into round discs and pickle them together with the florets!

Place all the cut cauliflower in glass jars and fill them to three-quarters full. Fill the jars with the hot pickling liquid. After the pickles cool down, place the jars in the refrigerator to store. The cauliflower pickles will be ready in 24 hours. Refrigerated, they will keep for 1 month.

I DON'T BAKE

我不喜欢烘培

Easy Stovetop Sweets and Desserts

I don't bake. It's not that I don't know how. I just don't have the patience when it comes to the exact measuring of every single ingredient. And then waiting in front of the oven for it to be ready. And I can't touch it or check on it during cooking time. But I am very good at making desserts; I have a very savory-chef approach when it comes to a plated dessert. My desserts always play with different textures, different temperatures and flavors; it is a very intricate balancing act.

Most of my desserts are on the lighter side. After a feast, I always want to finish with something sweet, but I am always really full and something light is what I crave. Most Asian desserts are made with fruit and starch. We are known for not using dairy, except in the northern part of China, which has an abundant amount of milk from the Inner Mongolian prairies. Ice cream was originally invented in Beijing for the Emperor around 200 BCE. I grew up eating "milk Jell-O," and later on I learned that it's the same as the Italian's panna cotta. Perhaps Marco Polo not only brought back pasta and pizza from China, maybe he brought panna cotta too?!

There are no cake, cookie or pie recipes in this chapter. Instead, you will find Jasmine Rice Pudding (page 170), Sweet Tapioca with Apple (page 181), Burnt-Almond Jell-O with Marshmallow (page 178) and Kaya Jam (page 177). This is the sweet ending to the book.

JASMINE RICE PUDDING WITH CHARRED PINEAPPLES

Making rice pudding normally is time consuming. By breaking the rice with a blender before cooking, we cut down the cooking time by more than half. There is also less chance of scorching the bottom. I love roasting fruit in butter for dessert. And I think I said it before; butter makes Chinese food better.

SERVES 6

Rice Pudding

1 cup (185 g) jasmine rice

3 cups (720 ml) water

2 cups (480 ml) coconut milk

3 tbsp (38 g) sugar

¼ tsp salt

2 tbsp (30 ml) condensed milk

Pineapple Topping

1½ cups (338 g) diced pineapple

2 tbsp (25 g) sugar

1 tbsp (12 g) unsalted butter

1 tsp minced ginger

½ cup (55 g) toasted sliced almonds

Blend the dry rice in a blender to break it up. You want about 60 percent of the rice as powder and the rest as small pieces. In a medium-size pot, bring the water to a boil on high heat. Drop all the rice in the boiling water, and then add the coconut milk. Stir constantly, and reduce the heat to low. Slowly simmer over low heat until the rice turns into a thick cream, about 15 minutes. Next add the sugar, salt and condensed milk. Chill the rice pudding in the refrigerator while you work on the pineapple topping.

Put all the pineapple in a mixing bowl, toss with the sugar and let it macerate for 10 minutes. Strain the pineapple with a strainer and save all the juices.

Heat up the butter in a medium skillet over high heat. After about 15 seconds, when the butter is brown, add the pineapple and ginger to the skillet. Char one side of the diced pineapple first, and then toss the skillet to flip them. When they are nicely charred and caramelized, reduce the heat to low, add the reserved pineapple juice and bring it to a simmer. When the pineapples are simmering, the topping is done.

To serve, spoon some charred pineapple sauce over the rice pudding. Sprinkle toasted almonds on top.

SWEET MOCHI WITH STRAWBERRY AND NUTELLA

Just so you know, glutinous rice has no gluten at all. It's very sticky, and that's how it got that name. So, when you are handling it, the best way is to dust potato starch everywhere—on your hands, on the table, roll the dough in it before you roll it out—so you won't create a sticky mess.

MAKES 6 MOCHI

Filling

6 strawberries

6 tbsp (90 ml) chocolate hazelnut spread, such as Nutella

Mochi Wrapper

1 cup (110 g) glutinous rice flour (sweet rice flour)

½ cup + 2 tbsp (150 ml) room temperature water

1 tbsp (13 g) sugar

½ cup (55 g) Japanese potato starch (for dusting)

Clean the strawberries, and remove all the stems and leaves. Smear 1 tablespoon (15 ml) of chocolate hazelnut spread on the stem side of each strawberry, and leave the point of the strawberries exposed. Set them spread-side up on egg trays and chill them in the refrigerator so the chocolate hazelnut spread is firmer and easier to wrap in mochi later.

Boil a pot of water on high heat. In a small mixing bowl, combine the glutinous rice flour and the room temperature water. Mix well until it becomes a dough. Portion the dough into 6 balls. They don't have to be perfect; we are making them into small balls so they will cook faster.

When the water is boiling, put the rice dough balls in the water and cook until they are all floating; this means they are fully cooked. Place these cooked rice balls in a food processor while they are still hot. Add the sugar, and blend until you have a big ball of sticky mochi dough. Let it cool down for 10 minutes.

Dust potato starch over your work surface and your hands, and portion the rice dough into 6 pieces. Flatten the dough with your hand into a disc, place a dipped strawberry in the center with the spread facing up, close the wrapper and pinch the ends together.

These are best eaten right away, and they should only be stored in the refrigerator for up to 1 day.

PANNA COTTA WITH MANDARIN ORANGE

Panna cotta is milk custard set with gelatin, and it has no eggs. It's one of the easiest desserts to make if you have the correct ratio—and now you do. The texture should be almost creamy, like a Greek yogurt, contrasted with the sweet and tart mandarin oranges. This is the perfect light dessert to end a feast.

SERVES 6

Panna Cotta

1 qt (946 ml) milk

¼ cup (50 g) sugar

1 thumb-size piece of ginger, sliced

5 gelatin sheets (silver)

Mandarin Orange

½ cup (120 ml) orange juice

¼ cup (50 g) sugar

1 pinch salt

1 tbsp (15 ml) lemon juice

Zest of 1 lemon

3 mandarin oranges, peeled and segments separated

Bring the milk, sugar and ginger slices to a simmer in a pot over low heat. Bloom the gelatin sheets in 3 cups (720 ml) of room temperature water. When they are completely submerged in the water and have become soft and gooey, strain them out and squeeze the extra water out of them.

When the milk is simmering, strain it into a bowl and whisk in the bloomed gelatin sheets. After the gelatin is completely melted into the milk, pour the mixture evenly into 6 rock glasses. Set the rock glasses in the refrigerator and allow the panna cotta to set, about 2 hours.

Bring the orange juice to a simmer in a small soup pot. Mix in the sugar. When the sugar is completely dissolved, take it off the heat and add the salt, lemon juice and lemon zest. While the sauce is still hot, add the mandarin oranges into the pot, mix well and cool it in the refrigerator.

To serve, spoon mandarins and sauce over the panna cotta.

PRO TIP: Gelatin sheets are cleaner and easier to handle than the powder form. We use them in the professional kitchens. You can find them online, or in any gourmet supermarket (such as Whole Foods) in the pastry section.

KAYA JAM (COCONUT-EGG JAM)

Oh, I can eat this yummy jam with toast, over vanilla ice cream or just take a big spoonful as dessert. It tastes like creamy coconut caramel candy. It will take some patience to stir constantly for 20 minutes, but trust me, it's well worth it.

MAKES 24 OUNCES (680 G)

5 eggs
1 cup (200 g) sugar
¾ cup (180 ml) coconut cream
½ cup (120 ml) coconut milk
1½ tbsp (10 g) cornstarch
1½ tbsp (23 ml) water
⅓ cup (67 g) sugar

Whisk the eggs, sugar, coconut cream and coconut milk together, and mix well. Use an electric hand blender to help make sure everything is combined. Slowly cook this mixture over medium-low heat in a soup pot, and constantly stir it with a wooden spoon for 20 minutes. The coconut mixture will start to thicken and become lumpy in the pot. Don't stop stirring, and make sure you scrape the bottom of the pot all the time so it does not scorch. When the jam is simmering, combine the cornstarch and water in a small bowl to make a slurry. Add the slurry into the simmering jam, and mix well to thicken the jam.

After your kaya jam is cooked, heat the sugar in a small pan over medium heat. When the sugar becomes golden brown, about 3 minutes, add this hot caramel into the jam and stir well; this will turn the color of the jam golden. Blend the jam in a blender until silky smooth, and put it into a jar. It will keep in the refrigerator for up to 1 week.

BURNT-ALMOND JELL-O WITH MARSHMALLOW

Ha-ha-ha, see the last time I baked, I burnt all the almonds! That's how I created this burnt-almond Jell-O. I didn't want to throw them away. And what a beautiful mistake it was! Toasted, nutty, burnt Jell-O, with sweet and gooey fluff, and juicy, crunchy pears to balance everything out. Maybe I should bake more?!

SERVES 6

Almond Jell-O

1 cup (110 g) sliced almonds, skin on

1 qt (946 ml) almond milk

⅓ cup (67 g) sugar

5 gelatin sheets (silver)

Topping

1 large Asian pear

1 tbsp (15 ml) lemon juice

12 tbsp (180 ml) marshmallow fluff

Preheat the oven to 400°F (200°C, or gas mark 6). Place the almonds on a baking sheet, and spread them in an even layer. Toast in the oven until they are all dark brown, about 10 minutes. Combine the burnt almonds, almond milk and sugar in a saucepan over medium-low heat. After it comes to a boil, remove it off the heat and allow it to steep in the refrigerator overnight.

Strain the almond milk the next day into a small pot, and bring it to a simmer. Bloom the gelatin sheets in 2 cups (480 ml) of room temperature water. After it's rehydrated, squeeze the extra water out. Melt the gelatin into the almond milk and pour it into 6 small bowls. Refrigerate for 2 hours to set the almond jelly.

To serve, leave the skin on the Asian pear and slice them into half-moon shapes. Toss the Asian pear with the lemon juice, then spoon it over the almond Jell-O. Place 2 tablespoons (30 ml) of marshmallow fluff next to the pears, and torch the fluff a little before serving.

PRO TIP: Gelatin sheets are cleaner and easier to handle than the powder form. We use them in professional kitchens. You can find them online, or in any gourmet supermarket (such as Whole Foods) in the pastry section.

SWEET TAPIOCA WITH APPLE

May peace and love come to your family: this is the message of an apple dessert in our culture. I end my book on this final sweet note. I hope you have enjoyed this glance at my journey as a Chinese kid growing up and cooking in the United States. Just like this dessert, the soulful Chinese flavors will always be part of me, but I am also taking on other cultures and techniques from the United States, this big melting pot.

SERVES 6

Sweet Tapioca

1 cup (150 g) small tapioca

1 cup (200 g) brown sugar

1 cup (240 ml) apple juice

Apple Topping

1 green apple

1 Fuji apple

Five-Spice Shaved Ice

2 cups (480 ml) apple juice

2 cups (400 g) sugar

¼ tsp Chinese five-spice powder

Boil 6 quarts (5.7 L) of water in a medium-size pot over high heat. When the water is boiling, add the tapioca into the water and stir like crazy to prevent the tapioca from sticking to each other and lumping up. Cook until all the tapioca becomes translucent and only has a small white dot left in the center, about 8 minutes. Strain the tapioca, and put it into a bowl. Combine the brown sugar and apple juice in a small soup pot, and bring to a boil over medium heat. Pour the brown sugar syrup over the tapioca, and mix well. Chill in the refrigerator.

To make the topping, cut the apples in half and slice them on a mandoline slicer into thin petals.

To make the shaved ice, heat up the apple juice in a small pot, and add the sugar and five-spice. When everything is dissolved in the juice, pour it into a shallow pan or dish. Freeze it completely, then scrape it with a fork to make "shaved ice."

To serve, spoon some tapioca in a small bowl. Top it with plenty of shaved ice and slices of apples.

ACKNOWLEDGMENTS

Growing up, I always dreamed of writing a Chinese novel. As a little girl from Beijing, I never imagined I would become a chef in the United States and I would be publishing my first cookbook. This is beyond my dream come true. So many people played an important part in my journey. If I left any one of you out here, you are in my heart!

Jimmy Lee, my husband, my rock, the person who always pushes me to be better, and the person who forced me to pursue my dream of becoming a chef: I wouldn't be here if not for you. Thank you for always being by my side; I love you an eternity.

Guiling Yu and Alvin Chung, mom and dad, thank you for bringing me to the United States, giving me the freedom to pursue my dream and understanding and supporting my nontraditional career path. I love you, even though you always shy away when I tell you!

Karen Chung, you are the best little sister any big sister can ask for. Your drive and your passion to serve society inspire me to be better every day! Now, will you please slow down a little on your medical school, surgical lab and all other over-achievements? Let your big sister have some thunder, too, sometimes?

Mark Hopper, my first chef, thank you for showing me the best fundamentals of cooking, setting me up for the rest of my cooking career.

Zach Allen, my best chef friend, thanks for "growing" up with me in the kitchen, showing me the roots of Italian cooking and helping mold me into my simple, soulful cooking style.

Ella Li, Helen Shin, Christin Gnadt, Sabrina Shin and Nikki Wong, my dear girl friends, thanks for always being here for me, never complaining about how I am never there for all your important dates because of my career. I can do what I do because of your friendship and support. Nina Compton, Brooke Williamson, Casey Thompson, Silvia Barban and Melissa King, love you, I want to cook with all of you til we are in our 90s!! The future is us, women chefs!! And thank you *Top Chef* family for connecting us and elevating our careers!

Sarah Monroe, thank you for cold emailing me, helping me with my writing and showing me how to talk less "cheffy" in my recipes. I wouldn't be able to finish this book without you.

Albert Law, Pork Belly studio, thank you for flying all the way from San Francisco to LA to shoot my book, for never making me pose and for understanding the stories behind my dishes! I am weird, and I am glad to have you by my side to realize my weird visions.

Most importantly, Silvia Siyi Liang. Grandma, nainai, look! I am publishing my first cookbook!! Everything I love about food started with you! Thank you for letting me be me, introducing the world to me. I have become a strong, independent woman like you. I love you. I miss you. I wish I could cook for you.

ABOUT THE AUTHOR

Born and raised in Beijing, China, chef Shirley Chung was exposed to international cuisine at an early age by her grandmother, Liang Si Yi, former director of The Red Cross in China. Shirley immigrated to the United States at age seventeen and worked in Silicon Valley for a few years after graduating. She then decided to follow her passion for food, so she left her career in high tech behind and enrolled in the California Culinary Academy in San Francisco. She is trained in classic French and Italian cuisine, and has worked and opened restaurants for Thomas Keller, Guy Savoy and José Andrés.

After she opened Carnevino as Chef de Cuisine for BBHG, Carnevino earned multiple awards for Best Steak House internationally. Prior to being a finalist on season 11 of *Top Chef* in New Orleans, she held the Executive Chef Position at China Poblano, by José Andrés, which was nominated for the Best New Restaurant Award by the James Beard Foundation in 2011. While working at China Poblano, she fell in love with Mexican cuisine and learned more about her own heritage.

In 2014, Shirley opened her first restaurant in Orange County, Twenty Eight, featuring modern Chinese cuisine. Recently, Shirley competed on season 14 of BravoTV's *Top Chef*. She used this opportunity to showcase her Chinese American cuisine during the competition and she was rewarded by being named the runner up of *Top Chef*. Shirley just opened her new concept in Culver City, California, Ms. Chi Café, an all-day café with her signature dumplings and other Chinese snacks!

INDEX

Medical Billing & Coding

Medical Billing & Coding

3rd Edition

by Karen Smiley, CPC

Medical Billing & Coding For Dummies®, 3rd Edition

Published by: **John Wiley & Sons, Inc.**, 111 River Street, Hoboken, NJ 07030-5774, www.wiley.com

For general information on our other products and services, please contact our Customer Care Department within the U.S. at 877-762-2974, outside the U.S. at 317-572-3993, or fax 317-572-4002. For technical support, please visit https://hub.wiley.com/community/support/dummies.

Wiley publishes in a variety of print and electronic formats and by print-on-demand. Some material included with standard print versions of this book may not be included in e-books or in print-on-demand. If this book refers to media such as a CD or DVD that is not included in the version you purchased, you may download this material at http://booksupport.wiley.com. For more information about Wiley products, visit www.wiley.com.

Library of Congress Control Number: 2019953067

ISBN 978-1-119-62544-5 (pbk); ISBN 978-1-119-62545-2 (ebk); ISBN 978-1-119-62546-9 (ebk)

Manufactured in the United States of America

C10015250_110119

Contents at a Glance

Table of Contents

Introduction

Welcome to *Medical Billing & Coding For Dummies!* Consider this your personal guided tour to the profession that all physicians, hospitals, and clinics rely on to get paid in a timely fashion. This book shows you the ins and outs of the medical billing and coding profession, from the differences between the two jobs to how to prepare for and land a billing and coding job to what to expect after you're safely in that office chair.

As you read this book, you'll discover that medical billing and coding is a vital cog in the healthcare wheel. After all, the medical biller and coder is the rainmaker of the healthcare industry, turning the healthcare provider's documentation into payment.

Medical billing and coding is way more than codes and insider jargon, though. It's also about working with people and knowing how to interact with each type of person or business you come in contact with, from patients and physicians to fellow coders and insurance reps — a virtual who's who of the medical world — and you'll be right in the middle of them all!

About This Book

The world of medical billing and coding, what with all the terminology you must master and the codes you need to know, can seem big and a bit daunting at times. After all, there's a lot to remember and so, so many codes. But don't worry: Parsing the ins and outs of all the details on how to enter the correct code is what those super-technical coding books are for. Think of *this* book as a friendly guide to all the twists and turns you'll encounter in your medical billing and coding world, from taking the certification exam and finding a job to working with insurance companies and deciphering physician documentation.

Not only do I share the ins and outs of the profession itself and what to expect on the job, but I also tell you what you need to know to succeed.

What this book isn't is a book of codes. Tons of great resources are out there that list all the codes you need to do your job properly, and I recommend that you have them handy. Instead, this book is a friendly take on the job as a whole. And, in this third edition, I give you all the details to get you started in this dynamic career, including new information on the 10th edition of the International Classification of Diseases (ICD-10), and fresh news on what is to come in the 11th edition of ICD. My main goal with this book is to introduce you to the wider world of medical billing and coding so that you are prepped and ready to scrub in for this challenging, evolving, and always exciting career.

Foolish Assumptions

In writing this book, I made some assumptions about you:

- You're a medically minded individual who is interested in pursuing a career in medical billing and coding and has no previous coding experience.
- You're a current medical professional who is looking to switch to the coding side of the industry.
- You're a medical billing and coding student who is looking for information on certifications, job hunting, and the career in general.

Regardless of why you picked up this book, you can find the info you need to pursue your medical billing and coding career goals with confidence.

Icons Used in This Book

As you read this book, you'll notice icons peppered throughout the text. Consider these signposts directing you to special kinds of information. Here's what each icon means:

TIP

This icon marks tips and tricks you can use to help you succeed in the day-to-day tasks of medical billing and coding.

REMEMBER

This icon highlights passages that are good to keep in mind as you master the medical billing and coding profession.

WARNING

This icon alerts you to common mistakes that can trip you up when you are coding or following up on a denial.

This icon indicates something cool and perhaps a little offbeat from the discussion at hand. Feel free to skip these bits.

Beyond the Book

In addition to the material in the print or e-book you're reading right now, this book also comes with a free, access-anywhere Cheat Sheet that has all the best tips on medical billing and coding. To get this Cheat Sheet, simply go to `www.dummies.com` and type **Medical Billing & Coding For Dummies Cheat Sheet** in the Search box.

Where to Go from Here

This book is designed to be easy to navigate and easy to read, no matter what topic you're interested in. Looking for information on certification exams? Head to Chapter 7. Want to know how to file an appeal? Chapter 14 has the information you need.

Of course, if you feel confident that you already know the basics on medical billing and coding and you want to dive into the middle of this book, feel free. That said, getting a strong idea of what the medical billing and coding job entails can be incredibly useful if you're a bit on the fence about whether this is the job for you. If that description fits you, start in Part 1, where you can find some really useful overview-type info.

Bottom line: Go wherever you want. After all, it's your life, it's your future, and this profession is yours for the taking. Go for it!

1

Getting to Know Medical Billing and Coding

IN THIS PART . . .

Get a high-level overview of the who, what, when, and where of the billing and coding profession along with an explanation of why the medical biller and coder are the lifeline of the industry.

Find out the difference between being a medical biller and being a medical coder.

Examine what you need to know now to enter and succeed in this field.

Get to know which job is right for you.

Discover where to begin to look for training in the areas you want to focus on.

» Deciding whether the job is right for you

» Choosing a certification

» Planning your education

Chapter 1

Dipping Your Toes into Medical Billing and Coding

Welcome to the world of medical billing and coding! No other job in the medical field affects more lives than this one because everyone involved in the healthcare experience, from the patient and front office staff to providers and payers, relies on you. You are, so to speak, the touchstone in the medical industry.

A lot rests on your shoulders as the biller and coder. With this responsibility comes great power, and that power must be treated with respect and integrity. In this chapter, I take you on a very brief tour of what medical billing and coding entails. I hope you find, as I have, that working as a medical biller/coder is a challenging and rewarding job that takes you right into the heart of the medical industry.

Coding versus Billing: They Really Are Two Jobs

Although many people refer to billing and coding as if it were one job function (a convention I use in this book unless I'm referring to specific functions), billing and coding really are two distinct careers. In the following sections, I briefly describe the tasks and functions associated with each job and give you some things to think about to determine which path you want to pursue:

» The medical coder deciphers the documentation of a patient's interaction with a healthcare provider (physician, surgeon, nursing staff, and so on) and determines the appropriate procedure (CPT) and diagnosis code(s) (ICD) to reflect the services provided.

» The medical biller then takes the assigned codes and any required insurance information, enters them into the billing software, and then submits the claim to the payer (often an insurance company) to be paid. The biller also follows up on the claim as necessary.

» Both medical billers and coders are responsible for a variety of tasks, and they're in constant interaction with a variety of people (you can read about the various stakeholders in Part 5). Consider these examples:

- Because they're responsible for billing insurance companies and patients correctly, medical billers have daily interaction with both patients and insurance companies to ensure that claims are paid correctly in a reasonable time.
- To ensure coding accuracy, coders often find themselves querying physicians regarding any questions they may have about the procedures that were performed during the patient encounter and educating other office staff on gathering required information.
- Billers (but sometimes coders, too) have the responsibility for explaining charges to patients, particularly when patients need help understanding their payment obligations, such as coinsurance and copayments, that their insurance policies specify.

» When submitting claims to the insurance company, billers are responsible for verifying the correct billing format, ensuring the correct modifiers have been appended, and submitting all required documentation with each claim.

In short, medical billers and coders together collect information and documentation, code claims accurately so that physicians get paid in a timely manner, and follow up with payers to make sure that the money finds its way to the provider's bank account. Both jobs are crucial to the office cash flow of any healthcare provider, and they may be done by two separate people or by one individual, depending upon the size of the office.

For the complete lowdown on exactly what billers and coders do, check out Chapter 2 for general information and Part 4, which provides detailed information on claims processing.

Following a Day in the Life of a Claim

When you're not interfacing with the three Ps — patients, providers, and payers — you'll be doing the meat and potatoes work of your day: coding claims to convert provider performed services into revenue.

Claims processing refers to the overall work of submitting and following up on claims. Here in a nutshell is the general process of claims submission, which begins almost as soon as the patient enters the provider's office:

1. **The patient hands over her insurance card and fills out a demographic form at the time of arrival.**

   The demographic form includes information such as the patient's name, date of birth, address, Social Security or driver's license number, the name of the policyholder, and any additional information about the policyholder if the policyholder is someone other than the patient. At this time, the patient also presents a government-issued photo ID so that you can verify that she is actually the insured member.

WARNING

   Using someone else's insurance coverage is fraud. So is submitting a claim that misrepresents an encounter. All providers are responsible for verifying patient identity, and they can be held liable for fraud committed in their offices.

2. **After the initial paperwork is complete, the patient encounter with the service provider or physician occurs, followed by the provider documenting the billable services.**
3. **The coder abstracts the billable codes, based on the physician documentation.**
4. **The coding goes to the biller who enters the information into the appropriate claim form in the billing software.**

   After the biller enters the coding information into the software, the software sends the claim either directly to the payer or to a clearinghouse, which sends the claim to the appropriate payer for reimbursement.

If everything goes according to plan, and all the moving parts of the billing and coding process work as they should, your claim gets paid, and no follow-up is necessary. For a detailed discussion of the claims process from beginning to end, check out Chapters 11, 12, and 13.

Of course, things may not go as planned, and the claim will get hung up somewhere — often for missing or incomplete information — or it may be denied. If either of these happens, you must follow up to discover the problem and then resolve it. Chapter 14 has all the details you need about this part of your job.

Keeping Abreast of What Every Biller/Coder Needs to Know

If you're going to work in the medical billing and coding industry (and you will!), you must familiarize yourself with three big must-know items: compliance (following laws established by federal or state governments and regulations established by the department of HHS or other designated agencies), medical terminology (the language healthcare providers use to describe the diagnosis and treatment they provide), and medical necessity (the diagnosis that makes the provided service necessary). In the following sections, I introduce you to these concepts. For more information, head to Part 2.

Complying with federal and state regulations

In the United States, as in many countries, healthcare is a regulated industry, and you have to follow certain guidelines. In the United States, these rules are enforced by the Office of Inspector General (OIG). The regulations are designed to prevent fraud, waste, and abuse by healthcare providers, and as a medical biller or coder, you must familiarize yourself with the basics of compliance.

Being *in compliance* basically means an office or individual has established a program to run the practice under the regulations as set forth by federal or state governments and the department of HHS or other designated agencies.

You can thank something called HIPAA for setting the bar for compliance. The standard of securing the confidentiality of healthcare information was established by the enactment of the Health Insurance Portability and Accountability Act (HIPAA). This legislation guarantees certain rights to individuals with regard to their healthcare. Check out Chapter 4 for more info on compliance, HIPAA, and the OIG.

Learning the lingo: Medical terminology

Everyone knows that doctors speak a different language. Turns out that that language is often Latin or Greek. By putting together a variety of Latin and Greek prefixes and suffixes, physicians and other healthcare providers can describe any number of illnesses, injuries, conditions, and procedures.

As a coder, you need to become familiar with these prefixes and suffixes so that you can figure out precisely what procedure codes to use. By mastering the meaning of each segment of a medical term, you'll be able to quickly make sense of the terminology that you use every day.

You can read about the most common medical prefixes and suffixes in Chapter 5.

Demonstrating medical necessity

Before a payer (such as an insurance company) will reimburse the provider, the provider must show that rendering the services was necessary. Setting a broken leg is necessary, for example, only when the leg is broken. Similarly, prenatal treatment and newborn delivery is necessary only when the patient is pregnant.

To demonstrate medical necessity, the coder must make sure that the diagnosis code supports the treatment given. Therefore, you must be familiar with diagnosis codes and their relationship to the procedure codes. You can find out more about medical necessity in Chapter 5.

REMEMBER

Insurance companies are usually the parties responsible for paying the doctor or other medical provider for services rendered. However, they pay only for procedures that are medically necessary to the well-being of the patient, their client. Each procedure billed must be linked to a diagnosis that supports the medical necessity for the procedure. All diagnoses and procedures are worded in medical terminology.

Deciding Which Job Is Right for You

If you think the idea of working with everyone from patients to payers sounds good and working a claim through the billing and coding process seems right up your alley, then you can start to think about which particular jobs in the field might be a good fit for you. Luckily, you have lots of options. You just need to know where to look and what kind of job is right for you. I give you some things to think about in the following sections.

Examining your workplace options

Before you crack open the classifieds, give some thought to what sort of environment you want to work in. You can find billing and coding work in all sorts of places, such as

- Physician offices
- Hospitals
- Nursing homes
- Outpatient facilities
- Billing companies
- Home healthcare services
- Durable medical good providers
- Practice management companies
- Federal and state government agencies
- Commercial payers

Which type of facility you choose depends on the kind of environment that fits your personality. For example, you may want to work in the fast-paced, volume-heavy work that's common in a hospital. Or maybe the controlled chaos of a smaller physician's office is more up your alley.

Other considerations for choosing a particular area include what you can gain from working there. A larger office or a hospital setting is great for new coders because you get to work under the direct supervision of a more experienced coding staff. A billing company that specializes in specific provider types lets you become an expert in a particular area. In many physician offices, you get to develop a broader expertise because you're not only in charge of coding, but you're also responsible for following up on accounts receivable and chasing submitted claims.

To find out more about your workplace options and the advantages and disadvantages that come with each, head to Chapter 3.

Thinking about your dream job

Although you can't predict the future, you can begin to put some thought into your long-term career goals and how you can reach them. Here are some factors to consider when thinking about what kind of billing/coding job you want:

- **The kind of job you want to do and the tasks you want to spend your time performing:** Refer to the earlier sections "Following a Day in the Life of a Claim" and "Keeping Abreast of What Every Biller/Coder Needs to Know" for more job-related tasks. Chapter 2 has a complete discussion of billing and coding job functions.
- **Where you plan to seek employment and in what kind of setting:** The preceding section gives you a quick idea of what your options are. Chapter 3 gives you more detail.
- **The type of certification potential employers prefer and the time commitment involved:** Many billing or practice management companies, for example, are contractually obligated to their clients to employ only certified medical coders to perform the coding.
- **The type of training program(s) available in your area:** Many reputable training programs are associated with the two main biller/coder credentialing organizations, the AAPC (American Academy of Professional Coders) and AHIMA (American Health Information Management Association), each of which tends to focus on a particular area. AAPC certification is generally associated with coding in physicians' offices, but it has recently updated its courses and now offers certification in both hospital inpatient and outpatient coding; AHIMA certification is generally associated with hospital coding. For information about finding a training program and your options, head to Chapter 8.

TIP

Take a few minutes (or hours!) now to think over these points. Trust me: It's time well spent before you jump on the billing and coding bandwagon.

Prepping for Your Career: Training Programs and Certifications

Breaking into the billing and coding industry takes more than a wink and a smile (though I'm sure yours are lovely). It takes training from reputable institutions and certification from a reputable credentialing organization. The next sections have the details.

Previewing your certification options

To score a job as a biller and coder, you should get certified by a reputable credentialing organization such as the American Health Information Management Association (AHIMA) or the AAPC (American Academy of Professional Coders). In

Chapter 7, I tell you everything you need to know about these organizations. Here's a quick overview:

- AAPC is the credentialing organization that offers Certified Professional Coder (CPC) credentials, as well as a myriad of other credentials. AAPC training focuses on physician offices, practice management, compliance, auditing, billing, and inpatient and outpatient hospital-based coding.
- AHIMA coding certifications — Correct Coding Specialist (CCS) and Certified Coding Associate (CCA) — are intended to certify the coder who has demonstrated proficiency in inpatient and outpatient hospital-based coding, while the Correct Coding Specialist—Physician-based (CCS-P) is, as its name indicates, for coders who work for individual physicians.

All sorts of other specialty certifications are also available, which you can read more about in Chapter 10.

TIP

To choose which certification — AHIMA or AAPC — best fits your career goals, first think about the type of training program you want. Second, examine your long-term career goals. What kind of medical billing and coding job do you ultimately want to do, in what sort of facility do you want to work, and how do you want to spend your time each day?

REMEMBER

To get certified, you must pass an exam administered by the credentialing organization. Head to Chapter 9 for exam details and information on how to sign up for one.

Going back to school

Sharpen your pencils, get a sweet new backpack, and shine up an apple for the teacher because you're going back to school. That's right, school. It's your first stop on the way to Medical Billing and Coding Land. The good news is that medical coding or billing is one of the few medical careers with fewer education requirements. Translation: You won't be spending decades preparing for your new career. Most billing and coding programs get you up and running in a relatively short amount of time, often less than two years.

REMEMBER

After you successfully complete a training program, you receive a *certificate of completion*. Note that this is different from achieving *certification*. To get your certification, you still have to take certification exams offered by the credentialing bodies after graduation. Fortunately, a solid medical coding and billing program provides you with the knowledge necessary to ace the exams and gain entry-level certification. Most programs offer training in the following:

- Human anatomy and physiology
- Medical terminology
- Medical documentation
- Medical coding, including proper use of modifiers
- Medical billing
- Claims filing
- Medical insurance, including commercial payers and government programs

You can read all about your educational options — from abbreviated study programs to more inclusive extended programs — in Chapter 8, where I highlight the advantages of some programs and the pitfalls of others.

Planning for the Future

As soon as you get your first billing and coding job — and probably even before that — you'll start hearing about something called ICD-10, which is the tenth revision of the International Classification of Diseases (hence, the ICD), the common system of codes used by the World Health Organization (WHO) that classifies every disease or health problem you code. These diagnosis codes represent a generalized description of the disease or injury that was the catalyst for the patient/physician encounter. As a biller/coder, you use the ICD every day.

ICD codes are also used to classify diseases and other health problems that are recorded on many types of health records, including death certificates, to help provide national mortality and morbidity rates. ICD-10 went into place October 1, 2015. Before that, the ninth edition of the ICD classification (ICD-9) had been used in the United States since 1979. Now, ICD-11 is on the horizon and is tentatively scheduled for a January 2022 release.

TECHNICAL STUFF

WHO uses the data gleaned from your coding to analyze the health of large population groups and monitor diseases and other health problems for all members of the global community. For your purposes, you can think of the ICD codes as the language you speak when coding so that organizations like WHO can do the work of keeping the world healthy.

The transition to ICD-10 increased the demand for medical coders due to the increased specificity. The healthcare workforce is predicted to continue growing, which should increase the demand for billing and coding professionals for the foreseeable future.

» Looking at the tasks that billers and coders must perform

» Determining which job is best for you

Chapter 2
Exploring the Billing and Coding Professions

Medical billing and coding specialists are the healthcare professionals responsible for converting patient data from treatment records and insurance information into revenue. They take all that complicated information and turn it into a language of codes the insurance companies and other payers can understand. The healthcare industry depends on qualified medical billers and skilled medical coders to accurately record, register, and keep track of each patient's account so that the docs get paid and the patients get charged only for services they receive.

Although they're frequently clumped together, medical billing and medical coding are actually two distinct jobs. In this chapter, I discuss each separately.

Note: In this chapter, I offer a very brief overview of the tasks that billers and coders perform. For a detailed discussion of the billing and coding process, head to Part 4.

Looking at the Medical Coding Job

The coder's job is to extract the appropriate billable services from the documentation that has been provided. The coder is given the office notes and/or the operative report as dictated by the physician. From this documentation, the coder identifies any and all billable procedures and assigns the correct diagnosis and procedure codes. The coder also identifies whether a procedure that is often included with another procedure should be billed on its own (or, in coder-speak, *unbundled*) to allow for additional reimbursement. To be eligible for unbundling, the documentation must indicate that extra time and effort was required or that a procedure that is normally included in the primary procedure was done at a separate site or time and was necessary to ensure a positive outcome for the patient.

REMEMBER

That's the nuts-and-bolts stuff. To do the job of medical coder well, however, you must be aware that medical coding requires a daily commitment to remaining ethical despite pressures from employers who are looking at the bottom line and don't understand the laws and procedural mandates a coder must follow. I have heard physicians tell coders to just use the code with the highest revenue potential. This philosophy may be what is best in the short term for the provider's bottom line, but when an auditor comes around to investigate, that money is going back with interest. So the first order every day for the coder is to be mindful of her ethical duty to the profession, physicians, and patients.

The key to optimal reimbursement is full documentation by the provider (the physician, for example, who sees the patient and performs the procedure) coupled with full *extraction,* or identification, of billable procedures by the coder. Everyone — from the doc to you, the coder — has to dot every *i* and cross every *t.*

In the following sections, I take you through the different tasks you'll perform as you prepare claims for reimbursement.

Verifying documentation

As noted earlier, the job of coder starts with the documentation provided by the physician. This documentation can take the form of an operative report or an office note.

REMEMBER

Physicians are trained to document their work, so consider them partners in the coding enterprise. They (or a member of their staff) note all the information needed to treat a particular patient before the paperwork hits the coder's desk.

Checking operative reports

An *operative report* is the document that is transcribed from the physician's dictation of the patient encounter. It describes in detail exactly what was done during a surgery. Operative reports are normally set into a template, which serves as an outline that identifies the reason for the procedure, what illness or injury was confirmed during the procedure, and finally the procedure(s) that were performed.

The basic format of an operative report includes the following:

- Patient name and date of birth
- Operating physician
- Assistant at surgery
- Date of service
- Preoperative diagnosis (the diagnosis based on the examination and preoperative testing)
- Postoperative diagnosis (new diagnoses based on what the doctor found during the surgery)
- Procedure(s) performed (an outline of the procedures done)
- Body of the operative report (a description of everything that was stated in the postoperative diagnosis and procedure performed sections)

Put simply, verifying documentation is a fact-checking gig. Here's what you need to check:

- That procedures stated as performed in the heading of the operative report are substantiated in the body of the report.
- The diagnosis provides medical necessity for the procedure and that the procedure(s) listed in the outline are documented in the body of the operative report. *Medical necessity* is simply the reason for the visit or surgery; it defines the disease process or injury (head to Chapter 5 for details). Before payers reimburse the provider, they have to know why the visit was necessary.

As a coder, you rely on the information in the body of the operative report to verify the documentation. If the body doesn't support the rest of the operative report (the operative report doesn't mention a procedure listed in the "procedures performed" section, for example, or the description isn't detailed enough), then you're responsible for asking the surgeon to clarify.

REMEMBER

If the doctor doesn't say it in the operative report, regardless of how obvious it seems, *it is the same as if it was not done,* because per coding guidelines, it cannot be coded or billed.

Checking office notes

All physician services are coded and billed based upon physician documentation. When coding office procedures or verifying the level of evaluation and management code that is appropriate for the visit, you rely on the physician's office notes. An office note typically documents the patient's symptoms, the physician's findings, and the plan for treatment, including a follow-up plan.

WARNING

If you believe that a higher level of service was performed, asking a physician for clarification is certainly acceptable, but coding a procedure that's not documented is not acceptable. Coding is not a job for those who like to second-guess. You can't assume you know what the doctor meant or intended and code based on your assumptions. Therefore, make sure you add "clarifying information" to your list of daily jobs as a coder.

IT'S A BIRD! IT'S A PLANE! IT'S SUPER-BILL!

A super-bill is a form created specifically for an individual office or provider. It normally is prepopulated with the patient's demographic information, including insurance copay, and contains the most common diagnosis and procedural codes used by the office. It may also have a section that indicates the need for follow-up appointments and should also have a space for the physician's signature.

The super-bill is a great tool for the provider for billing purposes and also proves helpful for keeping track of each patient's visit. In many offices, the super-bill has been replaced by the electronic health record (EHR), an all-electronic method of patient record keeping.

Super-bills, wonderful as they are, can also be the bane of the coder's existence. Although checking off billable procedures is certainly easier for the provider, they may overlook adding the detail necessary to support the procedures (and level of the visit) indicated on the bill. If the chart doesn't match the super-bill, it's back to square one for the coder.

Following up on unclear documentation

As I explain in the preceding sections, the physician documents all procedures he performs. If he doesn't state a procedure in his dictation (in his operative report) or note it in the physician's notes, regardless of how obvious it may seem, *it was not done.*

The chant of the medical coder always comes in handy. When in doubt or faced with incomplete documentation, remember: "If the doctor didn't say it, it wasn't done." Period.

When the documentation is missing or ambiguous, it's your responsibility to clarify with the physician. Although some physicians become defensive or irritated when the coder questions the documentation, those who understand that your questions can maximize their reimbursement will gladly amend the documentation to clear up the problem.

Assigning diagnosis and procedure codes

Time to play "Name that Illness!" Upon reading the operative report or office notes, you must identify the illness or disease and find the corresponding International Classification of Diseases (ICD) diagnosis code. The ICD codebook is the bible of coding, containing all the diagnosis codes.

After finding the diagnosis codes, you then look up the procedure codes that best describe the work done, using one of the following books:

- **The Current Procedural Terminology (CPT) codebook:** The CPT codebook contains all the procedure codes as determined by the American Medical Association (AMA) and includes the definition of each procedure. Physicians and outpatient facilities choose codes from the CPT book.
- **The ICD-10 Procedure Coding System (PCS) codebook:** Hospital inpatient procedures are chosen from the ICD-10-PCS reference.
- **Coming soon:** The next revision to the ICD codes, ICD-11, is tentatively scheduled to take effect January 2022. This revision will include an additional 40,000 codes for injuries, diseases, and causes of death.

Because so many different codes and corresponding procedures exist, you may suffer from "coding drama." Coding a procedure with a lot of moving parts can get a bit complicated. Sure, capturing all the procedures that were performed during a surgery is important, for example, but they each must be separately billable or have involved extra work by the surgeon in order to justify unbundling them (or billing them separately). The point? Coding can get pretty complicated. Before you panic, keep this in mind: Coding a procedure is simple if you remember to break it down into small bites.

Physician coding

Physician coding is just what it sounds like: coding diagnoses and procedures representing the work performed by a physician. Under certain circumstances, work performed in an outpatient setting, such as an ambulatory surgery center (ASC), also uses physician coding.

Physician offices, ASCs, and other outpatient facilities use the CPT code set to represent the procedure performed. Physician claims are submitted on the CMS-1500 claim form. (Although ASCs may be required to submit the older HCFA-1500 claim forms in certain states or to certain payers.) In most circumstances, facilities bill commercial carriers on the UB-04 claim form. Both of these forms are discussed later in this chapter.

Facility coding

Coding for facility reimbursement often pertains to hospital coding. Specific coding and billing guidelines exist for hospital billing. If you are working as a facility coder in a hospital, you will use the ICD-10-PCS codebook to identify surgical procedures done during an inpatient stay, and the CPT codebook for procedures done during an outpatient visit.

REMEMBER

Basically, facility coding is for the hospital inpatient setting. Outpatient centers, including those run by the hospital, use physician coding.

Transforming visits into revenue

After the procedure codes and diagnosis codes are entered into the office billing software, the billing process officially begins.

In many offices, the claim is out of the coder's hands at this point because the actual billing part of the process falls to the medical biller who takes the coding information and submits it for payment (you can read about that job in the next section). Nevertheless, the claim may return in the form of a denial from the payer.

Often, if a claim is denied for medical necessity (refer to Chapter 5), it is returned to coding for clarification or verification so that it can be resubmitted.

Determining whether medical coding suits you

As you decide whether medical coding is a job you'd like and do well at, consider these points:

- As a medical coder, you're responsible for extracting the correct procedure code from the physician's documentation. To do this task well, you must have a strong command of the medical terminology, be a good reader, and be very detail oriented.

  In fact, the job of coder is especially attractive to those who are skilled at analyzing data. Every procedure performed in a medical setting has a specific code assigned to it, and it needs to be coded properly to ensure correct billing and maximum reimbursement for the physician or facility.

- You're responsible for recognizing when information is unclear or missing from the documentation and for clarifying with the physician any ambiguous wording in the documentation.

- You must stay current on correct coding guidelines and the ever-changing procedure codes as determined by the AMA and the Centers for Medicare & Medicaid Services (CMS).

  TIP

  Check out `www.ama-assn.org` and `www.cms.gov` for the most up-to-date coding changes.

- As a coder, you may not have much interaction with insurance companies and patients because you will tend to spend most of your time in the office working on coding medical records. So if you think coding is the job for you, know that you'll have more face time with your computer than with patients.

Breaking Down the Medical Biller's Job

After the coder does his thing, it's time for the medical biller to step up to the plate. As the biller, you're responsible for billing insurance companies and patients.

When you submit claims to the insurance company, you're responsible for verifying the correct billing format, ensuring the proper modifiers are appended, and submitting all required documentation with each claim. In most offices, claims are submitted through billing software. Learning to use the software is essential to successful billing and will be a major part of your on-the-job training after you're hired. In the following sections, I highlight the key parts of your job as a medical biller.

A claim that has been well-documented and correctly coded and billed should generate a timely payment for the physician, which is the goal of both the medical coder and biller.

Knowing the payers and keeping up on their idiosyncrasies

Most providers have contracts with multiple commercial payers (basically insurance companies), as well as government payers, such as Medicare. Here's a very brief overview of the kinds of payers and organizations you'll work with as a medical biller:

- **Commercial insurance:** These are private insurance carriers, and they fall into a variety of categories, each of which has particular rules regarding what's covered, when, and how providers get reimbursed. Preferred provider organizations (PPOs), health maintenance organizations (HMOs), and point-of-service plans (POSs) are just a few you'll deal with.
- **Networks:** Some commercial payers and providers participate in networks. A *network* is essentially a middleman who functions as an agent for commercial payers by negotiating contracts with providers and pricing claims (that is, determining the fees for procedures) according to the terms of those contracts.
- **Third-party administrators:** These intermediaries either operate as a network or access networks to price claims, and they often handle claims processing for employers who self-insure their employees rather than use a traditional group health plan.
- **Government payers:** These include governmental insurance programs that offer benefits to particular groups. Examples of government payers include Medicare (the elderly and qualifying disabled people), Medicaid (low-income individuals), Tricare (military members and their families), and so on.
- **The Patient Protection and Affordable Care Act:** The Affordable Care Act (ACA for short) is the healthcare reform law in America. These plans can be purchased through open exchanges that are different in every state. As a result, a medical biller must verify the actual payer as identified on the patient's insurance card. ACA cards usually indicate that the plan is noncommercial and that provider commercial contracts may not be applicable. But to be sure, the front office must verify coverage type prior to seeing the patient. In most states, only providers who have enrolled with the state plan will receive payment for services.

Chapter 6 goes into a great deal of detail on all the things you need to know about these payers. What you need to know now is that each has its own rules and guidelines that must be followed to secure reimbursement. As a medical biller, you must be familiar with the eccentricities of each payer. You never know what you might need to know about a payer, such as which modifiers are accepted, how the payer views bilateral procedures, and what kind of documentation the payer requires. Most workers' compensation carriers, for example, require that procedural notes be included with *all* claims, even if doing so means they get the same operative report from the facility and the surgeon.

TIP

Taking the time upfront to learn what each payer requires can save you a lot of time when you're in the groove of billing. Who wants to get tripped up by not knowing a payer's documentation needs? Not you, rock star. So bone up on this information early and then hit your mental refresh button often by staying abreast of the latest payer information. You can read about the different payers in Chapter 6.

Billing each payer correctly

As with just about everything else in life, billing and coding is going paperless. Remember those giant sliding file cabinets in the doctor's office? They're either gone or are being used to store the office holiday decorations. The Health Insurance Portability and Accountability Act (HIPAA) now makes it necessary to bill most claims electronically.

Most payers accept electronic claims, although some still require paper claims. It's your responsibility to know which method will be accepted. This information is contained in the payer contract, but sometimes you need to call and ask how to submit the claim.

You'll encounter various formats or platforms of electronic claim submissions. For that reason, as the biller, you also need to make sure that the correct format is linked to each individual payer. Fortunately, this information isn't too difficult to find: The patient's insurance card normally has claim submission information on it, and of course, you can always call the payer to check prior to submitting a claim if you have any uncertainty.

For several decades, medical billing was entirely on paper. Then medical practice management software was developed and made claim processing more efficient. Although paper claims may soon be extinct due to the introduction of the HIPAA (covered in Chapter 4), certain payers are exempt and will continue to accept and possibly require paper claims.

In the following sections, I introduce you to the forms you'll encounter as a medical biller.

The CMS-1500 form

The Centers for Medicare & Medicaid Services 1500 (CMS-1500) form, formerly known as a Health Care Financing Administration-1500 (HCFA-1500) form, is the paper form used to submit claims for professional services (see Figure 2-1). Physicians and clinical practitioners submit their claims on this form, which is printed in red ink and contains spaces for all the necessary information. Directions for completing the form are printed on the back of each one.

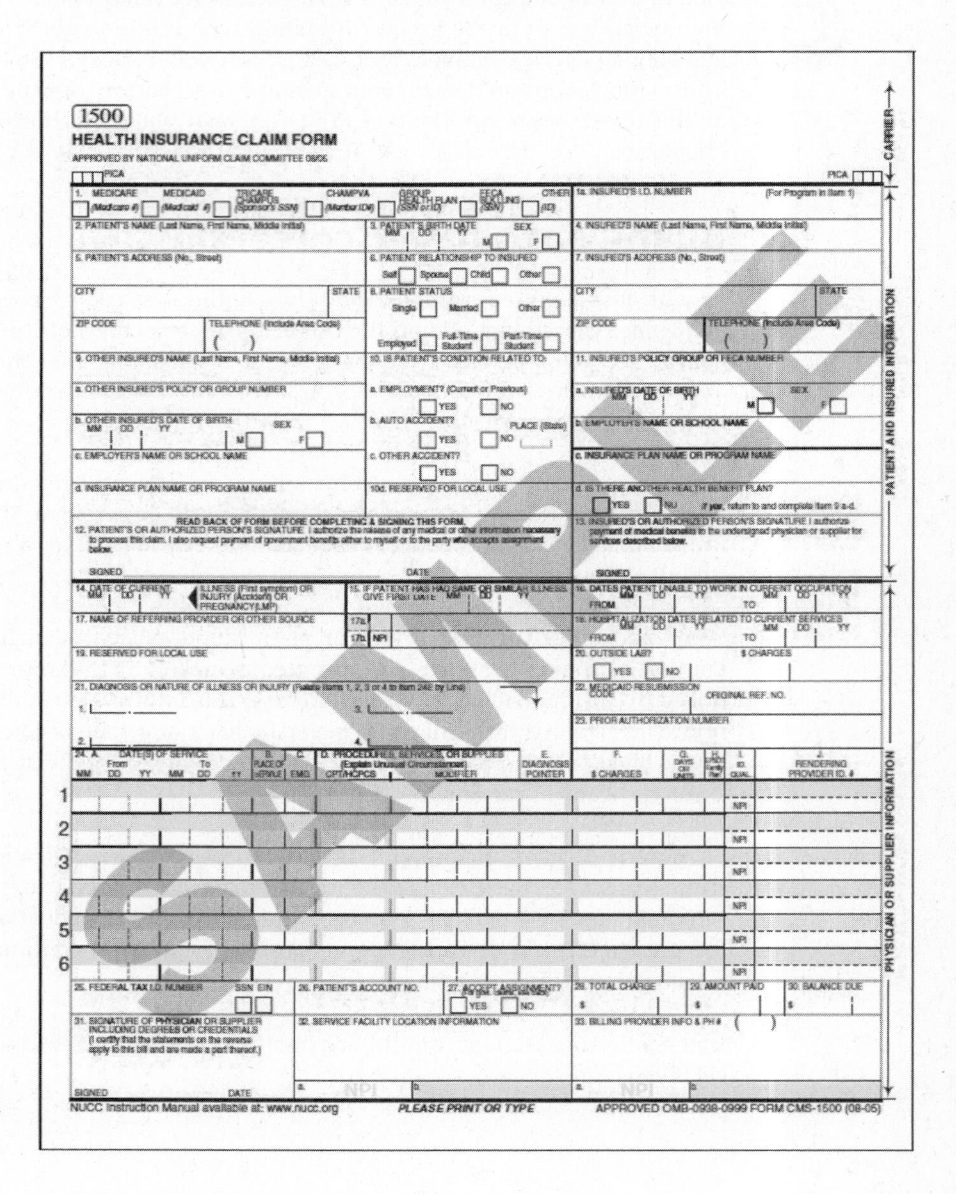

1500

HEALTH INSURANCE CLAIM FORM

APPROVED BY NATIONAL UNIFORM CLAIM COMMITTEE 08/05

PICA — PICA — CARRIER

1. MEDICARE (Medicare #) MEDICAID (Medicaid #) TRICARE CHAMPUS (Sponsor's SSN) CHAMPVA (Member ID#) GROUP HEALTH PLAN (SSN or ID) FECA BLK LUNG (SSN) OTHER (ID)
1a. INSURED'S I.D. NUMBER (For Program in Item 1)
2. PATIENT'S NAME (Last Name, First Name, Middle Initial)
3. PATIENT'S BIRTH DATE MM DD YY SEX M F
4. INSURED'S NAME (Last Name, First Name, Middle Initial)
5. PATIENT'S ADDRESS (No., Street)
6. PATIENT RELATIONSHIP TO INSURED Self Spouse Child Other
7. INSURED'S ADDRESS (No., Street)
CITY STATE
8. PATIENT STATUS Single Married Other
CITY STATE
ZIP CODE TELEPHONE (Include Area Code) ( )
Employed Full-Time Student Part-Time Student
ZIP CODE TELEPHONE (Include Area Code) ( )
9. OTHER INSURED'S NAME (Last Name, First Name, Middle Initial)
10. IS PATIENT'S CONDITION RELATED TO:
11. INSURED'S POLICY GROUP OR FECA NUMBER
a. OTHER INSURED'S POLICY OR GROUP NUMBER
a. EMPLOYMENT? (Current or Previous) YES NO
a. INSURED'S DATE OF BIRTH MM DD YY SEX M F
b. OTHER INSURED'S DATE OF BIRTH MM DD YY SEX M F
b. AUTO ACCIDENT? YES NO PLACE (State)
b. EMPLOYER'S NAME OR SCHOOL NAME
c. EMPLOYER'S NAME OR SCHOOL NAME
c. OTHER ACCIDENT? YES NO
c. INSURANCE PLAN NAME OR PROGRAM NAME
d. INSURANCE PLAN NAME OR PROGRAM NAME
10d. RESERVED FOR LOCAL USE
d. IS THERE ANOTHER HEALTH BENEFIT PLAN? YES NO If yes, return to and complete item 9 a-d.

READ BACK OF FORM BEFORE COMPLETING & SIGNING THIS FORM.
12. PATIENT'S OR AUTHORIZED PERSON'S SIGNATURE I authorize the release of any medical or other information necessary to process this claim. I also request payment of government benefits either to myself or to the party who accepts assignment below.
SIGNED DATE
13. INSURED'S OR AUTHORIZED PERSON'S SIGNATURE I authorize payment of medical benefits to the undersigned physician or supplier for services described below.
SIGNED

PATIENT AND INSURED INFORMATION

14. DATE OF CURRENT: MM DD YY ILLNESS (First symptom) OR INJURY (Accident) OR PREGNANCY(LMP)
15. IF PATIENT HAS HAD SAME OR SIMILAR ILLNESS. GIVE FIRST DATE MM DD YY
16. DATES PATIENT UNABLE TO WORK IN CURRENT OCCUPATION MM DD YY FROM TO
17. NAME OF REFERRING PROVIDER OR OTHER SOURCE 17a. 17b. NPI
18. HOSPITALIZATION DATES RELATED TO CURRENT SERVICES MM DD YY FROM TO
19. RESERVED FOR LOCAL USE
20. OUTSIDE LAB? YES NO $ CHARGES
21. DIAGNOSIS OR NATURE OF ILLNESS OR INJURY (Relate Items 1, 2, 3 or 4 to Item 24E by Line)
1. 2. 3. 4.
22. MEDICAID RESUBMISSION CODE ORIGINAL REF. NO.
23. PRIOR AUTHORIZATION NUMBER
24. A. DATE(S) OF SERVICE From MM DD YY To MM DD YY B. PLACE OF SERVICE C. EMG D. PROCEDURES, SERVICES, OR SUPPLIES (Explain Unusual Circumstances) CPT/HCPCS MODIFIER E. DIAGNOSIS POINTER F. $ CHARGES G. DAYS OR UNITS H. EPSDT Family Plan I. ID. QUAL. J. RENDERING PROVIDER ID. #
1 NPI
2 NPI
3 NPI
4 NPI
5 NPI
6 NPI
25. FEDERAL TAX I.D. NUMBER SSN EIN
26. PATIENT'S ACCOUNT NO.
27. ACCEPT ASSIGNMENT? (For govt. claims, see back) YES NO
28. TOTAL CHARGE $
29. AMOUNT PAID $
30. BALANCE DUE $
31. SIGNATURE OF PHYSICIAN OR SUPPLIER INCLUDING DEGREES OR CREDENTIALS (I certify that the statements on the reverse apply to this bill and are made a part thereof.)
SIGNED DATE
32. SERVICE FACILITY LOCATION INFORMATION a. NPI b.
33. BILLING PROVIDER INFO & PH # ( ) a. NPI b.

PHYSICIAN OR SUPPLIER INFORMATION

NUCC Instruction Manual available at: www.nucc.org PLEASE PRINT OR TYPE APPROVED OMB-0938-0999 FORM CMS-1500 (08-05)

SAMPLE

FIGURE 2-1: The HCFA/CMS-1500 form.

Various forms have been used in the past, and it's essential that you use the most current, or correct, edition when submitting a claim via a paper form.

The HCFA/CMS-1500 form is split into three sections. Section one is patient information. All this information should be in the patient's registration form. Section two is for procedural and diagnostic information, which should be on the superbill or coding form. Section three is for the provider information. See? Easy as 1-2-3.

The UB-04/CMS-1450 form

The Uniform Bill 04 (UB-04) claim form, also called the CMS-1450 or just plain UB in some circles, is used by facilities for health insurance billing. Hospitals, rehabilitation centers, ambulatory surgery centers (usually, but not always), and clinics must bill their services on the UB-04 form in order to get paid by commercial payers. There are 84 boxes on the UB-04. Required fields on the UB include revenue codes, bill type, and sometimes value codes in addition to much of the same information required in the HCFA. Just as with the HCFA/CMS-1500, the directions are printed on the back of the form.

Checking the claim over prior to submission

As I mention previously, as a biller, you'll receive the claim form from the coder and then prepare it for submission. In addition to knowing which submittal method to use — paper or electronic — you also need to check the claim over to make sure all the necessary information is included. This is one of the reasons why, even though you're not a coder, you need to understand the medical codes used.

In addition, you also need to know how to use modifiers correctly. The coder may be responsible for assigning modifiers based on correct coding edits, but the biller is ultimately responsible for making sure that payer-specific (or provider-specific) modifiers are on the claim prior to submission. For information on modifiers and checking the claim over before submitting, head to Chapter 12.

Assessing whether medical billing is the right choice for you

Medical billers are responsible for billing insurance companies and patients correctly. As a biller, you need to understand how to read claim forms and payer remittance advisories (RAs); you need to understand coding, even though you may not do that part of the job yourself; and you need to stay informed on the different claim submission standards for each payer.

In addition, this job often requires daily interaction with both patients and insurance companies. The responsibility for explaining charges to patients may fall to the biller, particularly when patients need help understanding their payment obligations (such as coinsurance and copayments) per their policy benefit. For that reason, billers need to have strong people skills both in person and on the telephone.

REMEMBER

As a potential biller, keep in mind that working with patients can present a challenge. Often, they're sick or hurt during your interaction with them. Not only may they be contagious, but emotions may be high or minds may be fuzzy as well. Do your best to stay friendly and patient — and wash your hands frequently! Another tip — have a "guest" pen for the patients. Keep the germs off of yours.

In Tandem: Working Together or Doing Both Jobs Yourself?

Although you often hear people refer to billing and coding in the same breath — see? I just did it — they're really two different jobs, as the preceding sections illustrate. After the coder has assigned the correct codes, the biller transforms the codes into a payable claim. As you pursue a career as a biller and coder, one of the things you should think about is whether you want to do both jobs or concentrate on just one. This decision may impact where you build your career, as I explain in the next sections.

Wearing both hats

Both billing and coding job functions typically occur in the same office, whether on- or off-site. The flowchart in Figure 2-2 encapsulates the key functions that make up a combined billing and coding job.

Some physician practices keep their coding and billing in-house, meaning it's done by their office staff. In these situations, there's no middleman, such as a practice management or billing company (discussed in the next section).

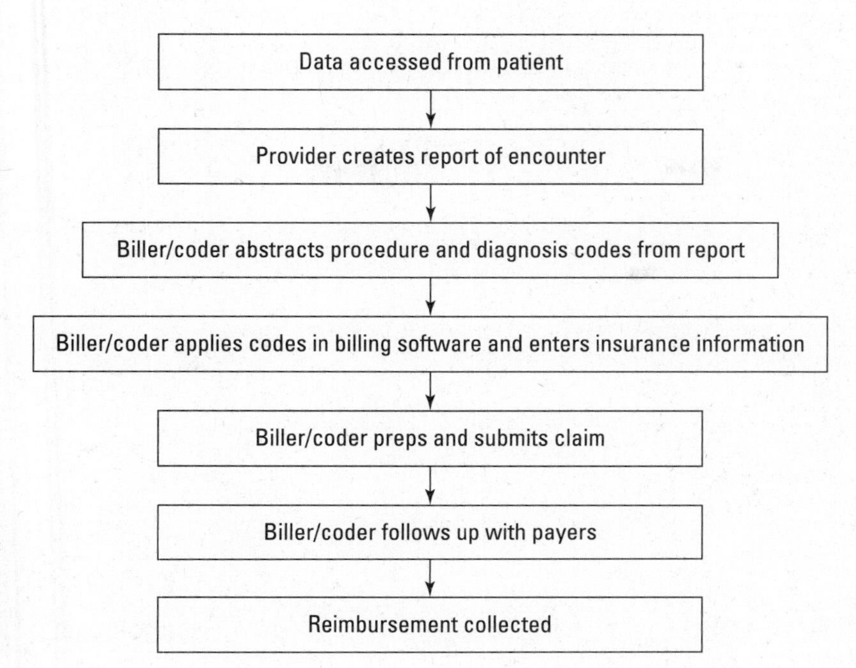

FIGURE 2-2: General functions associated with billing and coding.

In some small practices, one person — the office coder/biller — does both jobs. This individual is the key to the business's accounts receivable. Anyone considering accepting this type of position should have experience in both areas and should possess a working knowledge of payer contracts, which you can read more about in Chapter 11.

If you want to do double duty as a coder/biller, be prepared for twice the work and being twice as vital to the success of your facility. Wearing both the billing hat and the coding hat makes you the one multitalented sheriff in town!

Deciding which job is for you

The trend now is for physicians to use practice management or billing companies to facilitate their accounts receivables, and that makes billing companies a good place for a medical coder and biller to find work. These companies often employ several coders and billers, and it's definitely an environment in which you would do one job exclusively, due to the sheer volume of clients you service.

REMEMBER

Billing companies often use various types of coding and billing software, and they offer the best opportunity to get experience in different systems, in addition to allowing the novice coder to learn from the more seasoned coders.

» Working from home

» Creating your own corporate identity as a freelancer

Chapter 3

Weighing Your Employment Options

Translating the work performed by the doctor and the doctor's staff into payment is known as the *revenue cycle*. The entire cycle involves coding the procedures according to the documentation, billing the procedures with the appropriate modifiers and diagnosis codes, sending the claim to the appropriate payer, and receiving payment from the insurance company and/or the patient.

The processes of billing and coding in that revenue cycle provide all sorts of job opportunities, from those in physician offices to hospitals to insurance companies and government payers. So the job of billing and coding is a far-reaching one that affords you myriad opportunities, which is good news as you determine what sort of professional setting you most prefer.

Regardless of where you end up, medical billing and coding is a profession that isn't going away anytime soon. In fact, thanks to recent government efforts to convert to electronic health records, the opportunities are growing. Where you choose to plant yourself is entirely up to you. So hop on the cycle! It's going to be a great ride.

Choosing Your Environment: Doctor's Office, Hospital, and Others

Before you start job-hunting, give some thought to what sort of environment you want to work in. The possibilities are almost endless, and if you think about your preferences before you search for a job, you can narrow down your list of possible employers, saving yourself a boatload of time. Are you, for example, interested in the fast-paced, volume-heavy work that you'd likely find in a hospital? Or does the controlled chaos of a smaller physician's office seem more up your alley?

The good news is that all medical facilities and offices need some sort of billing and coding staff who can either work in the office or work remotely. Medical billers and coders are essential to the efficient processing of data, compliance with government regulations, and protection of patient privacy as required by the Health Insurance Portability and Accountability Act (HIPAA).

TECHNICAL STUFF

Currently, medical billing and coding jobs comprise one-fifth of the healthcare workforce, a number that is expected to grow. The transition to ICD-10, the updated version of the International Classification of Diseases that replaced ICD-9, increased the demand for medical coders because it made the coding and billing process more complicated (due to the increased specificity of the classifications) and more time-consuming. On the heels of ICD-10 is ICD-11, which is tentatively scheduled to become effective after January 1, 2022; ICD-11 will unlikely create concerns that were part of the ICD-10 delay. You can read more about ICD in Chapter 15.

In the following sections, I outline several places that hire billers and coders, plus I offer a tip for gaining access to your employer of choice.

REMEMBER

As you consider where you want to ply your trade, keep in mind that the environment you choose can impact how broad or narrow your exposure to the coding and billing profession is. For example, if you work for a general surgeon (an optimal — and most sought after — position for a coder), you get experience in most areas of coding. The surgeon may use evaluation and management codes in addition to procedural codes from every section of the coding book. In contrast, a position in a pathology laboratory may limit your experience to that area of practice. A coder with experience in all areas becomes more valuable as an employee to the bigger employers.

The doctor is in: Working in a physician's office

If you've seen someone buried under stacks of medical files as you take care of your copay in the doctor's office, chances are you're looking at a medical biller or coder. Just think — that could be you!

Several different kinds of physician offices employ their own coders and billers. Here are just a few possibilities:

- **Working in an office in which a group of physicians share a practice:** In a multi-physician office, the pace is usually a little faster, and more demands are placed on the administrative staff. Usually, a larger practice has an office manager in addition to the clerical staff.
- **Working in an office that has just one or two docs:** In this situation, the coder may function as the receptionist and biller as well. These offices can be great places to work. Due to size, you may find less office politics, and life usually tends to move at a slower pace when you're dealing with just one doc. The downside is that getting time off can be difficult, and your days off generally correspond to the physician's days off, so you have less flexibility with regard to personal time.
- **Working in an office in which the physicians do their own coding:** In this case, the physicians may use only the services of a biller. A certified coder is optimal to fill this type of position because, when the physician is out of her comfort zone from a coding perspective, a certified coder can assist with assigning the correct codes, as well as keeping abreast of code changes and other requirements. The downside to working in this environment is that your coding may not be as accurate as it should be (you may work with a physician who likes to "do it his way"), and moving to another job will be more difficult. Keeping providers like these on the right track is often a difficult and delicate position to put yourself in.

Hooking up with a hospital

Get all the images of *Grey's Anatomy* out of your head right now. Working in a hospital may be busy and exciting, but it's not always *that* dramatic, especially in the "back of house," where billers and coders do their stuff. That said, working in a hospital environment has a lot to keep you hopping.

Working in a hospital can be a rewarding experience for the coder. Hospitals are very departmentalized, with each department having its own coders. In most circumstances, the coding in a particular department is specific to a certain specialty or set of specialties, just as it would be if you were working in a physician's office. The difference is that the coding is for the facility, so expenses that are incurred by the facility — including drugs and implantable items such as stents or shunts, for example — are reimbursed through the hospital coding. In addition, most hospitals have a centralized billing department (or they may send the billing out to a billing company; see the next section).

Medicare and some state Medicaid plans reimburse hospitals based on diagnosis-related groups (for example, MS-DRGs or APR-DRGs) for inpatient claims. This means that the admitting diagnosis is linked to the severity of the patient's illness. The level of risk associated with the treatment can affect the level of reimbursement received from Medicare and other payers. In other words, the sicker the patient, the greater the risk, and the higher the level of reimbursement. Coding that drives diagnosis related groups (DRGs) is more complex than non-DRG claims. There are specific rules that govern sequencing diagnosis codes and also the documentation that is required to support using those codes.

Don't think that you can't create a niche for yourself in a larger hospital setting. You can, thanks to all the smaller sub-clinics and offices under the hospital umbrella that service the entire facility. For example, many surgeries can't be performed without anesthesia (well, they could, but it wouldn't be a popular choice!). So hospitals use anesthesiologists, who have to bill patients just like any other function of the hospital.

Focusing on a billing or practice management company

Other options for employment as a biller or coder usually involve working for a practice management or billing company. These companies provide various levels of administrative support, with some handling all of a provider's practice administrative duties (even though having someone on site who understands insurance is still important for every provider office).

Billing and practice management companies come in all sizes and specialties. The larger companies handle numerous clients and usually have a team of people working on one or two of the accounts. In addition, if the company provides practice management — including coding and billing for a physician or group — the work is the same as if the provider were handling this aspect of the practice in-house.

Work at a billing or practice management company may be a good bet for the novice coder or biller because it's a great way to learn the ropes under the tutelage of a more seasoned professional. It also provides an outlet for giving and receiving feedback and working through some of the stickier details with a coworker. In this work environment, you wouldn't be flying solo! As a general rule, bigger companies usually have more structure with regard to how they do things, and they provide the best on-the-job training. That being said, be mindful of companies that have internal training programs run by people who have only worked at that one company!

Just as with hospitals, you can find your own niche in practice management companies, too. Some practice management companies within larger organizations, for example, specialize in certain areas, such as anesthesia or radiological practices. Working for one of these companies enables you to focus on and gain expertise in those specialties. With anesthesia, for example, you would need to know *all* surgical and procedural codes, and radiology overlaps with cardiology because of the noninvasive cardiac procedures that are now common.

Many billing companies are contractually obligated to their clients to employ only certified medical coders to perform the coding. Although the AAPC (American Academy of Professional Coders) now offers a Certified Professional Biller certification, billers may often be trained on the job, but having knowledge prior to employment gives you an advantage as a job seeker.

Processing claims for an insurance company

You may decide that you want to work in claims. Working in a claims job is one way to stretch the limits of your billing and coding knowledge.

Major insurance payers use automated claims processing. The claims are received electronically and do not require a human touch unless there are problems. Smaller payers may either receive the information electronically or scan it into their processing software, where it is processed, ideally correctly. To ensure more efficient, yet timely claim processing, many of these companies also use a claims processor.

To be successful as a claims processor, you need to know medical claim coding, billing procedures, and insurance obligations. These processors carefully examine each claim to determine its validity and accuracy. The processor then refers to the patient's insurance policy benefit or plan to determine the correct level of payment for the claim. The processor also has software that contains the contracts that are linked to individual medical providers by their tax identification number or National Provider Identifier (NPI). They apply the plan provisions and payer contract to the claim to determine payment. After doing all this, the payment is issued accordingly. If the claim needs additional clarification or information, the claims processor sends a notice to the appropriate office to request the missing details.

In addition to payer-processing positions, insurance companies also need people to handle incorrectly processed claims when the providers appeal them. Again, solid knowledge of medical terminology, diagnosis, and procedural codes are valuable tools for these employees.

Considering the best of the rest

The possibilities are nearly endless in the billing and coding field. Even though you're most likely to find employment in a physician's office or in a larger facility like a hospital or clinic, here are a few other options you may find enticing:

- Nursing homes
- Outpatient facilities
- Home healthcare services
- Durable medical equipment providers
- Federal government agencies such as the Department of Health & Human Services, Social Security, Medicare, Tricare, or the Department of Labor

In short, billing and coding are important to any business that provides healthcare.

Getting your foot in the door

Whether you find work in a doctor's office, at the local hospital, at a practice management company, or for an insurance company, you have several options for jobs within those offices. Think of the world of billing and coding as a buffet, and you have a plate just waiting to be filled with a big, tasty job. The good news is that you get to pick based on your level of skill and your interests.

TIP

Still, finding employment as a novice can be a challenge. Many offices are fully staffed and may hesitate to hire a newly trained coder without any medical office experience. An excellent way to get your foot in the door is to accept a position that involves verifying each patient's benefits.

Remote Access: Setting up Off-Site

Working remotely — it's a good gig if you can get it! Some offices allow coders to work remotely. If you work off-site as a coder, you access the systems that contain the necessary documentation and then determine (or *abstract*) the correct diagnosis and procedural codes. You then return the codes to the billing department for claim submission.

In the following sections, I explain some of the things that make working remotely so enjoyable. But before you decide that working from home is for you, keep these important points in mind:

- **You must be able to ensure patient privacy.** When you work remotely, your office has less control over what you do and the environment in which you do it. For that reason, remote access places certain demands on you and the company to maintain HIPAA compliance. You must strictly follow policies and procedures to protect the privacy of the patients. For example, you need a private workspace that ensures that no one else — like guests and family members — can access patient information.
- **You must be able to work independently without supervision and still meet the company quotas that are normally imposed.** Companies that allow coders to work from home have the same expectations for their remote employees as they do for those working in the office. The remote worker normally is more productive if he or she exercises the same discipline that would be expected in the traditional office environment.

So take stock of your remote environment and your comfort level with shouldering that responsibility. If you feel comfortable that you can do both of the preceding, you may just find that working at home works for you!

Working in your PJs

One obvious perk to working from home is the casual dress option. Many offices have relaxed dress codes, but only within the confines of your own home is working in a robe and slippers even an option.

As pleasant as that sounds, keep in mind that you may have to dress like a grown-up every now and again. Most companies still require remote coders to attend office meetings, workshops, and other professional functions. Plus, because you want your boss to be able to put a face to your name and because you want to make yourself available for questions from the billing department or follow-up people (divisions that are dependent upon the coder when questions arise in claim submission and processing), you'll probably head into the office on your own occasionally.

The no-commute commute: Arranging a suitable workspace

One obvious perk to remote coding is that it eliminates the daily commute to an office, which saves energy, time, and money. The money you save on gas, clothes, lunches out, and wear and tear on your car (or a subway card) can go straight into the bank!

As a biller/coder, you need to make sure your workspace is equipped with a comfortable chair and a desk or table with room to spread out, a computer with Internet access, the appropriate software, and a telephone. Depending upon the company, you may also need a printer, in which case you will also need a shredder to properly dispose of any patient information. In addition, you need the appropriate coding books.

Although some companies supply all the materials you need, including the paper and toner (and pay part of your Internet and phone bills), others expect you to provide these things on your own. Be sure to clarify the company's expectations as well as your own before entering into an agreement.

REMEMBER

Some payers also allow people working in patient and provider support positions to work from home. Candidates for these positions must be able to maintain a professional demeanor from home, which means no barking dogs, crying babies, or other unprofessional background noises. If you have small children at home or you cannot secure a quiet room within your house (like a home office), then seriously consider setting up shop elsewhere. If, however, you've got a relatively quiet house during the day, then go for it!

Looking at the downside of working remotely

Every silver lining has a cloud, and working remotely is no exception. Although it may be a wonderful solution for some, it's not a wonderful solution for all. In the next sections, I address some of the pitfalls.

You don't get the benefits of being in the office

One downside to remote positions is that you have less interaction with coworkers. You may be the last to know when policies or procedures have changed. Working from home also does not offer the opportunity to cross-train in larger offices, which can affect your future employment options.

The employee with the most knowledge of office procedures and who is able to assist in other departments is a greater asset to the company. When you work remotely, you have fewer opportunities to prove your mettle within the office community. If you do choose to work remotely, try to find ways that you can keep that personal connection; otherwise, you may find yourself the first to be let go.

The big "but": Generally not a good idea for the novice

Remote coding is for the seasoned professional, not for the novice — no matter what they tell you in TV commercials for technical schools. Initially you may think that abstracting billable procedural and diagnosis codes is clear-cut. It's not. Because many providers document in conversational format, coders often need clarification on what exactly was done. Experienced coders need less clarification and normally have developed a method for performing a physician query with finesse, thus allowing them to get the information they need.

When you work in an office, you have access to an experienced coder who can often assist you in understanding the verbiage in the documentation. If you're a newbie, consider putting off your remote access plans for a year or two until you have some office experience under your belt.

Part of your responsibility as a coder is to make sure the documentation supports the claim being submitted for payment. If you're new to billing and coding, working in an office with the support of more experienced professionals can help you maintain that all-important accuracy. Think of it as a professional safety net. So if you do choose to fly the coop and ride solo, make sure you have strong support at the home office in case accuracy issues pop up.

Reviewing Other Work Options: Freelancing, Temping, and More

A well-seasoned coder may carve out a reputation that enables him to work on his own in a freelance or consultant capacity. As a freelancer, you may be hired by companies for particular projects or by individual providers who need temporary help. As a consultant, you may assist the provider with hiring support staff and training the new staff in areas of claim billing and submission. In either case — when the project is finished or after the office is up and running — your work is done.

As a freelance or consultant coder, you find your own employment and contract for the specified duties to be performed. Freelancing is an option only for the expert coder who is fully capable of working independently.

Temporary work is another avenue sometimes taken by the experienced professional. Administrative staffing companies employ individuals for short- and long-term assignments. You register with the agency and go to the assignments offered to you. Sometimes offices need help replacing an employee on medical or disability leave. Although choosing this option may allow you to gain perspective on what type of work best suits you, often the employers are quite specific about the type of temporary help they need and usually require someone with some experience.

REMEMBER

If you're new to billing and coding, freelancing, consultant coding, and temping are not good options for you, for the same reasons I outline in the earlier section "The big 'but': Generally not a good idea for the novice." If you need more convincing, read on.

Heeding a Word of Advice for New Coders

As I mention earlier, working independently — whether you're working off-site, as a freelancer, as a consultant, or as a temp — isn't a good idea for a novice coder. The liability for errors is too much of a risk to both you and the provider.

WARNING

Incorrect coding leads to incorrect billing, a situation sometimes known as *false claims reporting.* Fraudulent or false claims submission can be a criminal act with serious penalties ranging from payment being taken back by a payer to imprisonment (if evidence of intent by the provider exists) to exclusion from federal programs.

REMEMBER

Part of your job as a coder is to make sure submitted claims are supported by the physicians' documentation. If the documentation does not support the claim and the error is discovered, the provider is liable for the incorrect payment and possibly additional penalties and repercussions. If the provider for whom you work is penalized, the next head to roll will likely be yours. Making this kind of error doesn't make for a good reference, and it presents a definite challenge in any future job interviews. So be proactive about ensuring that your coding is accurate! If you choose to freelance, remain in close contact with the physician's office and remember that no question is too small. Getting the answers you need from the doc can you save you, and the provider, a lot of hassle when bills are due.

INTERNING? YES, PLEASE

Some vocational training schools work with local offices that allow students to do an internship. As an intern, you work in an office and are under direct supervision. Many offices have experienced coders and billers to serve as mentors. Sometimes, these opportunities evolve into regular employment. At a minimum, opportunities such as these give you experience and a professional reference.

Check with your school or professional organization about how to locate billing and coding internships in your area. Or check out the AAPC's Project Xtern program at `www.aapc.com/medical-coding-jobs/project-xtern/index.aspx` to find leads on internship opportunities.

The best thing you, as a novice coder, can do for yourself and future employers is to find work in a medical office, hospital, or billing company to gain experience in the medical profession. These environments introduce you to all areas of the claims process and make you more valuable to the company. In these environments, you learn the basics in a solid training program, and you learn the rest on the job. Physicians, if you work directly with them, and experienced coders can be wonderful mentors.

After you gain experience, you can branch out into alternative work scenarios. True, working in your PJs and having a 20-second commute from bedroom to home office is a lovely idea. But realize that you may have to pay some professional dues before your freelancing dreams can become a reality.

REMEMBER

There is no substitute for experience. Exposure to the claims process and experienced billers and coders is the key to shaping you into a fully seasoned and very valuable coder yourself.

2 Boning Up on the Need-to-Knows of Your Profession

IN THIS PART . . .

Grasp what compliance actually is and what it means when you're a medical biller or coder.

Get the full lowdown on the National Correct Coding Initiative edits. These edits identify what procedures may and may not be billed together — a major element in the medical billing world.

Get to know the importance of medical necessity. It's the link between procedures and payment.

Uncover the ins and outs of payer policies and provider contracts.

» Abiding by HIPAA rules

» Knowing the rules regarding bundling

Chapter 4

Compliance: Understanding the Rules

Compliance — it's such a serious word, and for good reason. When people in the healthcare industry speak about compliance by healthcare providers, they mean that an office or individual has set up a program to run the practice according to the laws established by federal or state governments and regulations established by the Department of Health & Human Services (HHS) or other designated agencies. The regulations are designed to prevent fraud and abuse by healthcare providers, and as a medical biller or coder, you must familiarize yourself with the basics of compliance.

Not only must you follow rules regarding how to process and bill claims, but you must also follow rules regarding the confidentiality of healthcare information. You can thank something called the Health Insurance Portability and Accountability Act (HIPAA) for setting the bar for compliance. This act was passed by Congress in 1996 and is sometimes called the Privacy Rule. It established the first national standard for use and disclosure of health information and guarantees certain rights to individuals with regard to their healthcare. HIPAA outlines how certain entities (health plan, clearinghouse, or healthcare provider, for example) can use or disclose personal health information, or PHI. In addition, under HIPAA, patients must be allowed access to their medical records.

In this chapter, I tell you who the key rule makers are and explain how you can stay on the right side of the law.

You Rule! Meeting the Rule Makers

The rule-making game has several players, and most of them are somehow related to good ol' Uncle Sam. The Department of Health & Human Services (HHS) is the primary U.S. government agency responsible for regulating the American healthcare industry. Medicare and Medicaid, part of the Centers for Medicare & Medicaid Services (CMS), are two of this agency's programs, and together they provide healthcare insurance for millions of Americans. This department's programs serve the United States' most vulnerable citizens.

The OIG protects the operations of the HHS. This oversight also extends to programs under other HHS institutions, including the Centers for Disease Control and Prevention (CDC), National Institutes of Health (NIH), and the Food and Drug Administration (FDA).

REMEMBER

The American Medical Association (AMA), which develops, maintains, and owns the copyright to the Current Procedural Terminology (CPT) codes, determines what the codes represent. CMS works with the AMA to determine code changes ("edits") and which codes are incidental to others.

As a biller and coder, you need to be familiar with these organizations. The following sections outline the key organizations that you'll work with as a medical biller and coder.

The Centers for Medicare & Medicaid Services (CMS)

As mentioned previously, the Centers for Medicare & Medicaid Services (CMS) is the home of two government healthcare programs: Medicare and Medicaid.

Originally, Medicare was intended to provide healthcare to the elderly at the age of 65. In the years that followed, the need for access to healthcare for others, including children, the disabled, and those with certain chronic illnesses, became apparent. Today, Medicare also includes those with physical or mental disabilities and those awaiting organ transplants, as well as prescription drug coverage.

Because these programs serve so many Americans and use taxpayer dollars to do so, the government has established rules governing what services are covered, the acceptable level of compensation for the service providers, and how claims should be processed.

Medicare policies regarding medical necessity, frequency of procedures, and other payment rules are often used as guidelines for commercial payers as well. For complete information about the policies for Medicare claims processing, check out the Internet-only manuals on the CMS website (www.cms.gov).

REMEMBER

Medicare policy rules change pretty frequently, and they affect payment for certain procedures. Take a procedure as simple as a lesion excision (removing a cyst or skin growth), for example. Medicare pays for this procedure only under a specific set of rules (the diagnosis must support medical necessity). If the rules regarding this procedure change, and if these changes affect your employer, it may be your job as a coder to keep the physician or staff informed.

The Office of Inspector General (OIG)

The Office of Inspector General (OIG) was established in 1976 to oversee programs administered through HHS. Much of the OIG's efforts focus on identifying waste, fraud, and abuse in Medicare, Medicaid, and other federal programs like Indian Health Services.

The OIG conducts audits and tracks how government funds are spent. The findings of these investigations are often the foundation for Medicare or Medicaid policy changes and procedural code changes initiated by CMS or the AMA. The OIG publishes the results of its investigation on its website (http://oig.hhs.gov).

If action is necessary to enforce compliance with laws and regulations, the Department of Justice or the FBI are called upon to execute.

REMEMBER

Even though most of these government organizations are sole entities, they typically rely on each other in one way or another. For example, because developments in medical technology and treatment options are usually far ahead of legislation, Medicare often discovers through an OIG investigation that taxpayer funds are not being used efficiently.

The individual payer (insurance company)

When you hear the term *individual payers*, you may assume it refers to individuals, but it doesn't. Individual payers are actually the insurance companies that provide group and individual coverage plans to patients. Each payer has its own policies and procedures, which are published and available for both patients and providers to review. The payer may be a plan administrator that is part of a pricing network or may serve as administrator for sponsored plans.

More often than not, CMS sets the bar when it comes to payer rules. As I mention earlier, Medicare follows a strict set of claims-processing policies that include correct coding edits, mutually exclusive procedures edits, modifier requirements, unit requirements, and numerous other specifications. In addition, Medicare requires that claims be submitted within 12 months of the date the services took place. Individual payers may follow the Medicare rules for payment, but they don't *have* to follow them. In fact, many often have their own policies.

Individual payers employ their own processing policies, including which edits they follow, which modifiers they recognize, and other payer-specific rules. As the coder and biller, you must be knowledgeable about each payer's policies when you prepare a claim for submission. If you don't follow the payer's policies, the claim may pay incorrectly or not at all.

In addition, most commercial payers have much shorter timely filing requirements than Medicare's 1-year limit, usually 90 days — which isn't a long time when crucial documentation is missing!

Also, you need to be mindful as to the type of private insurance the patient carries. Is it a fully insured plan? An ASO (administrative services only)? A Medicare replacement plan? Or maybe a Medicaid plan? Payment rules and policies vary within payers, depending upon which type of coverage the patient carries. Chapter 6 discusses the different types of commercial and government payers.

Complying with HIPAA

Strict regulations are necessary in billing and processing medical claims because the opportunity for fraud and abuse is ever present on both sides. The Health Insurance Portability and Accountability Act (HIPAA), passed by Congress in 1996, set a national standard for protecting health data and protecting the patient's rights.

Before HIPAA, individual state laws governed the privacy of health information, and these laws often varied from state to state. Under HIPAA, providers, plans, and all healthcare services must comply with federal standards. In addition, individual states still have the authority to regulate and set guidelines for insurance plans and provider practices that operate within their jurisdictions; they may be more stringent than the national standard, but they cannot be more lenient.

Here are the key provisions of HIPAA:

- **HIPAA guarantees everyone a basic right to privacy in addition to the right to have access to his or her own medical records.** Providers may charge a reasonable fee for access to the records and also may adopt policies with regard to compliance (for example, the process patients must follow to request records, or how the office is structured to ensure patient confidentiality).
- **HIPAA requires that all providers must inform their patients of their privacy practices.** These notices include a disclosure about how medical information is used and the patient's right to file a complaint with the Department of Health & Human Services Office for Civil Rights (OCR).

  As a general rule, protected health information (PHI) can be disclosed only with the consent of the patient. However, in some instances, PHI may be shared without the consent of the patient. Such circumstances include those that benefit the public, such as certain communicable diseases that must be reported to the CDC, records that are under subpoena in criminal cases, and the like.

- **HIPAA gives patients the right to know who has accessed their health records within the prior six years.** This disclaimer, however, doesn't need to include the people and other entities (such as clearinghouses and billing services) who see the records during the daily task of patient care. In other words, you don't need to let the patient know which clearinghouse the office uses, whether billing is outsourced, or other such practice information.

Organizations that are not bound by HIPAA rules include life insurance companies, workers' compensation companies, Social Security agencies, law enforcement agencies, researchers who are provided information by healthcare providers, companies that offer screenings at malls, and other such entities. Entities who are covered by HIPAA are responsible for implementing a compliance plan.

Under HIPAA, all reported breaches of compliance regulations must be investigated, and violators may face civil or criminal penalties. For that reason, it is essential that all cogs of the healthcare industry (including you as a biller and coder) be familiar with HIPAA rules.

Doing your part: Do's and don'ts of compliance

Even though HIPAA has changed privacy and data protection for the better, don't be fooled into thinking that information that should be held confidential between doctor and patient stays in the examination room. Patient information is exchanged in many places, so discretion on the part of all staff is imperative to protect the rights of your patients.

GOING BEYOND HIPAA'S CONFIDENTIALITY RULES

HIPAA does more than simply deal with confidentiality.

- Title I of HIPAA protects health insurance coverage for workers and their families who change or lose their jobs. Under HIPAA, a new group health insurance must provide coverage for most of the medical conditions that were covered by a patient's previous group policy. When an individual enrolls in a new group health plan, the plan may refuse to cover certain defined conditions for a period of 12 to 18 months. This exclusion is reduced by the amount of time that the patient had coverage under his or her previous group health plan. As the biller or coder, you must know this rule so that you can challenge an unlawful pre-existing denial by a commercial payer.
- Title II of HIPAA requires a national standard for electronic transactions and national identifiers for providers, insurers, and employers. These identifiers are known as Tax ID numbers (similar to an individual's Social Security number) and National Provider Identifier (NPI) numbers. Payers have payer identification numbers called payer IDs, 5-digit numbers that identify to which payer a claim is to be sent electronically. As a medical biller or coder, you must know and follow these standards to avoid violations for which your employer will be held accountable. (This is also the clause that contains the standards used to ensure the privacy of health information.)
- Title III of HIPAA addresses the way employers handle medical savings accounts, which are tax-deferred savings accounts that are used only to cover medical expenses.
- Title IV of HIPAA mandates that employers must allow employees to continue their health insurance when leaving their employ.
- Title V of HIPAA provides employers with ways to offset the cost of compliance, such as deducting life-insurance premiums from their tax returns.

Consider this: In earlier days, patient charts were kept in file cabinets or record rooms. Ideally, only those with a need to see those records were allowed access. Today, because of electronic data transfer, all patient information finds its way into data files. Without high levels of security, confidential patient information could easily find its way into the wrong hands.

Ultimately, all employees (this means you, too) within an organization bound by HIPAA are responsible for maintaining compliance to the best of their abilities. With regard to patient confidentiality, the general idea is really simple: Those who do not need to know should not be told. Patients in the waiting room do not need to know anything about another patient. They don't need to know another patient's name, address, phone number, Social Security number, birth date, or any other personal information. Nor do they need to know why that patient is there. Your office should have a process that allows every patient to relay this information without anyone else in attendance being privy to that information.

Your employer is responsible for having a compliance implementation plan and a way to monitor whether the plan is being followed. In small offices, one individual may be responsible for monitoring practices, like making sure computers are password-protected, making sure that sensitive areas are secure, and so on. Larger facilities normally have a number of people monitoring compliance within the practice. These individuals include informational technology specialists who make sure no software viruses or network breaches occur.

You also have an important role to play. Fortunately, the do's and don'ts of compliance are basic.

Here are the things on your Do list:

- Treat patients' personal information as you would like your own information to be treated: Keep it secure and respect their right to privacy.
- Use passwords that are not obvious (*password* is not a password; neither is *12345*), keep them in a secure place that is also password protected, and change them regularly.
- If you need to discuss patient care in locations where you can be overheard, be discreet. If you work in a surgery center, wear a uniform so that patients are not uncomfortable with a stranger in street clothes.
- Keep your voice down when discussing patient finances, both in person and over the phone.
- Be professional at all times.

And here are the Don'ts:

- Don't write your passwords on the side of your computer, share the passwords with other staff members for their use, or use the same password for everything. (Some offices may require that passwords be registered with a practice manager or compliance officer. Technically, a compliant office does not allow login and password information to be shared with anyone. Individuals are responsible for any and all activity logged under that individual's name and the consequences of a security breach must not be taken lightly.) So *do not share!*
- Don't discuss personal issues in the presence of patients.

In many offices, the coder is the one with the best resources for staying abreast of compliance regulations. These issues are often discussed at your professional organization's local chapter meetings, and they're the subject of articles in professional publications. The coder also needs to stay aware of Medicare policies, which include compliance issues.

ELECTRONIC SYSTEMS: CHARTS FOR THE 21ST CENTURY

First of all, let's be clear: You need to distinguish between two types of electronic systems: the electronic medical record (EMR) and the electronic health record (EHR). An EMR is just a digital version of a paper chart. It is not accessible by adjunct providers and can't be transferred electronically. These records must be printed out to be sent, just like making copies of the paper chart.

The future of medicine is the EHR. Use of the electronic records is intended to do away with the paper chart and make protecting and sharing information easier for providers. If a physician has access to the hospital's records, he or she can receive test results, pathology reports, and other information needed to treat the patient immediately.

EHRs are also considered to be more secure. They're password protected and can be programmed so that even those who have access to the records don't have access to the entire record, but only to those parts necessary to do their jobs. The front office, for example, may need full access to patient demographics and insurance information, but it may not need access to test results. Similarly, the nurse caring for the patient needs full access to health information but probably doesn't need to know the patient's Social Security number or address.

Not surprisingly, electronic records offer many advantages. Many types of record systems come with expansion modules that target specialties. These templates present mandatory data fields that must be completed before the record can be closed. This function eliminates the risk of missing information necessary for correct coding and billing (in addition to providing quality patient care).

Privacy is a major concern when a practice implements an EHR system. For that reason, privacy protocol must be followed. A misplaced paper chart may violate a single individual's privacy, but with EHRs, one data breach can violate hundreds of patients' privacy. Data loss is another potential issue with electronic records. A computer or server crash can erase several years' worth of data if the server isn't backed up daily. The use of cloud computing further complicates the issue. Primarily, cloud storage takes the PHI (personal health information) completely out of the provider's hands, making encryption essential.

Beyond your official responsibilities regarding compliance, keep in mind that, as part of the office staff, you can help guard confidentiality in other ways. For example, family members of the office staff don't belong in the secure areas of the office, and visitors to the office need to identify themselves and the reason for their visit. If you see people in areas they shouldn't be in, inquire why they're there and direct them elsewhere. (*Note:* Every office needs a form that obligates visitors to register and sign that they agree to protect any patient information that unintentionally finds its way to them.)

Uh-oh! Facing the consequences of non-compliance

Violating HIPAA is referred to as *non-compliance.* When HIPAA has been violated, the provider is subject to a fine and is responsible for fixing the problem.

Even accidentally or unintentionally releasing protected information can be a HIPAA violation. This type of violation varies in the level of severity, and the minimum penalty is $100, but if the violation is repeated, the fine can increase to several thousands of dollars. If the unintentional violation was a result of neglect and the provider doesn't take steps to correct the problem, the fine can rise to more than $1 million.

The penalties for intentional violations are even worse. Intentionally releasing protected information results in higher fines and may include a jail sentence. If the information is released for financial gain or malice, jail time may be up to 10 years and include a stiff fine.

To read more about possible repercussions of privacy violations, go to the HHS website (`www.hhs.gov/ocr/privacy/hipaa/understanding/summary/index.html`).

Unbundling the Compliance Bundle

Compliance rules also relate to billing practice. Being in compliance with billing practice means working within the correct coding edits (the NCCI edits). *NCCI* stands for National Correct Coding Initiative, which stipulates that, when you're coding multiple procedures, the extra procedure coded should have required that the physician perform extra work that is not normally part of the procedure.

The revenue cycle starts with the codes, and they must be the correct codes. Every CPT code represents a potential reimbursement, and you don't want payers making payment under false circumstances. But you do want the physician to be paid for the work he has done.

Looking at incidental procedures

Certain procedures are considered *incidental* to another procedure; that is, one procedure could not be completed without the other procedure and is, therefore, not a separate billable procedure (for example, suturing a surgical wound). The edits usually indicate that. When you check procedural codes, you see incidental procedures reflected as *bundled,* which means they're *inclusive* to another procedure. In other words, if a second or even third procedure is done through the same incision, the incidental procedure may not justify extra reimbursement.

That doesn't mean the provider can't get paid for additional work, however. When a procedure takes an extraordinarily long time or requires more than the accepted standard of work, you can apply a certain modifier, which may earn the physician additional reimbursement.

Other times, you can unbundle the procedure. When you "unbundle," or separately report procedures, you include additional codes on the claim to represent procedures that, although incidental to the primary procedure, actually merit additional reimbursement. The next sections give you the details.

Identifying when separately reporting is okay

Sometimes separately reporting normally inclusive procedures is supported. For example, if the provider performs a procedure that is listed as inclusive but does so through a separate incision, you can charge both codes. Perhaps the surgeon is working on more than one part of the body. If she performs a left knee meniscectomy (removing all or part of the *meniscus,* the pad of cartilage) and a right knee chondroplasty (shaving the cartilage), it is appropriate to separately code the chondroplasty, even though a chondroplasty is always considered incidental to a meniscectomy. Why? Because it's obviously not incidental when it's performed on a different leg.

The edits are there for a reason: Separately reporting procedures isn't always okay. In fact, it's often *not* okay. So how do you know what the edits are? You can find the Correct Coding Initiative (CCI) edits on the CMS website and in most coding software programs. These programs are a good investment for most companies that bill surgeries, partly because they let the coder know when reporting procedures separately is okay. Keep in mind, though, that some payers use their own editing programs that differ from the CMS version. If your employer is contracted with a payer, the contract usually defines which set of edits to follow. Certain medical associations also have their own ideas about procedures that may or not be incidental to the main procedure.

In general, follow the CMS edits; if the payer says to do otherwise, then follow the contract.

Recognizing when unbundling's not okay

Separately reporting procedures for the sole purpose of billing a higher dollar amount on a claim is never okay. Before procedures can be considered for additional payment, the physician must document the extra work. This documentation must be very specific and meet the guidelines for unbundling as outlined in the editing software and coding materials.

If something is unbundled incorrectly and the claim is audited by the payer, the physician or provider is obligated to return payment. In some instances, the payer may terminate the provider's contract. The payer may also ask for interest on wrongfully paid claims.

Defining exclusivity

Exclusivity means that one procedure is not possible under specific circumstances. Some procedures are gender-specific, and other procedures are not possible under certain circumstances. Read on for the details.

Understanding mutually exclusive procedures

Mutually exclusive procedures fall into two categories:

- **A procedure that can't be done in combination with another:** Because some procedures can't be successfully performed together, they are not going to be paid on the same claim. Here's an example (albeit an extreme one) that helps explain the concept: Imagine the patient has suffered severe damage to his arm. During surgery, the surgeon tries but fails to repair the arm and decides that amputation is necessary. You can't code for both a fracture repair and an amputation if both occurred during the same session. Nor is the insurance company going to pay for both the fracture repair and amputation in this situation. If the amputation was deemed necessary, then that is the procedure you code and bill for.

However, if the physician repaired the fracture and then three weeks later the patient returned with severe necrosis (tissue death) and was becoming septic — a life-endangering condition — and the surgeon amputates the arm, the provider can bill both procedures.

- **Procedures that are not possible under the present circumstances:** This type of exclusivity relates to procedures that are age- or sex-related. Men do not give birth. Women do not have prostate procedures. Exclusivity may be defined as not possible under the presented circumstances.

  Current federal anti-discrimination laws have caused payers to be hesitant to deny claims based on patient gender. So likely what would have in the past been a denial due to the patient's gender, may now come back as a medically unlikely denial.

Understanding contractual exclusions

Exclusivity may be a reference to procedures, as explained in the preceding section, or it may relate to contractual terms. Payer contracts may pertain to the type of plan — health maintenance organization (HMO) or preferred provider organization (PPO), for example — sponsored by that company. Each plan has different payment obligations that must be met for a claim to be paid.

HMOs, for example, require the patient to name a primary care physician (PCP) who acts as a gatekeeper for spending the insurance company's money. The patient is required to seek treatment from the PCP first. If that physician feels that the illness or injury requires the services of a specialist, then he may refer the patient to a specialist within the network.

Exclusivity may also refer to the network. Some plans do not allow patients to see out-of-network or non-contracted providers. Their coverage is exclusive to providers within the network. PPOs, for example, normally allow the patient to visit any provider that is contracted with the insurance company. If the patient visits a non-contracted provider, the claim is considered *out-of-network*, and the plan may pay for the services but at a much higher cost to the patient.

Contracts between payers and providers may contain fee schedules or payment agreements that are exclusive to various plans within their organization. These agreements are exclusive to the terms of the contract. They apply only to a certain payer under defined conditions, and claims must be filed within the terms defined in the contract(s).

SYMBOLIZING CODING

Coding books have symbols that serve as reminders with respect to the codes. They have symbols that indicate the number of digits in a diagnosis code. They have symbols that tell the coder whether the procedure is considered *unilateral* (applying to one side of the body only). They indicate whether the procedure is covered per Medicare regulations. They have symbols for female, male, and numerous other specifications. Other symbols alert the coder whether a code was added, changed, or may have been deleted at the beginning of the current year (a good reason to make sure you are using a current edition of the CPT and ICD codebooks).

The coding books, together with Medicare and payer websites, guide you when you abstract information from the medical record. Keeping current on code changes and updates to regulatory guidelines and legislation will keep the revenue cycle in motion and maintain the provider's compliance with both billing regulations and privacy obligations.

Getting the Most out of the Dreaded Audit

In the event of an audit by the payer, an internal auditor, or an external auditor, an auditing coder (someone just like you) recodes the audited claims. In doing so, he or she should be able to abstract the same information from the record documentation that you did. If the audit comes back with a different code, an explanation for the difference accompanies the audit. That discrepancy could be the result of a couple of things:

- A recent change in coding rules that you were unaware of.
- You missed certain codes.

If so, use the audit as a learning experience. But if the auditor sees a different code entirely or misses a code that you submitted, challenge the audit and explain your reason for coding the claim the way you did. The auditor may agree to your position or may be able to explain the flaw in your reasoning.

REMEMBER

Regardless of the differences, audits are about improving. They help you grow and improve as a coder, and they reiterate to the provider the importance of documenting procedures correctly. If the physicians you work for question your skill as a coder because you didn't fare well in an audit, ask to be allowed to attend a practice-specific workshop or webinar to help you become a better employee.

Distinguishing between internal and payer audits

Several different kinds of billing and coding audits exist, but all refer to an independent review conducted by a different person with coding background to verify the accuracy of your work. Providers conduct audits because, although they don't like to leave money on the table, they don't want to be paid more than they deserve. Carriers conduct audits to be sure they are not overpaying for services.

Most large practices have an internal auditing department, whose auditors randomly select charts to evaluate. Other providers, usually smaller ones, send quarterly audits to an outside consulting firm. The auditors look for under-coding, over-coding, and incorrect coding. Often, if an error is found during an audit, the result is to submit a corrected claim, possibly with a copy of the medical record and a letter explaining the reason for the request.

Other audits are *payer audits.* Most payer contracts contain a clause that allows the payer to request medical records, invoices, and other supporting documentation for claims paid within the past year (or, in some instances, farther back). Medicare is a payer that can just show up and request to see records on-site. Payer audits are performed to verify that claims submitted for reimbursement have the necessary supporting documentation, such as invoices, procedure notes, or test results.

Guarding against an RAC audit

Currently a bit of publicity has surrounded the Medicare RAC audits, which are being conducted by Medicare's Recovery Audit Contractors. The RAC audits are a result of the 2003 Medicare Modernization Act. As a result of this legislation, CMS and RAC auditors recouped more than $980 million from providers in the three initial states of Florida, New York, and California. The objective of the RAC audit differs from a traditional Medicare audit in several ways. First, the RAC auditors are essentially functioning as bounty hunters and are paid a commission equal to 10 percent of the amount recouped. The audits focus on CMS payment criteria, such as medical necessity relative to procedures. The RAC auditors also examine compliance with Medicare's payment criteria, documentation, and billing requirements.

The primary targets of RAC audits are hospital claims, for obvious reasons: That's where the big money is. However, don't be careless just because you work for a small provider. RAC audits can — and often do — target physicians and ambulatory surgery centers.

TIP

Most RAC audits are public information, so the recommended protection against a RAC audit is to implement a self-audit program. In other words, hire an outside auditor to perform an audit — or look at the coding from an auditor's perspective to see if there are errors or opportunity for payer recovery. Independent audits may duplicate the action of the RAC to ensure compliance.

Avoiding an audit: You can't

Audits are a necessary evil because they are usually the only system that enables a company to monitor and ensure coding quality. Normally, when you pay for a service, you see the end result, but not the insurers. Instead, these payers entrust the providers with the power to simply send a form and declare that the work was done. Audits keep everyone on their toes, which can only be good for both sides. Also keep in mind that when payers, especially Medicare, recoup money, they often ask for interest.

Bottom line: Audits are unavoidable, but they don't have to be miserable. In the next section, I explain how to ensure that the auditors don't find problems with your work.

Protecting yourself from an audit

If the documentation is clear, an audit is no problem, and documentation is the only way to protect yourself in an audit. Follow this advice:

- Make sure you understand the documentation needed to code and bill procedures.
- Make sure that you understand the payer contracts and submit claims according to the terms of that contract.
- Be especially careful with unbundling. Codes are bundled for a reason: because they should be included with the primary procedure that was performed. Sometimes, procedures are extra, usually for anatomical reasons. Then, coding both procedures separately may be okay, but make certain that the documentation supports both procedures.
- Make sure you code only what the documentation supports and that everything you do as a coder is part of the record. The phrase "That is what the doctor meant" can be a problem for obvious reasons. If a provider insists that, when he says "A," he means "B," then get it in writing. The same holds true for unbundling procedures. If the provider insists that certain procedures be submitted because he "wants to track them" or because "XYZ will pay it," *get it in writing.*

If you follow these guidelines, you can stop sweating and start getting your ducks in a row so you're prepared if and when the time comes to have your work audited. That way, you have no worries.

» Getting familiar with medical terminology

» Defining different procedure types

» Navigating the world of patient evaluation and management

Chapter 5

Not-So-Strange Bedfellows: Medical Terminology and Medical Necessity

In billing and coding, you've got to know as much about the language that helps create all those billing codes as you do about how to perform the coding. Two big building blocks help construct the basis for billing and coding: medical terminology and medical necessity.

Medical terminology refers to the words that describe illness, injury, conditions, and procedures. The majority of the word parts that make up medical terms originate in Greek and Latin. *Medical necessity* refers to the requirement that any procedures performed are necessary to diagnose or treat a medical condition while maintaining an acceptable standard of care. A whole group of other terms, called *diagnosis terms*, are the basis for the codes you enter to substantiate medical necessity.

Insurance companies are usually the parties responsible for paying the healthcare provider for services rendered. However, with few exceptions, such as for preventative care, an insurance company only pays for procedures that are medically necessary to the well-being of the patient, its client. For that reason you must link each procedure billed to a diagnosis that supports the medical necessity for the procedure. All diagnoses and procedures are worded in medical terminology. To accurately abstract (or identify) the correct codes, you must understand the verbiage used in the record, as well as the terms used to describe surgical procedures and evaluation and management procedures. This chapter tells you what you need to know.

Brushing Up on Basic Anatomy

The first class in most coding programs is a human anatomy class. *Anatomy* is the study of the human body structure. Anatomy is broken down into subtopics, including *gross anatomy*, which relates to the part of the body that can be seen.

Typical coding programs educate you in all areas of anatomy from the outside in, with a particular focus on the disease process and its effect on how the body functions. *Disease process* is defined as a deviation of the normal structure or function of a body part that is represented by symptoms.

In the following sections, I give you a crash course in body systems, illness and disease, and injuries.

REMEMBER

The disease process doesn't occur in a vacuum. It always affects a specific body system, which itself is made up of particular organs. While not expected to completely understand the complexities of medicine, coders do need to have a basic familiarity with anatomy and understand the disease process as it relates to procedures to be billed. The diagnosis code selected from the International Classification of Diseases (ICD) codebook represents the disease or injury. The diagnosis code that's linked to the procedure must show the necessity of the procedure being billed. You can find the procedure code in the appropriate section of the Current Procedural Terminology (CPT) codebook.

Getting familiar with body systems

A *body system* is a group of organs that perform a specific task. For example, the nervous system includes the brain, the spinal cord, and the nerves. Table 5-1 lists the major body systems you'll likely encounter on the job (and in your codebooks in the section devoted to that system).

Information about body systems matters to you because coding books are structured according to the body systems. These books contain the procedures as maintained by the American Medical Association (AMA), and they're updated each year; some codes are added, and some are deleted. The new codes usually become effective on January 1. So make sure you always use the most current editions!

TABLE 5-1 **Major Body Systems**

System	Organs Involved
Cardiovascular	Blood vessels, heart, and lymph system
Digestive	Structures inside the mouth, stomach, and intestine, all the way down to the rectum and anus
Endocrine	Thyroid, pancreas, parathyroid, and adrenal glands
Eye and ocular adnexa and auditory	Eyes and ears
Female genital (see note)	Ovaries, fallopian tubes, uterus, and external genitalia
Integumentary	Skin and nails
Male genital (see note)	Penis, prostate, and testes
Musculoskeletal	Connective tissue, muscles, ligaments, and bones
Nervous	Brain, spinal cord, and nerves
Respiratory	Airway and lungs
Urinary (see note)	Kidneys, bladder, ureters, and urethra

Note: *In some reference books, the male and female genital systems are combined with the urinary system and referred to as the genito-urinary system.*

After you identify the correct system code from the CPT codebook, your next step is to find the supporting diagnosis codes for the procedures. You can find these in the ICD-10-CM (International Classification of Diseases, Tenth Revision, Clinical Modification) codebook. Lucky for you, the ICD-10 codebook also categorizes diagnosis codes by body system (in addition to other sections that contain codes for illness and other nonspecific codes).

After you're familiar with the basic body systems, it's time to think about what can go wrong with them. When a system is not functioning properly, an illness or disease process is at work.

Getting a handle on illness and disease

Most of the codes you will encounter as a biller/coder have something to do with a patient's illness. *Illness* is a catchall term that refers to a feeling or condition of not being healthy. Although an illness may be due to a disease, a disease has measurable symptoms, and it affects normal body functions.

REMEMBER

Be sure you know the difference between *illness* and *disease*. Just as you may be ill but not be suffering from a disease, you may be suffering from a disease but not feel ill. A patient may have influenza, an illness, for example, but that doesn't mean she's suffering from a disease. Conversely, a patient may have Type 2 diabetes, a disease, but she may not feel bad or be experiencing obvious symptoms.

During a patient encounter, the physician examines the patient, documents his findings, and then determines the best course of action for treatment. When performing this type of service, the physician bills for an evaluation and management encounter (also known as an *E&M visit*), which is a fancy way of referring to a doctor's visit, or a *consultation* (a visit requested by another physician or healthcare entity). Whether a physician conducts an E&M visit or a consultation, he will report some sort of illness or disease-related term in the patient's record, even if the problem is something as simple as the common cold. (You can read more about E&M and consultation visits in the later sections, "Connecting with the World of Evaluation and Management Codes" and "Dealing with consultation visits.")

Encountering injuries

Many physician encounters are due to injury, and the difference between disease and injury can be blurred. A patient may suffer bruising due to disease, for example, but have no history of injury. This is why, for the purposes of coding, you want to be familiar with the varying levels of injury:

- **Acute injury:** Damage to the body incurred by accident
- **Chronic injury:** Damage to the body that is a result of overuse or aging

Treatment may differ depending upon whether the injury is acute or chronic. With an acute injury, the injury has just happened, and the tissue in question is still viable. A chronic injury, on the other hand, has occurred over time or is a once-acute injury that has only partially healed. Often, treatment of a chronic injury requires additional work: A surgeon may need to remove non-viable tissue or possibly use tissue grafts to successfully complete the repair. Thus, a chronic injury is often more time-consuming because the body's tendency to heal itself can result in scar tissue (called *fibrosis*).

If you have any question about whether the injury is acute or chronic, investigate further before choosing a procedure code. If the patient history is available for review, you can abstract the information you need to choose the correct code. In this case, you would review the patient history to see when the patient first came in for treatment, or you would look for the patient information page to see whether the patient indicated when the injury occurred. Many times, patients say that they have no idea why the problem occurred. In this situation, you probably have to use chronic injury-related codes unless the provider says otherwise.

Because the story may be more complicated than a one-time incident, don't assume that an injury is acute. When you're unsure, investigate. Check for clues in the report. For example, words such as *pathological* often indicate a disease process that would point to chronic, not acute, injury.

Say What? Deciphering Medical Terminology

Anatomy, illness, injury, and disease are all based in specific medical language and terms. By deciphering the medical terminology used in medical records, you can more easily assign the correct diagnosis and procedural codes. For that reason, a solid foundation in medical terminology is essential for the coder.

A whole world of medical terminology is out there for you to explore, and solid coding programs offer classes in medical terminology. In this section, I take you on a quick tour of the terminology you need to know. (For more detailed information, take a look at *Medical Terminology For Dummies*, by Beverley Henderson and Jennifer Lee Dorsey [Wiley].)

Most medical terms are two-parters; that is, they're made up of prefixes and suffixes. Some medical terms also have a word segment in the middle, but the majority of medical terms are built with the prefix/suffix combination. These word parts are almost always Greek or Latin in origin. If you have a background in these languages (or have studied words derived from Greek or Latin), you'll have a great head start in understanding medical terminology.

In the beginning: Knowing your prefixes

A *prefix* refers to the beginning segment of the word. The prefix of the word often is the first clue about which body part or which area the procedure relates to. Some examples of prefixes are *arthr(o)-* (joint), *hemi-* (half), *cardi-* (heart), and *bronch-* (air, airway). When you see a word beginning with *arthro-* (for example, *arthroscopy*), you know that it has something to do with the joint. Similarly, *bronchoscopy* has something to do with the airway (in the next section, I explain what the suffixes, or word endings, mean). Table 5-2 lists some of the more common prefixes.

TABLE 5-2 **Common Greek and Latin Prefixes**

Prefix	Meaning	Prefix	Meaning
a-	Absent or lack of	hyper-	Above
ab-	Away from	hypo-	Under
abdomino-	Referring to the abdomen	hyster-	Pertaining to the uterus
alb-	White	inter-	Among
ad-	Toward	intra-	Inside
angi-	Pertaining to vessels	leuko-	White
ante-	Before	macro-	Large
anti-	Against	micro-	Small
arthr(o)-	Joint	my(o)-	Muscle
aud-	Hearing	necro-	Dead
auto-	Self	neo-	New
brady-	Slow	nephro-	Kidney
bronch-	Air, airway	neuro-	Nerve
calc-	Stone	osteo-	Bone
cardi-	Heart	path-	Disease
cerebro-	Brain	sarc-	Flesh
chondr-	Cartilage	sub-	Under
circum-	Around	super-	Above
derm-	Skin	teno-	Tendon
dys-	Painful, difficult	tachy-	Fast
entero-	Intestine	thrombo-	Clot
gastro-	Of the stomach	trans-	Across
hemi-	Half	trich-	Hair
hepat-	Liver		

Sussing out the suffixes

The terms you encounter in the coding world have to end somehow, and that happens with a suffix, which has a special meaning all its own. *Suffixes* describe condition or action. For example, *-scopy* means to use an instrument to view. Therefore, you know that the word *arthroscopy* refers to looking into the joint with a scope (the prefix *arthro-* refers to the joint), and *bronchoscopy* refers to looking into the airway (*bronch-* means "air") with a scope. (Refer to the preceding section for common medical prefixes.)

Table 5-3 lists common suffixes and their meanings.

TABLE 5-3 **Common Greek and Latin Suffixes**

Suffix	Meaning	Suffix	Meaning
-algia	Pain	-ostomy	Opening
-asis	Condition or state of	-pathy	Disease
-cide	Destroy	-penia	Deficiency
-coele	Swelling or cavity	-pexy	Fixation
-desis	Bind together	-phasia	Speaking
-ectomy	Surgical removal	-pheresis	Removal
-emia	Blood condition	-plasia	Formation or development
-genic	Producing	-plasty	Surgical repair
-gram	A recording	-rhaphy	Surgical suture repair
-graph	A recording instrument	-scopy	Use of an instrument for viewing
-ia	Abnormal state	-stenosis	Narrowing
-itis	Inflammation	-stomy	Opening
-lysis	Destruction	-tomy	Cutting operation
-malacia	Softening	-version	Turning
-otomy	Surgical opening		

Eureka! Putting them together

It should be apparent at this point that doctors and nurses are not the only ones who need to understand medical terminology. Your understanding the differences in terms is essential, as well, so that you can assign the correct codes.

After you understand prefixes and suffixes, you've got to make sense of the word as a whole. When you take the parts and assemble them, you have a medical term. Common terms assembled from the basic prefix/suffix combinations include the following:

- **Chondromalacia:** *Chondro-* refers to cartilage; *-malacia* means "softening," so *chondromalacia* means "softening of the cartilage."
- **Arthritis:** *Arthr-* refers to the joints; *-itis* means "inflammation," so *arthritis* means "inflammation of the joint."
- **Osteopenia:** *Osteo-* means "bone," and *-penia* means "deficiency." Therefore, *osteopenia* means "loss of bone."
- **Nephritis:** *Nephr-* refers to the kidneys, and *-itis* means "inflammation." Therefore, *nephritis* means "inflammation of the kidney."
- **Myalgia:** *My-* refers to muscles, and *-algia* means "pain." Therefore, *myalgia* means "pain in the muscles."

REMEMBER

As you can see, the words can be mixed and matched as needed, and they take on different meanings as they are assembled. Adding to the potential confusion is the fact that many of the terms commonly used are quite similar and can seem deceptively close in meaning. To the untrained eye, they may actually seem to be the same. But the smallest of differences can make a big difference in reimbursement. The key to accurately charging the payer is a careful review of the record.

Here are a few examples of some similar-sounding terms that are actually different procedures. See whether you can spot the differences:

Term 1	***Term 2***
Arthrotomy (surgery that is done through an open incision into a joint)	*Arthroscopy* (a surgical procedure performed by inserting a scope into a joint)
Laparotomy (surgery performed via an open incision into the abdominal cavity)	*Laparoscopy* (a surgical procedure performed by inserting a scope into the abdominal cavity)
Tenodesis (repair of a tendon that has been cut or torn)	*Tenolysis* (release of a tendon that is constricted by fibrosis or scar tissue)

The same too-close-for-comfort issue is true of terms used to describe medical diagnosis (the topic of the next section); they may use similar terminology, but a minor distinction makes a big difference when you're coding. Here are some examples:

Term 1	*Term 2*
Hypertension (high blood pressure)	*Hypotension* (low blood pressure)
Bradycardia (slow heartbeat)	*Tachycardia* (fast heartbeat)
Angioplasty (technique to treat blocked coronary arteries)	*Angiography* (technique to visualize and diagnose arterial disease)

As the preceding examples show, you must read the record carefully to avoid costly errors.

Understanding Medical Necessity

As I explain earlier, both diagnosis and procedures are linked to payment, so thoroughly understanding the diagnosis terms serves you well when you have to report the circumstances documented in the record so that the payer can make an accurate determination as to correct payment under the terms of the patient's benefits.

Procedures and the reasons for performing them are at the heart of medical necessity. Put simply, the payer will absolutely, without fail, pay only for those procedures that are deemed medically necessary or are otherwise appropriate and covered services. For that reason, if you want the payer to approve payment (and you do), then you must make sure that the reason behind every procedure a medical professional performs is valid. For example, if the diagnosis code specifies a broken foot, the payer will pay only for the broken foot, not for a shoulder repair, even if both happened in the same accident. *The diagnosis must fit the procedure.* Seems pretty obvious, right?

REMEMBER

It's not your responsibility as the coder to make up a payable diagnosis; it's your responsibility to *verify* that the diagnosis in the chart supports the procedure being billed. If you think the chart does not reflect the correct procedure, ask for clarification. Never make an assumption about what you think the physician meant to say. Take the time to follow up on any questions you have about the chart in question. Doing so saves you time and trouble later.

Scrubbing In: Proving Medical Necessity for Surgical Procedures

When a physician plans a surgical procedure, no matter how simple or complicated, she makes a *preoperative diagnosis* based on test findings and examination. To confirm this preoperative diagnosis, the physician must be able to see inside the body cavity, either by cutting the patient open or by inserting a scope to see the inner workings. At that point, the doctor can make a *definitive diagnosis*.

You cannot code a surgical procedure from the preoperative diagnosis (also called a *preliminary diagnosis*); you can code the procedure only from the definitive diagnosis (also called the *postoperative findings*). Why? Because the physician can speculate about what she might find, but she can never really know until she performs the procedure.

You also need to examine the record closely to fully understand the approach the physician took and what she found. The approach lets you know whether the procedure was a traditional *open procedure*, one in which the patient's body is cut open, or a newer *endoscopic procedure*, in which a minimally invasive scope is used to perform a procedure inside the body. In the next sections, I explain the nuances of both types of approaches.

Checking out endoscopic procedures

Many surgical procedures that you code are performed through the use of scopes. This type of procedure is generally referred to as *minimally invasive surgery*. Some operations can be completed entirely through a scope, while others are assisted by the use of a scope but still involve making an incision.

Some of the most common scope procedures are arthroscopic surgeries and laparoscopic procedures. The following sections have the details.

Looking at arthroscopy

Arthroscopic surgery allows orthopedic surgeons to visualize, diagnose, and possibly treat injury or disease inside of a joint.

When a procedure is performed arthroscopically, the surgeon makes a minimum of three small incisions, called *portals*, into the joint. One incision is for visualization, one is for infusion of liquid for joint spaces, and the third is for the instruments, which are much smaller than traditional surgical instruments. Rather than directly view the surgical field (the area being operated on), the surgeon uses the scope to view the inside of the joint on a monitor. To make viewing the area easier, the joint is inflated with fluid, and additional portals may be created to view other areas within the joint.

Common arthroscopic procedures are performed on knees, shoulders, ankles, and hips. Small joints are also treated arthroscopically, but these procedures, such as carpal tunnel release, are less common and often are more time-consuming than traditional surgeries.

SCOPING OUT FAMILIES

REMEMBER

The AMA and American Academy of Orthopedic Surgeons (AAOS) categorize arthroscopic procedures into *scope families*. Simply put, scope families are procedures that go together.

Certain procedures are inherent to (automatically part of) other procedures that are performed. Because inherent procedures don't require additional time or skill by the surgeon, they're not eligible for additional reimbursement. Here's an example of a scope family procedure: In arthroscopic-assisted ACL reconstruction, the lateral meniscus is often torn as well, so arthroscopic meniscectomy can be billed at the same time. No modifier is necessary. But arthroscopic chondroplasty is considered incidental and is never allowed on the same knee.

REMEMBER

Different procedures that are performed in different compartments may be billable, depending on the documentation and the individual coding requirements for each compartment. The AMA and AAOS define what is separately billable and what is not. If you find yourself working in orthopedics, you need to learn what is and isn't considered a separate procedure. You can refer to the AMA website (`www.ama-assn.org`) and the AAOS website (`www.aaos.org`) for more information.

CODING ARTHROSCOPIC PROCEDURES

So how would you handle coding such a procedure? You've got to start with the documentation. The physician should document the surgery by compartment, clearly stating what he did in each compartment. The CPT codebook lists the different procedures that may have been performed. To be eligible for additional reimbursement, each procedure must have been fully documented as having been performed in different compartments. But be sure to check the edits because certain procedures — such as chondroplasty — are not to be separately reported unless they are the only procedures performed.

TIP

Sometimes a procedure is begun through a scope and then converted to an open procedure due to complications. When that happens, you code the open procedure only. Head to the section "Examining open surgical procedures" for details on open surgical procedures.

Defining laparoscopy

Laparoscopic surgery is a member of the endoscopy family, along with arthroscopy, except that laparoscopic surgery refers to the abdominal cavity (*laparo-* means "abdomen"); laparoscopic surgeries also include surgeries performed in the pelvic cavity. This type of procedure is another minimally invasive surgery that is sometimes called "Band-Aid surgery" because the incisions may have a suture, but they're often simply covered with a small bandage. Common laparoscopic procedures include gallbladder removal, appendectomies, ovarian cyst excisions, and numerous others.

UNDERSTANDING THE PROCEDURE

Here's how laparoscopic surgeries work: Procedures are performed through a set of small portals in the abdomen. Similar to arthroscopic procedures, the physician views the interior of the abdomen on a monitor. During a laparoscopy, the abdomen is inflated with gas, which creates space that makes the areas easier to see and gives the surgeon more room to work.

Common acronyms for laparoscopic procedures are

- **SPA:** Single Port Access surgery
- **LESSS:** Laparoscopic Endoscopic Single-Site Surgery
- **SLIT:** Single Laparoscopic Incision Transabdominal
- **OPUS:** One-Port Umbilical Surgery
- **NOTUS:** Natural Orifice Transumbilical Surgery
- **E-NOTES:** Embryonic Natural Orifice Transumbilical Endoscopic Surgery

You will always want to verify documentation for correct code assignment and make certain that you are using current editions of coding materials in the event that a new code was added. For ICD-10-PCS, the approach is essential to the correct code assignment.

REMEMBER

At the beginning of the surgery, the scope is inserted through an incision near the navel, and the surgeon views inside the cavity to make sure that it's safe to proceed. If, during this inspection, the surgeon sees any medical reasons to stop the laparoscopic procedure (called *contraindications*), the laparoscopic procedure is converted to a traditional open procedure (covered in the section "Examining open surgical procedures"). Contraindications include excessive inflammation or various other unknown risk factors.

If the surgeon feels that proceeding with the laparoscopy is safe, he creates additional portals for the specialized instruments needed to facilitate the necessary procedure(s).

Some procedures are *laparoscopically assisted.* An example is a hand-assisted laparoscopic surgery, in which the surgery is performed via a technique that uses a larger portal that allows for the insertion of a hand. This incision is larger than the traditional port but still smaller that a laparotomy incision. Surgeries performed laparoscopically normally require shorter recovery times and have fewer complications, compared to traditional open procedures.

BREAKING DOWN FAMILIES OF LAPAROSCOPY

Laparoscopic procedures that go together are sometimes referred to as *families.* As explained in the earlier section "Scoping out families," procedures that are performed together as part of the necessary procedures may not be separately billable.

One common example in the laparoscopic world is a *diagnostic laparoscopy.* A physician may determine that the only way to really know what is going on with a patient is to take a look, using a diagnostic procedure. If that's all the doctor does, then the diagnostic procedure is billable. But if during this look-see, the surgeon sees something else — say an inflamed appendix — and removes it via laparoscopic appendectomy, then only the appendectomy can be billed.

Examining open surgical procedures

Open surgery refers to traditional surgical procedures, which involve an incision made by a surgeon. Obvious differences exist between endoscopic and open surgical procedures from a coding position. The distinction between *-otomy* versus *-scopy* may seem minor, but it makes a big difference.

REMEMBER

Being able to recognize such subtle differences between terms is why a solid knowledge of human anatomy and medical terminology is so important. Without it, you won't be able to tell one type of procedure from another.

Coding the open surgical procedure

When you sit down to code an open procedure, you see the operative report, which includes the following:

- A heading that identifies the patient, the date and location of the surgery, the physician, his assistant, and other demographic information.

TIP

The first step in abstracting the billable codes from the medical record of an open procedure is to identify which body part was treated and why. After you have identified that, you know which area of the CPT codebook to check to begin the process of coding.

- A preoperative, or preliminary, diagnosis, which is the diagnosis based on preoperative testing and pertinent physical findings observed by the physician during the examination.
- The postoperative, or definitive, diagnosis, which is what the physician confirmed during the surgery.
- A summary or outline of the procedures performed.

WARNING

Do not code procedures from the outline in the report! These headings are merely previews of what is to come. Regardless of what the heading says, in order to correctly assign a code, that procedure must be documented in the body of the report.

- A full report containing the surgeon's description of everything that he did during the operation.

REMEMBER

The documentation for the procedure should always be described in the body of the report. If the body of the report does not contain something that is mentioned in the heading, then the physician must correct the documentation before it can be reported. Remember the mantra of the medical coder: "If the doctor didn't say it, it wasn't done."

Initiating a physician query

To get the missing information, you can initiate a physician query via a handwritten note (some facilities have a query form just for this purpose), or you can ask the surgeon directly for clarification if you work in an environment in which a direct query is possible. After you get an answer and if the record needs to be altered, the surgeon must dictate an addendum (add to the note), or he may dictate a corrected note.

WARNING

When initiating a physician query, make sure you don't lead the physician with regard to verbiage. Here are some examples of leading verbiage and more appropriate alternatives:

Leading	***Non-leading***
Did the mass invade muscle tissue?	How deep was the mass?
Did you excise over one centimeter of the clavicle?	How much of the clavicle did you remove?

Let the physician describe the work performed without putting words in his mouth.

Understanding incidentals and when procedures can be separately reported

The surgeon may indicate that a certain procedure was extra or required additional time and skill on her part. If this extra work is well documented, it may support separate reporting.

The ability to separately report procedures is affected by something called the National Correct Coding Initiative (NCCI) edits, which are the Medicare version of what is and isn't included or exclusive to other procedures. Most editing software programs are based on these edits. If the NCCI edits indicate that the procedures are bundled, then the physician must have documented that the procedures required additional skill and time before they can be billed separately.

For example, during a surgery, the surgeon has to make an incision, which is not billable. At the conclusion of the procedure, the surgeon needs to repair the incision, which is also not billable. Now, if the repair is more than what would be necessary to close the incision — say the surgeon has to rearrange tissue to improve the appearance of the scar — then the repair may be eligible for additional reimbursement, but the surgeon would have to document the additional work and the reason it was necessary. Otherwise, the procedure may be considered *incidental* and not separately billable.

As the coder, you're responsible for verifying which procedures are incidental and which ones are eligible to reported separately.

Using billing modifiers

Modifiers are two-character codes appended to the main CPT code that are used to provide additional information to payers. Certain modifiers are appropriate for surgical or diagnostic procedures; other modifiers are appropriate for claims submitted for reimbursement of office visits, referred to in the coding world as evaluation and management, or E&M, visits (covered in the next section). Here are the modifiers you're most likely to use:

- **Modifier 25:** You use this modifier when a procedure is performed on the same day an E&M visit occurred. This modifier indicates that the procedure wasn't necessarily related to the E&M visit, and the provider feels that additional reimbursement is warranted because the E&M was significant and separately identifiable from the procedure.

- **Modifier 51:** This modifier is used by Medicare. It is placed on the CMS-1500 claim form by the administrator and indicates a multiple procedure reduction should be applied to that line. Most Medicare contractors prefer that providers do *not* append this modifier, as doing so may trigger additional payment reductions.
- **Modifier 59:** You use this magic modifier to indicate that a procedure being billed is normally included with another procedure or encounter but warrants separate consideration.

  Note: Effective January 5, 2015, Modifier 59 was enhanced for better specificity as to why unbundling is supported. The Centers for Medicare & Medicaid Services (CMS) made this decision because modifier 59 had such a broad range of uses. It encompassed everything from separate encounters and different anatomic locations, in addition to distinct services. The modifier has become so widely used (or abused) that identifying exactly why an edit was being bypassed was difficult.

  The new second modifiers are as follows:

  - *XE Separate Encounter:* The service is distinct because it occurred during a different encounter.
  - *XS Separate Structure:* The service was performed on a separate organ or structure (body part).
  - *XP Separate Practitioner:* The service was performed by a different practitioner.
  - *XU Unusual Non-Overlapping Service:* A service was used that shouldn't overlap the usual components of the main service or procedure.

Correct reimbursement may depend upon using the appropriate modifier, and you're responsible for understanding which modifier to use when. But be careful. If you overuse or incorrectly use them, the provider can get into trouble.

Connecting with the World of Evaluation and Management Codes

Evaluation and management (E&M) codes are the most commonly billed codes. These are the codes for every office visit and personal encounter a physician has with a patient, which typically involve noninvasive physician services.

When you use these codes, you find that your knowledge of medical terminology and medical necessity really comes into play because everything has a code! Here's a general list of the kinds of things that have their own E&M codes:

- Office visits by new patients
- Office visits by established patients
- Emergency room visits
- Observation visits (when the patient is in the hospital but not admitted because he's just being observed)
- Consultation visits (visits that have been requested by another physician, provider, or healthcare entity; read more about this in the later section "Dealing with consultation visits")

Other codes include codes specific to hospitalized patients, codes for treating patients in nursing homes, critical care codes, and codes for assisted living/rest home visits.

The E&M visit may take place in a physician's office, nursing home, patient's home, hospital, emergency room, or clinic. *Note:* If the examination takes place during an office visit or a hospital visit, or if the patient has been referred for a specialized evaluation, the visit may technically be referred to as a *consultation,* which simply means that it's been requested by another physician or healthcare provider. Before you can bill a consultation, specific requirements must be met. I address those requirements later in this chapter. Another important note: Medicare does not reimburse consultation codes.

Looking at what happens during the run-of-the-mill E&M visit

As I explain earlier, E&M visits take place in multiple settings, but the basic structure is pretty much the same no matter the situation. Generally, you can break what happens during these visits down into three parts:

- **Gathering general information about the patient and the reason for the visit also known as the history:** The first part of an E&M visit normally involves the physician asking the patient about the reason for the visit. The report you ultimately look at when you're coding includes the history of the present illness, the patient's personal history, the patient's family history, and information about the patient's social habits.

REMEMBER

Patient history is a major component of the work involved in an E&M service, so the more detail that is documented, the higher the reimbursement may be.

- **Conducting the physical examination:** The exam may involve a specific area of the body or several different areas. The more areas that the physician examines, the more detailed the examination. As with the history, examining multiple areas involves more physician work and therefore a higher level of reimbursement if the exam is thoroughly documented and appropriate for the patient's condition.
- **Determining the appropriate level of service:** The physician determines the appropriate level of service based on the presenting problem, the history and examination, and the amount of medical decision-making involved in the visit. This part of the visit greatly affects how you code the visit. The diagnosis, the plan for treatment, and the risk involved in treatment of the patient's illness are all factors you consider when choosing the appropriate level of decision-making for the CPT code to use to report the encounter. A more complex treatment plan or one that involves greater risk may justify a higher level of reimbursement.

REMEMBER

The medical necessity of the presenting problem is the over-arching criterion for the level of service charged. If a patient has a cold, a doctor can take a full history and examine every single organ system and body part, but no medical necessity exists to charge a high level of visit because the patient just has a cold.

WARNING

Some electronic health record (EHR) systems may automatically assign E&M codes based on the number of diagnoses linked to the visit. Beware! If the EHR system is set up to leave the boxes checked, the visits will be upcoded and will likely draw payer attention.

Read on for a more in-depth look at what takes place in an office and hospital setting and how it affects the way you go about your billing and coding business.

Visiting the office

Office visits usually fall under the jurisdiction of E&M codes. Here are some things to pay attention to in order to ensure that the provider is reimbursed appropriately:

- **The reason for the visit:** This refers to the symptom(s) that caused the patient to schedule a visit with the physician. The physician documents the patient's initial complaint, along with his or her confirmation of the symptoms present.

» **The specific patient type (that is, whether the patient is new to the doctor):** As the coder, you must verify whether the patient is new to the doctor, as well as the reason for the encounter. New patient visits have different CPT codes because an initial visit usually requires more of the physician's time and is therefore reimbursed at a higher rate. (New patients are those who are either completely new to the doctor or who have not been seen by the doctor or another one in the same specialty within the same practice for the past three years.)

» **Who is performing the service:** Some offices have nurse practitioners or physician assistants who see patients independently of the physician. There are special rules for billing E&M codes performed by this type of provider depending on the insurance that the patient has. For many commercial carriers who do not credential non-physician practitioners these visits are reported under the practitioner's provider number. Depending upon the laws of individual states, a licensed physician normally must be present in the office suite or within a defined range. Some states simply require that the physician be available by phone when patients are being seen by other members of the staff. Make sure you know the individual state laws with regard to non-physician providers' scope of practice as well as individual payer preferences for billing them.

REMEMBER

The procedures or visit codes for physicians and non-physician practitioners are the same, but the payer often pays a different amount. Some payers want modifiers to indicate that the visit was with a member of the physician's clinical staff rather than the physician. It's your responsibility as the coder to be aware of individual payer requirements and bill appropriately as defined by the individual contracts. Some payers are finicky about paying for nurse practitioners or physician's assistants, so make sure you learn the individual payer rules and keep the staff advised as necessary.

Sometimes a patient may visit the office, and the E&M code is not reportable. For example, if a patient comes in merely to receive a vaccination administered by a nurse, then the vaccination administration code may be the only reportable service. Billing for the drug may also be necessary, but you won't use an E&M code. (You can find the code for administering the vaccination in the CPT codebook. Healthcare Common Procedure Coding System [HCPCS] codes are used to report certain drugs, blood product and other items, and other medical equipment not found in the CPT codebook.)

TIP

Many offices used super-bills. These coding and billing shortcuts listed the most common diagnoses and procedures performed by the practitioners. The physician checked the boxes to indicate what occurred during the visit. The coder would review the super-bill to ensure that all reported procedures are correctly documented in the record and that the indicated diagnosis supports medical necessity. ICD-10 and expanded use of EMRs have brought an end to the super-bill.

Visiting the hospital

Choosing codes to report hospital visits by a physician can be a challenge for even the most experienced coders. Over-coding these visits can be an invitation for unwanted attention from payer audits, so you want to have a firm grasp of the different types of hospital codes, discussed in the following sections.

Level-one, -two, and -three codes

Hospital visit codes have different levels:

- **Level-one codes (the patient is getting better):** This level of code is used to report the physician encounter that involves review of the patient's condition, both by examination and by the progress the hospital staff notes in the patient's chart. Normally, these visits are brief, and the level of decision-making is moderate, which means that, if the patient is recovering as anticipated, proceeding to the next step of treatment or recovery is okay.
- **Level-two codes (the patient isn't getting better):** With level-two codes, the patient isn't recovering as anticipated, so something else needs to be done. In this case, the physician discusses options with the patient and possibly issues revised orders for the staff; he may also order additional tests.
- **Level-three codes (the patient is declining fast):** This level of code is for the patients who have not responded to treatment or, worse, have continued to decline. Level-three visits require more of the physician's time and involve a higher level of decision-making, accompanied by a greater degree of risk for patient mortality.

REMEMBER

Each level of coding comes with its own qualifying criteria. The level of medical decision-making is determined by the number of diagnoses present, the options for managing the illnesses, the amount or complexity of tests or data that the physician must review, and the level of risk to the patient for complications or death. So when a patient is initially admitted, you use specific codes to reflect that level of service. Then you use inpatient visit codes for services rendered during the patient's hospitalization.

REMEMBER

If the patient is very ill, the higher-level codes may be justified; then as the patient's condition improves, you use lower-level codes.

In the event that the patient is critically ill and E&M codes are not appropriate, you use *critical care codes.* These codes are time-based and support a high level of reimbursement. Keep in mind, though, that they must be fully supported to be paid. So if you have inadequate documentation to support critical care, then the higher level of E&M code is probably a better choice.

Inpatient and outpatient codes

Another consideration that defines the correct code choice is whether the patient is an inpatient or outpatient. Curiously, being in the hospital overnight does not necessarily mean that the patient is an inpatient. Here's the distinction:

- **Inpatient:** An *inpatient* is a person who has been officially admitted to the hospital under a physician's order. The patient remains an inpatient until discharge.
- **Observation status:** A person admitted to the hospital with a physician order as with inpatient status, but with an expectation that the patient will be hospitalized for less than two nights.
- **Outpatient:** A patient who comes through the emergency room and is being treated or who is undergoing tests but has not been admitted to the hospital is an *outpatient*, even if she spends the night.

Because of coinsurance responsibilities associated with Medicare Part B claims, CMS has indicated that facilities are responsible for notifying patients of their admit status.

WARNING

Misrepresenting a patient's inpatient or outpatient status may lead to accusations of fraud and improper facility payments, although sometimes the misrepresentation is unintentional. Documentation of patient status can be difficult to interpret when the patient status changes. Physician payment is not affected by inpatient status, as long as he does not report services as performed in the office during a hospital stay.

Observation codes

Outpatient service codes to bill for the physician's time when the patient is being seen at the hospital but the decision whether to admit has not been made. For example, a patient may come to the emergency room with chest pain, breathing difficulties, dangerously elevated blood pressure, or any number of symptoms, and that patient may spend one or two nights in the hospital. But if the physician has not written an order to admit the patient as an inpatient, it is an outpatient visit, and observation codes are the appropriate choice.

Always verify that a written order is part of the patient record, regardless of how often the physician sees the patient in the hospital setting. Without the written order, the visits are outpatient, or they may be consultation visits if the billing physician is seeing the patient at the request of another physician (see the later section "Dealing with consultation visits" for more info on coding those visits).

Other hospital coding considerations

You must follow certain rules when reporting hospital visit codes. Some of these rules come from Medicare; others are specified contractually by the payer.

For example, if a provider visits a patient more than once in a calendar day, only one visit can be billed (this includes physicians from the same practice), but the level of reimbursement can be based on the documentation that supports the highest level. For example, if Dr. A visits the patient in the morning and his partner, Dr. B, stops by later in the day, you can bill only one visit to the payer if both doctors are in the same specialty. But if Dr. A is from the internal medicine office and Dr. B is from the cardiologist office, then they can both report the visit — as long as the visits are documented in the chart for medical necessity.

Similarly, some payers have limits on the number of physician visits they will pay for in one calendar day. If several specialists are simultaneously treating a patient, you need to know the payer guidelines with regard to number of visits, and each physician needs to document the reason for each visit.

REMEMBER

The key point? Always choose the code based on the documentation provided. If the documentation is unclear, verify with the physician and ask for clarification — in writing — especially when you are coding different levels of service.

Dealing with consultation visits

A consultation visit is simply a visit that's been requested by another physician, provider, or healthcare entity, such as a nurse practitioner, social worker, attorney, or even an insurance company.

With consultation visits, the most important thing for you to remember as a coder is to verify how the patient ended up seeing the physician. Most payers need to know that a visit to a consulting physician was medically necessary and requested by another provider because they want your doctor's opinion. In addition to detailing how the patient got connected to the consulting physician, the record must also document the request and reason for seeing the patient. The consulting physician must then send a report of his findings to the provider or healthcare entity that requested the consultation. The consulting physician may order tests or therapy as long as everything he does is included in a report back to the requesting physician or entity.

This game of "Who Got Here and How" isn't just confined to the clinical setting. It's also a big part of how you code what goes down in a hospital. When a physician puts on his consultation hat to see an inpatient, the request and reason for the consultation, as well as the consulting physician's findings, must be part of the patient record, which is shared in the case of an inpatient. When all this information is included in the patient's record, you can code these visits as consultations. (***Note:*** There is an exception: If all the treatment for a given problem is transferred to a consulting physician and she accepts the transfer before seeing the patient, the visit is not a consultation.)

TIP

If during a consultation the physician decides that taking over care of the patient is in the patient's best interest, he may still charge for the consulting visit. The key to deciding this is knowing what the requesting physician really wanted. Was it for the consultant to render an opinion and return the patient to his care or was it for the specialist to take over all or part of the patient's care? If he wanted to relinquish care of the patient, it's not a consultation.

Consultation visits are often time-consuming. If the physician invests a lot of time discussing test results, treatment options, and the like with the patient, a time-based consultation may be billable. When choosing one of these codes, the total time of the visit, along with the amount of time spent in counseling the patient, must be documented with the other required information. When documenting a time-based consultation visit, the record should indicate that at least half of the time reported was spent one-on-one with the patient, discussing test results, treatment options, and so on. A summary of the discussion should also be included in the record.

REMEMBER

Be sure to verify whether a patient encounter is a consultation or a new patient visit. Consultation codes are the higher-paid E&M codes; therefore, solid documentation in the record is essential to support the additional reimbursement. If a consultation visit is mistakenly coded as a regular office visit the reimbursement is lower than it should be. Conversely, if the patient is actually a new patient or a referred patient, then the service has been over-billed. (A referred patient differs from a patient sent for a consultation in that the referring physician does not make the request in writing, and the second physician will not necessarily send a report to the first physician.) Again, Medicare will *not* reimburse consultation codes.

Determining the level of billable service

The documentation that defines the services provided, the time spent with the patient, and the severity of the patient's condition determine the level of billable services. The sickness of the patient and the amount of work required by the physician is directly related to the level of reimbursement that is due.

The levels of service do not necessarily indicate the amount of time required to evaluate and treat the patient. The codes for those tasks — evaluating the patient's condition and deciding what steps are necessary to manage that condition — are the E&M codes; refer to the earlier section "Connecting with the World of Evaluation and Management Codes."

The appropriate level of service, however, *is* determined by how much work was required by the physician. As a rule, the sicker or more unstable the patient, the higher the level of service reported and coded — if the provider submits thorough documentation.

» Understanding the role of networks and third-party administrators

» Navigating the world of Medicare, Medicaid, and other government payers

Chapter 6
Getting to Know the Payers

After you complete the coding, your work doesn't just go out into the void of space. It goes to the payer. A *payer* is the entity that reimburses the provider for services. Payers fall into three general categories: commercial payers (like insurance companies), government payers (like Medicare and Medicaid), and third-party administrators like American Insurance Administrators, Chickering Claims Administrators, or Healthnet, to name a few. Regardless of the payer type, every encounter between a provider and a patient is submitted to the payer as a claim, unless the service is a "self-pay" (paid in full by the patient, such as for cosmetic procedures or patients without insurance).

To keep all these potential payers straight (as well as figure out who is supposed to pay you, how much, and when), you need to have the coding agility of a cheetah. Keep reading, and all will be revealed.

Wading through Commercial Insurance Payers

The past 50 years have seen the healthcare industry develop into the behemoth it is today, and to no one's surprise, commercial insurance companies, which pay the majority of insurance claims, have become major cogs in the industry — so much so, in fact, that the patient without insurance may have difficulty securing affordable healthcare. Because commercial payers loom so largely in the big healthcare picture (commercial insurance administers the group health policies that most employers provide or supplement for their eligible employees), you've got to make their acquaintance because they'll show up frequently on your desk.

In the following sections, I outline who the different private carriers are and what you need to know about these plans to get the proper reimbursement.

VALUE-BASED CARE: A PATIENT-CENTERED SYSTEM

The current trend in commercial healthcare is called value-based care (VBC), where the patient bears a greater share of cost. Fewer plans use office copays, and more plans apply the office visit obligation to the patient's deductible. The problem with this approach is that patients aren't quite as efficient at making payments as the insurance company is. First of all, in many instances, the provider doesn't know what amount the contract is going to allow for the service provided, which makes asking the patient to pay upfront a little tough. In addition, many of these plans come with an FSA (flexible spending account), an HSA (health spending account or health savings account), or even an HRA (health reimbursement account). Some patients may be skeptical paying with one of these cards when they have no guarantee that the payment is correct. Each of these plans has very strict usage guidelines, and only certain types of services or commodities are payable from these funds. If a patient overpays, the fund must be reimbursed, and that can be a nuisance for both the provider and the patient.

From a cash flow standpoint, these plans can be a problem. Various approaches are being tested; some offices ask for a flat down payment amount and bill the patient for the balance. Billing patients can be expensive, though, and vigilance of patient accounts becomes a much higher priority than in years past. For some time, many offices would carry a patient account for several months (especially if the patient was long standing or a "frequent flyer"), but with a VBC model, those policies will need to be revamped, and a more aggressive collection approach will likely be necessary.

Identifying the carriers

The commercial insurance world revolves on an axis of variety. In fact, an insurance plan seems to exist for just about every situation, and providers see a variety of plans in their daily practices: preferred provider option plans; point of service plans; exclusive provider option plans; health maintenance organizations; high deductible plans; discount plans; and ultra-specific plans that provide only prescription coverage, vision coverage, or other specialized coverage. In the following sections, I take a look at some of the more common of these commercial plans.

REMEMBER

The commercial insurance carrier is the company that writes the check to the provider, but the carrier may or may not be the one who prices the claim. Some carriers participate with payer *networks,* and the network prices the claims. Others may use third-party administrators (TPAs) to adjudicate, or price, their claims through their networks. To find out more about these entities, head to the later sections "Tuning in to networks" and "Choosing third-party administrators."

Preferred provider organizations (PPOs)

A *preferred provider organization* (PPO) is a network of healthcare providers (doctors, hospitals, and so on) who have contracted with an insurer to provide healthcare services at reduced rates. The network contracts define reimbursement terms for all levels of service for the providers in the network.

Usually, patients with PPO plans are responsible for lower copayments and deductibles when they use a network provider, although they usually either pay higher premiums or have larger out-of-pocket costs than members of other plan types. On the plus side, PPO patients usually do not need a referral to see a specialist, but they may need to have certain procedures authorized in advance.

Health maintenance organizations (HMOs)

Health maintenance organizations (HMOs), which gained popularity in the 1970s, are organizations that contract with all types of providers (general practitioners, specialists, labs, hospitals, and so on) to create a patient service network from which the patient can choose or to whom the primary care physician can refer.

One benefit of the HMO to patients is lower-cost healthcare. They usually have lower premiums and little or no copay obligations. However, they must access all healthcare through an assigned *primary care physician* (PCP) who functions as a gatekeeper to control costs to the insurance company. Before patients can see a specialist, the PCP must refer them. Even with the required referral in hand, patients are still restricted to providers within the HMO's network.

Some HMOs have no out-of-network benefits. In this case — and depending on the provisions of the plan — the cost for the out-of-network services provided may fall on the healthcare provider or the patient. If a PPO-only provider sees an HMO patient, the PPO contract may force the provider to absorb the cost of patient treatment. If the provider has no contract with the company at all and sees an HMO patient, then the patient may be fully responsible for all costs. As the biller/coder, you'll see the results of these choices firsthand.

Point-of-service plans (POS)

Point-of-service (POS) plans are a combination of PPO and HMO plans. A POS plan allows the patient to choose between PPO and HMO providers. POS members do not have to have a primary care physician, but they can if they want to. If they visit an HMO provider, they receive HMO benefits. If they choose to visit a PPO provider, they receive PPO benefits. POS patients usually have out-of-network benefits as well. Visiting a non-network provider increases the costs for the patients.

Exclusive provider organization plans (EPOs)

Exclusive provider organization (EPO) plans are similar to HMO plans in that they typically require the patient to choose a primary care physician. They also require referrals if the services of a specialist are necessary, and the specialists must also be a network-contracted provider. The only exception is in the event of an emergency when a network provider is unavailable.

High-deductible plans

The rising cost of healthcare has given birth to the high-deductible health plan. HMOs and PPOs started offering these plans in 2003. HMO and PPO deductibles are typically fairly low, but the premiums can become expensive. The high-deductible plans offer lower premiums but come with a high deductible. Deductibles in the $5,000 range are common. These plans are a smart choice for the young, healthy adult who rarely visits a doctor. But if that adult breaks a leg, the $5,000 adds up pretty darn quickly.

Some patients with high-deductible plans have health savings accounts (HSAs) or health reimbursement accounts (HRAs). HSAs are funded pre-tax by the insured; employers fund the HRAs. In addition, HRAs may or may not be handled by the same carrier; it depends on the group health plan provisions with the employer.

Discount plans

Probably the plans with the fewest advantages for both patient and provider are discount plans. These plans require patients to pay a monthly fee, which gives them access to participating providers. The problem is that the patients pay for the services, supposedly at a discounted price.

These plans are not true health insurance, and plan members are usually shocked when they need to use their "insurance." It bears repeating, especially in this case: Always verify patient benefits in advance to protect the provider and the patient.

Tuning in to networks

Some payers and providers participate in networks. A *network* is essentially a middleman that functions as an agent for commercial payers. The payers participate in networks that price claims for them. If a provider is contracted with a network and the insurance carrier is also part of that same network, then the network prices the claim, and the payer (carrier) pays the claim according to the network pricing.

Some carriers participate with several different networks and have the claim priced according to the network that is most advantageous to them. For that reason, you want to know which networks your patients' plans access for pricing so that you can avoid unplanned write-offs. An easy way to find this information is to look at the insurance card to see whether it shows various network symbols, which represent a pricing network that the payer accesses for pricing claims.

A *write-off* is the part of the claim that neither the payer nor the patient pays. This particular part of the debt is forgiven. Most contracts define specific payment allowances per procedure. Regardless of the billed amount, the remaining dollar amount is contractually obligated to be written off by the billing provider.

Choosing third-party administrators

Third-party administrators (TPAs) are intermediaries who either operate as a network or access networks to price claims. TPAs often handle claims processing for employers who self-insure their employees rather than use a traditional group health plan. Also labor unions who offer coverage for members usually use TPA pricing.

The TPA functions as a network to price claims and serves the provider, the patient, and the employer by keeping healthcare costs under control. The reality is that most small companies are not in the healthcare business. They offer coverage to their employees but want to control the cost. By self-insuring — which means that the company actually pays the healthcare providers from a company account — the small company is, in theory, able to save money.

Here's how the cost savings is supposed to work: When a small company provides healthcare for its employees through a commercial carrier, the carrier prices the policy based on the health history and ages of the employees. Typically, a small group health plan costs a company about $450 per month per employee.

If an employer chooses to self-insure and uses a TPA, the employer pays a fee to be part of the network but then pays only the cost of the individual claims. The TPA negotiates the price through network pricing.

The downside of this arrangement is that, in the event of a catastrophe that affects several employees, the company could be in a dire financial situation. The success of using a TPA depends, in part, on playing the odds that something that lands everyone in the hospital won't happen.

Most providers view TPAs as run-of-the-mill network contracts, which they essentially are, although some TPA networks are funded by all parties. The provider may be responsible for paying a fee on adjudicated claims as part of the network agreement, and the insurer also pays a fee to participate in the network.

Understanding the difference between an insurer and a TPA is important, especially when claims don't process as expected, because the nature of the problem determines whom you contact:

- If a TPA has incorrectly priced the claim, you need to address the issue through the TPA.
- If the payer didn't pay the claim according to the TPA pricing agreement, then you need to secure a copy of the claim adjudication sent to the payer and demand that the claim be reprocessed according to the pricing.

Check your checks and balances before you call — make sure you're barking up the right tree before you pursue a TPA claim.

Medicare: Meeting the Chief Government Payer

Beyond commercial payers (covered in the preceding sections) is good ol' Uncle Sam, who sponsors a variety of healthcare programs. The biggest is Medicare. (For information on other government payers, like Medicaid, Tricare, ACA (Affordable Care Act), and more, head to the later section "Working with Other Government Payers.")

Established in 1965 as part of the Social Security Act, Medicare provides insurance to people aged 65 and over, as well as to people with qualifying physical or mental disabilities. The program is financed by payroll taxes known as the Federal

Insurance Contributions Act (FICA) tax. Both the employee and the employer pay this tax.

In the following sections, I outline the key things you need to know about Medicare.

TECHNICAL STUFF

The first Medicare beneficiary was former president Harry Truman. Actually, you don't really need to know this, but it's a fun fact anyway!

Examining Medicare, part by part

As mentioned previously, four types of Medicare exist — Parts A through D — and each serves a particular purpose. The different types of Medicare and the fact that participation is automatic in some cases but not in others can lead to a lot of confusion with the plan's beneficiaries. Make sure you verify exactly which parts of Medicare are applicable to the patients you're dealing with before services are provided. I explain what you need to know in the following sections.

Medicare Part A

Medicare Part A covers expenses for inpatient care in hospitals, skilled nursing facilities, hospice, and home healthcare.

REMEMBER

Spending the night in a hospital does not necessarily mean that the visit is a Part A claim. The patient must have been admitted under physician orders to be an inpatient. Refer to Chapter 5 for information on the requirements that must be met to qualify as an inpatient.

Medicare Part B

Medicare Part B helps pay for services deemed medically necessary that are not covered under Part A. These services include physician services (including some preventative services like flu shots), outpatient hospital services, durable medical equipment, and home health services. Beneficiaries must enroll in Part B, and they pay a monthly premium. In addition, beneficiaries are responsible for paying an annual deductible and 20 percent coinsurance for Medicare-eligible services.

TIP

Some patients do not realize that Part B is optional, and they may mistakenly believe that they have it simply because they qualify for Medicare. Make sure you see the patient's Medicare card to verify Part B benefits.

Technically, enrollment in Part B is optional, but if you are eligible and don't enroll when you're supposed to, you may incur a penalty if you decide to enroll at a later date. If a person continues to work after age 65, enrollment may be deferred (that is, you can skip enrollment without penalty). Those who are no longer employed but fail to enroll have a 10 percent per year penalty added to the monthly premium. Eligible recipients who are still covered by group health coverage can delay enrollment in Part B until their group coverage ends. However, those individuals still need to be aware of the enrollment period that applies.

Medicare Part C

Medicare Part C refers to replacement plans (also known as Medicare Advantage Plans) that some patients opt to enroll in. These replacement plans are offered by Medicare-approved private companies. Medicare replacement plans cover Part A and Part B services. Some plans also offer drug and vision coverage as well.

Medicare pays a fixed amount each month to companies that offer replacement plans, and in return, the companies agree to follow the rules set by Medicare for administration of the replacement plans. Each plan can charge out-of-pocket costs and can establish rules for plan use, such as requiring referrals to see specialists or requiring that the patient see only network providers.

Medicare-eligible patients who prefer private insurance enroll in Part C replacement plans. Some larger companies that historically have allowed retiring employees to stay on the company health plan are now offering Part C replacement plans to eligible enrollees. Some companies with employees who are Medicare eligible offer these employees Part C plans as well.

When coding for services provided to these patients, make sure you verify coverage and plan restrictions prior to any encounter. Commercial plans follow commercial contract obligations, and the Medicare plans have to follow Medicare payment guidelines unless the commercial contract contains a Medicare Part C reimbursement clause that obligates the payer to a specific payment or fee schedule different than standard Medicare.

You can avoid unnecessary denials by verifying Part C enrollment early in your coding process. Verification of Medicare patients is fairly simple. Some of the Medicare contractors have websites that let providers check patient benefits. Others have *interactive voice response* (IVR) telephone systems that providers can call to check patient coverage.

Medicare Part D

Medicare Part D is Medicare's prescription drug plan. Medicare-approved companies run these plans. To participate, qualifying individuals must enroll in a plan and adhere to plan restrictions.

Part D normally does not affect healthcare providers or their staff. But some patients can be confused and think they've enrolled in a Medicare supplement (explained in the next section) when what they have is a Part D plan to cover prescription drugs. In these situations, you may find yourself explaining to the patient the difference between another major medical plan and a Medicare supplement plan.

Looking at Medicare supplement policies

Medicare supplement policies cover the charges that Medicare doesn't pay. Normally, Medicare pays 80 percent of allowed expenses after the participants meet the annual deductible. Many patients enroll in secondary coverage to make up the difference. For example, these plans may cover the annual Medicare deductible and the 20 percent coinsurance left over by Medicare. These supplements don't cover expenses that Medicare doesn't approve, however.

CROSSING OVER

Some Medicare supplement policies accept claims directly from Medicare, a practice known as *cross-over claim submission.* Patients with these plans need to let Medicare know that they have a Medicare supplement plan, the details of that plan, and the effective date. Then, after Medicare processes a claim, it sends the claim directly to the secondary payer, and the provider is paid in a more timely fashion. Ta-da! Cross-over claim at work.

Some other supplemental Medicare carriers' claims will cross over, but they are not automatic. These are known as *Medigap policies.* To get Medigap policies to cross over, a provider needs to enter the policy holder, policy number, and name of the plan on the HCFA-1500 or UB-04 along with the carrier's assigned Medigap number.

Secondary complementary claims or Medigap claims don't automatically cross over to the secondary carrier if the claim is totally denied, a duplicate claim, an adjustment claim, a claim that has been reimbursed by Medicare at 100 percent, a claim that is submitted to Medicare outside the eligibility dates, or a claim for a provider who doesn't participate with Medicare. (***Note:*** When the cross-over action is automatic, you don't have a chance to correct an error on a claim.)

A true Medicare supplement serves as a gap coverage to pay what Medicare approves but doesn't pay. Medicare patients do not usually benefit by carrying a second major medical plan such as those discussed earlier in the chapter, and they are surprised when faced with unplanned medical expenses. Your best bet is to verify secondary coverage in addition to Medicare eligibility prior to any patient encounter. The question you need to ask as a coder is "Does this secondary plan cover what Medicare approves but does not pay?"

Coding and processing Medicare claims

It probably comes as no surprise to you that coding and processing Medicare claims can get pretty confusing. In the following sections, I give you the lowdown.

The coding criteria

Medicare strictly adheres to the established National Correct Coding Initiative (NCCI) edits, along with procedure/medical necessity protocol. In addition, its claims processing system is highly refined. Any claim that is submitted with errors or without the correct information does not process, period. For detailed information on how to submit an error-free claim, head to Chapter 12.

Rules regarding payouts

Congress legislates how Medicare claims are paid out to providers. Here's what you need to know:

- The payer has what is called a *payment floor,* a set length of time to complete and process claims. When the service dates have been released for payment, then Medicare pays.
- Medicare prefers to pay with electronic funds transfer (EFT), which helps solidify Medicare's reputation as a good payer that pays most claims without incident if they are submitted correctly.

Make sure you're familiar with the Medicare contractor's claim submission preference and submit claims accordingly because Medicare is not going to adapt to provider needs; the provider does all of the adapting!

The role of MACs, LCDs, and ABNs

Through Medicare, the Centers for Medicare & Medicaid Services (CMS) sets the rules for the country, but Medicare claims processing happens in regional areas. CMS contracts with private companies, called Medicare Administrative Contractors (MACs), to process Medicare claims. MACs have replaced the former system of fiscal intermediaries (who processed Part A claims) and the local carriers (who processed Part B claims).

As Medicare contractors, MACs may develop or adopt policies in the following circumstances:

- When no national coverage determination regarding a specific procedure exists. (Basically, *national coverage determination* refers to a nationwide determination of whether Medicare will pay for a service or not.)
- When a need to further define a national coverage determination exists.

When a local contractor adopts such a policy, it is known as an LCD, or *local coverage determination.* The Medicare Program Integrity Manual contains the guidelines for LCD policy development. You can check it out at `www.cms.gov/manuals`.

If a service or diagnosis is not covered by CMS, the MAC can't agree to cover it. A provider who furnishes a service that Medicare probably won't cover can ask the patient to sign an *advanced beneficiary notice* (ABN). By signing an ABN, the patient agrees to be financially responsible for the service if Medicare denies payment. If the provider doesn't offer the ABN or the patient doesn't sign the notice before services are rendered, the patient doesn't have to pay for that service.

REMEMBER

As a coder, you must be familiar with the local coverage policies of your Medicare contractor so that you can submit claims correctly. If a service is provided that is processed incorrectly, a solid knowledge of payment rules can help you resolve the issue.

Working with Other Government Payers

Medicare may be the biggest but it isn't the only government payer. Some of those with the greatest presence are Tricare (for military personnel and their dependents), the Department of Labor (for injured federal workers), ACA policies (known as "Obamacare" in the news), and Medicaid (for low-income individuals). Each has its own individual billing requirements. Keep reading for the details.

Patient Protection and Affordable Care Act (ACA)

The new kids on the block are the policies being sold as a result of the Patient Protection and Affordable Care Act, commonly called the Affordable Care Act (ACA). This law protects individuals who previously didn't have healthcare coverage but didn't qualify for Medicaid.

Under the ACA, health plans can no longer deny benefits for treatment of preexisting conditions, and young adults under age 26 are allowed to be covered under a parent's health plan. The ACA also protects individuals from arbitrary decisions by commercial payers, including retroactive cancellation of coverage due to an honest mistake, and gives patients the right to request reconsideration if a claim is denied.

Other features include a ban on lifetime coverage limits for new health insurance plans and a requirement that insurance companies make unreasonable rate hikes public.

Consumers buy these policies through the Health Insurance Marketplace during open enrollment, which occurs annually from November 15 through February 15 each year. Special enrollment is available outside this period for people who experience life-changing events, such as the birth of a child, the death of a spouse, and others.

As a coder, you need to learn about the plans being offered in your state. Many of the plans function like HMOs, and only providers who have enrolled with the plan are eligible for claim payment. *Enrolled in* is different from *accepts;* though your office may accept a plan, the provider may be considered out of network if it isn't enrolled as a provider in that plan. Also, from a practice management perspective, knowing who your payers are is important when scheduling appointments.

The front office should be educated in the difference between a commercial plan and an ACA plan that is a product of the same company. Usually, the ACA plan card has slightly different filing instructions (it may say that non-emergency services should be provided within the state, and so forth), and it may not have a group number and/or employer name like commercial cards. When scheduling appointments for consumers with ACA cards, the office may need to probe a bit in order to identify who the actual payer is.

REMEMBER

Every patient deserves to be treated; the mantra of the healthcare profession is "It's *always* about the patient." Knowing whether the provider is right for the patient is just good practice management. These individuals are already paying a hefty price for coverage; they shouldn't be saddled with an unplanned medical bill because they were not made aware that the provider was out of network.

Medicaid

Medicaid, like Medicare, was created by the 1965 Social Security Act. Its purpose is to help low-income people pay for part or all of their medical bills. Medicaid is federally governed but locally administered.

Medicaid falls into two general types:

- **Community Medicaid,** which assists eligible beneficiaries who have no (or very little) medical coverage, and
- **Medicaid nursing home coverage,** which pays for nursing home costs for eligible recipients. These beneficiaries pay most of their income toward nursing home costs.

In the next sections, I explain how Medicaid is funded and administered, who qualifies for the program, and what you as a coder need to pay attention to when dealing with Medicaid claims.

Administering and funding Medicaid

The Medicaid program is administered through the U.S. Department of Health & Human Services (HHS) through CMS. Each state is responsible for implementing its own Medicaid program, although CMS establishes the program requirements and monitors the programs to ensure compliance with federal policies and procedures. Participation in Medicaid is voluntary, yet every state participates and is required to follow the CMS protocol for service quality and eligibility standards.

REMEMBER

Federal regulations define the minimum medical services that must be provided to a Medicaid patient. These services include inpatient hospital treatment, pregnancy and prenatal care, and surgical dental services. Individual states may provide additional care when funding allows.

Several states combine Medicaid programs with other insurance programs, such as those directed at children. Some states use private health insurance companies to administer their Medicaid programs. These providers are essentially HMOs that contract with the state Medicaid department to provide services for an agreed-upon price. Other states work directly with the service providers.

The federal government and the states share funding for Medicaid. Some states receive additional funding assistance from counties.

Perusing program eligibility

Program eligibility is determined primarily by income and access to financial resources. For example, having limited assets is a primary requirement for eligibility. In addition to demonstrating eligibility due to financial status, though, eligible recipients must fall into another eligibility category as defined by CMS. These categories include age, pregnancy, disability, blindness, and status as a U.S citizen or lawfully admitted immigrant. Special exceptions are made for those living in nursing homes and disabled children residing at home. A child, for example, may be eligible regardless of the eligibility of the parents or guardians.

Individuals who meet other eligibility requirements but don't meet the income or asset requirement have a *spend down*, in which they reduce their assets so that they can qualify for Medicaid. Federal guidelines permit spend downs, but not all state programs allow them. Patients having a spend down pay for healthcare costs out of their own pockets, using their own resources, until their asset levels fall enough to qualify for Medicaid coverage.

Watching for special concerns when coding Medicaid claims

Most Medicaid plans only accept claims from enrolled providers; some plans won't even provide submission information to nonparticipants. Also, in most states, once you bill Medicaid (other than spend down obligation), the patient is no longer responsible for charges.

When billing for a Medicaid patient, you need to research the state's Medicaid billing requirements. Some carriers want certain modifiers; others don't. Verifying a patient's eligibility status with Medicaid is usually difficult. Generally, you can only verify whether the patient has it and whether a referral is needed. The spend down, if there is one, can't be determined until after the claim has been submitted for consideration.

Many Medicaid policies are secondary to Medicare. If the patient has kept Medicare advised, the claim usually crosses directly from Medicare to be processed. Unlike other secondary payers, however, Medicaid usually pays per its fee schedule, regardless of what the primary payer pays. For example, if a primary commercial insurance contract obligates a claim to pay $1,000, but the Medicaid fee schedule obligates the same procedure to pay $500, Medicaid will pay only up to $500 less any amounts paid by the primary insurance and the issue is closed.

Tricare (Department of Defense)

Tricare, funded by the U.S. Department of Defense, is the healthcare system used by active military personnel and their dependents.

Different Tricare programs address the needs of specific segments of the military:

» **Tricare Select:** Active duty military, retired active duty military, reserve military retirees, and eligible family members use Tricare Standard. These members can use any civilian healthcare provider and usually have a coinsurance responsibility and a deductible.

- **Tricare Prime:** Tricare Prime serves the same segment of the military population that Tricare Standard does, except that Tricare Prime is more restrictive. Tricare Prime patients are allowed to seek treatment only from network providers. All active military are required to enroll in Tricare Prime, but for eligible dependents, it's a less expensive option.
- **Tricare for Life:** Tricare for Life is essentially a Medicare supplement available to retirees who were formally Tricare members that became Medicare eligible. (Go to "Looking at Medicare supplement policies" for more information.)

TIP

To put it in insurance terms, think of Tricare Standard as the military equivalent of a PPO. Tricare Prime, which is more restrictive, is the equivalent of an HMO. Think of Tricare for Life as a Medicare supplement policy.

In the United States, Tricare benefits are administered through regional contractors known as Tricare North, Tricare South, and Tricare West. Overseas claims are processed through the Tricare Overseas Program.

Tricare follows the same claim editing programs that Medicare uses, and it pays according to Tricare fee schedules. A provider who treats a Tricare patient can expect the claim to process per the appropriate fee schedule; in return, Tricare trusts the provider to accept the fee schedule pricing and not to send the balance to the patient to pay (a practice called *balance billing*), regardless of a network contract.

TIP

The fee schedules are updated regularly; you can access them through the Tricare web portals.

CHAMPUS VA (Department of Veterans Affairs)

CHAMPUS (Civilian Health and Medical Program of the Uniformed Services) VA patients are those who are not eligible for Tricare: spouses or dependents of veterans disabled in the line of duty and surviving spouses of veterans who had been disabled or died from a service-connected disability. (Occasionally a surviving spouse or child of a military member killed in the line of duty may have CHAMPUS VA, but normally they are eligible for Tricare.)

REMEMBER

CHAMPUS VA plans are always secondary when another payer exists. When CHAMPUS VA is the primary payer, it functions mostly like an HMO. Always verify patient coverage prior to any scheduled encounters to secure any necessary referrals or prior authorization for treatment.

In prior years, both active and retired military beneficiaries and their dependents were treated exclusively at military facilities. Due to budget restrictions, the Department of Defense started to contract with civilian providers for their members' healthcare needs. This program was originally known as CHAMPUS. Later, CHAMPUS became CHAMPUS VA, which is now funded by the Veterans Administration.

Office of Workers' Compensation Programs (Department of Labor)

The U.S. Department of Labor's Office of Workers' Compensation Programs (OWCP) administers disability compensation programs to injured federal workers or those who acquire an occupational disease. Workers' compensation claims can be a bit tricky. Here's what you need to do when you work with these types of claims:

- **Follow the filing requirements established by the Department of Labor (DOL).** First, providers must enroll, after which point they are assigned a DOL provider number. Second, DOL claims always require prior authorization for each procedure (even though pre-authorization doesn't necessarily guarantee reimbursement), and each procedure must be supported by the approved condition being treated (medical necessity). Only the approved diagnosis for the patient's treatable condition is accepted on these claims.
- **Prior to treating a patient who tells you he has been injured on the job, verify workers' compensation claim information with the patient's employer or the workers' compensation carrier if you have that information.** Verify the claim number, date of injury, and the body part approved for treatment. Also get the adjuster's name and contact information and verify the submission address for the claims.
- **Verify the approved diagnosis code.** The workers' compensation carrier has one or two approved diagnoses that must be used for all claims submissions. The treating physician must know what these approved diagnoses are so that the treatment administered is supported by medical necessity. If you vary from these diagnoses, your provider may not be paid.
- **Make sure all reportable procedures have been pre-authorized.** All OWCP claims need to be pre-authorized. Although pre-certification does not guarantee payment, failure to pre-certify guarantees no payment.
- **Include the medical records with the claims.** Any treatment to be paid for must be a result of the injury. If the workers' compensation patient with the injured shoulder also has bronchitis, for example, the bronchitis is probably not an approved diagnosis.
- **Provide regular follow-up.** As with any other government program, you must navigate through the maze associated with each individual claim.

Similar to other federal insurance programs, OWCP processes claims based on a fee schedule. The DOL fee schedule, in addition to CCI edits, are used to process DOL claims. You can access the DOL fee schedule via a link on its website (`http://owcp.dol.acs-inc.com`). To access this portal, the provider must register and request a login. Also, payments for DOL claims are made via electronic funds transfer (EFT). Prior to submitting any DOL claims, part of the enrollment process is to also enroll for the EFTs.

With workers' compensation claims, not only are you billing and coding for the benefit of the provider or payer, but you are also coding something that will affect whether someone receives proper compensation for a possible at-work injury. A lot is at stake for everyone involved. For that reason, you've got to be on top of your coding game, even more so than usual. For specific information regarding OWCP claims, go to the Department of Labor's website (`www.dol.gov`).

TECHNICAL STUFF

The DOL has the three divisions:

- **Federal Employees' Compensation Act (FECA):** This covers the majority of DOL claims.
- **Division of Coal Mine Workers' Compensation (DCMWC):** This division is dedicated to coal workers' claims.
- **Division of Energy Employees Occupational Illness Compensation (DEEOIC):** This division is dedicated to the claims involving federal employees of the Division of Energy.

3 Becoming a Professional: Getting Certified

IN THIS PART . . .

Find out the difference between the two certifying organizations, AAPC and AHIMA.

Uncover the types of certifications offered and which is right for you.

Understand the big difference between a certificate and a certification.

Get tips on bolstering your credentials through specialty programs and continuing education.

» Identifying the certification that best fits your career goals

» Knowing what to expect for each type of certification exam

Chapter 7
Your Basic Certification Options, Courtesy of the AAPC and AHIMA

For success as a medical biller and coder, you've got to be certified by a trusted credentialing organization like the AAPC or AHIMA. Each organization is different and has its own unique credentialing requirements.

Each type of certification offered by these organizations has different benefits, depending on what you want to do in your billing and coding career. Some gear you up for work in a physician's office; others prepare you for the hospital environment. Plus, the type of certification you decide to pursue affects what kind of training program you end up in, because many of the training programs are specifically geared to particular types of certification exams. For those reasons, you need to give thought to what you want to do in your career before you make that all-important certification choice.

In this chapter, I introduce you to these credentialing organizations, explain the basic certifications they offer, and give you a general idea of what to expect on their certification exams. (You can read about specialty certifications in Chapter 10.)

Introducing the Two Main Credentialing Organizations: AAPC and AHIMA

The AAPC (American Academy of Professional Coders) and the American Health Information Management Association (AHIMA) are the two primary credentialing organizations. AHIMA certification covers coding in hospitals, and AAPC certification covers everybody else. *Note:* AAPC has added a new certification called the Certified Inpatient Coder (CIC), which is its only certification dedicated to inpatient hospital or facility coding (see the section "AAPC and its basic certifications: CPC, COC, CPC-P, CIC" later in this chapter for more details).

AAPC was founded in 1988 with two goals: providing education and professional certification to medical coders working in physicians' offices and setting a higher standard of coding by adhering to accepted standards. AHIMA's certifications are primarily directed at coders working in hospitals. Founded in 1928, AHIMA's original goal was to improve the quality of medical records; today it continues to strive for excellence in medical record integrity with the evolution of electronic medical records. Both AAPC and AHIMA offer educational resources and programs including certifications.

REMEMBER

Prior to applying for membership in either organization and registering to take a certification exam, research each one to see which best fits your needs and your budget. You also may want to find out when and where the local chapter meets and attend a meeting or two to get the feel of the organization's culture. And feel free to press some flesh and talk people up: Both organizations offer network and mentoring opportunities.

Going with AAPC

AAPC is widely recognized for credentialing both physician- and hospital-based coders; it now also offers physician training services to practices. Its training programs are offered throughout the United States. The organization also offers access to continuing education opportunities and a jobs database. In addition to regional conferences, AAPC has HealthCon, a national annual healthcare conference, where you can find both educational and networking opportunities. (The smaller regional conferences offer similar opportunities and are usually more economical.)

Choosing AHIMA instead

AHIMA is highly respected in the area of hospital and physician coders. The organization offers a variety of training programs, has an annual convention, and conducts workshops lasting several days in a variety of locales. If you choose to be credentialed by the AHIMA, you'll have access to training and networking opportunities throughout your career.

Although it offers entry-level credentials, AHIMA doesn't offer apprentice-level certifications as AAPC does. AHIMA certifications are intended for those already intimately familiar with coding.

Being a joiner: The benefits of membership

In today's world of privacy and compliance concerns, certification is the industry standard. Because certification shows that you are proficient in your area and are committed to quality healthcare by disseminating quality information, it's one of the first qualifications employers look for when they review you as a potential candidate, and it's an asset when you're negotiating a salary. In addition, the majority of billing companies have contracts with their clients that obligate them to hire only certified coders.

As a member of one of the two main credentialing organizations — AHIMA or AAPC — you're privy to different professional goodies. Both organizations provide numerous networking opportunities. In addition, AAPC members receive discounts on certification tests, preparation materials, workshop fees, and numerous other products. Similarly, AHIMA members enjoy membership perks such as access to professional publications, discounts on books, and other training opportunities open to members only.

Joining one or both: The pros and cons of multiple membership

You may be wondering, since certification offers so many benefits, whether you can compound your advantages by having more than one certification. Very possibly. But before you sign up for every certification possible, consider the pros and cons of having multiple certifications.

Pros:

- **Potentially higher salary:** Theoretically, the more certification levels you achieve, the higher the salary you can expect. In reality, *experience* plus certification improves your marketability tenfold. In other words, don't go certification crazy without earning some real-world experience to go along with all those acronyms.

- **More access to networking opportunities:** Multiple memberships mean increased network opportunity. If you attend local chapter meetings and become an involved member, when a job becomes available, someone with influence may suggest you or serve as a reference.

Cons:

- **Increasing costs to achieve multiple certifications:** One big disadvantage of multiple certifications is cost. The initial cost of taking the test(s) can be a drain on your personal finances. In addition, each certification requires a certain number of continuing education units (CEUs) within your chosen specialty. (Chapter 10 has more information about continuing education.)
- **Higher membership dues:** The other disadvantage is the cost of membership. Some employers may reimburse your dues or other costs, but don't count on it, especially in the beginning.

Looking at the Basic Certifications

As I explain earlier in this chapter, if you want to get ahead as a medical biller and coder, certification is a must. The trick is knowing which certification organization is most appropriate for you and whether you'd be best served by having multiple certifications.

AAPC and AHIMA are the most well-known (read: trusted) organizations, so their certifications likely open more doors. Choosing the right certification depends on your experience and eligibility to take the exam(s). In the following sections, I discuss what each organization offers and other things you need to think about. (*Note:* Both organizations also offer specialty certifications. You can read about those in Chapter 10.)

AAPC and its basic certifications: CPC, COC, CPC-P, CIC

Starting at the top of the heap, you'll want to think about AAPC certification and what it can or can't do for your coding career. The basic certification level for AACP is the Certified Professional Coder (CPC) certification. This certification indicates proficiency in reading a medical chart and abstracting the correct diagnosis codes, procedural codes, and supply codes. It's the certification level most members first attain.

As a CPC-certified coder, your best fit is in a physician's office, billing office, or certain other outpatient environments (although the AAPC has ventured into inpatient hospital coding as well through its Certified Inpatient Coder [CIC] certification). In those places, you're expected to have a thorough understanding of anatomy and medical terminology and be able to apply procedural codes and the supporting diagnosis codes. Other basic CPC certifications include Certified Outpatient Coder (COC) and Certified Professional Coder-Payer (CPC-P). You can see a quick description of all these certifications in Table 7-1.

Visit www.aapc.com for additional details.

TABLE 7-1 **Basic AAPC Certifications**

Certification	Related Skills and Competencies
Certified Professional Coder (CPC)	Proficiency in reading medical charts and assigning correct diagnosis (ICD-10) codes, procedure codes (CPT), and supply codes (HCPCS)
Certified Outpatient Coder (COC)	Proficiency in assigning accurate codes for diagnosis, procedures, and services performed in an outpatient setting; understanding compliance and outpatient grouping systems; and completing a UB-04, the billing form used for facility claims, with appropriate modifiers
Certified Professional Coder-Payer (CPC-P)	Proficiency in understanding the claim adjudication process; possessing basic knowledge of coding-related payer processes, including the relationship between coding and payment
Certified Inpatient Coder (CIC)	Proficiency in inpatient hospital facility coding; specializing in ICD-10 coding and knowledge of DRGs and the Inpatient Prospective Payment System

WARNING

You may encounter coders who say they are "ICD-10 certified," but there's no actual ICD-10 certification. Prior to ICD-10 implementation, those who held credentials were obligated to recertify under the new code sets. But "ICD-10 certified" was not, and is not a credential.

AAPC has stringent eligibility requirements for full certification. If you have at least two years of coding experience before you take the exam, you'll be fully certified upon passing. If you don't have experience in coding prior to sitting for the exam for any of these certifications, you'll earn an apprentice status: CPC-A, COC-A, or CIC-A. You can request that the A be removed by following either of the following processes:

» **Send a request, along with two letters verifying that you've had at least two years of experience using the coding books.** At least one letter should be on letterhead from your employer, and the other may be from a coworker. Both letters must be signed and should outline your coding experience and amount of time in that capacity. Alternatively, to speed the process up, your references can fill out the Apprentice Removal Template available on the AAPC website. However, letterhead and signatures are still required.

- **Prove that you have completed at least 80 hours of coding education and have completed one year of on-the-job experience using CPT, ICD, and HCPCS codes.** This can be a certificate of course completion, a letter from your instructor on school letterhead, or a transcript that states that you have completed a minimum of 80 hours of classroom training. If you choose this option, you also must provide one letter on letterhead that has been signed by your employer that verifies you have completed one year of on-the-job experience.

AHIMA and its basic certifications: CCA, CCS, CCS-P

Although AHIMA certification is most desirable for hospital-based coders, this certification is also accepted in physician practices or practice management companies.

Here are the basic certifications offered by AHIMA:

- **Certified Coding Associate (CCA):** This certifies the coder has demonstrated proficiency in inpatient and outpatient hospital-based coding. It's a nice overall certification that prepares you for multiple environments.

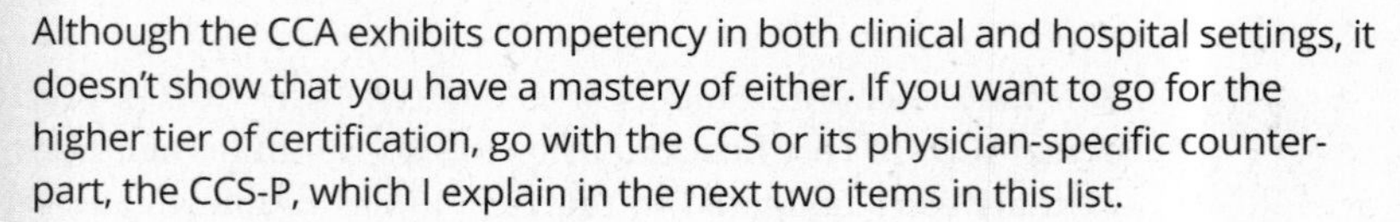

  Although the CCA exhibits competency in both clinical and hospital settings, it doesn't show that you have a mastery of either. If you want to go for the higher tier of certification, go with the CCS or its physician-specific counterpart, the CCS-P, which I explain in the next two items in this list.

- **Correct Coding Specialist (CCS):** This is the main certification offered by AHIMA. It indicates you have competency in hospital coding, and it requires a higher level of expertise in diagnosis and procedural coding than the CCA certification does, because as a CCS, you are able to abstract codes from patient records.

  People who attain this certification are also experts in both Current Procedural Terminology (CPT) and International Classification of Diseases (ICD) coding systems. And just like CPC-certified coders, the CCS possesses a strong knowledge of medical terminology and human anatomy. The CCS curriculum also contains instruction in the disease process and pharmacology. Whew! That's a lot to take in. But, hey, if working in a big hospital is your bag, then you're going to interface with all kinds of people and situations. The CCS helps you get ready for all of it.

- **Correct Coding Specialist–Physician-based (CCS-P):** This certification indicates that you specialize in physician settings, such as physician offices, and are responsible for assigning ICD-10 diagnosis and CPT procedure codes based on patient records. You have thorough knowledge of health information and are dedicated to data quality and integrity because data submitted to insurance companies determines the level of reimbursement to which the physician is entitled.

There are a number of options to obtain AHIMA certification. The certification process is regulated by the Commission on Certification for Health Informatics and Information Management (CCHIM). The Exam Development Committees are composed of experienced, credential-specific subject matter experts. In addition, unlike the AAPC, a number of the certification levels have academic qualification requirements and require completion of an approved AHIMA program prior to submitting an application to take the certification exam(s).

For details, visit www.ahima.org.

Choosing the Certification That's Right for You

Deciding which type of certification best fits your career goals is really a two-step process. Think about these two factors when you are selecting a certification type:

- **The type of training program you want:** How much time can you dedicate to a training program? What's your budget? What sort of curriculum interests you?
- **Your long-term career goals:** What kind of medical billing and coding job do you ultimately want to do? In what sort of facility do you want to work? How do you want to spend your time each day?

Your answers to those questions can help you choose what kind of certification will most benefit your long-term goals and short-term educational needs. Read on for more details.

REMEMBER

The thing you need to remember about AAPC and AHIMA when choosing a type of certification is that each organization's certifications are designed to help you fit in the career niche of your choice. (*Note:* You can attain several other types of certification, including numerous specialty certifications you can add on top of your primary certification. To find out about these certifications, go to Chapter 10.)

Examining the educational requirements

Some certifications require you to earn a four-year degree prior to taking the exam, while others require little more than a short-term program under your belt. Both AHIMA and AAPC recommend you complete some type of accredited training program. These accredited programs provide the education and training you need to work in the healthcare industry and to pass that exam. Your other pre-test training options include vocational training schools and online programs.

Most programs offer training in subjects like human anatomy and physiology; medical terminology and documentation; medical coding, including proper use of modifiers; medical billing; and more.

Each training option has its pros and cons, but the most important qualities to look for in a training program are accreditation and the expertise of the instructors teaching the classes. Head to Chapter 8 for a complete discussion of training programs, the degrees offered, and how to choose a program that's right for you.

Prioritizing your career needs

Although you can't predict the future, you can put some thought into your long-term career needs when you're thinking about the type of training program you want. The last thing you want is to get stuck in a program that prepares you for a certification exam that doesn't match up with how you want to spend the rest of your career. As you talk your way through this decision, consider these factors:

- Where you plan to seek employment (hospital, physician's office, and so on)
- The kind of job you want to do (coding, medical billing, charge posting, or accounts receivable follow-up)

TIP

Coders tend to be introverted and detail-focused and are happiest working quietly on their own. If that appeals to your personality, then coding may be a good choice, as would other positions that tend to attract people with those same qualities, like medical billing or charge posting. If you're more social, you may be happier in accounts receivable follow-up because this position requires constant interaction with others (payers).

- The type of certification potential employers might prefer
- The availability, quality, and cost of the training programs in your area

Seeing what employers in your area want

Where you want to work and what kind of job you want to do will probably carry the most weight in your decision-making process. After all, you want to make yourself the most marketable candidate for the jobs you want most. Try these tips for tracking the ins and outs of potential employers and, by extension, the certifications they require:

- Check with local employment recruiters and see what type of credentials their clients prefer.
- Take note of the credentials displayed in local medical offices that you visit.
- Look through the local job listings and see what kinds of certifications are mentioned in jobs that appeal to you.
- If you have your heart set on working for a particular company, find out what kind of coders it prefers. If the local hospital only uses AHIMA-certified coders and records clerks, then you want to find an AHIMA-accredited program and take an AHIMA exam. On the other hand, if that same hospital employs both AAPC- and AHIMA-certified professionals, then you need to find the program that best prepares you to take the exam that'll give you the best chance to score a job.

Examining the Exams: A Quick Review of the Main Tests

After you've given thought to what sort of medical billing and coding career you want and have an understanding of what the standard educational path for a medical biller and coder is, you're ready to research the main certification exam options. And — no big surprise here — you can start by getting to know the exams offered by the AAPC and AHIMA: the Certified Professional Coder (CPC) exam, offered by AAPC, and the Correct Coding Specialist (CCS) exam and the Certified Coding Associate (CCA) exam, both offered by AHIMA.

The following sections give you a brief overview of the main certification exams. For more information about preparing for the exams, head to Chapter 9.

The CPC exam (AAPC)

To ensure that you can perform all the necessary job requirements out in the field, the CPC certification examination itself tests for strength in all areas, including the following:

- Anesthesia
- Systems of the body (head to Chapter 9 for information on these)
- Radiology
- Pathology and laboratory coding
- Medicine, including injections, psychotherapy, and other office procedures, in addition to heart catheterizations and more
- Evaluation and management service guidelines, including how to work with new patients, existing patients, consultations, and so on
- Diagnosis coding
- Medical terminology
- Healthcare Common Procedure Coding System (HCPCS) codes (which relate to implants, certain *biologicals* [drugs or vaccines], and other items used in patient care)
- Coding guidelines, including bundling and modifier use (which you can read about in Chapters 11 and 12)

A reputable study program prepares you for all these areas so that you can both pass the test and perform well on the job.

TIP

To prepare for the exam, take advantage of resources offered by AAPC. You can purchase CPC-specific study guides through the AAPC website (`www.aapc.com`). These study guides contain coding examples, give sample questions, and offer tips for taking the test. Practice tests designed to give you a look at actual test questions are also available to buy. The same people who made up the certification examinations prepare these simulated exams. So you're getting the inside scoop on what to expect in the testing room when you take the sample tests from AAPC. You can also sign up for an exam review class, sponsored by local AAPC chapters (you can find these online by state and locale).

Prerequisites and more

Lucky for you, you don't have to jump through a lot of prerequisite hoops before you sit down to take the CPC certification exam. In fact, AAPC doesn't have eligibility requirements to take its certification exam, period. The organization simply advises you to be academically prepared, but you aren't required to show proof that you completed a program. Don't interpret this to mean that you should just forgo your education and walk in the testing room without any prior knowledge, though. After all, you want to pass with flying colors!

REMEMBER

The level of prior experience you have when you take the exam affects the credential you earn. To earn the full CPC designation after passing the CPC examination, you must have experience in coding. If you don't already have experience, you are eligible for only the apprentice level certification, the CPC-A. For more on what CPC-A is and how to gain full CPC designation, refer to the earlier section "AAPC and its basic certifications: CPC, COC, CPC-P, CIC."

Test specs: Cost, format, and more

And now for the polite introductions. In this section, I cover the vital information you need to know about the test that you'll spend countless hours prepping for.

- **Cost:** You may want to start saving your pennies now. Exam costs and prerequisites continue to change. I recommend checking the AAPC website (`www.aapc.com/certification/cpc`) for current costs, prerequisites, and exam locations.
- **Number and types of questions:** The CPC examination consists of 150 multiple-choice questions.
- **Time:** You are allowed 5 hours, 40 minutes to complete the test.
- **Resources you can use during the test:** You are allowed to use approved coding manuals as long as the writing in them (that is, your chicken scratch in the margins) doesn't contain notes such as word definitions and specialty advice from coding resources, and no papers can be taped or pasted inside them. Not allowed in the room: electronic devices with an on/off switch (cellphones, smartphones, tablets, and so on) — failure to comply with this policy may result in disqualification of your exam.

REMEMBER

The books you can use during the test are current year and/or previous year CPT codebooks. (Although books from the previous calendar year are allowed, the questions are based on current books, so I advise you to use current manuals instead.) You can use only the standard or professional editions of the CPT codebooks published by the American Medical Association (AMA) — no other publisher is allowed. So when it comes to CPT codebooks in the testing room, it's AMA or the highway! You can also use officially published errata updates (which list errors in a book and furnish the appropriate revisions). As for ICD and HCPCS coding books, it's your call: These books don't have to be a particular edition or from a particular publisher.

The test proctors check the code books as you enter the test area. Be sure that you remove any nefarious notes before you get there. You don't want to get pinched for cheating just because you left in a note or two by accident.

- **ID:** You need a government-issued photo ID.
- **Receiving scores:** After you take the exam, the results are available online between five to seven days after the proctor receives them (go to your own member area at www.aapc.com). Hard copies of the scores are mailed within two weeks of receipt from the proctor. Unfortunately, you can't get your results by phone.

The CCS exam (AHIMA)

The CCS examination consists of multiple-choice and fill-in-the-blank questions that are based on medical terminology and coding examples and that include questions based on pharmacology (drugs and the conditions they're prescribed to treat). You prepare for this test in the same way you prepare for the CPC examination (refer to the earlier section).

Prerequisites and more

If you want to take the CCS examination, you must have a very basic paper in hand: your high school diploma or an equivalent, such as the general education diploma (GED). Beyond that, AHIMA recommends (but doesn't require) that you have a minimum of three years' experience in a hospital setting coding for multiple types of inpatient and outpatient cases.

AHIMA, much like AAPC, also recommends that you are proficient in anatomy, pharmacology, and the disease processes. You'll also want to have a demonstrated proficiency in abstracting pertinent data from patient records. Why? Well, the CCS is able to assign procedure codes and the supporting diagnosis codes. Because of that, healthcare providers rely on competent coders to report data that is used for reimbursement. Also, public health agencies and research organizations use data derived from your coding patterns to identify developing needs of the industry. So your coding has lasting effects that go well beyond reimbursement for the provider.

Test specs: Cost, format, and more

Here are the vital stats for the CCS:

- **Cost:** At the time of this writing, the cost for CCS examinations is $299 for AHIMA members and $399 for nonmembers — which is why it pays to be a member of AHIMA before you sign up for the CCS test. Who wants to turn down $100 savings right off the bat?

- **Number and types of questions:** The CCS exam consists of 97 multiple-choice questions that require you to choose the best response from four options. Next are eight clinical case scenarios each with two or three questions (one asking for principal diagnosis and the others asking for additional diagnosis and/or procedure codes), for a total of 22 questions associated with clinical cases. To help you out, screenshots of the CCS tests are available on the AHIMA website. (Bonus! Of the 97 multiple-choice questions, 18 are considered "pre-test" questions. The pre-test questions aren't counted in your score; they're used to assess the usability of the test itself. Think of these as questions that test the test!)

TIP

- **Time:** The test lasts 4 hours, with no breaks. So ease up on the coffee and be sure to make time for using the restroom *before* you go in the exam room!
- **Resources you can use during the test:** During the test, you can use approved books (listed on the AHIMA website: `www.ahima.org`), but you can't use any kind of coding software, so leave that at home. Other things not allowed: cellphones or other electronic devices, food or drinks, or purses.
- **ID:** To get into the test, you need two forms of signed identification, at least one of which has a picture of you. Examples of acceptable IDs include a valid driver's license, military ID, passport, Social Security card, credit or debit card, and so on. Go to the AHIMA website (`www.ahima.org`) for more information on acceptable forms of ID.
- **Receiving scores:** After you take the test, you have to wait until AHIMA releases your test results, and times may vary. You can contact AHIMA directly to get an approximate turnaround time. Contact information is available on the website.

If, for some reason, you don't do as well as you'd hoped, you have to wait at least 91 days before you can apply for a re-test. The re-test requires another test fee, and you have to go through the whole application process again.

The CCA exam (AHIMA)

As I note earlier, the CCA credential is a certification that shows you have demonstrated the ability to abstract the correct procedural and diagnosis codes in hospitals and physician practices. This credential indicates proficiency in all areas of coding, both hospital- and physician-based. Here's what you need to know:

- **Prerequisites:** To be eligible for this credential, you must have a high school diploma or equivalent. AHIMA also recommends that you have at least six months' experience working for a healthcare organization in a position that requires use of coding materials. If you don't have that experience, you must show that you've completed a formal training program instead. (An AHIMA-accredited program isn't required, but it does provide the most appropriate preparation for this examination.)

- **Cost:** At the time of this writing, the cost of the CCA exam is $199 for members and $299 for nonmembers.
- **Number and types of questions:** This exam has 100 multiple-choice questions, including ten non-scored pre-test questions. Test content includes demonstrating proficiency in the clinical classification systems, reimbursement methodologies (this category includes code sequencing and DRG assignment), health record content (is the record complete?), compliance (including ethics and thorough documentation), information technologies (use of software, including the infamous EHR), and confidentiality (HIPAA and patient privacy). To find out more about the CCA, go to the AHIMA website.

» **Mapping out your time commitment**

» **Weighing your education options**

» **Avoiding diploma mills**

Chapter 8

The Path to Certification: Finding a Study Program

After you familiarize yourself with the basic types of medical billing and coding certifications (the topic of Chapter 7), you're ready to choose the right educational path to help you reach your goals. The good news about becoming a medical coder? It has fewer educational requirements than other medical careers. So you don't have to spend decades preparing for your new career. Most billing and coding programs get you up and running in a relatively short amount of time, often less than two years; having a bachelor's or master's degree is only required for some of the upper level American Health Information Management Association (AHIMA) certifications. (Head to Chapter 10 for more about certifications that require college degrees.)

In this chapter, I explain the various educational paths open to you and highlight the things you need to know to choose the program that best suits your goals.

REMEMBER

The certificate issued by a training program is *not* certification; it is nothing but a piece of paper saying you went through a program. True certification can only be given by one of the credentialing organizations like the AAPC (American Academy of Professional Coders) or AHIMA.

The Big Picture: Thinking about Your Degree and Career Objectives

A famous proverb goes something like this: A journey of a thousand miles begins with a single step. True. But something needs to come before that first step; otherwise, you could end up going in circles or someplace you had no desire to be.

Before you begin your journey to a career as a medical biller and coder, you first need to think a bit about what you want to do.

Prioritizing your career needs

Although you can't predict the future, you can put some thought into your long-term career needs when you're thinking about the type of training program you want. The last thing you want is to get stuck in a program that prepares you for a certification exam that doesn't match up with how you want to spend the rest of your career. As you talk your way through this decision, consider these factors:

- Where you plan to seek employment (hospital, physician's office, and so on)
- The kind of job you want to do (whether you prefer the quiet work of a coder, the data entry routine of the biller or charge poster, or the daily interaction required of an accounts receivable representative)
- The type of certification potential prospective employers prefer
- The availability, quality, and cost of the training programs in your area

TIP

Where you want to work and what kind of job you want to do will probably carry the most weight in your decision-making process. After all, you want to make yourself the most marketable candidate for the jobs you want most. Try these tips for tracking the ins and outs of potential employers and, by extension, the certifications they require:

- Check with local employment recruiters and see what type of credentials their clients prefer.
- Take note of the credentials displayed in local medical offices that you visit.
- Look through the local job listings and see what kinds of certifications are mentioned in jobs that appeal to you.
- If you have your heart set on working for a particular company, find out what kind of coders it prefers.

Determining what kind of program better meets your needs

The type of certification(s) you want — AHIMA or AAPC, but there are others, too — may affect the type of education path you choose. Some schools cater to specific certification options, while others offer a more rounded education that focuses on the general knowledge you need to take most certification exams. So spend some time thinking about what kind of program can best prepare you for the career you want. Consider these examples:

- **AAPC certification** serves best those individuals who are interested in pursuing a career in physician-related coding and billing, and the AAPC certification test includes more coverage of Current Procedural Terminology (CPT) codes, the codes physician-based providers use when billing payers. As a result, AAPC programs cover more of the physician-specific codes than AHIMA programs do.
- **AHIMA credentials** are normally associated with hospital coding and billing. Its test includes more about International Classification of Diseases, Tenth Revision, Procedure Coding System (ICD-10-PCS) codes, which are used when billing hospital inpatient services. AHIMA programs put more emphasis on the ICD-10-PCS codes than AAPC programs do. (You can read more about ICD codes in Chapters 5 and 15.)

REMEMBER

Don't misinterpret the distinctions between AHIMA and AAPC programs to mean that an AAPC-certified coder wouldn't be able to find work in a hospital setting, or that an AHIMA-certified coder couldn't work in a physician's office. Just be aware that the initial learning curve on the job may be a little steeper because the certification test is not specifically focused on the area you find yourself in.

Either program focus you choose will get you off to a solid start, so go with your gut about what best fits your goals, schedule, and learning style. If the local community college program fits your budget and schedule and happens to focus on AHIMA educational needs, then you'll likely find yourself on the AHIMA-certification path. Similarly, if the local vocational school has a well-respected AAPC-based program, you may go down the path toward AAPC certification. Either way, a job is likely waiting for you at the end of the road!

REMEMBER

When you consider potential programs of study, keep in mind that solid medical coding and billing programs provide their students with the knowledge necessary to ace entry levels of certification. When you complete the coursework, the technical school or community college will issue you a certificate of completion. This certificate is not the same as *certification*. Although you will receive some sort of certificate or degree from your institution, you still have to take certification exams after you graduate.

Deciding whether you want to pursue a degree

The type of certificate or degree you earn depends entirely on the type of school you attend. Some of the community college programs offer associate's degree programs. Make sure the program you choose offers the degree you want to attain.

The degree or certificate you earn may not be as important to you as the certifications you want to master, but be mindful that getting an actual degree does have advantages:

- **It increases your earning potential.** Some employers provide better wage incentives to those with both a degree and certifications. Some employers may hire coders without any certification credentials at all, but the wage potential is greater for certified coders.
- **It increases your employment options.** The majority of billing companies are contractually obligated to employ only certified coders to perform client coding.

Considering the Time Commitment

Time is a factor in anything you do, and it's no different when choosing a course of study. I'm going to bet that, like most people, you don't have all the time in the world to study at your leisure and take years to complete a degree. Perhaps you are embarking on a second (or third or fourth) career. Perhaps you have children or a parent to care for. Maybe you have to go to school while working at another job. Any number of time-related factors can affect what program you choose to pursue.

Looking long term, you want to consider how long you can afford to be in school — whether that means attending classes at night while you hold down a day job or taking a year off work to devote yourself 100 percent to getting your degree and certification. In the short term, you need to decide how much time you actually have available to devote to studying.

In the following sections, I walk you through some considerations to keep in mind as you create your long-term plan of action and your short-term plan of daily study.

Planning for your time-to-degree

Although becoming certified in medical billing and coding requires only that you pass a five-hour exam, you can expect your training to take between one and two years. Then, following certification, you should plan on an additional two years of on-the-job training. The next sections have the details.

Allotting for time in the classroom

The amount of time you need to fully prepare for a billing and coding career depends upon your pre-existing knowledge of the field and the amount of education or training you need to prepare for a job. In general, the greater the educational or training requirements, the longer the program. If you're unfamiliar with computers or a bit rusty in your English and math skills, you may need additional classroom training to update your skill set in the basics. On the other hand, if you already work in a healthcare environment, you may find a program with less instruction in basic skill sets quite adequate.

TIP

Don't shortchange yourself just because you want to get through the program quickly. If one program doesn't offer training in all the skill sets you need to be successful, rule it out. Getting a little more training than you need is better than struggling because you lack the foundation necessary to process the class materials, and you'll be the better prepared candidate when the time comes to interview for jobs.

REMEMBER

The important thing is to find a program that meets your individual needs as well as your time constraints. Don't be afraid to ask questions of school admissions counselors whose job is to find students who best fit their program. These counselors can also help you determine whether the school fits your needs in terms of time-to-degree.

Allowing time for on-the-job training

Classroom instruction provides you with the tools of the trade, but on-the-job training teaches you how to use them. So remember to account for a year or two of this kind of training in your planning. The more experience you have in the healthcare industry prior to formal training, the shorter your post-program, on-the-job training period. For the novice with no healthcare experience, a minimum of one or two years of on-the-job training will likely be necessary.

On-the-job training is a great way to learn the nuances of billing and coding. Plus, you get paid to learn! Be sure to investigate programs that offer this as a post-grad option.

WARNING

Some employers are willing to hire novice coders, but doing so can be a disservice to the novice if no on-site mentor is available. Before you say yes to a job offer straight out of school, make sure you inquire about the type of mentoring and support you can expect.

Anticipating your day-to-day schedule

Most vocational school programs involve about 10 hours per week in the classroom. For every hour you spend in class, plan on at least 2 hours of study time. Grand total for this scenario? About 30 hours per week for class and study. But that's not all you need to consider as you think about your daily schedule. You also need to include time to commute and time for family and household responsibilities.

TIP

If you've not been in school for a while, let me offer you a refresher course in time management. Calculate approximately how many hours you need to spend on each of those activities, add them up, and then multiply that number by a factor of ten. That's how long accomplishing all these tasks each day will take. Okay, okay. I'm exaggerating. But the point is spot on: When you're in school, these tasks take longer than you anticipate. So from now on, make your mantra "Overestimate, overestimate, overestimate." Build in extra time for both study and all the other activities.

Here's some advice to help you maximize your time and stay sane in the process:

- **Dedicate ample time to study.** Regular study is essential for success. The number of hours you need depends on your current level of familiarity with the medical curriculum. If you are a registered nurse, then the only new material you'll encounter in a coding program will be the method of medical record abstraction (basically, which codes are where and how to choose them). If, on the other hand, the last time you read the word *patella* was in middle school, then mastering medical terminology and anatomy in addition to learning the methods used in coding books may require a bit more study. Plan for the scenario that's most appropriate to your situation.
- **Plan a time and place to study.** Pick a quiet time and place where you can concentrate on your work without distraction. Give your study time the same importance as your other daily tasks.
- **Take care of yourself.** Make time for ample rest and relaxation. A well-rested brain is a powerful brain. Staying up all night to study for the next day's test is counterproductive. I offer lots of study tactics in Chapter 9.

REMEMBER

If you have a plan and the tools to study efficiently, you'll be prepared for the job, not just the test(s) and subsequent certification exams.

First Things First: Squaring Away Your Prerequisites

Nearly every course of study has a list of prerequisites, things you need to know or skill sets you need to have, to be successful as an incoming student. In the case of medical billing and coding, you don't necessarily need to know all the ins and outs of the medical industry, but you do need to sharpen your basic building-block skills — reading, keyboarding, and arithmetic, in particular — if you want to take your career to the next level. These basic requirements promote success in the classroom and on the job.

Preparing for your training program

General prerequisites for medical billing and coding success are strong keyboarding skills and strong reading skills. You also need to know basic math skills.

Brushing up on reading and keyboarding skills

To process codes clearly and effectively, you must be able to read fairly quickly, and you must have good retention. You also need to enter data accurately with a keyboard. (In billing and coding, accuracy takes preference over speed.)

TIP

Want to be a faster reader? Use a ruler to help your eyes quickly skim down a page. Want to increase your typing speed? Try one of the free online typing tutorials to refresh your fingers.

Making the most of math

On the math side of the fence, you need to have a fairly solid proficiency in math because some positions require higher-level math skills. For example, you may have to compute reimbursements by using relative value units (RVUs) and then applying a conversion factor.

RVUs are numbers that represent the amount of work and cost involved in performing a procedure. They are based on three factors:

- The amount of physician work involved in the procedure
- The estimated cost to a practice in order to perform the procedure
- The malpractice insurance costs associated with the procedure

Because these costs can vary depending on the geographical location of the practice, the assigned RVU is adjusted based on where the procedure was performed. The logic behind this conversion factor is that the overhead is higher — and it therefore costs more to run an office — in a metropolitan area (New York City, for example) than it does in a rural area (like Grover City) so the reimbursement will be higher.

To perform the math skills you'll learn in your billing and coding program, you need to have a solid grasp of math basics down first — things like addition, subtraction, and multiplication, which are part of the daily coding and billing world. Also, a basic grasp of fractions and decimals is needed for choosing the correct Healthcare Common Procedure Coding System (HCPCS) codes for specified drugs or injectables. If you're unsure about your math-related bona fides, ask your program admissions counselor about recommendations for refresher math courses at the local community college.

Getting ready for the certification test

After you complete your training program, you're going to want to take your certification test(s). Some of these tests have prerequisites, too.

The major prerequisite for certification testing (which comes, ideally, after you complete a course of study) is a solid knowledge of medical terminology, anatomy, CPT codes, ICD-10 codes, and rules of reimbursement as well as a basic knowledge of compliance. As a medical biller and coder, your job is to make sure that the numbers are right when you submit them for reimbursement: the procedure code numbers, the diagnosis code numbers, the insurance policy numbers, the billing address, and every other number and letter that crosses your desk.

In addition to the preceding, other prerequisites may be necessary for AHIMA and AAPC certification. In the following sections, I explain what these prerequisites are. Before you register for these certification examinations, check out the organizations' websites — `www.ahima.org` and `www.aapc.com` — for more information about each organization's certification requirements.

Prerequisites for AHIMA certification tests

The most basic entry-level AHIMA certifications require that you have a high school diploma or equivalent before you can sit for the examinations. Other AHIMA certification levels require bachelor's degrees or higher to sit for the certification examinations.

TIP

Medical billing and coding training programs themselves have no enrollment requirements. You can enroll, for example, fresh out of high school, after years as a stay-at-home parent, or as a college graduate. But as I make clear in the preceding paragraph, the exams for some certification levels do have educational prerequisites. Therefore, before you enroll in a particular training program, make sure you understand the actual certification requirements that you'll encounter when you sign up for the certification tests.

Prerequisites for AAPC certification tests

AAPC certifications don't specify high school graduation or its equivalent as a prerequisite for certification eligibility, but they do recommend it. Similarly, to take exams for specialized certification levels, the AAPC recommends that you have experience in the area of specialization prior to applying for certification.

Picking a Program of Study

Certification may open the door to your new career, but you need to understand the workings of the industry to succeed in the billing and coding business. That's where your program of study comes in.

By attending classes and studying under professionals who know the ins and outs of the industry, you can have a competitive edge over job candidates who study independently for the certification tests.

REMEMBER

Wherever you choose to enroll, make sure the institution offers classes in, at minimum, anatomy, medical terminology, ICD-10-CM and ICD-10-PCS coding, CPT coding, and billing practices. These subjects represent the minimum you must know to pass a certification exam and get a job in billing and coding. Ideally, full programs also offer classes that explain the different types of insurance, describe how clearinghouses operate and what their function actually is, and introduce you to the types of coding and billing software that medical practices commonly use. Your best bet is to make a list of these subject areas and keep them close by when you're looking online at potential schools or speaking with school representatives.

The path to certification can be costly; it pays to research any and all programs before making a commitment. Whether you enroll at a community college, a vocational school, or an online program, you want to weigh the pros and cons carefully to decide what best fits your needs, goals, and lifestyle so that you can move on to the next big step — taking that certification exam.

In your backyard: Community college

Community college programs vary in cost and number of hours required for a certificate of completion.

A solid community college program includes instruction in medical terminology, anatomy, physiology, and diagnosis and procedure coding. A good program also includes instruction in medical billing programs in addition to an introduction to medical clearinghouse practices.

Some community college programs send you out the door with an associate's degree, which is a diploma that usually represents completion of a two-year course of study. Others offer certificates of completion, which indicate that you have successfully completed the program. Programs offered by community colleges have both pros and cons.

The advantages of a community college

Community college billing and coding programs give you credibility because they're known to offer programs with a solid and diverse course of study. The associate's degree or certificate of completion you receive has an air of authority that you may not get from a for-profit school. Following are some other benefits:

- **Commitment to its students:** A community college is invested in the success of its alumni and often offers post-graduate services such as job search support and alumni resources for networking. Also, community college programs have ample resources to assist potential students with planning a course of study.
- **Affordability:** Community college programs are based on the normal fees of the local college; an average program costs around $2,500. Financial aid is usually available in the form of grants, scholarships, or loans, and the interest rate on a student loan can be quite attractive.
- **Possible externship or internship opportunity:** Many local instructors work in the industry and have the resources to offer on-the-job training opportunities.

THE INS AND OUTS OF INTERNSHIPS AND EXTERNSHIPS

Internships (on-the-job training that takes place while you're in school) and externships (on-the-job training that takes place after you graduate) are generally a result of an agreement between local businesses and local community colleges or vocational schools. The availability of these positions serves as a selling point for the school and also provides local businesses with potential future employees (that's you!) who have been given the skill sets necessary to be an asset to the company.

Participating in an internship or externship has a number of benefits:

- **You get real on-the-job experience.** The necessary skills to become a medical coder and biller are learned in the classroom, but implementation of those skills happens on the job, and there's no substitute for job-related experience.
- **The exposure you receive during an internship can open the door to a paid position.** These positions often result in job offers just at a time when you're looking for a job (students serving in these positions are normally in the final steps of their respective programs or have recently completed them).
- **Internships and externships serve as an avenue to networking.** If you don't find employment with the current company, someone who has been working alongside you may very well know of an opening elsewhere or would be willing to serve as a professional reference in the future.

Many vocational schools have connections to the community and are able to assist with externships or internships. Check with your program's career counselors or individual instructors to find out about possible internships or externships.

Tip: Often instructors of the programs also work for the companies offering the internships, and the instructor's recommendation often results in the opportunity for the student. If you are interested in one of these opportunities, let your instructor (or advisor) know and then be the kind of student who gives the instructor the confidence to recommend you.

The disadvantages of community college programs

Community college programs have certain drawbacks:

» **Scheduling issues:** Community college programs are usually structured to coincide with the typical college semester or session term (usually an August start for fall term and a January start date for spring). In addition, individual classes are usually structured in a series of tiers, with tier-one classes being prerequisites for the tier-two classes and so on. If life intervenes and interrupts your participation in the scheduled classes, the interruption can result in a delay of a year, which is particularly a problem when the program participation is small, because the program cycles are less frequent.

Although you can't predict what happens in life, be sure your community college's term schedule fits with your overall lifestyle before you commit. Otherwise, you may find yourself treading water for a full year until you can take some required classes again.

- **Lack of flexibility:** As I explain in the preceding bullet, the community college curriculum is normally structured in class blocks that serve as prerequisites to the next class. The structure is such that the classes follow in order and may not offer much flexibility with regard to times and frequency. For the student already working, the lack of flexibility can be a major roadblock.
- **Having to purchase your own books:** Many community college programs use a book rental system for students, but in a coding program, you want to keep your books so that you can use them later to study for the certification exam. Unless the cost of materials is built into your tuition, you need to purchase your own books, which can get pretty expensive. Here's why: You need the coding books to take the certification exam, and the books change every year! If the year (and coding books) changes, you need to purchase more books. The exam schedule indicates which coding books should be used to find the right answers.

  Note: Procedure codes that are found in the CPT codebook are added and deleted annually, and the ICD-10 coding books add new diagnosis and procedure codes every year. So someone — either you or your employer — will need to buy new books annually. Although there are online versions available, nothing replaces the printed book for the seasoned coder.

If you use an older book (say, one you buy from an online reseller) while you're in school or to take your certification exam, it may not do much damage. But in the actual work of coding, numbers are everything. After you begin your job, you absolutely must use the right book.

Vocation station: Technical school programs

Vocational schools offer an alternative to the community college route. Some of these programs offer excellent training. In the following sections, I go over some of the most common pros and cons of technical school programs.

TRAINING THE TRAINERS

Your first priority right now is making sure you get the training that will best prepare you for the certification exam. But don't forget that the people who train you have to be trained as well.

AAPC offers a Certified Professional Coding Instructor (CPC-I) certification, for those who successfully complete the Professional Medical Coding Curriculum (PMCC) training. Individuals who hold this certification have received additional instruction above and beyond what you ultimately get, have taken a specialized teaching exam, and must have passed the certification tests they teach. These individuals are also specially licensed by the AAPC. To be eligible to take the preparation course for the exam, potential CPC-Is must be members in good standing of AAPC and have a minimum of five years of coding experience.

The preparation course itself includes instruction in understanding the process of teaching adults. The PMCC instructor must also demonstrate a thorough knowledge of coding disciplines and their practical applications. The PMCC certification examination includes a written portion in addition to a 15-minute presentation, which is evaluated by the student's peers.

After having earned the CPC-I certification, the instructor may teach accredited courses, either as an employee of a teaching institution or by offering individual instruction. So as you investigate potential training programs, be sure to sniff out who the CPC-Is are in the school and make sure they're part of the staff.

The pros of a technical school

Attending a vocational or technical school program offers certain advantages:

» **The programs are usually more subject specific and take less time to complete.** The more specialized vocational programs usually focus on subject matter that is directly related to the program, such as medical terminology, anatomy, how to use coding materials, understanding insurance, and an introduction of various coding and billing software programs. They also tend to cycle more often (that is, the programs are offered more frequently), which eliminates a longer waiting time to begin a program.

REMEMBER

Although the abbreviated course schedule means less time from enrollment to certificate of completion, don't assume that it means less commitment to study. If the program is complete but shorter, you have less time to learn the material because you're covering the same amount in a shorter time frame, which may translate to a greater need for out-of-class study time.

- **The specialized curriculum makes for smaller classes and promotes more interaction with the instructors.** This is a bonus for you as a student. More face time equals more personal instruction.
- **Vocational and technical schools often have lower out-of-pocket costs.** Many vocational programs include coding materials with the cost of tuition, and many AAPC programs also include a student membership and the certification examination fee. This represents a significant out-of-pocket savings (at the time of this writing, the cost of a typical certification exam is $260 to $350 for students with student memberships — and the books at a bundled price are about $160). A student membership is offered at a discount to individuals enrolled in an AAPC-accredited program. Yes, you're still paying for these items through tuition payments, but it tends to hurt less when it's all rolled into one payment.

  Note: Having lower out-of-pocket expenses doesn't necessarily mean that these programs are less expensive. In fact, they may be more expensive. The next section has the details.

The cons of technical schools

Following are the disadvantages of vocational or technical school programs:

- **Vocational school programs often are more costly.** Unlike community colleges, vocational schools are purely self-supporting and for-profit institutions. Programs may cost closer to $10,000 (this cost usually includes material costs and the fees to sit for a certification examination).

  TIP

  Make sure exam fees are included in your tuition and that, at the end of the program, you can take the certification exam as an inclusive part of your paid program. (A major marketing tactic these programs use is to boast that 90 percent of their graduates receive certification upon completion, which is one reason the cost of the exam is rolled into the tuition. The thinking is that students are more likely to study for and take an exam that they've already paid for.)

WARNING

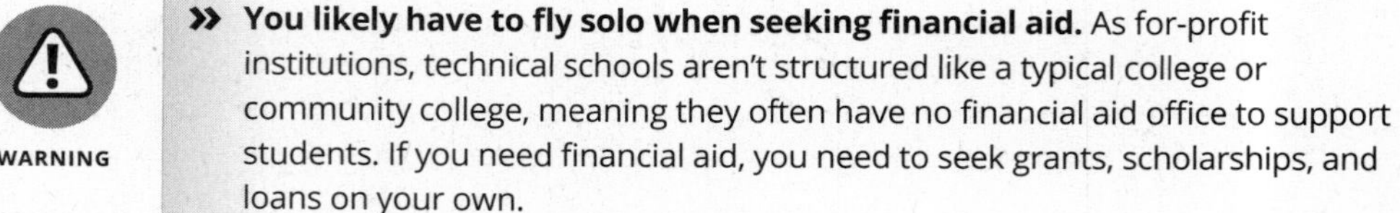

- **You likely have to fly solo when seeking financial aid.** As for-profit institutions, technical schools aren't structured like a typical college or community college, meaning they often have no financial aid office to support students. If you need financial aid, you need to seek grants, scholarships, and loans on your own.
- **They may not be accredited.** Unfortunately, as the field of medical coding and billing rapidly grows, so do the number of scams and diploma mills. The onus is on you to seek out accredited programs that require study in the necessary topics. To find out how to tell good programs from bad, head to the section, "Caveat Emptor: Watching Out for Diploma Mills" later in this chapter.

Clicking the mouse: Online training

You can prepare for a career in medical coding and billing through an online program. If you're self-motivated or if you're already working in the medical field, online training may be just what you need. Like the community college and vocational school programs, online study has advantages and disadvantages, which I explain in the following sections.

REMEMBER

Online education is no substitute for student-instructor interaction, but it is a good alternative for people who already have a billing and coding knowledge base and want to go it alone.

Benefits of online programs

Here are the advantages that an online program has to offer:

- **Scheduling flexibility:** The biggest advantage online study provides is flexibility. With online studies, you attend classes at your own convenience. A quality online study program sets deadlines for completing the classwork, but it's up to you to work it around your schedule. You decide when to log in for class, be it noon or midnight. You just log in and go, which is a great benefit if you have a full-time job, kids, or other responsibilities that don't allow you to participate in a typical day-to-day class schedule.
- **Access to programs regardless of your location:** Online programs are not geographically restrictive. You don't have to live in an urban area to enroll in a training program. You can live on the North Pole and attend class via an online portal. Having access to any online program is especially beneficial if you live in a rural area or don't have reliable transportation to a college campus.
- **Less costly:** Online programs tend to be less costly than community college or vocational programs due, in part, to the fact that the school has less overhead. Fewer needs for physical facilities, resources, and higher faculty salaries help lower the costs for online programs. Plus, many online programs are a cog in the wheel of a larger bricks-and-mortar institution, so on-campus or commuter student tuition already covers much of the overhead, allowing for lower costs for online participants.

MAKING THE MOST OF THE WEB FOR AAPC AND AHIMA COURSES

The AAPC offers an online bundle for both Certified Professional Coder (CPC) or Certified Outpatient Coder (COC) courses of study (see Chapter 7 for specifics on these certifications). The bundle includes the following:

- An online preparation course that teaches necessary coding skills for the specified area (CPC or COC) and prepares the student for the certification examination. The course is designed to be completed in four months or less.
- Course-related materials, including a textbook and accompanying workbook. *Note:* These are not coding books; you must purchase those separately.
- Up to three practice examinations.
- The cost of taking the certification examination. You must take it within one year of enrolling in the course.

You can find out more about this bundle training at www.aapc.com.

AAPC also now offers an exam to be a Certified Physician Practice Manager (CPPM). The CPPM credential is intended for someone who wants to oversee the business end of the physician's practice. Some practices are quite large, and a lot of money moves through them; all practices need to have someone in charge who is keeping abreast of regulations that affect the healthcare industry. These individuals manage the revenue cycle, the human capital — employees, and all the nuances associated with daily operation, including HIPAA and vigilance over data security. As of this writing, the exam costs $350 and consists of 200 multiple-choice questions; you can't use any reference materials. This test is all about what you know, not what you know how to look up.

AAPC suggests that applicants have a minimum of an associate's degree, and it requires they have current AAPC membership before applying to take the exam. You must get 36 continuing education units (CEUs) every two years to maintain certification.

AHIMA also offers an online training program, called the Coding Basics Program. This 12-course program is broken down into clusters that are made up of specific courses. The program is more in-depth than other online programs and is structured closely to instructor-led classrooms. To enroll in the online program, you must meet one of these prerequisites: proof of a C grade or better in a college-level basic human anatomy and physiology course, or completion of AHIMA's qualifying course. You can find more information about the program on the AHIMA website at www.ahima.org.

Although a novice is eligible to enroll in either of these programs, the programs are really a better choice for individuals who are already familiar with healthcare.

Drawbacks of online programs

Although saving big bucks and going to class in your jammies are real boons, online programs have some obvious drawbacks:

- **You have limited access to educational support.** Online students must be able to work independently and without the structure provided by a traditional classroom. With online instruction, you have less student-teacher interaction. If you're working at 3 a.m. and have a question, for example, an instructor is probably not going to be available for a discussion. Although you may be able to communicate with your instructor via message boards or email, you'll still need to wait for an answer before you can proceed with your assignment.

  REMEMBER

  Mastering the art of self-directed learning can be a challenge for some. It can be especially frustrating for a student who is unfamiliar with the healthcare industry. Online instruction is probably a better choice for a student who is already working in healthcare. Access to a mentor is an asset that isn't always included with online tuition.

- **You need to be technically savvy.** Online students need to be able to correct the myriad issues that arise when working online. Let's face it: How many times do you forget to hit "Save"? To succeed online, you need to know your hardware, your software, and the quirks that go along with them. If locating the Power button is the extent of your technical knowledge, you may want to steer clear of the online option.

  WARNING

- **Online programs have a higher incidence of being scam operations.** Do not enroll in an online program that is not accredited by either AAPC or AHIMA. The same organizations that lend credibility to vocational programs also have tools that allow you to verify the credibility of online programs, and the same organization accreditation standards apply to online programs as classroom training.

  REMEMBER

  Quality online programs offer the same curriculum as any accredited programs. They also allow students to communicate directly with the instructor, either through live chat sessions or e-mail. Although the communication isn't face-to-face, the level of accessibility with your instructor should be the same as it would be in a typical classroom setting. For more things to look at when investigating the credibility of a program, head to the later section, "Caveat Emptor: Watching Out for Diploma Mills."

- **You have less opportunity to network with other students and faculty.** Don't care about the social aspect? Think about this: Who would you be more likely to recommend: your online classmate or the person sitting in the next desk?

TIP

If you enroll in an online program, locate the local professional chapter of the credentialing organization you want to join and start attending the meetings. Doing so is a great way to add the networking component that online programs lack. You can locate local chapters through the national organization websites or by calling AAPC (800-626-CODE [2633]) or AHIMA (312-233-1100).

- **Materials necessary to complete the program can be costly.** Online programs usually require that you purchase coding books just like community college programs do, so the costs can add up. Unfortunately, you can't get coding books in many places, and the only discounts you can get are by purchasing bundles; see the sidebar, "Making the most of the web for AAPC and AHIMA courses" earlier in this chapter for details.
- **Certification exam costs are not included in the program cost.** Certification exams can be costly (refer to Chapter 7), and as I explain earlier, you need the most current materials when you take the tests. Unlike programs offered at vocational schools, the cost of the exam probably won't be included with your online tuition. So be prepared to pony up the costs after you get through your online program.

Caveat Emptor: Watching Out for Diploma Mills

One of the biggest drawbacks to the increasing need for billers and coders is the rise of programs that are nothing but diploma mills. These unscrupulous companies take your money and leave you with a piece of paper but no true marketability. Here are some clues that the program isn't a good one:

- Their ads claim that, in just a few weeks' time, you'll be operating your own business out of your home, and clients will be beating down your door. Reputable medical billing and coding programs may tout some of the ways you can use a degree, but they don't make big promises about riches and fame.
- They promise that you can get certification of completion with a minimal amount of study or classwork. Quality programs — whether college, vocational, or online — require both classroom time and self-study time. In addition, the material covered is similar across the board and includes instruction in anatomy, medical terminology, coding, insurance rules for both Medicare and commercial insurers, and billing software programs.

TIP

How do you tell a credible program from ones that are just scams? Start by checking with AHIMA and AAPC. Both organizations' websites list accredited training programs, those that offer the correct curriculum, have instructors certified to teach, and use a curriculum that follows the guidelines established by the organization. For more on each organization's accreditation criteria, go to their websites: AHIMA (www.ahima.org) and AAPC (www.aapc.com). Both organizations also have search tools that assist in finding certified training programs. These groups can recommend a program that fits your needs without taking you to the bank.

If you're researching schools on your own, get answers to these questions:

- How long has the school been in business?
- Is the school accredited?
- How many students are in each class, and what is the student-to-teacher ratio?
- Can you reach the instructor outside of class?
- If the curriculum does not suit you, what is the refund policy?
- Does the school have a placement department to help graduates find jobs?
- What is the program's placement rate for graduates?
- What are the credentials of the instructors, and what is the ratio of full-time versus adjunct instructors?

You can also ask to see the school's business license. In addition, legitimate schools have financial aid advisors to assist prospective students with finding a way to finance their training. Ideally, the financial aid pays for books and supplies. Some grants even pay for room and board. These financial aid packages are the same ones that community college and four-year-college students are given.

WARNING

If the school representative seems less than truthful or tries to convince you that, after six weeks, students are suddenly inundated with job offers, walk away. If the representative tells you that completion of the program prepares students to open a home office and start a business, *run* away. These are all signs of diploma mills. Another indication that the school is a possible scam is that it has changed its name several times or has moved from state to state.

Bottom line: If it smells fishy or sounds too good to be true, it is.

» Sharpening your focus on specific topics

» Reviewing ways to relieve pre-test jitters

» Registering for the exam

Chapter 9

Signing Up and Preparing for the Certification Exam

The time to rock that certification exam is near! You've taken the classes (if you haven't, Chapter 8 helps you find a study program), and you've determined the type of exam you want to take (see Chapter 7 for a breakdown of different tests). Now, the only task left for you to do is study, study, and study some more before you sign up for that exam and ace it.

In this chapter, I provide all sorts of advice to help you make the most of your study time and stay sane while you do it. I also tell you what you need to know to sign up for the exam(s).

Establishing a Study Routine and Strategy

The saying "Work smarter, not harder" truly applies to certification exam study techniques. To do well, you need to comprehend a lot of material, so much so, in fact, that you'll be better off if you prioritize what you need to study and when.

Your success in a medical and billing program depends on your ability to learn new material quickly and efficiently.

Everyone has his or her individual style of studying, but certain techniques have proven to be effective. One of the best ways to increase retention, for example, is to do the assigned reading, listen as the material is discussed, and then make notes that translate the material into your own words.

TIP

Understanding what kind of learner you are is helpful, too. Are you a visual learner, someone who remembers what she sees? Or are you an auditory learner, remembering what you hear? Maybe you learn best when you can associate movement with concepts. Whatever your learning style, practice retention exercises in a way that best suits you. Whether you use flashcards, podcasts, videos, or write out your own study notes, go with what works for you.

Before you dig into those books, though, you've got to carve out some space, both physically and mentally, and you have to make time, which I discuss in the next sections. After all, your success is directly related to the advance planning you do and the amount of work and energy you invest in your studies.

Setting up your own space

Efficient study requires concentration, so you need to set aside a space to do just that, even if all you can find in your house is a quiet corner of the living room. Here are some pointers:

- **Choose an area that works for you.** If you're like many people who believe that they study better and retain more if they simulate a classroom environment, choose an area that lets you sit at a desk or table in a firm chair. If you're more likely to curl up in a chair to study, make sure the chair isn't so comfortable that you fall asleep.
- **Select an area that's free of distractions.** When you're preparing to take a test, you want all your senses directed toward the thinking process.

  WARNING

  Some people find background music helpful when they study, but that doesn't mean playing music that makes you want to sing along. As soon as you start to sing along — or even become aware of the music — you're distracted and not putting all your attention on your studies.
- **Set up the study area with the necessary supplies.** You should have paper, pencils, highlighters, ruler, and a trash can nearby so that you don't have to go hunting for these things when you need them.
- **As often as time allows, study in your designated study area.** By using a familiar environment to study and then test, you can recall material more easily.

Clearing your calendar for study

As you progress through the program on your way to the big exam, keep track of important dates. Most course schedules indicate the dates on which topics are to be introduced and when the big certification test is scheduled. With this information, you can rearrange your schedule to avoid conflicts with other activities and set aside the time necessary to study.

WARNING

Last-minute cram sessions make life stressful and don't help you learn the material. In addition, memorizing material just to pass a test isn't in your best interest. To bill and code correctly on the job, you need to know all the material they teach you. It's not like you can forget anatomy or diagnosis codes when the test is over. Every course taught in a coding program and everything covered in the certification test is essential to the revenue cycle process.

REMEMBER

To be a successful biller and coder, you must understand the body, the disease process, and illness and injury, all of which require a foundation in human anatomy and physiology. Without this foundational knowledge, the medical terminology is nothing more than random words. You may be able to link key words to the correct procedural and diagnosis codes, but when you have to fully decipher an operative report and abstract all reportable procedures, you'll be in trouble. So in your long-term test-prep planning and calendar clearing, allow ample time for the proper instruction.

Developing a study strategy

When you finally score some dedicated space in your house and time on your calendar, you can sit down and start studying. But, you say, "Where do I start? There is *so much* information!" True, you do need to know a lot (I give you a brief overview of the key topics in the next section, "Focusing on the Right Topics"). Here, I list some helpful study techniques and strategies that can help you retain important information:

- **Focus on the key ideas and concepts.** How do you know what these are? Simply look over the review exercises at the end of a chapter or section before you begin reading. By looking at the review questions first, you'll be more focused on the main ideas of the assignment as you read.

TIP

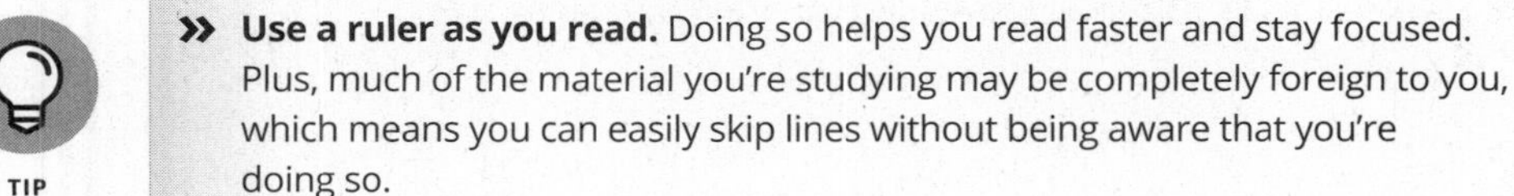

- **Use a ruler as you read.** Doing so helps you read faster and stay focused. Plus, much of the material you're studying may be completely foreign to you, which means you can easily skip lines without being aware that you're doing so.
- **Rewrite the key ideas in your own words.** If you understand the topic enough that you can explain it in your own words, you're good to go.

» **Mark up your books.** When you come to something important in the text, use a highlighter to make it stand out. Write notes in the margins to serve as reminders.

TIP

Anatomy books are full of diagrams and illustrations. Pay special attention to how these relate to the text, and make any notes that can help you remember.

WARNING

Although you can and should make notes in your coding books, keep in mind that books you use on your certification examinations can't have definitions or notes that supplement other parts of the examination. The exam proctor may not let you use it if there are or seem to be cheat notes. For example, when you're taking the medical terminology portion of the exam, your notes in the CPT or ICD books shouldn't have terminology definitions. However, after the test, feel free to mark away!

» **Regularly review topics you studied previously.** If you don't have much time to devote to studying on a particular day, use what time you do have for review of past lessons. If you mark up your textbook as I suggest in the preceding bullet item, you don't need to reread the old chapters entirely; you can hit the highlights, literally!

Focusing on the Right Topics

To learn everything you need to know in the time you have available, you need to focus your study. Otherwise, you'll be the academic equivalent of a chicken with its head cut off, just running around all crazy-like.

The good news is that the certification test you take pretty much determines the information you need to know. Beyond that, all certification examinations assess competency in all areas of health information. You can be sure that your training program (see Chapter 8) is going to prepare you for questions covering many of the primary billing and coding subject areas, such as

» Medical terminology

» Human body systems, their structure, and their normal function

» Disease process and various treatments

Identifying body systems

The majority of medical billing and coding training programs begin with basic human anatomy and physiology, more commonly referred to as *body systems.* You need to understand how each organ within a particular body system works, how disease or illness affects the system, and why the treatment was necessary.

Most textbooks contain diagrams specific to each body system. These diagrams show the organs within each system and describe the function of each organ as it relates to the individual system. In addition, you'll see illustrations showing cells, tissues, and several different types of disease processes. As you read the text, closely study the illustrations. Doing so not only clarifies the general concepts, but it also reinforces the information. The human body has ten systems, each of which is made up of specialized organs that must work together for the human body to function properly and efficiently. When one system is affected by illness, all the other systems are affected in some way. I give you a quick introduction to the systems of the human body in the following sections.

A solid foundation in human anatomy and physiology is a huge asset when taking the certification examination. In fact, it's a prerequisite for most American Health Information Management Association (AHIMA)–accredited programs and is suggested (but not required) for AAPC (American Academy of Professional Coders) programs. But knowing human anatomy and physiology is important for more than just passing the test. Without a thorough understanding in anatomy, you'll have a difficult time locating the correct procedural codes. After all, you need to know which part of the body is being treated so you can apply the proper codes.

The circulatory system

The circulatory system transports nutrients and gasses to all cells of the body. There are two parts of this system:

- **The cardiovascular system** is composed of the heart, blood vessels, and blood (see Figure 9-1).
- **The lymphatic system** is made up of the lymph nodes, *lymphatic vessels* (which carry the lymph fluid), the *thymus* (the gland that helps produce T-cells, which are a type of white blood cell), and the spleen, as well as other parts (see Figure 9-2).

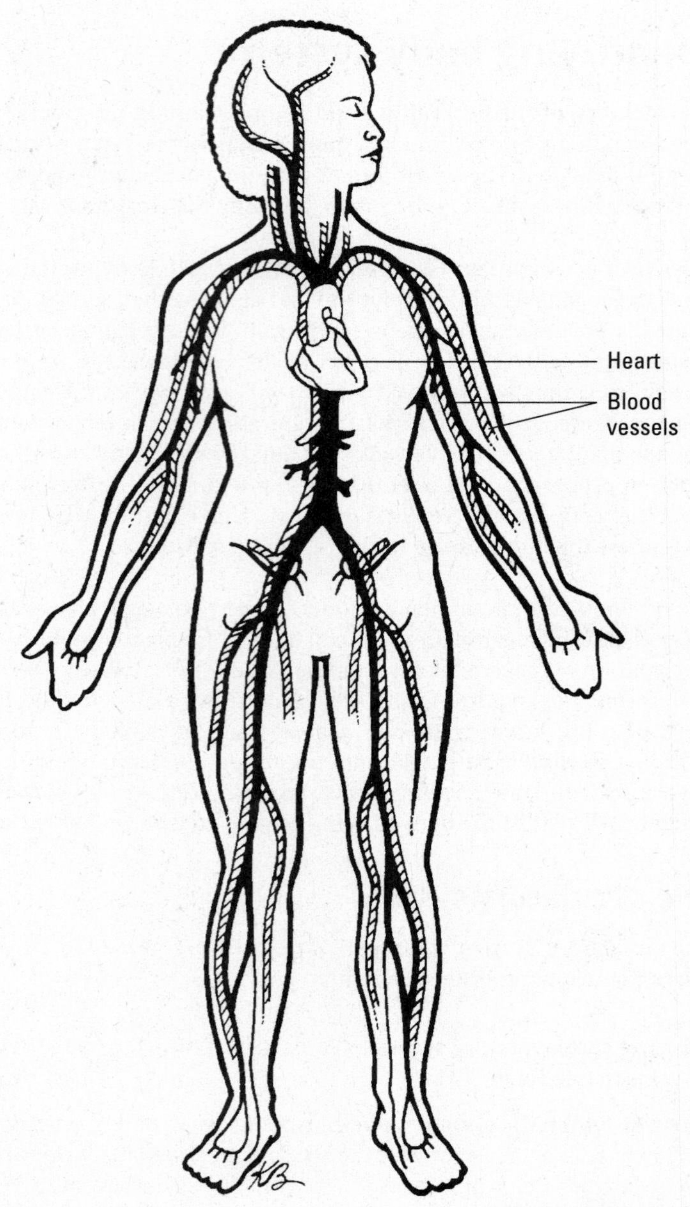

Illustration by Kathryn Born, MA

FIGURE 9-1: The cardiovascular system, the heart of the circulatory system.

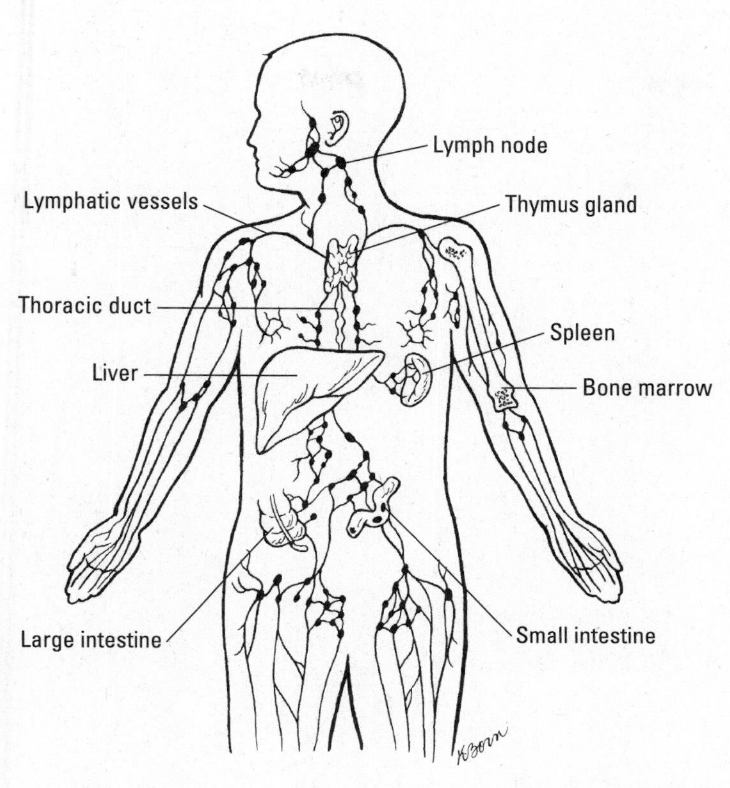

FIGURE 9-2: The lymphatic system, another part of the circulatory system.

Illustration by Kathryn Born, MA

The digestive system

The digestive system, shown in Figure 9-3, converts food into nutrients that the body can use (or *metabolize*). The primary organs of this system are the mouth, stomach, intestines (small and large), and the rectum. The system's accessory organs (organs that assist the system in performing its function) are the teeth, tongue, liver, and pancreas.

The endocrine system

The endocrine system maintains growth and *homeostasis* (a fancy way of saying the body's "status quo"). It is made up of the pituitary gland, *pineal gland* (the gland that secretes melatonin, the hormone that regulates the sleep-wake cycle), thyroid gland, hypothalamus, adrenal glands, and ovaries in the female and testes in the male, as well as some other parts. Figure 9-4 shows the endocrine system.

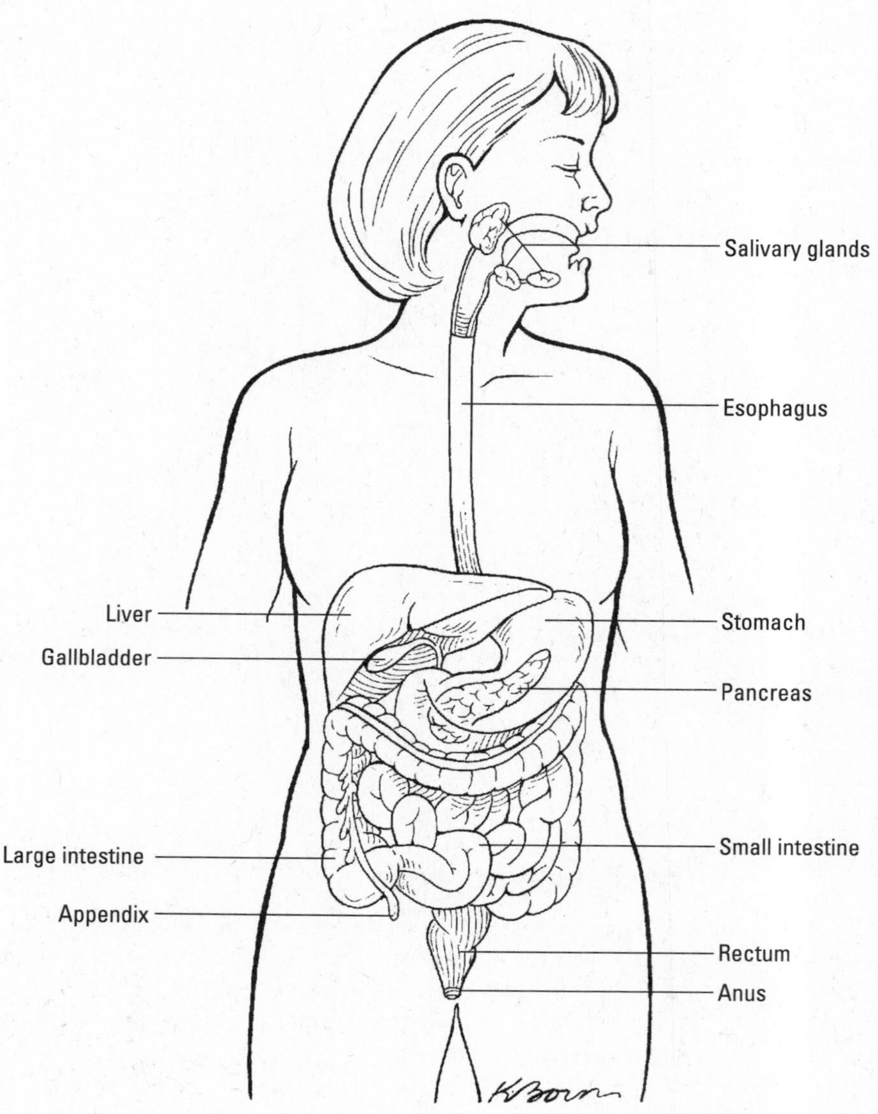

FIGURE 9-3: The digestive system.

Illustration by Kathryn Born, MA

The integumentary system

The integumentary system protects the internal organs from damage, protects the body from dehydration, and stores fat. It is made of skin, hair, nails, and sweat glands.

The musculoskeletal system

The musculoskeletal system is made up of two systems: the skeletal system and the muscular system.

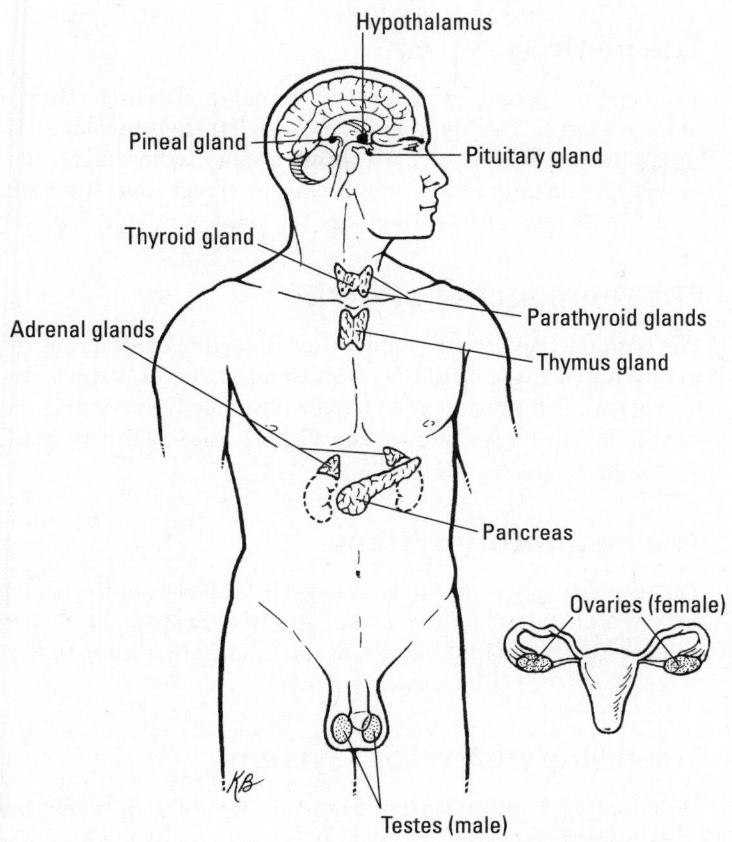

FIGURE 9-4: The endocrine system.

Illustration by Kathryn Born, MA

The skeletal system protects the body and gives it its shape and form. It's made up of bones, joints, *ligaments* (fibers that connect bones to other bones), *tendons* (fibers that connect muscles to bones), and cartilage. The muscular system is made up of — you guessed it — muscles, tendons, ligaments, and cartilage. It enables the body to move. The muscular system has three kinds of muscles:

- **Cardiac muscle:** This is the heart muscle.
- **Smooth, or *involuntary,* muscles:** These muscles make up several internal organs. They're called involuntary muscles because we don't control their movements (the movement of the intestinal walls, for example).
- **Skeletal, or *voluntary,* muscles:** These muscles allow us to move. They're called voluntary muscles because we control them.

The nervous system

The nervous system monitors the internal (body temperature, pulse rate, and so on) and external (sights, sounds, and smells) environment and sends messages to the individual organs or systems to respond accordingly. It is made up of the brain, spinal cord, and nerves. Messages travel from the brain down the spinal cord to nerve receptors throughout the body.

The reproductive system

The reproductive system enables the production of offspring. The male reproductive system is made up of the testes, scrotum, penis, *vas deferens* (the passage way for sperm), and prostate. The female reproductive system is made up of the ovaries, fallopian tubes, uterus, and vagina. The mammary glands are considered accessory organs.

The respiratory system

The respiratory system provides oxygen to all cells of the body by performing gas exchanges between air and blood gases. It is made up of the nose, trachea, lungs, and *bronchi* (the main passages of the trachea that leads to the lungs), as well as other parts (see Figure 9-5).

The urinary/excretory system

The urinary/excretory system, shown in Figure 9-6, removes wastes and maintains water balance in the body. It is made up of the kidneys, urinary bladder, *urethra* (the passage from the bladder that transports urine outside of the body), and *ureters* (the passages from the kidneys to the bladder).

Understanding medical terminology

The coding certification examination is an assessment of your readiness to be a medical coder. All the components of the certification program are targeted toward this exam. Your knowledge of medical terminology is part of the assessment, as well as an integral part of understanding all the other things you need to know, both to pass the exam and to succeed on the job. Remember, the AAPC exam contains a specific section on medical terminology. The AHIMA exams are a little different, but they still require a solid understanding of the terminology used in the healthcare profession.

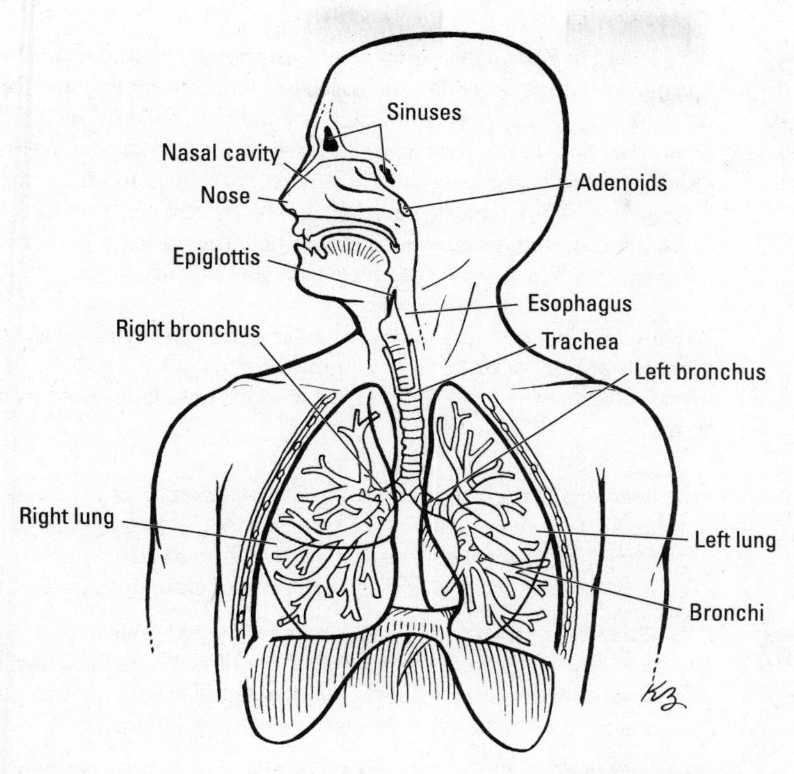

FIGURE 9-5: The respiratory system.

Illustration by Kathryn Born, MA

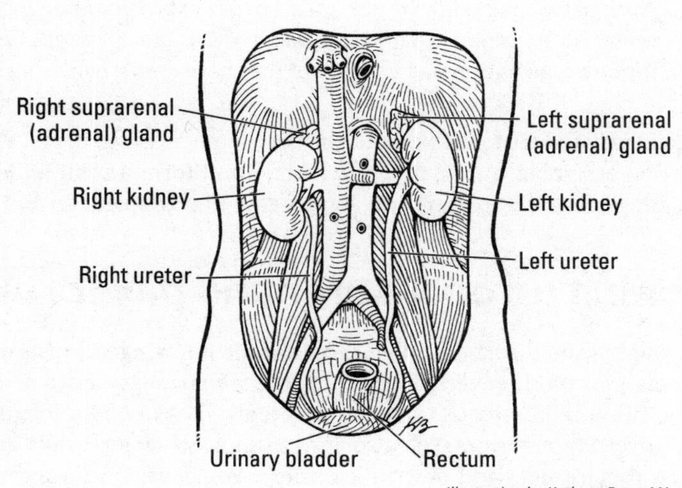

FIGURE 9-6: The urinary/excretory system.

Illustration by Kathryn Born, MA

REMEMBER

Why is a firm knowledge of medical terminology so important? Why not just look up the words you need? Because doing so will take you about five times as long to do your job. Before you can assign a diagnosis code to an illness or injury, you need to be able to identify it in the medical record. Physicians are trained to provide diagnosis verbiage in all patient records. Your job is to abstract the correct diagnosis and procedural codes by translating the verbiage in the medical record. Knowing the prefixes and suffixes and how they work together will clue you in to what you need to know to properly code a procedure.

When you study the terminology, pay attention to the prefixes and suffixes, most of which are Greek or Latin in origin. Here's a quick heads-up on what you need to pay attention to (see Chapter 5 for more details on how to decipher medical terms):

- **Prefixes:** The prefix, or beginning part of a word, gets you started with understanding what is going on. It normally tells you where in the body something was done. If the first part of the word, for example, is *nephro-,* which means "kidney," you know that the relevant body part is the kidney.

  REMEMBER

  When billing and coding, you want the diagnosis prefixes and the procedural prefixes to match up. For example, if the record were to contain the word *tarsal* and then switch to *carpal,* you'd want to investigate, because *carpal* means "hand" and *tarsal* means "foot." Big, big difference.
- **Suffixes:** The suffix, the ending part of a term, usually indicates what was done or how it was done. There are fewer suffixes than prefixes, but they are essential when identifying the correct codes to be submitted for reimbursement. For example, *-ectomy* (surgical removal), *-otomy* (surgical cutting), and *-ostomy* (opening) are all similar, but they have entirely different meanings.

TIP

A good way to learn prefixes and suffixes is to use index cards. With this method, you can assemble words, mix and match, and form a solid understanding of the meaning of each word part and, eventually, the complete term.

Boning up on insurer and payer rules

Although a small part of coding certification, knowing the insurer and payer rules is a big part of biller certification. In that arena, you want to be familiar with the basic filing requirements and the different types of claim forms for commercial and government payers. You also need to know when modifiers are necessary (and when they're not) and how to use them. For general information on when and how to use modifiers correctly, head to Chapter 12. Payer-specific filing requirements are usually found in the contract or may be found in the payer's policies (located on the payer's website).

Preparing Yourself for Test Day

Even if you know what topics to expect on the exam, have adopted all my study suggestions, and have practiced, gone over, and reviewed all your notes and books, a couple things may still trip you up when the time comes to actually take your certification exams. Those things? Stress (your mind doesn't work so well when it's frozen in panic) and improper notes in your coding books (which means you can't use the book you've been counting on during your exam). In the next sections, I tell you how to avoid either scenario.

Finding ways to stress less

If you are one of those people who suffers from test anxiety, in the following sections, I share some test-taking strategies that may help you feel less stress.

Doing one last review of coursework

If you take the advice I give earlier in this chapter and budget your time so that you have sufficient time to study, you're already ahead of the game. When exam time approaches, do the following:

- Ask your instructor to specify the areas that will be emphasized on the test. Focus on these areas during your final review.
- Review any material from practice tests, workbook exercises, sample coding exercises, review material, the textbook, and class notes.
- Make sure you're familiar with the way the sections are arranged in your International Classification of Diseases, Tenth Revision (ICD-10) and Current Procedural Terminology (CPT) codebooks.

  The materials you've been using to practice your coding skills — the ICD-10 and CPT books — are the same materials you use for the certification examination. So make sure you're familiar with how and where to look for the information you need. You can find more on this topic in the section "Knowing how to use your resources." The books come with tabs that you can personalize; however, once you have some experience, it is unlikely you will need them.
- Review your practice tests results and make sure you understand any errors you made. Taking as many practice tests, preferably timed ones, is an important and extremely helpful step in preparation for the actual test. Remember: Each test you take helps prepare for the next. For more on where to get practice tests, head to the section "Signing Up for and Taking the Big Test."

Mastering tricks to avoid — or reduce — stress

Here are a few things you can do to stay as stress-free as possible:

- Make a list of materials you need — everything from pencils to codebooks — and get these things ready the night before so that you don't have to rush around searching for them the day of the exam.
- Bring ID. You need two forms of ID; both AHIMA's and AAPC's websites list acceptable forms of identification. Don't forget them!
- Wear comfortable clothing and arrive early for the examination.
- Keep a positive mindset that you're going to do your best.
- Don't pay too much attention to the other test-takers. Stress can be contagious.

Knowing how to use your resources

As the test time nears, look through your ICD-10 and CPT books. Make sure you're familiar with all the sections and highlight the areas you want to focus on. If you prefer, you can put identifying tabs on the book to help remember different sections. (*Note:* Professionals don't tab their books. Books with tabs imply a lack of experience and familiarity with the material. Tabs are fine for the test, but remove them after you clear that hurdle.)

Here's how to use these resources effectively:

1. **Look up the documented disease, injury, or condition in the ICD-10-CM codebook and then refer to the tabular list to ensure completeness of the diagnosis code.**

   The ICD-10-CM codebook contains all the diagnosis codes, broken down by disease or injury type. The front of the book contains the alphabetical index as well as coding guidelines in the front of the book that are specific to each section (for example, documentation for sepsis, seventh-character specificity for injuries, and so on). These guidelines are important; they are not just there for reference (although they are to be used as such).

   Make sure you don't leave off a specificity digit. The ICD-10-CM codebook guides you to the correct diagnosis code, but it may not provide the complete diagnosis code. Don't try to save time and code from the alphabetic index. Always code from the Tabular List.

2. **After you have the diagnosis code, refer to the CPT book for the procedural code(s).**

   Determine which part of the body the procedure(s) involve; then refer to that section of the CPT book.

   The CPT book has an index, but it's not particularly useful when you're looking for procedures. For that reason, look directly in the appropriate section of the book to identify the code that reflects the procedures.

3. **Check to make sure the diagnosis code supports medical necessity for the procedural code you're submitting.**

   For example, if you are reporting a hernia repair, make sure the diagnosis is a hernia.

WARNING

The test proctors examine all materials brought into the testing area. Make sure you haven't written any notes in your CPT or ICD-10 codebooks that will bar you from using them during the exam. Highlighted areas are acceptable, and personal notes may be okay, but definitions of medical terms aren't. If you've noted something like "measles, mumps, rubella" next to MMR vaccine, you either need to erase it or use a book the proctor provides. Also forbidden are notes that involve information from sources other than the approved coding materials. (This is another reason to attend local chapter meetings. The examination proctors are normally chapter officers, and they're more than happy to advise you with regard to the acceptability of your books.)

Here are some other things not allowed into the test areas: reference or study materials, sticky notes, loose-leaf paper notes, calculators, smartphones, or any materials that give you an unfair advantage.

Signing Up for and Taking the Big Test

When you decide that the time is right to take the certification examination, check the website of the organization whose test you have prepared to take. AHIMA has testing information on its website (`www.ahima.org`), and AAPC has the necessary information on its website (`www.aapc.com`).

The training program you enroll in will direct you to its certification examinations. If your program does not include certification testing arrangements, you need to register and pay for any and all examinations that you plan to take.

REMEMBER

Plan ahead! Both AHIMA and AAPC require prepaid registration several weeks in advance of the scheduled examinations. In addition, the tests are scheduled at the convenience of the certification organizations. Although they are available year-round, a limited number of seats are available at each session. The tests are also dependent upon volunteer proctors whose time is to be respected. Oh, and don't be late! Proctors lock the door before the test begins, and no one is allowed in after that point. Actually, AHIMA candidates are asked to report to the test center 30 minutes before the scheduled appointment; those who arrive 15 minutes after the scheduled appointment can't take the test and forfeit the prepaid fee.

TIP

Both organizations offer practice tests that you can purchase prior to the actual examination. Consider taking one to see how you do. In addition, local AAPC chapters often hold review classes before an exam to help those taking the exam practice their skill and timing. Experienced officers or other members with a solid background in teaching often lead these classes.

In the following sections, I give you a general idea of the kinds of questions you can expect, explain when you can expect your score, and offer several test-taking tips.

Taking a quick peek at the exam

The tests are shipped to the exam proctor prior to the testing date. The seal on each test remains unbroken until the examinee is ready to begin or you're given permission to begin. Then you're allowed a specified amount of time to complete the exam (5 hours and 40 minutes for AAPC's CPC test, for example, and 4 hours for AHIMA's CCS exam). The test format is multiple-choice or a combination of multiple-choice and fill-in-the-blank.

Following are some examples of possible types of questions that may be on the certification examination(s).

A section on medical terminology will ask questions such as

> What does MMR stand for?
>
> What is the meaning of homeostasis?
>
> What is a ROS?
>
> What is an H&P?
>
> What is medical necessity?

The section on human anatomy may include questions such as

What are the parts of the circulatory system?

Are the bronchi part of the (A) skeletal system, (B) muscle system, (C) integumentary system, or (D) respiratory system?

The spleen is an organ found in the ___________system.

The Achilles tendon is part of the _______.

The metacarpal is found in which part of the body?

Also expect to find coding-specific questions that ask you to identify the correct diagnosis code(s) as indicated by the terminology in the question. Here are some examples:

What is the correct ICD-10 code for carpal tunnel syndrome on the right wrist: (A) G54.01, (B) G54.02, (C) G54.03, or (D) none of the above?

What is the correct ICD-10 code for closed fracture, left radius (alone) unspecified part, initial encounter: (A) S52.509, (B) S52.502A, (C) S52.531D, or (D) none of the above?

Does ICD-10 diagnosis code S42.001K represent (A) mal-union or (B) non-union of the clavicle?

In which section of the CPT book is a splenectomy found?

An arthroscopic left knee medial meniscectomy is reported with CPT code _____________.

Chondroplasty is always included with arthroscopic knee procedures. True or False?

You may also be presented with scenarios that ask you to employ your coding skills. Here's an example scenario:

Preoperative diagnosis: left Achilles tendon rupture. Postoperative diagnosis: Same. Procedure: Left Achilles tendon repair.

Consent was obtained and the patient received a regional block prior to administration of general anesthesia. A tourniquet was placed on the left thigh and inflated. An 8 cm longitudinal incision was made over the rupture. Sharp dissection was used to tunnel through the subcutaneous tissue to expose the rupture. Two #2 fiber wires were used to repair the tendon. The incision was then closed with 0-vicryl, the tourniquet was deflated, and the dermis was closed in the usual fashion.

Please supply diagnosis and procedure codes for the above.

For specific information about the kinds of questions you'll find on either the AAPC exams or the AHIMA exams, refer to Chapter 7.

Making the grade — or not

A passing score for the AAPC exams is 70 percent or above. AAPC test scores are usually released within 7 to 10 business days and are available online in your AAPC account.

AHIMA has made some changes in the way it administers and scores tests. AHIMA contracted an independent agency to assist in developing and administering its certification examinations, thus formalizing the testing process. After finishing the exam, candidates complete and turn in a report to the test center staff to receive their test results. If the staff suspects a computer malfunction or candidate misconduct, test results may be held pending an investigation.

REMEMBER

If you don't do well on the certification exam despite all your prep, you can retake the test. AAPC allows one retake within one year of the original test without additional fees, although you do have to register for the examination again, just as for the initial sitting. If you need to take the AHIMA test again, you must pay the fee again after a 91-day waiting period has elapsed.

Tackling test-taking tips

Successful test-taking requires careful preparation and the ability to avoid making careless mistakes. Following are some tips that can help ensure that you get the highest score possible:

- **Carefully read the directions for each section.** Doing so helps you avoid careless errors.
- **Quickly look through each section of the test for an overview and scan for keywords.** The keyword identifies which part of the body is being treated.
- **Answer the easy questions first to build confidence; then go back and answer more difficult ones.** If you get stuck on an answer, skip it and come back to it later if time permits. It is helpful to be conscious of the time available so that you don't stress over one question and ignore others you may know.
- **On the multiple-choice questions, eliminate obvious incorrect answers.** Then choose the best option from those remaining. For example, if the question references the right side, you should know that the diagnosis code will likely end with a 1. (followed by the encounter indicator).

» **On the operative note section, read carefully and note the primary procedure first.** Then note the diagnosis that supports medical necessity. It is a good idea to review the questions prior to reading an op note or other lengthy documentation. That will help understand what information is going to be needed in advance.

» **Don't leave blanks.** A non-answer is an incorrect answer, so if you are not sure, guess.

» **If you have extra time, check your answers.** Resist the urge to leave immediately after you complete the test. Check to make sure you have answered all the questions and that you haven't mismarked any answers.

TIP

As you go along, you may come across information in a later question that indicates you answered a previous question incorrectly. If so, go back and change your earlier answer!

» Investing in your career with continuing education

» Finding free resources

Chapter 10
Adding Street Cred: Specialty Certifications and Continuing Ed

Consider credentials the golden tickets to your medical billing and coding career. They give you credibility as a coder. In Chapter 7, I explain the basic certifications offered by AAPC and AHIMA (the CPC, the CCA, and the CCS, for example). In this chapter, I introduce you to these organizations' specialty certifications.

Specialty certifications indicate extensive knowledge in particular areas of coding. These certifications are obtained by taking exams specific to the certifying organizations. Yet so many specialty certifications are available that picking one can seem overwhelming, but it really isn't that hard: Just pick what best bolsters your bona fides as a coder.

Beyond the specialty certifications are continuing education opportunities that keep you abreast of what's going on in your field. This chapter has the details.

Introducing Specialty Certification Options

Both AAPC (American Academy of Professional Coders) and the American Health Information Management Association (AHIMA) offer specialty certifications that you can achieve as you develop your career. Earning a specialty certification shows an employer that you're striving to become an expert in your profession and an asset to the position. Adding specialty certifications also makes you highly marketable in your field.

Other organizations offer certifications as well. These include the Board of Medical Specialty Coding and Compliance (BMSC) and the Professional Association of Healthcare Coding Specialists (PAHCS) among others. Note that neither of these have the history of AAPC or AHIMA, but they are options. The BMSC, for example, was created to offer people who already have basic certification a way to credential their specialty knowledge. It's not an organization from which a novice would normally benefit.

REMEMBER

Certifications are only as credible as the organization that gives them. Do your homework to find the most appropriate and reputable for your situation.

Eyeing AAPC trademarked certifications

AAPC offers several trademarked certifications. Some of these specialty certifications do not require you to get a Certified Professional Coder (CPC) certification (refer to Chapter 7), although each requires continuing education specific to the defined specialty. Thorough knowledge of medical terminology, anatomy, and physiology is also a must. These certifications, listed in Table 10-1, are beneficial to those already working in a medical office.

Showing off specialty AHIMA certifications

Much like its kissing cousin, the AAPC, AHIMA offers several types of specialty certifications. It's a veritable alphabet soup of acronyms and designations, but fear not: I explain them all in the following sections.

TABLE 10-1 **Trademark AAPC Certifications**

Certification	Related Skills and Competencies
Certified Ambulatory Surgery Center Coder (CASCC)	Ability to read and assign the correct codes and modifiers to procedures performed in an ambulatory surgery center (ASC); understanding rules for ASC reimbursement, including the multiple procedure discount coding for discontinued procedures
Certified Anesthesia and Pain Management Coder (CANPC)	Proficiency in selecting the highest based anesthesia CPT code for surgical cases and assigning the appropriate American Society of Anesthesiologists (ASA) codes; correctly using anesthesia modifiers and determining base units for cases; having a good grasp of procedures performed by physicians specializing in physical medicine, rehab, and pain management
Certified Cardiology Coder (CCC)	Proficiency in coding cardiovascular tests and procedures, including heart catheterization, coronary interventions, and vascular procedures, that are performed by cardiologists
Certified Chiropractic Professional Coder (CCPC)	Proficiency in coding procedures performed by licensed chiropractors
Certified Emergency Department Coder (CEDC)	Proficiency in coding surgical procedures performed by emergency department physicians; awareness of evaluation and management guidelines and time-based code protocol
Certified ENT Coder (CENTC)	Proficiency in coding ENT (ear, nose, throat) procedures, as well as determining appropriate evaluation and management codes by reading office notes and operative reports (which may document surgical procedures performed by otolaryngologists)
Certified Evaluation and Management Coder (CEMC)	Expertise in assigning the correct evaluation and management codes by identifying the level of visit based on the three key components of history, exam, and medical decision-making
Certified Family Practice Coder (CFPC)	Expertise in determining the correct kind of evaluation and management codes to capture the level of visit; proficiency in coding minor surgical and ancillary procedures that a family practitioner may perform; full understanding of relative value unit (RVU) sequencing; and a knowledge of preventive care services coding
Certified Gastroenterology Coder (CGIC)	Proficiency in coding procedures performed by gastroenterologists; determining evaluation and management codes
Certified General Surgery Coder (CGSC)	Proficiency in coding surgical procedures performed by general surgeons; knowledgeable in global periods and RVU sequencing
Certified Hematology and Oncology Coder (CHONC)	Proficiency in coding surgical and therapeutic procedures performed by hematologists, oncologists, and members of their staff
Certified Internal Medicine Coder (CIMC)	Proficiency in determining billable procedures based on physician office notes, including office procedures (injections, vaccinations, and so on) and minor surgical procedures (such as joint injections)

(continued)

TABLE 10-1 *(continued)*

Certification	Related Skills and Competencies
Certified Interventional Radiology Cardiovascular Coder (CIRCC)	Expertise in interventional radiology and cardiovascular coding for procedures performed under imaging guidance, such as proficiency in coding cardio-related items (like diagnostic angiography), cardiac catheterizations, and nonvascular procedures
Certified Obstetrical Gynecology Coder (COBGC)	Proficiency in coding obstetric services and surgical procedures normally performed by OB/GYNs
Certified Pediatric Coder (CPEDC)	Proficiency in coding office procedures and surgical procedures performed by pediatricians, as well as determining correct evaluation and management codes based on office notes
Certified Physician Practice Manager (CPPM)	Expertise in business processes, including fraud and compliance, medical office accounting, revenue cycle, and human resource management as well as HIPAA and data security, including health information technology (IT) and electronic medical records (EMRs; see Chapter 11)
Certified Plastics and Reconstructive Surgery Coder (CPRC)	Expertise in coding surgical procedures performed by plastic and reconstructive surgeons, as well as the ability to identify procedures considered cosmetic
Certified Professional Biller (CPB)	Expertise in different insurance plans and payer policies (including LCDs and NCDs; see Chapter 17) and knowledge of coding guidelines, healthcare industry regulations, and the revenue cycle, including claim follow-up
Certified Professional Coder in Dermatology (CPCD)	Proficiency in coding surgical procedures (including various types of lesion excisions) performed by dermatologists
Certified Professional Compliance Officer (CPCO)	Proficiency in understanding the requirements necessary to develop and implement a compliance protocol for a medical office
Certified Professional Medical Auditor (CPMA)	Proficiency in coding and documentation guidelines; being able to offer advice to improve a facility's or practice's programs to assess and maintain documentation coding quality and reduce risk revenue cycle; possessing advanced knowledge of medical documentation, fraud, and abuse as well as a familiarity with penalties for violations based on government regulations
Certified Rheumatology Coder (CRHC)	Proficiency with evaluation and management codes and surgical procedures performed by rheumatologists
Certified Urology Coder (CUC)	Expertise in coding office and surgical procedures performed by urologists

Registered Health Information Administrator (RHIA)

As a Registered Health Information Administrator (RHIA), you are an expert in managing medical records, including patient information and computer systems. You also have in-depth knowledge of ethical and legal requirements and standards with regard to the healthcare industry.

To be eligible for this certification, you must

- Have completed an accredited Health Informatics and Information Management (HIIM) program or have graduated from an HIIM program approved by a foreign association with which AHIMA has a reciprocity agreement.
- Have a degree from a Commission on Accreditation for Health Informatics and Information Management (CAHIIM) program. A directory of these programs is available on the CAHIIM website (`www.cahiim.org`). CAHIIM is the organization that accredits associate, bachelor's, and master's degree programs in health information management.

HIIM? HIIM WHO?

Health Informatics and Information Management (HIIM) deals with just about everything associated with the information created, disseminated, and shared by the healthcare industry, soup to nuts. From local information technology and interpersonal digital relations between physicians, clinics, and hospitals to coding information for Medicare and Medicaid, information management plays a role in how all the healthcare pieces work together. Making sure that patient data is managed with the utmost integrity is paramount, and it is part and parcel of an ongoing national effort to reduce medical errors and high costs for both physician and patient.

A strong foundation in HIIM is important for anyone wanting to earn certification in a related field. The impending total shift to electronic health records promises a secure future for anyone involved in the health information and informatics industry, so getting a degree in HIIM is going to be a win-win.

To talk nuts and bolts, the HIIM-related degree preps you for all sorts of career opportunities. For example, according to the University of Tennessee's Health Science Center, its Master of HIIM degree prepares you for careers in healthcare administration, data security oversight, strategic and operational information resource planning, clinical data analysis, clinical classification systems and support systems, information systems development, and even electronic health records implementation and management. In short, the HIIM world is your oyster. Don't wait — get on the HIIM bus ASAP.

Registered Health Information Technician (RHIT)

As a Registered Health Information Technician (RHIT), you are certified to ensure completion and accuracy of medical records, including proper entry into computer systems. You may also specialize in coding medical records.

This certification is often held in combination with a bachelor's degree. To be eligible, you must have completed an accredited HIIM program (accreditation is through the Commission on Accreditation for Health Informatics and Information Management Education) or have graduated from a HIIM program approved by a foreign association with which AHIMA has a reciprocity agreement.

Certified Health Data Analyst (CHDA)

To achieve the Certified Health Data Analyst (CHDA) certification level, you must demonstrate expertise in health data analysis. As the healthcare industry becomes more data driven and the use of electronic medical records continues to increase, practitioners will need individuals who can focus on the future of their practices and develop strategies to stay viable. To be eligible for this certification, you must have either of the following:

- A bachelor's degree or higher and a minimum of five years of healthcare data experience
- A RHIA credential and a minimum of one year of experience in healthcare data

Certified in Healthcare Privacy and Security (CHPS)

The Certified in Healthcare Privacy and Security (CHPS) certification identifies you as competent in protecting privacy and security programs in all types of healthcare information management. To be eligible for this certification, you must have any of the following:

- A bachelor's degree with a minimum of four years of experience in healthcare management
- A master's degree (or equivalent) with a minimum of two years of experience in healthcare management
- A HIIM credential of RHIT or RHIA with a bachelor's degree or higher and a minimum of two years of healthcare management experience

Perusing the best of the rest

AAPC and AHIMA aren't the only games in town. Although they are perhaps the most well-known, you may discover that your professional goals would be better met by getting certified by another organization or by adding certifications from other organizations onto your AAPC or AHIMA certifications. In the following sections, I discuss two reputable certifying organizations: the Board of Medical Specialty Coding and Compliance (BMSC) and the Professional Association of Healthcare Coding Specialists (PAHCS).

Board of Medical Specialty Coding and Compliance (BMSC)

BMSC is a lesser-known provider of specialty medical coding certifications and training for coders, compliance officers, and clinicians. BMSC certifications encompass those who work in physician offices, as well as home healthcare professionals.

Because the levels of education required in coding and compliance build from one certification level to another, BMSC certification helps coders and other professionals move up the career ladder.

The BMSC's certifications include the following:

- **Specialty Coding Professional (SCP) and Advanced Coding Specialist (ACS),** both of which offer specialty certification in numerous areas
- **Certified Compliance Professional-Physician (CCP-P),** a certification for compliance professionals in physician offices
- **Home Care Coding Specialist-Diagnosis (HCS-D)** for home care coders with experience in that area
- **Home Care Clinical Specialist-OASIS (HCS-O)** for home healthcare clinicians

REMEMBER

All the BMSC certifications are directed to those who already have experience in the specified areas. Recertification requires taking an exam every two years and renewing your membership annually.

Professional Association of Healthcare Coding Specialists (PAHCS)

PAHCS is a support organization that functions as a communication network for members. This organization serves primarily as a support system for coders working in a medical practice, but membership is open to all coding professionals.

Certification by this organization involves submitting an application and completing a written examination that shows proficiency within the ambulatory healthcare delivery system. If you've been certified by other organizations, you may receive PAHCS certification by showing proof of current certification and paying a membership fee and a processing fee.

Building on Your Cred with Continuing Education

Regardless of which certification(s) you choose, you've got to participate in some continuing education to maintain it. The healthcare industry is constantly evolving. Codes change. Rules change. Medicare policies change. A claim form that's been used for several years is replaced. Every year, diagnosis codes and new CPT codes are added while older codes are retired. Continuing education keeps you up to date on all the pertinent changes.

Adding up the continuing ed units (CEUs)

The number of continuing education units (CEUs) you need varies based on the type of certification(s) you have. Each specialty certification requires units in that specialty in addition to the basic certification requirements. Table 10-2 shows the current CEU requirements for AAPC certifications.

TABLE 10-2 AAPC CEU Requirements

Number of Certifications	CEUs Required
1 certification	36 CEUs every two years (see note)
2 certifications	40 CEUs every two years, with specialty-specific requirements (see note)
3 certifications	44 CEUs, with specialty-specific requirements (see note)
4 certifications	48 CEUs every two years (see note)
5+ certifications	52 CEUs every two years, with specialty-specific certification requirements (see note)

Note: *The CIRCC, CPMA, and CPCO certifications (mentioned earlier in this chapter) require that at least 16 of the CEUs in a two-year period be credential-specific. The CPPM certification also requires that 16 CEUs be related to practice management. Also, there must be 8 CEUs specific to each specialty.*

TIP

Ask your credentialing organization about how many CEUs are needed for each credential before you decide which program to go with. Knowing how much time is involved later may help you make the wisest decision now.

AHIMA continuing education requirements differ slightly. They require completion of CEUs in addition to mandatory annual coding self-assessments (available through AHIMA). The level of certification dictates the number of CEUs required per two-year cycle: CCA, CCS, and CCS-P require 20 CEUs in addition to two self-assessments per cycle. RHIA, CHDA, CHP, and CHS each require 30 CEUs. The RHIT requirement is 20 CEUs.

Multiple AHIMA certifications require different numbers of CEUs, depending on the individual certifications. You can find out about specific requirements on the AHIMA website (www.ahima.org).

Earning the units you need

You earn CEUs by attending workshops, professional boot camps, and webinars and by taking quizzes linked to professional articles in coding magazines or technical publications.

The credentialing organization determines the number of CEUs the various activities offer after evaluating the educational content of a program. The number of CEUs associated with an activity normally coincides with that activity's time commitment. One hour equals one CEU. Exceptions are meetings and workshops. Often, organization meetings earn you one CEU for each hour of learning, minus any breaks, lunch, or networking time with vendors.

REMEMBER

Make sure your credentialing organization has approved the activity you want to use as a CEU. Approved articles, quizzes, meetings, webinars, and so on display the organization's approval seal, along with the number of CEUs you can earn.

Each time you earn a CEU, you receive a certificate that has an index number that you register with AAPC. This number verifies that the CEU is authentic. Go to AAPC's online CEU tracker (available to members) and enter the index number into the tracker. Be sure to hold on to the paper copies of your certificates, though. You'll need them in the event that you're randomly selected for a CEU audit.

Digging up complimentary CEU resources

Some free CEU resources are available if you know where to look. Read on to find out more.

Quizzing your way to free AAPC units

Membership in the AAPC includes a subscription to the organization's magazine, *Healthcare Business Monthly.* Each month, the AAPC website includes an online quiz covering articles in that month's publication. Complete the quiz, and your CEU is automatically linked to your account. How's that for healthcare information management?

Other free resources may be local chapter opportunities or attendance at certain lectures. You can contact the AAPC directly to inquire about opportunities in your area.

Training your sights on free AHIMA units

AHIMA offers five recorded webinars that are related to its Program for Evaluating Payment Patterns, which is aimed at hospital management. Check out `www.ahima.org/events` for links to the webinars, as well as audio resources, event and conference listings, and a host of other professional resources geared toward coders.

Taking advantage of Medicare's web-based training

Medicare offers web-based training, organized into a series of modules. The web modules offered by Uncle Sam are quite informative, and you can complete them at your own pace. These training exercises are relevant to current coding and processing issues, and Medicare updates them regularly, keeping you abreast of the latest developments and changes. After you complete the web training, you take an online quiz. Pass the quiz and earn a free CEU.

REMEMBER

You need to enter these CEUs into your AAPC CEU tracker account yourself. If you are earning CEUs toward other organization certifications, you need to follow their protocol for submitting them. Check out `www.cms.gov/Outreach-and-Education/Medicare-Learning-Network-MLN/MLNEdWebGuide/Downloads/MLNWBTs-for-CE-Credit.pdf` for more information about this great resource.

Getting the most bang for your buck with CEUs

You often need to earn CEUs on your own time (and your own dollar), in which case you want to make sure you're getting the most benefit for the cost. In the next sections, I offer advice on which activities provide a good cost-to-CEU ratio.

Workshops

Attending a one-day conference or workshop that offers 8 or 10 CEUs can be an economical use of your time, given that you need at minimum of 18 units each year. Attending a conference or workshop is a good idea especially if the meeting is relevant to your current position or to the position you hope to get.

Both the AAPC and AHIMA offer workshops that allow coders to not only earn CEUs but, most importantly, also learn about updates to policies, procedures, and diagnosis codes. Attending these can be costly (check with your employer to see whether it will subsidize your attendance), but the price is often worth it. Compared to online learning or reading articles, attending a workshop gives you the opportunity to ask questions and network with the instructors and other attendees. Medicare also hosts training through a program called Provider Outreach and Education. The goal of this program is to educate providers and their staffs about fundamentals of Medicare, including policies, procedures, and changes to the Medicare program.

Medicare also offers numerous training opportunities: live training through seminars, teleconferences, and webinars; on-demand training through audio and audiovisual presentations including educational materials; and online training through the Medicare Learning Network, a web-based program that targets different provider types. These opportunities are usually free if you sign up in advance.

Boot camps

Boot camps are learning-intensive workshops. They normally span a two- or three-day period and can supply you with a lot of CEUs. Check with AAPC or AHIMA to find out about boot camps in your area.

Paid subscriptions

A host of paid subscriptions target specialty areas from anesthesia to urology. Subscribers to these publications or websites normally have the opportunity to earn CEUs by completing online quizzes that cover current and past articles. The good thing about subscribing to these resources is that you can review them on your own schedule and as often as you like. The downside is that, if you need clarification, you have to write a letter or send an email to the editor(s) and wait for the answer. If you tend to be impatient, you may want to keep some other resources at your disposal as well.

4 Dealing and Succeeding with Nitty-Gritty On-the-Job Details

IN THIS PART . . .

Trace the necessary steps to ensure correct claims processing, from patient encounter to revenue.

Discover the clinical documentation verification needed before a claim can be billed.

Get tips for following up on underpaid or unpaid claims and the appeals process.

Find out what part the World Health Organization plays in medical billing and coding.

Get details on how improved documentation is needed to work in the ICD-10 world and how to help your clinician with this task.

» Securing authorizations

» Working with billing software

» Handling an appeal

Chapter 11

Processing a Run-of-the-Mill Claim: An Overview

As a biller and coder, you perform magic daily by converting physician- or specialist-performed services into revenue. You perform this feat through the fine art of claims processing. *Claims processing* is the industry term that refers to the general process of submitting and following up on claims. Of course, you can break this general process down into particular tasks, like gathering the necessary demographic information from the patient, abstracting the codes themselves from the provider's documentation of the patient encounter, entering the codes into the billing software, and so on.

In this chapter, I outline the general claims submittal process from beginning to end to give you a solid foundation in how things work and who does what along the way. For detailed information on actually preparing a claim for submission, head to the other chapters in this part.

Dreaming of the Perfect Billing Scenario

Although every billing scenario is a bit different, they all follow, to a large degree, the same general process. In this section, I explain what the ideal billing situation looks like. When everything goes according to plan and all the moving parts of the billing and coding process work as they should, you end up with a fully paid claim that doesn't require follow-up on your part.

Completing the initial paperwork

When you walk into the office of any healthcare provider, be it a family physician, a testing lab, or the emergency room, what's the first thing you do? You walk up to the desk and check in, of course. As a biller and coder, this initial interaction is the first step in the billing scenario.

During the check-in, a couple of things happen:

- **The patient completes a demographic form.** This form identifies the patient name, birth date, address, and Social Security number or driver's license number. The form should also indicate who the policyholder of the insurance is and what that person's relationship is to the patient. If the policyholder is someone other than the patient, then the same information (name, birth date, and so on) should be obtained about the policyholder as well.

  TIP

  Copy the patient's insurance card at each encounter, both front and back, when you request the demographic form.

- **You verify the patient's identity by asking for a government issued photo ID.** Thanks to a proliferation of insurance fraud and identity theft (thanks, technology!), you need to make sure that the patient who brings in an insurance card is actually the insured member.

  WARNING

  Using another individual's insurance coverage is fraud, and a provider who submits a claim that intentionally misrepresents an encounter in order to obtain payment is also committing fraud. So be alert and double-check the ID the patient hands you, because every provider is responsible for verifying patient identity and could be held liable for fraud committed in the provider's office.

- **You verify whether the patient needs a referral or a preauthorization.** To find out more about what these are and why you need to check them early, hop to the later section "Covering Your Bases: Referrals and Preauthorization."

- **You verify benefits.** Here are some benefit-related questions to ask up front:
  - **Is there a copay?** If so, the provider is normally expected to collect that amount up front.
  - **Is there any unmet deductible?** If the patient has an unmet deductible, the provider may want to ask for all or part of that up front.
  - **Is the patient out-of-network, and if so, what are his out-of-network benefits?**

- **You collect any copayments, deductibles, or coinsurance obligations.** If the provider encounter is a procedure to which a deductible or coinsurance obligation may be incurred, these amounts may also be collected up front.

Getting the documentation about the patient encounter with the provider

After the initial paperwork is complete, the next step of the revenue cycle is the actual patient encounter with the service provider or physician.

Following the encounter, the provider documents the billable services. This documentation includes what was done, the reason the service was medically necessary, and any additional information that the physician feels is relevant to the patient's care. In the past, the charts were paper, and the documentation was usually handwritten. Today, providers are moving toward electronic health records. These records contain the same information and are much easier to read than handwriting.

Entering the codes into the billing software

With the patient information gathered at check-in and the provider documentation of the patient encounter, you have the information you need to enter the correct Current Procedural Terminology (CPT) and International Classification of Diseases (ICD) codes into the billing software. This is the general procedure:

1. **You enter the patient information into the billing software.**

   This information includes patient demographics, payer information, and financial guarantor information (see the earlier section "Completing the initial paperwork").

   TIP

   If the patient has two insurances, one is primary and one is secondary. Some patients may have more than two carriers. If so, you enter that information into the billing software, too, along with the order in which the insurance carriers should be billed.

2. **You abstract the billable codes based on what the physician documentation says.**

3. **You enter the information — the CPT (procedure) and ICD (diagnosis) codes — into the appropriate claim form in the billing software.**

4. **You send the claim off.**

   In most cases, the claim is electronically uploaded to a medical clearinghouse to then be sent to the appropriate payer. In some cases, the claim is sent directly to the payer. To find out more about billing software, jump to the later section "Working with billing software."

TECHNICAL STUFF

   Many carriers have claims submission portals on their websites that allow providers to submit claims directly. However, because the process can be time-consuming (due to having individual websites for each carrier), this system isn't efficient for larger providers. Also, medical billing software and clearinghouse software provide code-editing services that help prevent claim rejections due to clerical or coding errors — an advantage you miss if you submit claims directly.

REMEMBER

To get the provider paid, you have to submit every single claim as obligated by the payer contract. Unfortunately, every payer seems to have different rules, and you'll encounter thousands of little billing and coding peculiarities unique to each payer — too many to mention here, in fact. The best way to find out about these rules and payer-specific peculiarities is to become familiar with the contract and payer reimbursement policies or call the payer relations line to verify submission requirements.

Show me the money! Letting the payer take its turn

After the payer receives the claim, the payer reviews the claim to determine the following:

- Whether medical necessity has been met.
- Whether the services billed on the claim are covered by the patient's plan.
- What the reimbursement allowance is. To determine this, the payer references the contract that may be in place with the service provider.

After the terms of the contract have been met, the claim will process and pay under the terms of the patient's plan.

REMEMBER

What makes this scenario perfect? The patient is insured, the provider has a contract with either the payer or the network to which the payer belongs, and the claim is clean (that is, it can be processed using only the information provided, it contains no errors, and the correct contract is loaded into the payer claims software). The point? A lot of things impact how smoothly processing a claim goes.

Delving into the Details: Contract Specifics

Every payer has its own policies and procedures manual, and as the coder, you need to be knowledgeable about individual payer requirements. The best place to find that payer information is in the contract. The contract also defines the levels of payment for each of the network providers. As a biller and coder, one of the most important parts of your job is understanding contracts and how they determine the amount of reimbursement the provider receives.

Normally, you have access to the payer contract: It will be programmed into your billing software. Ideally, the payer contracts are pre-loaded into the software, allowing you to view the contract on a network drive. If not, you can print a paper copy. As you read through the contract, you see that each set of policies contains subsets that apply to the various plans sponsored by the payer or that apply to the network that the payer participates in. Examples of subsets include the plan benefits available to health maintenance organization (HMO) members versus the plan benefits available to preferred provider organization (PPO) members.

Understanding who's contracting whom?

In the case of contracts, the payers (insurance companies) are in charge. They offer various levels of coverage to their members. When contracting with the insurance company for employee group coverage, the patient's employer often selects the level of coverage it will offer its employees. In this case, the insurance company is *underwriting* the plan, which means that the employer pays the insurer, who is then responsible for paying the covered services within the confines of the contract.

Some employers find that underwriting their own policies is more cost-effective. In that case, the employer may contract with a network or third-party administrator for pricing of claims, but the actual payment comes from the employer. Sometimes this type of coverage is indicated on the patient's card as ASO (administrative services only), and the plan coverage may differ from the payer providing the administrative services. In this case, the payer is not actually providing insurance, but rather is only acting as the financial agent of the patient's employer. Always make sure to call the number indicated on the card to ensure that the benefit verification is correct. Check out Chapter 6 for more information about third-party administrators.

The insurance company or network also contracts with healthcare providers to participate within the network. Here's the idea: The company directs patients to providers in its network, thus increasing the number of patients (and payments) these providers get. In return, the providers help keep the payer costs under control by limiting the amount of reimbursement they receive for each encounter. By staying within the payer network, the patient saves the insurance company or employer money while still receiving quality healthcare.

Whenever possible, providers try to participate in the plans or networks that underwrite the majority of the local population (that's a cost savings).

Looking at standard contracts

Many payers or networks have standardized contracts that they offer to healthcare providers. A well-defined contract does the following:

- Defines the number of days after the encounter that the provider has to submit the claim. This is called *timely filing.*
- Specifies how many days after receipt of the claim the payer has to make payment. Some states have prompt claim pay laws, and it's important to know what each state requires. If the payer is not compliant with either the contract or state laws, penalties are usually applied in the form of interest that compounds daily.
- Specifies which of the payer plans are included, the frequency of services that it will cover (for certain procedures), and the type of claim that is to be submitted by the provider.
- Identifies special circumstances that may affect either the provider or the payer, such as
  - How unlisted procedures are to be reimbursed (these procedures end in "99" and are usually worded in a way that states "other unspecified procedure")

WARNING

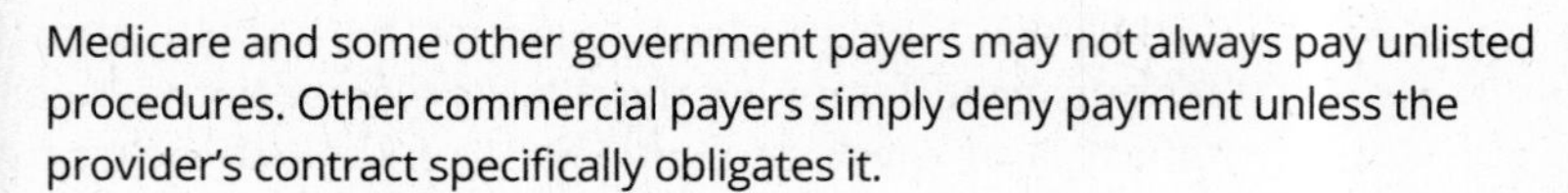

Medicare and some other government payers may not always pay unlisted procedures. Other commercial payers simply deny payment unless the provider's contract specifically obligates it.

  - The appeals process.
  - Procedures that are carved out of the fee schedule to be paid a set amount (see the next section for more on carve-outs).
  - The number of procedures that the payer will pay per encounter.
  - The multiple procedure discount (the discount applied to procedures that are paid in addition to the initial procedure).
- Identifies cost intensive supplies or procedures that may need to be paid. This may include such items as implants, screws, anchors, plates, rods, and so on.

Even though they're standardized, every payer contract is different in one way or another. Make sure you read each contract carefully and familiarize yourself with each set of payer circumstances.

Cutting through reimbursement rates and carve-outs

As I explain in the preceding section, despite their differences, contracts tend to be fairly boilerplate. These contracts are similar to Medicare's fee schedule, and they may be based on that schedule. They may pay 110 percent or 125 percent of what Medicare allows. They may even pay less than Medicare allows, which sometimes happens with large networks or payers who have so many insured members that providers risk financial disaster by not participating. (In such a case, providers can't really afford to not participate because the number of patients in the practice will fall drastically.)

Providers who want to become part of a specific network first identify which services they expect to provide and how much they need to be paid to be profitable within the network. The providers also factor in all overhead costs (rent, utilities, staff, commodities, and salary) associated with each type of service. They also may identify specific services that they'd like to be carve-outs of the contract.

A *contracted carve-out* is a special clause in the contract that stipulates a different payment rate from the normal rate for a specified procedural code. These carve-outs are important parts of provider contracts. Although they should result in a profit for the provider, they often delay correct claims processing because they require special handling by the payer. To put it simply, the carve-out isn't a simple line item that the payer's computerized processing system can automatically assign payment for; instead, it's a clause that requires additional care when coding *and* paying.

Covering Your Bases: Referrals and Preauthorization

Contracted providers should know what services each payer does and doesn't cover. Some payers, for example, don't pay for procedures that are considered investigative or experimental; others don't pay for unlisted procedures. Medicare may not pay for any procedure that is unlisted, and many payers follow Medicare guidelines as a matter of course.

That's why, prior to a patient encounter, you must check the patient's plan benefits in addition to the provider contract. Doing so lets you identify potential reimbursement issues in advance and know what, if any, special protocol needs to be followed. Two of the more common scenarios you'll encounter involve checking referrals and securing preauthorization.

Checking for referrals

If the patient's plan requires a referral, make sure a referral was given. Check in the record to ensure that the referral is noted (it is usually an alphanumeric entry that must be included on the claim). For certain HMO plans, the primary care physician submits the referral to the payer prior to the specialist encounter; then, when the payer receives the claim, the payer knows that the visit was authorized.

REMEMBER

Although many plans place the responsibility for obtaining the referral on the patient, it's in the best interest of both the patient and the provider for you to assist in this endeavor. The provider is the professional and in the best position to understand what steps are necessary to treat the patient.

Dealing with prior authorization

Prior authorization (also known as *preauthorization*) is the process of getting an agreement from the payer to cover specific services before the service is performed. Normally, a payer that authorizes a service prior to an encounter assigns an authorization number that you need to include on the claim when you submit it for payment.

Getting the correct CPT code beforehand

The key to a solid preauthorization is to provide the correct CPT code. The challenge is that you have to determine the correct procedural code before the service has been provided (and documented) — an often difficult task.

To determine the correct code, check with the physician to find out what she anticipates doing. Make sure you get all possible scenarios; otherwise, you run the risk that a procedure that was performed won't be covered. For example, if the doctor has scheduled a biopsy (which may not need prior authorization) but then actually excises a lesion (which probably does need prior authorization), the claim for the excision will be denied. What's a coder to do? Authorize the excision! It's better to authorize treatment not rendered than to be denied payment for no authorization. No penalty is incurred when a procedure has been authorized but is not completed, so err on the side of preauthorization.

In rare cases, information about the patient's insurance coverage and/or prior authorization requirements is not available prior to an encounter. This scenario most often occurs in emergency situations, due to an accident or sudden illness that develops during the night or on weekends. When this happens, the servicing provider must contact the payer as soon as possible after services are provided in order to secure the necessary authorizations.

REMEMBER

Although you are the coder in charge of assigning the appropriate codes, the burden of obtaining necessary authorizations is largely on the provider, because it's the provider who'll be denied payment as expected. Getting preauthorization takes only a few minutes, and it can save countless hours on the back end trying to chase claim payments. Preauthorization also results in faster claims processing and prompt payments.

Proceeding when you don't get the necessary preauthorization

Who gets stuck with footing the bill when preauthorizations don't pan out? It depends. The determination as to who is responsible is often defined by the patient's insurance plan. If the plan benefits outline specific services that are not covered and the patient seeks those services, the responsibility for payment falls to the patient. On the other hand, if a provider fails to authorize treatment prior to providing services to a patient and payment is denied by the insurance company, then the provider may be obligated to absorb the cost of treatment, and no payment is due from the patient.

WARNING

Many payers don't issue retro authorizations, even when the failure to get preauthorization was a mistake. Some may overturn a denial on appeal, but they're under no obligation to make payment if the proper process was not followed.

Some payers may assign full financial responsibility for a procedure that didn't get the necessary preauthorization to the patient. This is almost a guarantee if the patient is out of network with the provider. In this case, the provider has to make a decision about whether to pursue collecting the payment from the patient. Some swallow the loss. Others send the unpaid bill to the patient, but doing so is bad business. Patients are both unaware of the process and not in any sort of position to guess what CPT code should be submitted to the insurance company. This is yet another reason to do your homework as a coder and make sure those preauthorizations are in place prior to submitting your claims.

WARNING

Occasionally you run into a situation in which the patient's coverage was verified prior to services, and the patient's employer terminates benefits retroactively. This usually happens when there is a termination of employment that is challenged in court or when an employer learns that a covered employee was in violation of his or her contract during employment. In these very unfortunate situations, the patient is responsible for the medical fees, but collecting the debt can be quite difficult.

Tracking Your Claim from Submission to Payment

As noted earlier, the claims process begins when you enter the CPT and ICD codes into the billing software, but it certainly doesn't end there. Your claim will take a (potentially arduous) journey on the path to payment. In the following sections, I explain the stops and possible perils along the way, from billing software to the clearinghouses to the payer.

Of course, not all submissions have happy endings; they get stuck along the way. In that case, you may need to submit corrected claims or file an appeal. For details on that process, head to the section "Fighting for Proper Payment: Filing an Appeal with the Payer" later in this chapter.

Working with billing software

Everything that happens in the claims process is reliant on the software you use to code and bill. Consider this software the backbone of what you do. It prepares the claim to be submitted to the claims clearinghouse (covered in the later section "Passing from provider to clearinghouse . . .").

Exploring features of the software

Many different types of billing software are available, but they all allow you to enter the procedure codes and diagnosis codes, as well as the provider's fee for each code, the patient's insurance information (policy number and group number), and the payer's address. The software also links each payer to a specific payer ID.

Most of the newer versions of billing software are compatible with electronic medical records (EMRs), in which case the billing modules of the software are included with the clinical modules of the patient's record. What this means is that the clinical staff enters the clinical information and provides additional documentation of medical necessity.

Here are some other features you may encounter:

- Some offices use billing software that links into their electronic medical records, while other offices have encounter-specific information (encounter times, names of clinical staff involved in the encounter, and so on) stored in the billing software. This information is useful for inventory purposes, to determine the cost of each patient's care, and in the event of any legal inquiries.
- Some offices have security edits in place that allow access to various parts of this software based on the employee's need to know or clearance. Access to the patient's personal history, for example, may not be viewable by the billing staff, and access to patient demographic information, such as Social Security number, may not be viewable by the charge-nurse.

Numerous types of billing software systems are available, and the one you use depends on the provider's needs and budget, but the primary purpose of all billing software is to serve as a platform to prepare the claim to begin its journey, which ends when the provider receives payment from the insurance company or other payer.

Making sure the correct contract is loaded into the billing software

Normally, payer contracts are already loaded into the office billing software so that, when you enter information, the software automatically links each procedure to the appropriate payment obligated by the payer contract.

Having the correct contract loaded saves time because it facilitates payment posting on the back end of the claim. Here's why: When the insurance company makes a payment, the payment is posted to each patient account. The person responsible for posting payments is referred to as the *payment poster*. If the contract isn't loaded correctly, the payment poster must verify each payment to make sure that it's correct.

In small companies, the payment poster may be the office manager or other front office associate. Larger companies, including most billing companies, have employees whose job is limited to just posting payments to the correct accounts.

Passing from provider to clearinghouse . . .

Companies that serve as intermediaries who forward claims information from healthcare providers to insurance payers are known as *clearinghouses*. In what is called *claims scrubbing*, clearinghouses check the claim for errors and verify that it is compatible with the payer software. The clearinghouse also checks to make sure that the procedural and diagnosis codes being submitted are valid and that each procedure code is appropriate for the diagnosis code submitted with it. The claim scrubbing edit helps prevent time-consuming processing errors.

Each provider chooses which clearinghouse it wants to use for submitting claims. Most clearinghouse companies charge the providers for each claim submitted, and they also charge an additional fee to send a paper claim to a certain payer. Some of the larger payers may own their own clearinghouses.

Clearinghouses may submit claims directly to the payers, or they may have to send a claim through other clearinghouse sites before reaching the payer(s). The claims may go through other clearinghouses for the following reasons:

- **The provider billing software isn't compatible with the payer processing software, and the information needs to be reformatted prior to being sent to the payer.** Because of the potential difficulties caused by incompatible software, clearinghouses require an initial enrollment period prior to sending claims for the first time. During the enrollment period, which can take up to four weeks, the clearinghouse tests the compatibility between the provider software and the payer software. Providers need to be mindful of this process so that their claims are not delayed. When using a new clearinghouse, verify the enrollment process before you actually need to submit live claims. (Also check the clearinghouse's payer list. You want to choose a clearinghouse that already has a relationship with your payers.)
- **The payer isn't enrolled in the same clearinghouse the provider uses.** The provider pays the clearinghouse, and the insurance companies pay the clearinghouse. Each payer is identified by its clearinghouse *electronic data interchange* (EDI) number. This number serves as the payer's "address," or identifier, and it tells the clearinghouse which payer to send the claim to. If the payer isn't enrolled in the same clearinghouse as the provider, the claim is sent to a clearinghouse that the payer is enrolled with. Take a look at a couple of examples:
  - **Example 1:** Provider Smith uses ABC billing software. Provider Smith then enrolls with XYZ clearinghouse. ABC software sends the claims entered into it to XYZ clearinghouse. Payer Gold is enrolled with the same XYZ clearinghouse. So XYZ receives Provider Smith's claims and sends them directly to Payer Gold. This is a simple exchange, and the claim is paid fairly quickly.
  - **Example 2:** Provider Smith uses ABC billing software and enrolls with XYZ clearinghouse. Payer Gold isn't enrolled with XYZ clearinghouse; it's enrolled with JKL clearinghouse. So XYZ clearinghouse must send the claims to JKL clearinghouse before they can be sent to Payer Gold. This exchange takes longer to get the claim from the provider to the payer and may delay payment.

Obviously, if a clearinghouse has to send a claim to other clearinghouses, the claims process takes longer. In addition, exchanges like this can perpetuate, with your claims going every which way before reaching the intended payer. And every time the claim is transferred, the chances of it being stalled or lost increases. And round and round you go! To avoid this carousel of billing chaos, you need to know where the claims are going after they leave the provider.

If you are enrolled with a clearinghouse that seems to always send the claims to other clearinghouses, shopping around may be wise. Enrolling with a larger entity may cost a little more, but doing so is usually worthwhile if it gets the payment in sooner.

It's always a good idea to keep your clearinghouse reports. You may need them should the need to prove timely filing arise down the road.

. . . And going on to the payer

After making its way through the clearinghouse, the claim finally ends up with the payer. The payer is responsible for paying the provider for services rendered to its client, the patient. Refer to Chapter 6 for information about the various payers.

Recognizing how claims are processed

The payer enters the claim into its processing software. What happens next depends on the claim. Claims that are compliant with the provider contract and patient's plan guidelines are usually paid promptly.

Claims that involve high dollar amounts or that need supporting documentation usually require *manual processing*. Unlike most claims, which are processed by computers, claims requiring manual processing need to be reviewed by a human. In addition to simply looking at the procedures, the payer reviews the diagnosis and other applicable documentation. For example, if the provider contract includes a carve-out for, say, implants (refer to the earlier section "Cutting through reimbursement rates and carve-outs"), then the payer may need to see the invoice(s) in order to calculate the correct payment for that line. Or if a provider has billed an unlisted code and the contract allows payment for this code, then the payer may need to review additional information, such as an operative report, to determine which procedure the unlisted code represents. As you may guess, manual claims processing takes longer.

Each state has an insurance department or commissioner, and any commercial payers who violate state prompt pay laws or contractually obligated payment timelines may be reported to the appropriate official. When this happens, the department investigates the complaint and may take action either by serving notice to the payer that payment must be made immediately or, if deemed appropriate, revoking or suspending the payer's license to do business in that particular state. Keep in mind, however, that, even though payers are obligated by contracts to pay claims within a specific time period, that obligation is not enforceable if the provider doesn't submit the claims correctly or completely. Also of note, federal government payers and ASO plans do not fall under the jurisdiction of state insurance regulators and therefore may not be required to adhere to these laws.

Understanding claims matching

To pay for services rendered, the payer relies on the claims to be correct and truthful, often using a method called *claims matching.* When specific services are performed, several providers submit claims for the same patient. Here's an example: Say that a patient has a surgery. The surgeon submits a claim; the hospital or facility submits a claim; and the anesthesiologist submits a claim. Each claim is slightly different, of course, because each provider rendered a different service, but the surgeon's bill, the anesthesiologist's bill, and the facility's bill should match — that is, the surgeon, the anesthesiologist, and the facility should all agree on the type of surgery that was performed.

WARNING

If the bills don't support one another the payer may request supporting documentation from any or all providers. In addition, if the surgeon and facility each bill for a completely different body part than that submitted on the anesthesia claim, an inquiry will likely occur. (***Note:*** Some payers won't pay for facility charges or the anesthesia charges until after they've reviewed the surgeon's bill.)

Working together with other providers gets claims paid faster. And that should always be your goal: coding correctly and efficiently to secure accurate and prompt payment for your provider. If additional information is requested from a payer, promptly provide it. Failure to cooperate delays not only your claim but all related claims as well.

Scoring the payment or going into negotiation

If the provider and payer have a contract in effect on the date the service was rendered and if the claim moved through the process as it should, the payment that the payer issues to the provider should be correct. If the payer and provider don't have a contract, the payer may send the claim to be priced by a third party in a process known as *negotiation.*

Some payers use third-party pricing companies to negotiate pricing for out-of-network claims. These companies serve as intermediaries in the negotiations between payer and provider. The intermediary contacts the provider and offers a negotiated settlement amount that is specific to an individual claim. Normally, this settlement offer also includes a prompt payment clause. After the provider signs the settlement, the payer sends the agreed upon payment. (You can read more about third-party administrators in Chapter 6.)

In a negotiation, the intermediary may do the following:

- **Arbitrarily price a claim and state that the pricing is "usual and customary" based on the geographical area where the services were provided:** These claims are often underpriced, so be prepared to challenge the pricing.
- **Submit a settlement request to the provider:** These settlement agreements normally obligate a discounted payment to be sent within a specified time, usually 10 days or less.

These negotiation attempts are just that — attempts. The provider isn't obligated to accept the offer. In fact, providers should counter any initial offer they receive from a payer in these circumstances:

- **When a contract exists between provider and payer:** If the claim doesn't pay as specified by the contract, you should immediately notify the payer of the issue. Often, you can simply send the claim back with a notation explaining how the claim should have processed.
- **When no contract exists between payer and provider:** In this situation, the payer isn't entitled to a discount, even though the payer looks for a discount in most cases. If the provider hasn't accepted a pre-payment price reduction but the payer takes one, immediately notify the payer *in writing* that the payment is not acceptable. This written notice, sent upon receipt of an under-paid claim settlement, is known as a *claim appeal*. The important part of the appeal is to know the payment rules and stand firm on them. I go into more detail on appeals in the next section.

The verbiage on these "offers" is that the claim will be processed under the accepted pricing. If the provider is out of network (and it will be), that just means said provider has agreed to accept a reduced fee. It is likely that this reduction will *not* exceed the patient's out-of-network deductible and there will be no "expedited" payment from the insurance company.

WORKING OUT THE WORKERS' COMP CLAIM DETAILS

Each state has its own guidelines for workers' compensation claim payments. Some states have fee schedules; others don't. In states that have workers' compensation fee schedules, these fee schedules function the same as a provider contract; the claim processes according to the fee schedule. If the provider treats a workers' comp patient, the payment guidelines that apply are those where the patient's employer filed the claim, not where the provider is.

Check out this example. Patient Bob works for a company that is headquartered in Kentucky. Bob lives in Illinois (which has a workers' compensation state fee schedule) but has surgery in Missouri (which has no workers' compensation fee schedule). The Kentucky employer files the claim with its carrier in Kentucky, and the Missouri provider is obligated by the payment guidelines of Kentucky.

Therefore, if you're coding the payment for a workers' compensation claim settlement, educate yourself and possibly your employer about the workers' comp laws of the state where the claim was filed. Most states have this information on their websites. You can also obtain the necessary information by calling the State Department of Injured Workers.

If the state-legislated payment rules are violated and a commercial payer (refer to Chapter 6) sends incorrect payment, then the provider has grounds to file an appeal, and it's your job as the coder to appeal, appeal, and appeal again until your provider has been paid correctly. If no contract or pre-payment agreement exists, then the provider is under no obligation to accept the payment as full claim settlement. Bottom line: Know before you file.

Fighting for Proper Payment: Filing an Appeal with the Payer

If something goes haywire during the claims process and your provider doesn't get paid or doesn't receive the amount contracted, you need to file an appeal with the payer. Another point you may have to appeal is violation of prompt pay statutes.

Prompt pay statutes define how long a payer has to pay a claim after having received it. The prompt pay statutes are different in each state, so make sure you know the statute that applies to your provider. If the payer doesn't pay within the legislated time frame, the statute usually obligates additional payment of interest, which accrues on each claim. Often, this accrual is per day.

REMEMBER

If the payer delays or stalls payment, interest is due. Because the interest amount is usually small, providers often overlook it. Don't. Enforcing the prompt payment rules keeps payers accountable. Plus, if the situation were reversed, don't think for one minute that the payer(s) would not enforce the interest penalty.

When you file an appeal, make sure you base the appeal on facts. The phrase "It's not fair!" isn't sufficient grounds for appeal — but, of course, you already know that. If a contract exists between payer and provider, you need to quote the verbiage of the contract in the appeal. If the payer is refusing to honor a negotiated agreement, you refer to the agreement. If the payer still refuses to settle the matter to your satisfaction, then you may need to take the issue to the state insurance commissioner, an attorney who specializes in this area of the law, or the Department of Labor.

For detailed information on how to file an appeal (as well as how to resolve disputes), head to Chapter 14.

REMEMBER

Remember the two golden rules of appealing a claim, and you'll be just fine in the coding world: First, keep impeccable documentation of every interaction you have with a payer. The paper trail you create might serve you well later when questions arise about the claims you process. And second, always, always keep your cool, on the phone and in writing. Think Dragnet style — just the facts, ma'am!

» Ensuring all billable codes are included

» Seeking clarification when the documentation is unclear

» Double-checking your work

Chapter 12

Homing In on How to Prepare an Error-Free Claim

Is any day better than payday? Personally, I think not. And I'm betting providers don't think so, either. That's why they hired you: to make sure all the coding is right-on so they get paid right away. Let's face it: Money talks. As the coder, you're the one who converts the healthcare provider's work into revenue. The more accurate the coding, the better the revenue.

Your goal as a biller/coder is to make sure every encounter is documented properly. The codes must accurately represent the work performed. If you undercode, for example, you're leaving money on the table: Work was done, but you didn't request the fair payment. Similarly, if you submit codes that the documentation doesn't support or you unbundle procedures for the purpose of extra payment, you're committing what is known as fraudulent billing.

Your goal, then, is to make sure you bill for every service for which your provider is entitled to be reimbursed. To do that properly, you need to know which services merit separate reimbursement (and which ones don't), how to gather the information you need to abstract the codes from the documentation, and what to check to make sure everything has been accurately represented. In this chapter, I tell you how to do all those things.

Assigning CPT Codes

To get your provider paid, you've got to start somewhere, and that somewhere can be found by looking no further than the Current Procedural Terminology (CPT) procedure codes you submit on each claim. The more accurately you assign these codes, the more money the payer sends to the provider. But the earning potential of each claim depends on much more than just assigning codes and crossing your fingers. Instead, your coding must be accurate, without *undercoding* (leaving billable codes off of the claim) or *upcoding* (submitting codes that are not supported by the medical record), both of which can be considered fraudulent billing.

The magical little codes that help you turn patient encounters into cash for your provider are the most powerful part of each claim you code. They help prove to a payer that a medical product or service should be paid for.

Getting the lowdown on CPT codes and fee schedules

Each payer assigns a specific dollar amount to each CPT code; this lets the payer know how much to pay for the service rendered. Put all the codes and all their associated fees in a list, and you have a fee schedule.

Medical fee schedules are built from CPT codes that are often either priced individually or categorized into tiers:

- **Fee schedules with individual pricing:** Medicare and other payers, such as Tricare, price codes individually, and their fee schedules list each individual code and the payment assigned to that code.
- **Fee schedules with categorized pricing:** These contracts are built around a tier system that groups procedural codes into specific tiers and assigns payment obligation to each tier. The procedures within each tier are normally of similar complexity and require a similar level of time, skill, and expertise. Each payer has its own tier system, although the more complex procedures earn higher reimbursement from the majority of commercial payers.

Knowing the rules governing which codes you can use

When you're coding, you just look at the fee schedule, find the CPT codes you need, and include them all on the claim form, right? Wrong. Not every code can be grouped or classified similarly, so you have to know what kind of code you're dealing with:

- **Codes that can't be billed with other codes:** Codes that represent different procedures to the same body part often can't be billed together. For example, an open reduction (or repair through an incision) of a fracture of the radius can't be billed with a closed reduction (setting the fracture without an incision) of the same body part. In these cases, only the more complex procedure is billed. When would such a situation occur? Suppose the physician tries a less invasive procedure but is unable to attain the desired results, so she ends up performing a more invasive or complex procedure. Only the more invasive or complex procedure is billable.

  To understand what can and can't be billed separately, you need to understand bundling. The later section "Paying attention to your bundle of joy" has the details.

- **Codes for procedures that can't be billed under specific circumstances:** Men can't get hysterectomies, so if a claim for a male patient lists a code for a hysterectomy, the payer isn't going to pay the claim. For obvious reasons, a hysterectomy is a procedure that is only payable if the patient is female. In today's lingo, the denial will likely indicate a medically unlikely procedure.
- **Codes that can only be billed to a patient once in a lifetime:** We only have one of some things (like gallbladders, spleens, and uteruses); therefore, a patient can have such an organ removed only once. If the payer system is up to date, additional claims for these types of one-time-only procedures are always rejected.
- **Codes that require specific conditions to be met before they can be billed:** Some codes are age-related, others are sex-related, and still others are the one-time-only codes (explained in the preceding item in this list). For example, various procedures (such as tonsillectomies or adenoid removals) are appropriate only for specific age groups. The CPT codebook indicates when a procedure code has such a condition.
- **Codes that aren't compatible with other codes (at least in theory):** Sometimes codes just can't be combined because performing both procedures would 1) be impossible, 2) not make sense, or 3) represent a service

or procedure that is incidental to another. For example, you wouldn't submit a procedure code for a right foot bunion repair during the same session when the right foot was amputated. Why would a physician bother with the bunion if the foot's coming off anyway? Well, he wouldn't, which is why you simply can't combine those codes. The same holds true with a cataract extraction for an eye that was removed the previous month, or an appendectomy performed on a patient during the same session as a colectomy (colon removal). These codes can't be combined because the procedures can't be done at the same time.

You can find out more about these code pairs through the Medicare National Correct Coding Initiative (NCCI) edits. These edits are available on the Centers for Medicare & Medicaid Services (CMS) website (`www.cms.gov`) and on most Medicare contractor websites.

Linking your CPT codes to ICD-10-CM codes

Remember your good friend, medical necessity? (If you don't, refer to Chapter 5.) Medical necessity plays a big role when it comes to the viability of the procedure codes you use. Every CPT code billed must be supported by a corresponding diagnosis code that supports medical necessity for the procedure that was performed.

REMEMBER

One diagnosis may support several procedure codes. A patient who presents with ankle instability may require as many as three billable procedures to stabilize the joint, and all three of these procedures will be paid. All of this information is part of the medical record; you just need to play Sherlock Holmes to find the coding clues to identify any and all billable codes.

Making your code as specific as possible

In addition to choosing the right code, you also need to ensure that the assigned code is specific to the procedure. Just as you rely on the physician to be as specific as possible in his or her documentation, the physician relies on you to assign the most accurate codes possible.

For this process to work as it should, two things need to happen in the following order: First, the physician needs to document correctly so that you can choose the appropriate procedural code. Second, you need to choose the correct CPT code using the physician's documentation. The next sections have the details.

REVVING UP FOR REVENUE CODES

Revenue codes are four-digit codes that are used on UB-04 claim forms, the forms used by facilities to bill most commercial payers. Revenue codes are only used on UB-04 claim forms; they're also used in addition to CPT codes. They let the payer know what kind of procedures the submitting provider is contracted or licensed to perform and bill. For providers, such as a hospital with multiple locations, the revenue code identifies the department in which the procedure was performed.

Providers that submit revenue codes have the accepted revenue codes specified in each vendor contract. The specific revenue codes listed in the contracts are discussed on the AAPC (American Academy of Professional Coders) website (www.aapc.com) and are also discussed in the Medicare Internet Only Processing manual, which you can access on the CMS website: www.cms.gov.

Although the majority of facility claims are submitted on UB-04 claim forms, professional claims are submitted on HCFA/CMS-1500 claim forms, which represent the services performed by a physician or other professional healthcare provider.

I discuss the differences in the forms in Chapter 2. What's important to remember here is that, although revenue codes only show up on the UB-04 form, they are somewhat related to what can be found on the HCFA/CMS-1500, and both kinds of forms must be as accurate as possible.

The doc's job: Documenting diagnosis and procedure

In the physician documentation, the physician must clearly state and describe the procedure that was performed. Here's an example of good documentation; it has everything you need to select the correct codes:

> A longitudinal incision was made to the radial aspect of the DIP joint of the left index finger. Subcutaneous dissection was blunt. An obvious ganglion was identified. The connection to the joint between the extensor tendon and collateral ligament was identified. The joint was opened, and the cyst was removed in its entirety, leaving the ligaments intact. The wound was irrigated. A vicryl stitch was placed between the tendon and the ligament. The skin was closed, and a dressing was applied.

Seems simple enough, right? Unfortunately, you'll occasionally encounter the following problems, which need to be resolved before you can assign the proper codes:

- **A physician simply dictates that she performed a specific procedure, but instead of describing the procedure, she uses a CPT code.** For example, "I then performed a CPT 29828." This type of entry doesn't satisfy documentation requirements. The physician must describe the procedure in detail before you can code and bill it. Proper documentation of a surgical procedure includes a brief history of the patient's problem, a good dictation of the approach taken, any structures affected by the approach, a clear description of what was done while inside the patient, any complications that may have arisen, and an explanation of the closure and recovery.
- **A physician may consistently fail to document a particular procedure, saying, "That's what I always mean when I say that."** Unfortunately, his intentions don't constitute proper documentation. The physician must clearly state and describe the procedure that was performed each and every time he performs it.
- **A physician may inadvertently clone a patient's record as a result of electronic health records (EHR).** This may happen following a surgical procedure, when the patient is seen postoperatively, or it may happen when a patient is seen on a recurring basis for a chronic condition. If the clinician isn't careful when entering patient information for the visit, procedures from previous encounters may be pulled into the current record. The result: incorrect billing. You may see injections that didn't occur, drugs that were not administered, or more than one evaluation and management encounter. You *may* even see surgery performed in the office. Coders must review these records prior to routine import into the billing software. The OIG (U.S. Office of Inspector General) and commercial payers all frown upon false claims, and such claims may have serious consequences.

TIP

If you're dealing with a doc who habitually makes these documentation assumptions, you may have to produce the necessary documentation — that is, show him the description of the procedure as published by the American Medical Association (AMA) or CMS — so that he agrees to comply. Doing so is more work for you, but it pays off big time later when you file that clean claim.

REMEMBER

In these situations, you need to get the missing information; after all, it's the physician's job to describe procedures, and it's your job to code them, not the other way around. However, how you go about filling in the documentation blanks is very important. You can't ask leading questions, for example, because doing so can lead to fraudulent coding and excessive reimbursement. Head to the later section "Setting the record straight: Physician queries" for strategies you can use to get the info you need.

The coder's job: Choosing the correct CPT codes

Most of the procedural codes are well-defined by the American Medical Association. They describe specifically how physicians have been trained to perform the procedures. For example, CPT code 25609 is the open reduction with internal fixation of an intra-articular (in the joint) distal radius fracture. (In plain English, this is a surgical procedure in which a broken arm is repaired through an incision.) This description reflects the industry standard regarding how the procedure is performed.

Every CPT code has a specific description. The documentation should fully support the use of each CPT code you submit for payment. In this game, close isn't good enough. The code has to be exact; you can't choose a code that's merely similar. Occasionally, however, you may have to use an *unlisted code* (which is pretty much what it sounds like — a code that is used when no other specific code fits).

Unlisted codes exist because the CPT codes aren't set in stone. As technology evolves, so do procedural codes. When a new technique is developed or modified as a result of new technology, the previously used code may no longer be appropriate. With an unlisted code, you compare the pricing to a similar specified code. For example, arthroscopic biceps tenotomy (cutting the tendon) currently doesn't have a specific CPT code, so when that procedure is performed, coders use CPT code 29999 and compare it for pricing purposes to CPT code 23405, which is the code that would be used if the procedure had been done through a traditional incision.

Paying attention to your bundle of joy

You can link some services together when you code because a physician may have performed one service as the result of doing another. As luck would have it, there's a handy-dandy term for grouping services under one code: *bundling*. Other times, codes describing services considered to be inclusive of another (that is, performed as part of a single procedure) can be billed separately if they are documented accordingly.

Knowing what to bundle or not is a skill that comes with practice and learning the ins and outs of your coding resource books. Refer to Chapter 4 for detailed info on bundling. In the next sections, I give you a quick overview.

Breaking down bundling basics

Whether procedures can be billed separately or not depends on what goes on during the encounter: An example would be laboratory panel codes. Panels are comprised of certain individual tests; the panel code can be used if all parts of the panel were performed. Otherwise, individual codes would be appropriate.

- If additional skill and time are required to do the extra work, then the other procedure may qualify for additional reimbursement. For example, closure of a surgical opening is part of the surgery. But if the closure is a complex procedure that involves an extensive amount of time and skill, then you may be able to separately report those services. Unbundling means that one or more codes that are normally incidental to another can be billed separately. To do that, you apply the individual codes and a modifier to bypass the edit.
- If the physician performed a procedure because he was already working on that part of the body, because that procedure incidental it is *not* separately reportable. For example, if a surgeon is performing abdominal surgery and decides to remove the patient's appendix as well, you can't bill for the appendectomy because the surgeon was already in the abdomen, and in some (if not all) states the appendectomy is mandated.
- Bundling can refer to a procedure that had to be done to successfully complete the primary procedure. Think about incisions and repairs. Before a surgeon can enter the body, an incision has to be made; therefore, it's not really a separate procedure. After the physician completes the surgery, the incision needs to be closed. Closure is not separate; it's incidental and a pretty important part of the procedure.

If you use coding software, the software indicates when two or more codes are mutually exclusive or when one is incidental to another. If you don't use coding software, you can go to the Medicare website and most Medicare contractor websites to find out whether or not the payer considers one code incidental to another.

The NCCI policy manual provides detailed rationale for understanding when incidental or mutually exclusive codes may be appropriately reported. Modifiers indicate when a procedure has been modified or altered. They should not be used to seek additional reimbursement. To find out more about modifiers, head to the later section "Applying Modifiers Correctly."

Dealing with bundling errors

Most payer processing software programs identify bundling errors, or more accurately, they identify procedures that have been unbundled improperly. They don't identify procedures that *should* have been included but that are missing. (After all, payers don't want to pay more than they must. If you unbundle for additional reimbursement, and the payer doesn't agree that the extra reimbursement is supported, it won't pay for it.) It's your responsibility as the coder to review the medical documentation and identify all billable procedural codes.

WARNING

Not all payer processing software identifies bundling errors. If you submit claims to those payers, the claim will pay as you billed it. Keep in mind, however, that this doesn't give you carte blanche to overcode. When you *overcode*, you take advantage of payers by submitting procedures that will pay but that are not supported in the record. The provider you work for is bound by ethics to submit truthful claims. Just because a payer will allow it doesn't mean you should bill it when unbundling is not supported.

Applying Modifiers Correctly

You use modifiers to alter the description of a service or procedure that has been provided. You can use modifiers in circumstances such as the following:

- **The service or procedure has both a professional and technical component.** An example would be radiological procedures: One provider (the facility) owns the equipment and bears the cost of maintenance and other things, but the physician must interpret the findings of the radiological procedure.
- **The service or procedure was performed by more than one physician and/or in more than one location.** For a complex procedure that requires more than two hands, an assistant surgeon may be used.
- **The service or procedure has been increased or reduced.** For example, a procedure that normally takes an hour requires two hours because of scar tissue, or the description of a procedure notes that another procedure is included but that other procedure wasn't necessary and therefore wasn't performed.
- **Only part of a service was performed.** A procedure that is bilateral by definition (that is, it is performed on both sides) is performed only on one side.
- **The service or procedure was provided more than once.** An example would be excising lesions on different areas of one body part through separate incisions.
- **Events occurred that were unusual to the circumstances.** For example, the patient had an adverse reaction to anesthesia, which resulted in early termination.

Note that you can use two types of modifiers: *informational modifiers*, such as "laterality"; and *payment modifiers*, such as "22," "25," or "59" (and the new more descriptive "x" modifier). Whenever you attach a modifier, make sure it's appropriate. Adding a modifier just because you know it'll get the claim paid is never okay.

Payer organizations revise modifiers annually, with some being added and others deleted, and each payer can determine whether and how the modifiers must be used for its own organization. For example, Medicare discontinued the SG modifier, which it once used to indicate that a claim was for a facility, but various Medicaid and workers' compensation payers still require it. For this reason, you must keep abreast of individual payer preferences with regard to required modifiers. In states that require ambulatory surgery centers to bill on HCFA/CMS-1500 forms instead of UB forms, the SG modifier is alive and kicking.

Some payers may have contracts and/or policies that have other requirements for modifiers above and beyond the standard coding usage.

Because commercial payer policies differ, make sure you have access to their contracts so that you can code the claims correctly with the required modifiers. You're also responsible for remaining current with regard to modifiers your employer uses. You can find modifiers in the CPT codebook, on the CMS website (`www.cms.gov`), and on Medicare contractor websites.

In the following sections, you can read about how modifiers relate to commercial payers as well as government ones. Other government payers such as the U.S. Department of Labor, Medicaid, and Tricare have specific modifier requirements for various classifications of providers and procedures.

Using modifiers for commercial payers

To apply more specific payments to procedures, many commercial payers require modifiers. Keep in mind, though, that how the modifiers are used differs from payer to payer. The following sections show some examples.

Modifiers 50, 52, RT, and LT

Certain procedural codes are bilateral in their description (that is, the procedure is performed on both sides of the body), while others require the use of a modifier to indicate laterality. Modifier 50 indicates that a procedure was performed bilaterally. For example, if a provider performs a bilateral procedure on one side only, the coder must apply modifier 52 to indicate that the services were reduced.

Some commercial payers recognize modifier 50 (bilateral procedures), essentially agreeing that the procedure was performed twice, once on each side — and process accordingly. Other providers require that the procedure be listed twice on the claim, first with the LT modifier (left) and then again with the RT modifier (right).

TC modifier and modifiers 22 and 26

Commercial payers commonly use the TC modifier and modifiers 22 and 26:

- **TC modifier and Modifier 26:** TC means "technical component." When a radiology service is being billed, for example, the facility that owns the equipment can bill for its use by applying the TC modifier to the appropriate procedural code. The physician who interprets the X-ray or other product of the radiology service can report his services by billing the same procedural code with modifier 26, indicating that the physician who didn't own the equipment did this work.
- **Modifier 22:** This modifier is used when a procedure is more extensive or required more time and skill than normal.

Managing modifiers for Medicare

Medicare claims always require the use of appropriate modifiers such as the following:

- Modifiers that indicate laterality.
- Modifiers that indicate services were provided by resident or intern in training. Some surgeries performed in a training hospital may also require a specific modifier to indicate that the reason another physician assisted was because a resident physician was unavailable. (*Resident physicians* are no longer medical students but are still in the learning phase of their careers. They have MD behind their names but continue to work with supervision before taking board examinations.)
- Modifiers to indicate that a non-physician practitioner, such as a nurse practitioner or a physician assistant, provided a service. Another modifier indicates that a non-physician who assisted a physician is seeking a separate reimbursement (applicable only if the procedural code is one that has been determined to require the additional assistance).

For additional information about Medicare modifier requirements, go to the CMS website (`www.cms.gov`).

Utilizing modifiers for other government payers

In addition to Medicare, other government payers require modifiers, as the next sections explain.

Tricare

Tricare, funded by the U.S. Department of Defense, insures active military members and their eligible dependents, as well as retired military members who have chosen to exercise the option to remain covered and their dependents. The options available to patients depend on their military status and where they live.

Tricare's processing software accepts all current modifiers, so when you bill this carrier, you want to make sure that you use all applicable modifiers. For example, a patient may have surgery for a hernia, which has a 90-day global package. (Tricare *global packages* specify the number of days and the services — preoperative assessment, postoperative visits, and so on — included with the reimbursement for the procedure.) That same patient may later see the same physician for a different ailment that requires a separate and appropriate modifier in order to be paid.

REMEMBER

Tricare benefits are administered through three Tricare area administrators: Tricare North, Tricare South, and Tricare West. Each of these administrators maintains a website that allows providers to verify fee schedules, check on required modifiers, and view other payer specific information.

Workers' comp (the Department of Labor)

The U.S. Department of Labor (DOL) recognizes current modifiers as determined by Medicare, but it still determines payment based on the approved procedure and diagnosis codes regardless of the modifiers. What this means is that when a DOL injury has been "approved," the body part that sustained injury is the only part covered. For example, a fracture of the left wrist will have the approved diagnosis code. If surgery is required, a specific CPT code is submitted for approval and that is the only code that will be paid under that claim. If during the surgery a nerve injury is identified, regardless of the documentation or modifier, repair of that nerve will not be paid unless that procedure defined by a specific CPT code had been approved prior to the surgery.

Using retired modifiers

Certain payers use older claims processing systems. Many of the Medicaid payers and some of the smaller workers' compensation payers still use these older programs and, as a result, still require the use of retired modifiers. *Retired modifiers* are those that were removed from the Medicare list.

One retired modifier that is still routinely used is the SG modifier, mentioned earlier. This modifier was used to indicate that the procedure code on the claim was being submitted by an ambulatory surgery center to represent the facility's charges for the service provided.

You're responsible for knowing which modifiers the payer requires. If you submit a claim without the appropriate modifier or with a new modifier that isn't programmed into the payer's processing software, the claim may be rejected. To prevent this from happening and to get the claim paid faster, always check with the payer prior to submission. If the payer is one of those who doesn't answer the phone or hasn't updated its website with current policies, you need to follow up with a letter. In the letter, request a summary of claim filing requirements.

Looking for Money Left on the Table

Your responsibility as a biller/coder is to abstract all billable codes from the medical record. Failing to identify billable codes (*undercoding*) is referred to as leaving money on the table. And leaving money on the table will get you fired. Want to understand and avoid undercoding? Read on.

As bad as undercoding is, overcoding is just as bad. When payers discover later that a claim was overpaid, they'll ask for the money back, usually in the form of a demand letter that describes the overpayment and explains why the payment should be returned. If the payment isn't returned, the payer uses the overpayment as an offset to future claims, sort of like a credit, in what is known as a *take-back.* Take-backs are a challenge to the payer, but they're even more of a challenge for the provider because convincing a payer that the overpayment doesn't actually exist can be difficult. When the payer has already used the perceived overpayment toward future claims, the ledger can get pretty messy.

Some states have laws that define the number of months that can pass in which an overpayment refund can be requested. These state laws don't apply to federal government payers or to ASO plans. Some state laws also define the time frame in which carriers can request payment returns. Make sure you know the laws of your state.

Turning a critical eye to the record

You must catch any and every service in the provider's record and code it accordingly. Unfortunately, although the coding software your provider uses may help you identify a lot of oddities in the claim, such as unbundling, it won't help you identify undercoding. To do that, you have to rely on your coding skills, because you're the last line of defense against leaving money on the table.

TIP

If your employer doesn't use coding software, the NCCI edits are available on the Medicare website as well as on most of the Medicare contractor websites. Other sources include coding companion publications that usually indicate procedures that are inclusive to a particular code.

REMEMBER

Undercoding and overcoding errors often result from a misunderstanding about what can and can't be bundled. Although you don't want to overcode, you do want to look critically at every procedure so that you can determine whether you can code it separately.

Overriding published edits

As the coder, you can override — or bypass — a published edit in the software, if you know how. The most obvious way to bypass a published edit is to assign a modifier to a code. This modifier gives the payer more information about the procedure in question. As I explain earlier, modifiers indicate when a procedure has been altered from its published description and should be reimbursed accordingly. They may indicate that a normally bundled procedure was actually separate or that a procedure required additional time and work by the physician or required assistance of a co-surgeon or assistant surgeon among other things.

In some circumstances, you can't use a modifier, even though, when reviewing the record, you can clearly see that the provider performed extra work. In this situation, if you're dealing with a commercial payer, you may be able to convince the payer to allow the additional procedures. Keep in mind, though, that if these payers base their argument on edits found in their own claim editing software, and the edit says "no," then the answer is "no."

TIP

Payers use claim-editing programs that may differ from the NCCI edits and can be frustrating to providers. Usually the payer contracts identify which claims editing software they use for processing. Some payers use more than one type of editing software and apply the one that allows them to pay the least. Again, this situation is frustrating for providers, and if it's in the contract, it can be very hard to challenge successfully.

Setting the record straight: Physician queries

Suppose you are looking at documentation and it does not seem to be complete. Sometimes, dictation does not capture everything the physician said, or he may have been interrupted and lost his train of thought. There may also be conflicting information within the record (for example, the physician references the right arm in paragraph 1 and the left arm in paragraph 2). Either way, incomplete documentation needs to be addressed. It is time to query the physician.

Knowing when a physician query is necessary

When you ask for clarification, you're performing what is known as a *physician query*. A physician query is necessary when you encounter an implied procedure or a missing procedure:

- **Implied procedure:** In this situation, a procedure may be listed in the heading of a record, but it's not documented in the body of the record.
- **Missing procedure:** A missing procedure is one for which a diagnosis is listed but no treatment is noted.

The missing or implied procedure may have been a result of the physician being interrupted during dictation, or it may be an error in transcription. Most physicians and facilities use transcription services. The physician dictates, and the transcriptionist listens to the dictation and types the words into a document. Sometimes the transcriptionist uses templates and fails to import the correct one. Other providers use voice recognition software. The physician dictates, and the words are entered automatically into a document. These notes have frequent errors, and clarification of the medical record is important for legal reasons.

WARNING

If you work with a particular physician for an extended time, you'll be so familiar with what the doctor does and how he does it that you'll essentially be "in the doctor's head" every time you read the documentation. It's vitally important that you remain cognizant of the need for clear documentation and are careful about not coding a procedure that likely was done but is omitted from the documentation.

Conducting a physician query

A physician query is simply a note to the physician that asks for clarification of the record. Some offices have a query form you can use to seek clarification when a procedure has been implied or is obviously missing. Many of these forms, which are common in hospitals or large offices, list the most common omissions and a line for "Other." You simply check the box you need more information for.

If you work for different providers, you need to familiarize yourself with the various query procedures of each office. If you're working with a small office or practice, you can leave the note or chart in question on the physician's desk with a note that says something like: "Which arm was it?" or "How large was the lesion?"

In other practices, you can simply ask the physician a non-leading question, and the provider will then dictate an addendum to the record that clarifies or corrects the issue at hand. Knowing how to approach the physicians now can help you produce sparkly clean claims later.

When you ask a physician for clarification about a record, beware of putting words in the doc's mouth. Any and all clarification about records must come straight from the physician — not you. Don't make assumptions about what he meant. Question the documentation, but don't lead. Here are some examples of good versus bad queries:

Instead of This	Say This
It was the left arm, correct?	What arm did you perform the procedure on?
Was the tumor more than 5 cm?	How large was the tumor?
Did you excise more than 1 cm of clavicle?	How much clavicle was removed?
Did you debride to bleeding bone?	How extensive was the debridement?

Checking and Double-Checking Your Documentation

Just as carpenters "measure twice, cut once," before you send out a claim, you need to check and double-check your work to increase your chances for success (read, getting the requested reimbursement) the first time around.

Submitting a claim correctly with all necessary information required for prompt processing is known as filing a "clean" claim. A clean claim is one that can be processed without the payer needing to request additional information from the provider or a third party.

When you review each record during your final check for accuracy, remember to do the following:

- Make sure the patient's name, address, date of birth, identification number, and group number are correct and populate the correct fields.
- Check to see that all billable codes are documented.
- Verify that the form contains no expired or deleted codes and that the codes have been entered correctly (no transposed digits).

» Verify that medical necessity has been met.

REMEMBER

You must make sure that the documentation is relative to the diagnosis. The record should always include the reason for the patient encounter (medical necessity, which you can read more about in Chapter 5). In addition, any and all procedural codes submitted for payment must be supported by the appropriate diagnosis code that supports medical necessity. When a diagnosis is entered into the record, a decision regarding treatment usually follows it, if it wasn't actually treated at that time. Diagnosis codes such as these that are part of the medical record but that are unsupported by documentation or appear to be irrelevant to the services provided may be subject to physician query. If a billable procedure is obviously missing, indicate that to the physician. Ask her to clarify the record. (Refer to Chapter 2 for information on verifying documentation.)

» Make sure the record is complete and that all fields are populated.

» Check that all required signatures are dated, especially physician signatures. Electronic signatures also show a time and date stamp.

» If the physician completed a super-bill (a billing form used in many providers offices that includes the most frequently performed procedures), verify that the procedures indicated on the bill are documented in the record.

» Verify the prioritization of the codes in relation to the payer-specific contract. Know which codes are obligated for higher reimbursement. (The payer may want the highest paying code listed first on the claim.)

» Check for bundling/unbundling issues. You can find out more about these in the earlier section "Paying attention to your bundle of joy."

» Make sure the payer is correctly identified, including the right payer identification number and payer mailing address.

After you make sure that all these elements are in place, you submit that puppy! The preferred method of submitting claims is electronically. Electronic submission is faster, and it allows the provider to verify that the payer accepted the claim. The clearinghouse will acknowledge the receipt of each claim and will also generate an acceptance report if one is returned by the payer after the assigned payer has accepted the claim. For more information on what happens in the clearinghouse and beyond, head to Chapter 13.

» Decreasing the time your claims linger in accounts receivable

» Using RA documentation to verify proper payment

Chapter 13
From Clearinghouse to Accounts Receivable to Money in the Pocket

As the preceding chapters make clear, a lot goes into getting a claim ready, and nearly an entire village has had its fingers in the pie. The front office staff has gathered all the necessary demographic and insurance information. The physician has seen the patient and documented all provided services in the medical record. You have carefully abstracted all billable services and supported them with diagnosis codes that support medical necessity, entered the insurance and demographics information and the codes into the billing software, reviewed everything to make sure all the *i*'s are dotted and *t*'s crossed, and then sent the claim on its way with a kiss, a wave, and silent prayer that it doesn't take to drinking or get caught up with the wrong crowd.

Yes, a lot can happen to a claim once it leaves your conscientious hands. In this chapter, you take a look at the kinds of things — beyond coding errors — that can impact whether your claim generates the payments your provider deserves. I also explain some of the things that impact the final reimbursement amount.

Spending Time in the Clearinghouse

When the claim is ready to be submitted, you upload it to the clearinghouse to be sent to the payer. What, exactly, happens once your claim reaches the clearinghouse? The next sections explain.

Scrub-a-dub-dub: Checking for errors

At the clearinghouse the claim is *scrubbed,* or checked for errors. Some errors identified by the clearinghouse can be corrected online so that the claim can be forwarded on. This type of error includes mistakes regarding revenue codes or other clerical issues. Other errors, however, are not so easily fixable. For these, the claim needs to be fixed at the provider's office and then resubmitted. Errors of this type include attempting to submit to a payer who is unknown to the clearinghouse. This situation can occur because some smaller payers don't accept electronic claims and aren't registered with any of the clearinghouse companies. In this case, you must submit a paper claim directly to the payer. (Directions for claim submission are always noted on the patient's ID card.)

Matchmaker, matchmaker: Sending the claim to the right payer

The clearinghouse directs the claim to the payer, according to the payer identification number, in a process known as *payer matching.* During the provider's original enrollment with the clearinghouse, payers are matched to the correct payer identification number following the first claim submission. The payer ID is the electronic address of the payer, and it tells the clearinghouse where to send the claim. Every time a claim is submitted to a new payer, the clearinghouse flags the claim for payer matching.

The provider is responsible for telling the clearinghouse which payer should receive the claim. If the provider identifies the wrong payer, the claim won't be paid. (Payers don't take claims that belong to other insurance companies and send them on. Instead, the payer usually rejects the claim and sends notice of that rejection to the submitting provider through the clearinghouse.)

The payer processes the claim and determines the reimbursement according to the codes submitted on the claim. For information on what goes on after the claim is in the payer's hands, head to the later section, "Payment or Denial: Being in the Hands of the Payer."

TECHNICAL STUFF

Revenue codes are not usually assigned by the coder, but they are programmed into the billing software and are based on the type of provider submitting the claim.

Generating reports

Every clearinghouse keeps track of the claims that pass through its system. Reports are available that show claims that were sent, which payer they were sent to, and when all these transactions occurred. Also available are reports that indicate when a problem occurs with claim submissions. You can find these reports on the provider's clearinghouse web page. Most payers also send files back to the clearinghouse that report the status of the transmitted file(s).

REMEMBER

Sometimes a provider submits an incorrect claim, isn't notified of an error, and the claim just seems to disappear. This is why follow-up is so important. Be sure to check the clearinghouse acceptance reports and verify them with the billing software submitted claims, also called the *batch report,* daily. If a claim is on the batch report but not on the acceptance report, find out why.

TIP

Daily verification of the rejected reports is also important. Part of your office routine should be to check the rejection report and fix all claims on the same day if possible. By following up immediately, you can prevent timely filing denials (that is, having your claim denied because you failed to submit it within the payer's published time frame). If you are faced with a timely filing denial, the clearinghouse report may be just the evidence you need to have the denial overturned.

Facing Factors Affecting Reimbursement Amounts

Claims are submitted to generate reimbursement. Each provider determines how much it will charge for services provided, but that is not necessarily the fee that the payers will pay. When a provider and payer have a contract, reimbursement is based entirely on the obligation that is contractually defined. Without a contract, reimbursement depends on different factors, which I discuss in the following sections.

Understanding relative value units

You may wonder how Current Procedural Terminology (CPT) codes correspond to a dollar value and why. The system used by Medicare and many health maintenance organizations (HMOs) is called the Resource-based Relative Value Scale (RBRVS). Every CPT code has been assigned something called a relative value unit, or RVU, that determines the cost of a service.

Determining the RVU

The RVU is determined by first adding up three components:

- **The work required by the physician:** This component takes into consideration the amount of time, skill, training, and intensity that was necessary to perform the procedure. Each CPT code is reviewed at least every five years to determine whether this value should remain the same.
- **The cost of doing business or maintaining a practice:** This includes rent, equipment, supplies, and staff.
- **The malpractice expense or liability expenses borne by the provider:** Malpractice/liability expenses vary among providers. Certain specialties such as obstetrics tend to involve higher malpractice premiums than a primary care physician is likely to face.

These three RVU factors are then multiplied by a geographical adjustment that creates the compensation level for the service in that exact location. (This geographical adjustment explains why a procedure done in New York City is worth more than the same procedure done in Boise.) The geographically adjusted RVUs are then multiplied by a conversion factor that converts the RVU into a dollar amount, which determines the price that Medicare or the HMO pays. Using this formula, any entity can calculate the price it'll reimburse for any given procedure.

Reviewing RVUs and contract details

Make sure you know the contract details for each payer, because the differences between payers can be huge. For example, depending upon how the contract is structured, the providers may still find themselves paid per RVU rather than contract allowance.

Also, when multiple procedures are billed on a claim, they are prioritized for payment, and a discount, called the *multiple procedure discount* (MPD), is often applied. The procedure that is obligated at the higher allowance is paid at 100 percent of the allowed amount; the second procedure may be paid at 50 percent; and so on. On contracts that are based on RVUs, the higher the RVU, the higher priority for payment. (You can read more about prioritization of payments in the next section.)

Not all contracts are RVU-based, and procedures that are obligated to pay higher according to the contract may have a lower RVU. This sometimes occurs when the contract contains several commonly performed procedures that have been carved out. With this tactic (which is referred to as *strategic contract management*), specialty providers identify certain procedures that are routinely performed and ask that one or two (or more) of the related procedural codes be *carved out,* or especially identified as payable at a flat rate that isn't linked to RVUs or any other fee schedule. A surgeon who performs 300 laparoscopic cholecystectomies (gallbladder removals) each year may try to have that specific procedural code carved out of one or two of his network contracts to pay a flat rate.

Prioritizing procedures

The payment poster, the person who posts the payments to the account ledger, needs to know the correct order in which to post the payment. He gets that info from the claim form.

Procedures are billed by order of expected payment. The procedure that is expected to reimburse the greatest amount needs to be the first one listed on the claim, the procedure that is expected to reimburse the next greatest amount is next on the claim form, and so on down the line.

How this order is established varies. Many offices have the contract pricing programmed into their billing software. If the software is programmed correctly (that is, the contracts are loaded correctly, and the claim is linked to the correct payer contract in the billing software), the claim will be submitted in the correct order. (***Note:*** The program should be updated every year and every time the contract is revised.)

If the software is not programmed, then the responsibility for prioritization of procedures falls to you. That is why you need to know the contractual obligation for each procedure — so that you can identify which procedure is to pay at 100 percent and so on.

Most payers have processing software that recognizes the correct prioritization of the procedures and processes the claim to pay in that order, but some payers pay claims based solely on the prioritization established by the billing provider. That's why it's important to know whether the payer is contracted. If so, the highest reimbursable procedure will likely be listed first on the claim, followed by the next higher, and so on. But if the payer contract is RVU-based rather than procedural based, the procedure with the highest RVU is first.

If an error occurs in claims payment, the problem may be the prioritization. If the provider thinks a certain CPT code should be paid at 100 percent of the allowed amount, but that CPT code has a lower RVU and the payer software processes per RVU, a dispute is certain. In such cases, the contract prevails, so you need to know the contract and your priorities — literally! In the end, the payer is the one who decides whether to make payment. Most contracts contain arbitration clauses that outline the process of dispute resolution. When no contract is in place, the dispute can escalate to a legal issue to be decided by a judge.

Payment or Denial: Being in the Hands of the Payer

After you submit the claim to the clearinghouse and the clearinghouse acknowledges the receipt of the claim and sends it off to the payer, you wait. Every payer has its own timetable and, depending on how clean your claim is (refer to Chapter 12), will choose to push things through the system or deny your claim.

Diligent claim follow-up on your part can accelerate prompt payment. This process needs to begin the day that the claim is uploaded to the clearinghouse. Be sure to verify and archive all transmission reports. These reports are your proof that the claim was sent, and they serve as proof of timely filing should a dispute occur later.

After accepting the claim (either in electronic or paper form), the payer either rejects it or sends it for processing. When the payer enters the claim for processing, it is referred to as a *pending claim,* which means it's waiting to be reviewed for payment. Fortunately, you can do things to shorten the wait time, which I explain in the next section.

After that, the claim will either be paid or . . . not. If your provider gets paid, you're golden. If not, you have to deal with rejection or the big D — denial. The following sections have the details.

Reducing your time in accounts receivable

The practice of following up on claims after submission can reduce the number of days from submission date to payment date. Ideally, the claim should leave your hands within 72 hours after the date of service. That is when the payment clock starts and when you can start looking for that check to show up in accounts receivable (AR).

To help reduce your claim's time in AR, state payment laws legislate the number of days in which a payer must pay a clean claim. Payer contracts usually have prompt pay clauses, as well.

Your billing software can help you keep track of how long a claim has gone unpaid by giving providers access to a number of reports. One of those is the *aged collection ledger.* This report reflects the individual payers and the patient accounts that are associated with each payer. The report also indicates the age of the account in number of days: 30 days or fewer, 31–60 days, 61–90 days, 91–120 days, and so on. The report also shows the number of days allowed in AR per payer.

When looking at the report, look at the abbreviated version, which is the age of the accounts per payer, and do the following:

1. **Beginning with the payer with the largest number of accounts receivable outstanding, look at the payer's accounts that are 30 days or fewer.**

   Verify that these claims have been received. Doing so helps prevent timely filing issues later on.

2. **Looking at the oldest accounts, call each payer and check the status of each account.**

   Here are some questions to ask each payer you call:

   - "What is the payer-specific claim number?"

     Note: The incoming claim receives a claim number from the clearinghouse called an ICN (incoming claim number). Make note of that number as well and verify it with your submission report.

   - "What is the status of this claim?"
   - "When can we expect payment?"
   - "Are there any issues causing the claim to be delayed? If so, how can we fix them?"
   - "Is additional information needed?" If so, get a fax number and send the necessary information; then call back and confirm the receipt of the fax.
   - "With whom am I speaking, and what is the reference number for this call?"

3. **Work your way through the aged account ledger by looking at the accounts as they have aged and get the claims in process to pay.**

   If you are responsible for the financial state of the aged accounts, the fewer the days in accounts receivable for each claim, the better you look.

Overcoming rejection

With a rejection, essential information is missing from the claim that prevents the payer from entering the claim into its system. Common reasons for rejection include missing or incorrect patient identification number or demographic information such as sex or birth date. Your goal with a rejection is to provide the missing info in a thorough and timely manner.

If a claim doesn't process correctly as result of a coding error, you need to submit a corrected claim. Many payers have specific forms that you must use to facilitate this process. Usually the form asks for the original claim number and includes a field you use to identify the reason for the corrected claim submission.

WARNING

If you notice that a claim was coded or billed incorrectly, it's the provider's responsibility to notify the payer of the error. Failing to notify a payer when a claim has been erroneously submitted may result in charges of fraud. Other types of fraud include knowingly submitting incorrect information or filing a claim for services that were not provided.

In some cases, the payer may request a refund of the incorrectly billed claim. Medicare has a voluntary refund form on the Centers for Medicare & Medicaid Services (CMS) website, as do most carrier websites. This form is used when a provider wants to return a Medicare payment, and it allows the provider to simply submit a new claim. Commercial payers vary in their policies when dealing with an incorrectly submitted claim, so check with the individual payer to verify the process prior to sending back a payment.

Dealing with denial

Reimbursement is a direct result of the provider's tenacity in following up the claim submission and submitting claims correctly. Claim errors result in either rejections (covered in the preceding section) or denials. With a denial, the claim was processed by the payer but is not being paid for some reason. Claims deny for a myriad of reasons, such as omission of policyholder information (name, birth date, and relationship to patient) when different than the patient, failure to obtain an authorization number or referral, not checking the "Accept Assignment" box, or missing or incomplete provider information, such as the physical address where services were rendered.

When you're faced with a denial, you don't take it lying down. Instead, you gather together your wherewithal, your documentation, and anything else you need and file an appeal. Chapter 14 has the details.

Breaking Down the Remittance Advice

After a claim processes, payment follows. Each payment is accompanied by a *remittance advice*, or RA. An explanation of benefits (EOB) is sent to the patient and an RA is sent to the provider to show how the claim processed. It also lets the provider know whether any remaining balance is due by the patient. As a biller/coder, you want to review this documentation to verify that the claim was processed and paid correctly.

Getting familiar with the RA

The RA generally contains the details explaining how the claim was processed, although some payer remittances show only the total claim amount along with the total provider write-off and the total allowance. When this happens, it is up to the payment poster, or designee, to break the payment out to show the detail by line.

On the RA, payments are posted by line item. If a claim lists four CPT codes, the payment is allocated among the payable four lines to show how much reimbursement was received for each procedure.

Here are the kinds of postings you see on the RA for every CPT code listed:

- Amount of the procedure before any discounts are applied
- Amount the patient is responsible for
- How much the contract allows for the procedure
- The type and amount of any discounts that apply
- The final amount of the reimbursement after all discounts, deductibles, and so on, are applied

REMEMBER

As a coder, you need to pay attention to the details on this form to make sure the provider received the reimbursement to which she was entitled. Here are some things to look for:

- That the right payment allowances were applied
- That discounts were applied appropriately
- That no procedures were improperly denied
- If no payment was received, whether it was due to the entire amount being applied to the patient's deductible, the claim being denied, or some other reason

If anything is amiss — the payment allowances aren't correct, for example, or a procedure that should have approved was denied — then you need to appeal the claim and provide medical records and other necessary documentation to support your claim. Head to Chapter 14 for more on making an appeal.

Another issue with an remittance advice can be blamed on payer processing changes. Payers sometimes split or combine lines from the original billing, such as a procedure billed with modifier 50, *Bilateral Procedure,* appended and 2 units. The payer remit may show as two lines, RT and LT. Posters need to be attentive to these issues when using an autopost payment system (included in some software) because the payment will not balance.

Meshing the COB with the RA

Your RA may address something known as *coordination of benefits* (COB), which has to do with how benefits are paid when a patient has more than one insurance plan that covers the service, as in the case of dependents or children who are covered under both their parents' insurance. If, for example, both parents are employed and have benefits, either one or both of the parents will have dependent coverage on the children. When both parents exercise this option, confusion often ensues. Here are some of the key issues that arrive with COB claims:

- **When both parents exercise this option, whose plan is the *primary payer* (the first payer to be responsible for claim processing)?** Most payers make this determination based on what is known as the *birthday rule,* which states that the parent with the earlier birthday (by month and day, not year) is the primary payer. So if Mom's birthday is January 6 and Dad's birthday is May 31, Mom's insurance is the primary payer.
- **If a claim is submitted to Dad's insurance when Mom's plan is the primary payer, what happens?** Dad's insurance usually denies payment as the responsibility of another payer. If you submitted the claim to Dad's insurance after Mom's insurance paid, you also need to submit the RA from Mom's insurance along with the claim to show that the claim was paid or priced by the correct payer.

Dealing with two-parent or dual coverage of an adolescent gets more complicated when a divorce is a factor in determining responsibility. Some divorce decrees assign responsibility for medical coverage to a certain parent, and this decree may conflict with the birthday rule. When this happens, getting the claim paid correctly takes tenacity, and you may need assistance from the parent(s). Similarly, when a responsible parent remarries and that spouse or stepparent becomes the primary carrier, getting claims paid correctly can take months.

» **What happens if, for some reason, the primary payer's plan no longer insures the child?** In this case, the parents need to contact the correct payer and update the records so that the claim will pay correctly. (***Note:*** You can prevent this situation by verifying at check-in whether the insurance is the primary payer; refer to Chapter 11 for information on the kinds of things to check during check-in.)

Surveying subrogation

Insurance companies do not want to pay claims for which they are not responsible. There may be times that the patient's insurance pays the claim, then subrogates the claim with another company after determining that responsibility is that of another payer. *Subrogation* happens when a third party takes on the responsibility of another's legal right to collect the payment, which means that company A paid the original claim and then went to company B (maybe a homeowner's insurance) and asked to be reimbursed. When this happens, you may see an RA come across your desk that shows the claim reversed but still paid.

TECHNICAL STUFF

Subrogation can be financially advantageous to a third-party payer who bears financial responsibility because it allows the non-contracted third party to benefit from the contracted pricing. After all, the third party is simply reimbursing the amount the insurance company paid, which, because of contracted discounts and fee schedules, may be much less than a non-contracted payer would otherwise pay. The end result is usually a huge savings on claim settlement.

» Identifying when an appeal is necessary

» Crafting an appeal that gets results

» Managing Medicare appeals

Chapter 14
Handling Disputes and Appeals

Filing that first claim is a great feeling. High-fives all around. But just when you thought your job was done, you realize it's only just begun. After you master the front-of-house operations, you're ready to button things up on the back end, which, in the claim cycle, refers to following up outstanding claims and is just an insider's way of saying *collections.*

At this point, you also may find yourself dealing with disputes with the payers. Maybe the payer didn't process the claim correctly. Maybe it denied payment entirely. In either case, your job is to figure out the cause of the dispute and work to resolve it. In this chapter, I tell you everything you need to know about the appeals process.

Dealing with Disputes Involving Contract and Non-Contracted Payers

Most, if not all, disputes arise when the provider, your employer, is underpaid. Ideally, payer contracts clearly define a firm payment structure. Often, these contracts are based on Medicare fees, and as long as you're participating in the patient's plan, all is good. Sometimes a contracted payer processes a claim incorrectly, a kind of dispute that is easily remedied. Other types of disputes require more work. In the following sections, I explain what you can expect when handling disputes involving both contract and non-contracted payers.

TIP

You can prevent many issues by verifying the patient's coverage prior to the encounter. Some plans require that certain procedures be authorized prior to being performed, for example; other plans (HMOs especially) may require a referral from the primary care physician before seeing a specialist. When you verify coverage, make sure you understand what, exactly, has been approved. A referral may be just for a visit, for example, and if surgery or another procedure is deemed necessary, the patient may need another referral to be treated. So check because a little effort on the front-end may save a lot of effort on the back end.

Contract payers

Contract payers are those with whom your provider has a contract or who are part of a network with which the provider has a contract. The contract identifies the payment structure for each procedure and defines such issues as the following:

- The number of procedures that are to be paid per service date
- The reduction formula, often referred to as the multiple procedure reduction

  REMEMBER

  With *multiple procedure discount* (MPD), the first procedure is paid at 100 percent of contractual allowance; the second may be paid at a reduced rate, often 50 percent; and the third at whatever percentage is deemed appropriate per the contract. Medicare sets the standard by stating that the first procedure is paid at 100 percent and additional procedures are paid at 50 percent of the allowance. Some payers reduce subsequent procedures to 25 percent of the allowed amount, and others may limit the number of procedures that will be paid.
- Other payment guidelines, such as revenue code allowances and implant allowances (implants are plates, screws, anchors, and other hardware used to secure orthopedic repairs)
- The timely filing limit (Medicare is one year, but many commercial payers have shorter limits)
- The appeals process

If a payer fails to pay a claim as defined by contract, the appeals process is pretty simple: You simply write a letter that details the way the claim should have paid according to the contract. If the claim didn't pay as expected due to an ambiguity in the contract, you need to outline your expectations, refer to the contract, and stand firm. A well-structured contract averts any ambiguous processing.

Non-contracted payers

Non-contracted payers are those with whom the provider does not have a contract. Payment for these claims is what is known as *out-of-network*, and you need to carefully investigate them prior to any patient encounter because some plans don't allow for out-of-network services.

Plans that don't allow payment for out-of-network providers may process the claim to make the entire billed amount the patient's responsibility, or they may pay the claim without applying a discount. Often, if a provider doesn't participate in a certain network, the payer negotiates through a third-party pricing agent and tries to obtain a discount from the provider. Other times, if a provider contacts an out-of-network payer prior to a patient encounter, the payer asks for a one-time agreement for payment.

TIP

In cases where the payer denies payment and the plan provisions stipulate that the patient is responsible for all charges, most providers try to work with the insurance company to get the claim paid. Therefore, before sending the patient a bill, try to talk to the patient's insurer to find out whether the issue can be resolved. You also want to let the patient know that her insurer has denied payment and see whether either she or her employer can assist in resolving the issue.

When you deal with non-contracted payers, you need to rely on correct claims processing guidelines (published by the Centers for Medicare & Medicaid Services [CMS]) and the pre-encounter verification. Commercial payers can always cry "NCCI edits" when processing an out-of-network claim. After that, they are bound by the provisions of the patient's coverage plan.

REMEMBER

Patients are responsible for ensuring that any medical provider they seek treatment from accepts their insurance. However, as a principle of good customer service and sound business practices, a provider should, whenever possible, verify patients' coverage prior to treating them so that the patients will be aware in advance of the extent to which they will be financially responsible for payment.

Knowing When to File an Appeal: General Guidelines

After you submit a claim to the payer, you can reasonably expect a response within 60 days. Often, larger payers respond within 15 days. If everything goes the way it should, the payer processes the claim as you anticipated, and the payment is correct. If either of these two things doesn't happen, you need to follow up.

When general follow-up doesn't yield a timely payment

Following up may be as simple as calling the payer to see whether the claim has been received and where it stands in the adjudication process. (*Adjudication* refers to the payment obligation outlined in the patient's insurance benefits with regard to a claim.) Sometimes, the claim just isn't there, and you need to resubmit it and start the calendar again. Other times, the payer may need additional information from your office, another provider, or the patient.

If the payer needs information from your office, you can provide it simply enough. If the payer needs information from another provider, you may need to contact that other provider to see whether the payer's request has been received and whether the provider has responded. If information is needed from the patient, you probably need to contact the patient and ask her to contact her insurance company. If a claim does not pay as obligated by contract, you need to start the appeals process, explained in the section "Going through an Appeal, Step by Step."

When mix-ups in accounts receivable result in a delay

Accounts receivable (AR) is the industry name for outstanding payments. All companies monitor how many days their numerous accounts have been in AR. For most companies, an average age of 30 to 45 days is acceptable, but this can vary depending on provider specialty and the types of payers the practice accepts. Some billing companies may find 90 days tolerable, but going beyond that gets undesired attention from above. Outstanding AR can be a result of a slow payer, and most contracts contain language that obligates payment within a certain time. Many states have prompt pay statutes aimed at preventing claim stalling.

Often the cause of a high number of accounts receivable days is that the payer has not paid as expected. This may be due to poor billing and follow-up work by the practice than due to payer claims processing. Claims processors use claim adjudication software to price claims. For payment to occur in a timely manner, the correct contract must be loaded for each claim. Sometimes, that doesn't happen, and the claim doesn't process according to contract. At that point, you must appeal the claim.

The Art of the Appeal: Understanding the Basics before You Begin

Preparing an appeal to correct an incorrectly processed claim is an art. You have to know enough about the details of the claim and the individual quirks of the payer to find a workable, timely solution. In the case of an appeal, the burden of proof is on the provider to show why the claim has not processed correctly.

How you approach an appeal has a big impact on how smoothly and quickly the process goes. In the following sections, I explain how to approach an appeal so that you maximize your chances of getting the reimbursement the provider is entitled to.

REMEMBER

An appeal that is based on the contract and that clearly defines how the claim should have processed usually results in a reprocessed claim, especially if the contract has a prompt pay clause. If the payer failed to process the claim according to the contract and the error resulted in a delay of prompt payment, the payer may have to pay interest on the late dollars. Because this kind of error can cost payers a lot of money, they want the error fixed as much as you do.

Recognizing who you're dealing with

The primary contact between a provider and a payer is the provider representative. In most cases, however, your first point of contract is actually with the provider relations department, otherwise known as *provider services.* If you are responsible for claim follow-up, prepare to spend a lot of time on the phone with these individuals.

Provider services

The people who work in provider services can check to see whether a claim was received, can usually provide a processing time, and can sometimes facilitate correcting an improperly processed claim. When a claim processing is not in compliance with the payer contract, often the remedy is a simple phone call. If the payer has loaded the contract correctly (refer to the earlier section "When mix-ups in accounts receivable result in a delay"), the provider services representative can identify the problem — usually with coaching from you — and send the claim back to processing with instructions regarding what needs to be done.

If your contract was not loaded correctly, then calls to provider services for resolution are useless because these representatives rely on the information loaded into their systems, and they have no way to verify contract specifics. In this case, you need to turn to your provider representative.

Provider representative

If your contract wasn't loaded correctly, you address the problem through your provider representative, who is the individual responsible for making sure that the contract between the payer and the provider has been correctly loaded into the payer claims processing system(s).

In this situation, you need to contact the provider representative to let him know that the claims are not paying as agreed. Normally, you can get the name of the provider representative from the provider relations department or the payer website.

REMEMBER

Your provider representative generally tries to assist with contract or claims issues, particularly issues that may cause several claims to pay incorrectly for the same reason — which is usually a contract problem. If you have a contract with the insurance company, disputes should be easily resolved. Without a contract, things can get difficult, so be sure to have all of your *i*'s dotted and *t*'s crossed.

Knowing what to say and what not to say

During the appeal process, you want to keep to the facts. If a contract exists, refer to the language of the contract. If the problem is a bundling issue (one or more of the CPT codes on the claim are considered incidental or inclusive to another; refer to Chapters 4 and 12), then describe the extra work — be sure to include the extra time involved — and why this time investment was necessary. In addition, let the payer know what payment you are expecting or what payment agreement will be acceptable to close the claim.

Keep your emotions in check in these situations. The old saying that you can catch more flies with honey than vinegar totally applies here. Try to keep your comments positive and use appropriate, formal language on the phone and in written communications. Some effective phrases to use during appeals include:

- **"Our contract obligates CPT code 55555 to allow $1,234."** Say this if you didn't receive the amount you should have or the payer disputes the amount owed.
- **"This service was authorized prior to the date of service by ABC, and this is the authorization number: 1234."** Say this when you want the claim to be reprocessed because it was denied for lack of precertification. (But make sure the correct procedural code was authorized! For more on prior authorizations, refer to Chapter 11.)

REMEMBER

Although payers will usually make the disclaimer that prior authorization is not a guarantee of payment, do not allow them to use this as an excuse for an incorrect payment. Remind the payer, "We asked first, and you said yes." In some states, an authorization extends to other services that were deemed necessary once surgery begins.

- **"We are aware of the edits; however, this procedure should not bundle because it required access through a separate incision."** This provides an explanation for your request for extra reimbursement.
- **"I can send a written appeal. Can you provide a fax number and address please?"** This information ensures that the claim gets to the right place.
- **"What do I need to do to facilitate this issue?" or "Who should I speak with about this problem?"** These questions alert the person on the other end that you plan to do what needs to be done to resolve the claim.

TIP

Avoid using phrases such as "It's not fair" or "We didn't know the surgery wasn't covered." Here's a news flash: The payer doesn't care. Payers are running a business, and disputes regarding payment are just that — business — which is what they should be to you, too. So follow the payer's lead and keep things professional.

Using the resources at your disposal

When you're appealing a claim, your primary resource is right in your filing cabinet or on your hard drive: It's your payer contracts. If, for example, a contract obligates claim payment of a certain amount, you would word your appeal to remind the payer of the contractual obligation: Basically, Payer XYZ agreed in the contract to pay $1,000 for procedure 23456 but paid only $700. Pretty straightforward stuff. A reminder of the contract should be all you need to have the situation corrected.

Other resources include the National Correct Coding Initiative (NCCI) edits, professional newsletters including *CPT Assistant*, and numerous other coding guidelines. ***Note:*** Many specialties have published payment rules that may be different than the NCCI edits. Therefore, if your provider is a specialist, you can use this documentation to reference reasons for demanding that the claim be processed differently. Whatever specialty newsletters or coding guidelines you reference, if possible, send the written documentation with any appeals.

REMEMBER

Although NCCI edits are the most widely recognized, other editing systems exist. Look in the contracts to see which edits a payer follows, and verify which edits were followed when processing the claim(s).

Going through an Appeal, Step by Step

When a claim does not pay as accepted, the first course of action is usually a phone call. Ask the representative whether the issue can be resolved; if not, seek direction to initiate the appeal or reconsideration process. If you're dealing with a commercial payer, the payer may have a reconsideration form on its website that providers can use to challenge a payment decision. If not, then the formal written appeals process begins. The next sections take you through these steps.

Making the initial call

In most cases, the most efficient first step in the appeals process is to make a phone call to the payer. Writing letters takes time, and then it takes even more time for the recipient to read the letter, verify the argument, and then forward the claim to be corrected. If the problem is simple, you may be able to have the claim sent back simply by calling the payer. (For more complicated issues, you may need to begin with a letter; head to the next section for details about these situations.)

REMEMBER

Before discussing the claim with you, the provider representative — the person employed by the payer to work with you regarding disputes — verifies your need to know. Expect the representative to ask for the following information:

- Your name.
- The name of your company and tax ID number or the NPI (National Provider Identifier) number.

  The NPI is the ten-digit number required by HIPAA (Health Insurance Portability and Accountability Act) to identify providers in electronic transactions.
- The patient's ID (the identification number assigned by the payer), name, and date of birth.
- The date of service in question.
- The billed amount of the claim. (This is the dollar total of the claim, not what you are expecting to be paid.)

After you verify your need to know, you have the opportunity to tell the provider representative why the claim has not processed correctly. Often the representative can look at the claim, look at your contract, and verify what needs to be done. If that happens, the representative can usually send the claim back to the processor with instructions to reprocess. Sometimes, the phone call alone may be enough to resolve the issue. If it's not, you need to follow up with a letter, as the next section explains.

TIP

Make sure you document all phone conversations in the patient system or billing software. Note who you spoke with, what the agreement was, and the reference number (get this number from the provider representative; it documents the conversation on the payer's end). This kind of documentation is essential when a potential filing issue arises.

It's in the mail: Composing an appeal letter

Sometimes, a phone call just isn't enough. The issue may be complicated and easier to document in writing. For example:

- If the problem is a bundling issue, a written appeal is always necessary. You can't argue unbundling without supplying the documentation that supports the request for additional payment.
- If you are dealing with a third-party pricing issue, you may need to send a letter to the payer and the third-party pricing agent.
- If taking legal action becomes necessary, you need the written proof of your attempt to secure correct payment.

Including the pertinent information in your letter

In your appeal letter, be sure to include the claim number, patient name and ID number, the date of service, and the amount billed.

Begin the body of the letter by outlining your expectations for claim settlement. Then explain why the claim should pay per the expectations you describe. After that, reiterate your expectations, including the time frame that payment is expected and the follow-up action you'll take if the claim doesn't reprocess as you've outlined. Figures 14-1 and 14-2 show requests for reconsideration, one for a contracted payer, the other for a non-contracted payer.

TIP

Be prepared to follow through on any implied actions. If you say that the matter will be referred to your attorney in 30 days, then send it as promised. Similarly, if you say that the issue will be sent to the insurance commission in 30 days, do it.

Payers take department of insurance complaints very seriously. Make sure you are on solid ground. If you are, forward on!

April 10, 2020

Global Health United
12345 Business Parkway
Bigtown, TX 54321

Claim appeal – Or Request for reconsideration

RE: Patient Name: John Q. Public
ID (or Claim) #: 55555
Service Date: 2-1-2015
Billed Charges: $1,200.00

To Whom It May Concern:

The above claim was not processed correctly. Our contract obligates this claim to be paid as follows:

CPT 12345 is obligated to pay $1,000 per contract. This amount is due at 100% of obligation. CPT 78901 is obligated at 50% of the $400 contractual obligation, or $200.

Please verify the above in our contract and reprocess correctly. If I can be of further assistance, please do not hesitate to contact me between the hours of 8AM and 5PM CST at (555) 555- 5555.

Respectfully,

Mary Smith, CPC

FIGURE 14-1: A request for reconsideration for a contracted payer.

Using reconsideration request forms

Some commercial payers or insurance companies have something called *reconsideration request forms* available on their websites. That's just a fancy way of saying "claims form," but you get the picture. Depending upon the company's preferences, you can submit some forms online; others must be mailed or faxed.

These standard forms are for simple appeals — called *first-level appeals* — that are contractually based and need very little argument. If this initial appeal is denied, you need to file a formal second-level appeal, which is a letter that outlines your request and the reason for your position along with the supporting documentation. (You can read more about the different levels of appeals in the section "Maxing out your appeals.")

March 13, 2020

Global Health United
12345 Business Parkway
Bigtown, TX 54321

RE: Claim number: 123456789
Patient Name: Jane Doe
ID Number: 55555
Service Date: 2-1-2015
Billed Charges: $1,234.00

To Whom It May Concern:

The above referenced claim was not paid correctly. We do not have a contract that obligates us to accept this discount. Please identify the contract accessed when pricing this claim, along with documentation that supports any association with that contract to this provider. If no contract was utilized, then please identify the methodology used to price this claim.

Stall tactics such as this that delay correct claims processing is a violation of Indiana Statute 987 and as such will be reported to the State Insurance Commissioner thirty days from the date of this notice if the issue is not promptly resolved to our satisfaction.

We will settle this claim upon receipt of $1,110.06, which represents 90% of billed charges.

Sincerely,

XYZ Billing and Coding

On behalf of Dr. Jones

FIGURE 14-2: A request for reconsideration for a non-contracted payer.

Remembering important aspects of sending an appeal letter

When you send an appeal, keep the following points in mind:

- Notify the intermediary, if one was involved, that the payer has refused to honor the negotiated settlement.

» Prior to sending the appeal, call the payer to verify where the appeal should be sent. If the claim was priced by a network and paid by a commercial payer, send the appeal to both and let them know that each has been notified of the payment deficiency.

» Check to see whether the network priced the claim or whether the payer simply accessed the network itself.

On the phone again: Following up when the check doesn't arrive

If the appealed claim does not bear fruit in the form of a check, you may start to get a little nervous. At this point, put on your happy voice and call for a follow-up to check on the status of the check. When you do speak with a payer, just as when you compose the appeal letter, always base your argument or appeal on facts found in contracts, agreements, professional publications, and your resources about medical necessity.

REMEMBER

Always be clear with regard to the reason for your call and have all of the necessary information at hand. You need the provider's NPI number and/or tax ID number. The payer uses these numbers to verify your identity and that you have a right to make the inquiry. You also need the patient's ID number, his or her date of birth, the date of service, and the billed amount of the claim (the total dollar amount).

Fully document all conversations with payers or patients in the patient record, which is usually part of the billing software. Clearly state what was said and by whom, and get the name of the person with whom you are speaking.

In the following sections, I list the kinds of questions and information you should gather. In all these cases, verify how long resolving the issue will take and set up a tickler system to remind yourself, or your staff, to follow up if that date passes and the issue hasn't been resolved as promised. Base your timing for the next follow-up call on the feedback from the representative. But always check at least every 30 days on all outstanding claims.

TIP

A *tickler system* gives unprompted reminders. You can use a calendar, as long as you can remember to look at it. Even better, if your office uses a program like Microsoft Outlook or Gmail, you can set up these automatic reminders in the system's calendar, and they'll pop up on the appointed date and time.

General follow-up questions

When following up with payers, ask the following questions and document the answers in the file:

- **When was the claim received?** Don't assume the claim reached its destination. Each lost claim is lost revenue. Therefore, within 30 days of initial claims submission, make sure you follow up with the insurance companies to verify that the claim was received and is in process. After the 30-day deadline, the next deadline is 60 days. Any claim that is approaching 90 days old should be investigated as a priority in order to prevent a potential timely filing denial.
- **Has the claim been assigned a claim number? If so, what is it?** Make a note of this number. This claim number is different than the number in your clearinghouse report and may change at the payer based on the number of times the claim is touched. Keep note of all relevant numbers. The initial number is the ICN — the incoming claim number. The ICN stays with the claim, but is not always easily located. During processing, the payer may assign a platform claim number. Every time the claim is touched, it may trigger an updated claim number.
- **Is any additional documentation needed to complete the claim processing?** If additional information is requested, make arrangements to submit that information. After you send it, follow up in a week or 10 days to make sure that the claim is again in process.
- **What is the anticipated completion date for the processing?** Make a note of this date; payment should follow.
- **What is the reference number for this call and the name of the person with whom you're speaking?** This information lets you document all calls going forward.

Questions to ask if the rep tells you that the claim has been paid

If the representative tells you that the claim has been paid, ask these questions:

- What is the check number or electronic funds transfer (EFT) number?
- What is the allowed amount of the claim? If the allowed amount is not correct, ask the representative whether the claim can be sent back for correct processing. Repeat the obligation as defined in the contract and restate why the allowance is incorrect.
- What is the amount of the check or EFT?
- Does the patient have any responsibility for claim payment, such as copay, coinsurance, or unmet deductible?
- When was the check/EFT sent?

» Where was the check/EFT sent?

» What is the reference number for the call? Document this in the billing software.

Notes to take when the claim hasn't been paid as expected

If you are calling because a claim has not paid as expected, note the following:

» Why the claim processed the way it did.

  If a contract was utilized and pricing was incorrect, notify the representative of the correct obligation according to your records.

» The claim editing software that was utilized to process the claim.

» The correct address to send a written appeal. (Also, note the account and keep a copy.)

» The representative you're speaking to.

Maxing out your appeals

In a perfect world, claims always get paid on the first go-round. And if a claim does not pay correctly at first, you can either call or send a written appeal, and the payer will recognize his error and process the claim correctly. Alas, we don't live in a perfect world. Sometimes, even after the phone call and letter, the claim still isn't processed. In that case, you need to follow the appeals process as outlined in your contract.

Some payer contracts outline their appeals process. Several define the process in steps such as first-level appeal, second-level appeal, and request for outside review as the final level. I explain these levels in the next sections.

TIP

When sending a written appeal, whether it's a first- or second-level appeal, send medical records and a copy of the claim along with a copy of the remittance advice (RA) that was included with the payment. The RA shows how the claim payment was calculated. Including the RA helps the payer identify the claim, including the individual processor. If you don't include a copy, make sure that the claim number is on the appeal so that the payer can identify the correct claim. (See Chapter 13 for more about sending RA documentation.)

First-level appeals

A first-level appeal may just be a reminder that, according to your records, the claim should have processed a certain way. It's basically a friendly reminder that the contract wasn't followed or a discount was applied without a contract. If the problem is purely a pricing issue, this reminder may be all you need, and the payer will correct the error without further delay.

If the problem is that the claim was denied for medical necessity or anything of that nature, include all documentation with your first-level appeal. When you do so, the payer (hopefully) will reverse its decision and reprocess the claim correctly. If your first-level appeal defines the reason for the request along with any supporting documentation, it may be the only appeal you need.

The response time to appeals is often included in your contract and varies among payers. In cases where the payer has implemented new processing software and has multiple claims paying incorrectly (or not at all), the backlog can quickly become months. If you have not had a reply within 30 days, follow up to make sure that the appeal has been received. Each state has its own prompt payment statute, so your timing also depends on the statutes for your individual state.

Second-level appeals

Sometimes, the payer denies your request. In this case, you need to send another request. The second request is called a *second-level appeal.* You may need to send this appeal to a different address, or you may be able to simply mark it "second level" in order to identify that you have asked for resolution once already.

A second-level appeal is more formal. In it, make sure you do the following:

- **Clearly define the problem and note that you have asked once already without success.** You may even include a copy of your original appeal.

  In a second-level appeal, if you can state your case in a different way, try to do so. Sometimes simply rephrasing your words makes a huge difference in the success of a second-level appeal.
- **Include all documentation.** This documentation would include things like the RA, medical records, applicable invoices, and a copy of the contract (or the applicable section of the contract). (***Note:*** If you send a copy of the claim, make sure to mark it "COPY.")

Check your contract before sending a second-level appeal. Some payer contracts specify that the second-level appeal is the final level, and if it is denied, no further appeal options are possible. In this case, check your contract for options. The contract may identify a third-party mediation process for disputes if the dollar value is high enough. If you're dealing with a non-contracted payer, you can involve an attorney. Most offices have an attorney who specializes in healthcare and can handle the matter for you.

Appealing Medicare Processing

The Centers for Medicare & Medicaid Services (CMS) has a defined process for appealing. This process is easy to follow and quite efficient. You can find all the necessary forms on the Medicare website (www.medicare.gov) and individual contracted Medicare carrier websites.

The preferred method for submission is online. You can also submit additional documentation as well. The Medicare online appeal site provides a cover sheet that you can use to mail or fax the documentation to the appropriate address for consideration.

REMEMBER

Medicare tends to see everything as black and white and makes all decisions based on the policies that were in effect on the service date. So as long as you or your software stays current with regard to Medicare policy, then appealing to this payer is quite painless.

In the following sections, I take you through the Medicare appeals process.

Request for redetermination

The request for redetermination is a friendly reminder that the Medicare processing does not reflect the local fee schedule. You can find the initial request form at www.medicare.gov. Most Local Coverage Carriers or Medicare contractors have links to this form on their individual websites, and many allow the appeal to be submitted online with supporting documents faxed, using the assigned cover sheet.

TIP

My advice is to submit online if possible to avoid any potential timely appeal issues. According to Medicare rules, an appeal must be submitted within 90 days of the initial determination. If you submit online, you have proof of timely submission.

If the contractor doesn't grant your request or provide solid evidence that the claim has already processed correctly, the next level of appeal is to a Qualified Independent Contractor.

Qualified Independent Contractor (QIC) reconsideration

If your request for redetermination doesn't resolve the problem, next up is the Qualified Independent Contractor (QIC) reconsideration. You must submit this request within 180 days of the receipt of your redetermination reply. The instructions for submitting this appeal are on the redetermination notice. With this form, you can also submit additional evidence.

The QIC is the last level of appeal that allows you to submit additional evidence, but the best approach is to submit *all* evidence with the initial request for redetermination. When you submit evidence later, you have to include with the evidence an explanation as to why you didn't submit it with the original request and why it's now relevant.

To file a QIC, you must use the reconsideration request form (CMS-20033) which you can find on the CMS website (`www.cms.gov`). If you choose not to use this form, be sure to include the following information on your request:

» Beneficiary (patient) name and Medicare number.

» The specific service(s) or item(s) for which the reconsideration is being requested, along with the date of service.

» The name and signature of the provider. As the representative of the provider, you use your name and sign the form.

» The name of the Medicare contractor who made the redetermination. To save time, you also want to include a copy of the redetermination.

» An explanation of why you still disagree with the processing.

» Any additional evidence, along with explanations for why you didn't submit this information earlier and why it's relevant now. (Medicare may exclude evidence that has been submitted late unless you can show good cause for submitting it late.)

The QIC written decision is normally received within 60 days and contains an explanation of the ruling and information regarding whether an additional level of appeal is available. The next level is to take your appeal to an Administrative Law Judge. Additional evidence is not allowed at the upper level of appeal unless you have a documented reason why the evidence was not previously submitted.

Administrative Law Judge (ALJ) Hearing

If you are not satisfied by the two previous levels of appeal, then you may request an administrative law judge (ALJ) hearing. You can find the necessary form (everything requires a form!) at `www.medicare.gov`. But you can also present your case in writing. In this request, outline the area in dispute, along with the case number assigned by the QIC, the Medicare number of the patient, the original claim number assigned by the Medicare contract, and all evidence previously submitted. You must also identify the claims processing rules that support your request and the reason you feel the process has not been followed.

Currently, the amount in dispute must be a minimum of $130 before an ALJ hearing can be requested. This amount may increase annually based on the consumer price index.

When conducting a claims review, the judge conducts a hearing, reviews all the evidence, and makes a decision based upon Medicare rules and the law. Most hearings are held via videoconference or telephone, although you may request a hearing in person. The judge decides whether a hearing of this type is warranted. You may also request that the judge make a decision without a hearing, based solely upon the written evidence submitted. Medicare and its contractors are also notified of the hearing and are allowed to participate.

Hearings are conducted in person and over the phone. You may also request that the ALJ review the evidence and make a ruling. In a hearing, both parties are entitled to attend, although Medicare usually declines and leaves the decision in the hands of the ALJ. The burden of proof is on the provider. For this reason, some providers rely on legal representation if the amount in question is large. The ALJ level of appeal is not for the novice.

The ALJ normally makes a decision within 90 days, although this time frame is often extended for several reasons, including a heavier than normal case-load and evidence being submitted late.

If your claim is denied by the ALJ and you still feel that your claim has been processed incorrectly, the next level of appeal is the Medicare Appeals Council.

The Office of Medicare Hearings and Appeals (OMHA) was created by the Medicare Modernization Act of 2003. The purpose of this office is to streamline the appeals process and make it more efficient. The people in this office include a Chief Administrative Law Judge and the regional or Associate Chief Administrative Law Judges, each of whom has an assistant known as the Hearing Office Director. OMHA is responsible for the level-three Medicare appeals process.

Medicare Appeals Council and Judicial Review

The Medicare Appeals Council is part of the Departmental Appeals Board of the Department of Health & Human Services (HHS). It is independent of the other appeal boards.

To submit a request, you use form DAB-101, which you can download from the HHS website (`www.hhs.gov`). You can either submit the appeal online (doing so requires that you register with the Departmental Appeals Board electronic filing system on the HHS website), or you can submit a request in writing.

Make sure the written request includes the following:

- » Beneficiary (patient) name and Medicare number.
- » The specific service(s) or item(s) for which the reconsideration is being requested, along with the date of service.
- » The date of the ALJ decision and a copy of the decision.
- » The name and signature of the provider. As the representative of the provider, you use your name and sign the form.

After you complete the form, you can fax it to (202) 565-0227 or mail it to the following address:

Department of Health & Human Services

Departmental Appeals Board

Medicare Appeals Council, MS 6127

Cohen Building Room G-644

330 Independence Ave., S.W.

Washington, DC 20201

REMEMBER

You must file the appeal within 60 days after receiving the ALJ's decision. The appeals council assumes that you received the decision 5 days after the date on the decision itself. Therefore, timeliness is a huge factor, and if your appeal is late, you need good cause.

The council may dismiss, deny, or grant your request. It also has the option of returning the issue back to the ALJ for reconsideration. Most providers opt not to pursue the Medicare Appeals Council level.

If the reimbursement amount in question is above the current minimum requirement (it changes annually), then the next level of appeal is by Judicial Review in a Federal District Court. The notice received from the Council provides information needed to file a civil action, which represents the final level of appeal. At this level, the provider will benefit by using an attorney, and the legal costs will likely outweigh any perceived wrongs.

Appealing a Workers' Comp Claim

Often an out-of-network payer is responsible for paying a workers' compensation claim. Many states have legislation in place or fee schedules that outline how workers' compensation claims will be paid. Other carriers participate in networks that offer pricing for these claims. Some organizations, referred to as *silent PPOs,* price claims for carriers who don't have a contract with the service provider as though the provider participates in the network. The provider has the right to fight these discounts.

Workers' compensation claims demand upfront work. Someone in the provider's office should be responsible for verifying benefits, and this person should also verify the workers' compensation eligibility of the patient prior to any procedure being performed. (Coders are very good at verifying benefits because they have a thorough understanding of planned procedures and supporting diagnosis codes.)

Each workers' compensation patient has a caseworker, who is usually the coordinator for medical care, and this caseworker's name appears on any paperwork you receive. When dealing with workers' compensation, you also work with an adjuster, who is responsible for coordinating the provider claims. Most workers' compensation claims have a set amount that has been approved to pay for medical expenses related to the worker's injury. The adjuster keeps track of these funds as they are paid out and may need to go back to the carrier or employer and ask for additional funds (if any are available). Get the adjuster's name upfront and give him a call to make sure that you know where to send the claim and what additional documentation you must submit.

In addition to communicating with the caseworker and adjuster, you also want to verify the claim number, date of injury, and the body part that relates to the claim. Many carriers also require that all claims be submitted with the approved diagnosis code, so make sure that you and your employer know what diagnosis is covered.

When the claim is paid other than expected, referencing a network with which the provider is not familiar and taking a discount that the provider has not agreed to, then the appeals process begins. Often these underpriced claims are sent to the provider's attorney for a fair settlement. Depending on the office structure, the office manager or administrator is usually the one who sends the claim to the company attorney for action.

» **Familiarizing yourself with ICD-10**

» **Understanding the 5010 platform for claims submissions**

Chapter **15**

Keeping Up with the Rest of the World

Many parts of your job, particularly those that involve codes, coding software, and procedures, are established and maintained by large organizations. One of the biggest of these is the World Health Organization (WHO), an organization that evaluates and responds to world health trends. The coding standards you must adhere to play a large role in how WHO accomplishes its mission, because it uses these codes to gather and analyze data on what's going on in the world. And where do these all-important codes come from? The International Classification of Diseases (ICD), the common system of codes that, up until this point, you may have thought had no other purpose than to overwhelm you with a zillion technical-sounding acronyms.

As a biller/coder, you play a key role in helping these professional governing bodies keep everything on the up-and-up and collect data that impacts just about every decision made in the healthcare field, from how to improve coding functions to what to spend research dollars on.

In this chapter, I explain how the healthcare industry is moving toward being more specific when reporting diagnosis codes that support medical necessity, the players involved with that big change, and how it will affect you.

WHO's on First: Providing Data to the World Health Organization

You already know that your job as a biller/coder is to capture all billable procedures from the medical record and to make sure that each procedure you bill has a diagnosis code that supports medical necessity and justifies the procedure being billed. (If you don't know this already, read all about it in Part 2.) But what you may not know yet is that the information you communicate from the provider to the payer is also used to compile important health statistics that are used by the WHO, as well as by other national and international organizations involved with health issues.

TECHNICAL STUFF

WHO makes identifying, monitoring, and containing infectious disease outbreaks (like the HIV/AIDS outbreak in the early 1980s) possible at the international level, which has resulted in millions of saved lives. WHO has also been instrumental in the development and distribution of drugs, vaccines, and other disease-fighting efforts. The United States is one of almost 200 countries that is a member of this organization.

When it was founded in 1948, the original purpose of WHO was to identify methods that would provide better health to people worldwide. This goal has led to standards for safe drinking water, better sanitation methods, access to vaccinations, free birth control, and programs to combat hunger. Following are some of WHO's primary goals today:

- Facilitating health development in impoverished areas, focusing specifically on chronic and tropical diseases
- Fostering health security, including preventing disease outbreaks and addressing epidemic threats
- Improving logistics, such as access to medicine, training medical staff, and helping more people access care
- Interpreting research for new policy ideas and organizing resources into collaborative efforts

Although WHO does not conduct research itself, it does support and coordinate research efforts throughout the world by arranging conferences that encourage collaboration among researchers worldwide.

REMEMBER

WHO works very hard to keep the world population healthy. To do that, WHO needs the data you supply to be as specific as possible. As a coder, you are the individual responsible for abstracting the data that will eventually find its way into the WHO database.

HELPING THE WORLD'S NEEDIEST CASES

Monitoring the health of the entire globe is a big job, and WHO doesn't want to leave any country behind when it comes to disease management. That's why WHO works hard to enable healthcare access to underdeveloped countries. To address this need, WHO announced an agenda that challenged member countries to implement a system for a universal healthcare plan and to identify methods, such as increasing taxes and implementing improved budget guidelines, for raising funds to finance these healthcare plans.

WHO also encourages the improvement of healthcare in the most impoverished countries by working to improve access to primary care providers (preventative care reduces incidents of disease and allows for the treatment of minor illnesses before they can progress) and to prenatal care (to promote healthier pregnancies and healthier babies and to reduce maternal mortality). Perhaps one of WHO's biggest challenges has been the fight against HIV/AIDS.

WHO has made Africa the focus of efforts to address current health issues like these. Why? Because Africa remains the continent with the highest incidence of diseases in the world. Despite awareness of the spread of HIV and AIDS, it is still the leading cause of death among the citizens of this continent. The statistics are staggering: The estimated overall HIV prevalence rate in 2018 was approximately 13.1 percent among the South African population. For adults aged 15 to 49, an estimated 19.0 percent of the population is HIV-positive. So, it's no wonder that WHO has made this disease, as well as the general health of developing countries, a very high priority.

Charting Your Course with ICD

The International Classification of Diseases (most commonly known as ICD) classifies any disease or health problem you code. Basically, ICD is the common system of codes you use every day in your billing and coding work. Each diagnosis code provides a general description of the disease or injury that led to the patient/physician encounter.

ICD codes are divided into two categories:

- **ICD-CM (Clinical Modification):** Clinical modifications are diagnosis codes that all healthcare providers use.
- **ICD-PCS (Procedure Coding System):** The procedure codes are used only for inpatient reporting (hospital billing and coding).

These codes are not only used by billers and coders when they fill out claim forms, but they're also used by others to classify diseases and other health problems on many types of health records, including death certificates, to help provide national mortality and morbidity rates.

REMEMBER

WHO (which I discuss in the preceding section) uses the data gleaned from the codes you submit to analyze the health of large population groups and monitor diseases and other health problems for all members of our global community. For your purposes, you can think of the ICD codes as the language you speak to communicate with organizations like WHO so that they can keep the world healthy.

The Tenth Revision of ICD (ICD-10) went into effect in the United States in October 2015. The United States was the last industrialized nation to implement ICD-10 and managed to stage a 10-year delay as it continued to use the 30-plus-year-old Ninth Revision (ICD-9) codes. Opposition to ICD-10 was primarily based on the timing of initial costs (for things like reprogramming software and IT platforms and training all the personnel involved in medical billing or coding), particularly at a time when the United States was trying to control the rising cost of healthcare. However, the ICD-10 codes provide WHO with more specific data than the old ICD-9 codes, which in turn assists WHO in its effort to identify viral mutations and other health threats that may affect people all over the world.

Understanding the differences between ICD-9 and ICD-10

Repeat after me: ICD-9 is to ICD-10 as VCR is to DVR. In other words, ICD-9 was the old-school coding classification system, while ICD-10 is the new kid in town.

The differences between the two are fairly significant. Here are a couple of areas where they differ:

- **Number of codes:** ICD-9 had just over 14,000 diagnosis codes and almost 4,000 procedural codes. In contrast, ICD-10 contains over 68,000 diagnosis codes (clinical modification codes) and over 72,000 procedural codes.
- **The information conveyed by the code:** ICD-9 codes contained three to five digits beginning with either a number or a letter, with a decimal point placed after the third digit, and the ICD-9 book indicates the level of specificity for each code. ICD-10 codes, on the other hand, are up to seven digits in length. The first three digits are similar to the corresponding ICD-9 code, with a decimal point after the third digit. But the digits that follow the decimal point have specific meaning. For medical and surgical procedures, for example, the digits that follow are specific to body part, surgical approach, and other

qualifiers needed for billing. Similarly, the ICD-10-CM (Clinical Modification) codes that represent diagnosis codes also have seven digits (each digit may be replaced by a placeholder if it is not needed). The first three are similar to the ICD-9 code, but the additional codes add specificity to the code such as laterality, chronic versus acute, and so on.

- **Code assembly:** ICD-9-PCS (Procedure Coding System) codes are pulled from a book or coding software. ICD-10-PCS codes require the coder to do some assembly. The coder needs to break down the codes as follows:
  - First character: Section
  - Second character: Body system
  - Third character: Operation
  - Fourth character: Body part
  - Fifth character: Approach
  - Sixth character: Device
  - Seventh character: Qualifier

  All seven places are necessary; you populate blanks (places that don't apply to the service at hand) with the letter *x*.

  Most of the terms you use to construct the codes are defined within the system, but the coder is responsible for deciding which of the PCS definitions the documentation supports. That's why clinicians must be trained to thoroughly document what they have done.

The move to ICD-10 involved more training for coders because ICD-10 codes are more complex and more specific than ICD-9, and also because they have their own unique set of rules and guidelines (sometimes known as "coding conventions") for how they are to be used. If a specific "place" in the code isn't to be used, a placeholder character (x) *may* replace it. This represents an entirely different way of coding and was a challenge to even the most seasoned professionals in the early stages.

Even though this all sounds a little complicated (and it is), jumping on the ICD-10 bandwagon was good for several reasons. Proponents of ICD-10 argued that the improved data you get from using ICD-10 and subsequent coding changes will ultimately reduce healthcare costs such that the ICD transition will pay for itself. ICD-10 documentation will result in greater specificity in patient medical records, which will assist in assessment of treatment risk and frequency of procedural complications. It may also make documenting medical necessity for certain treatments easier.

Working on the 5010 platform

Part of the transition to ICD-10 happened on the technical end of things, particularly with the transmission platforms your coding software uses to push claims through to the clearinghouse. In preparation for ICD-10, providers, clearinghouses, and payers transitioned to claims transmission platforms that adhere to the Version 5010 electronic transaction standards outlined by the Health Insurance Portability and Accountability Act (HIPAA).

Using the 5010 platform, claims are transmitted electronically, and information that is entered into the billing software is then sent to the clearinghouse. In this system, each part of the claim can be pictured as a layer (or level), like this:

- The first layer (or level) contains information about the patient.
- The second layer contains information about the procedures and diagnosis codes.
- The third layer contains payer-specific information: the payer name, payer ID number, patient ID number, group number, and so on.
- The fourth layer contains the provider information, including name, address, and National Provider Identifier (NPI) number.
- The final layer is a view of the entire claim.

When a problem exists with the claim due to any of these transmission levels, the IT people fix it. Usually all you can do as a coder is identify where in the claims process the problem may be. In other words, you'll need to have your IT person on speed dial!

Moving beyond ICD-10

Now that the United States has made the transition to ICD-10, don't think you can sit back in the happy glow of having mastered ICD-10 requirements in your billing and coding. Consider that the World Health Organization is now expected to have the initial version of the Eleventh Revision of ICD (ICD-11) ready for public viewing in 2020. Although, it will come with much less fanfare and worry than ICD-10 — it is merely an addition of cause of injury and morbidity codes.

TIP

As a coder, always focus on continuing education that not only reinforces current procedures but that also prepares you for the next level. For example, coders who have already achieved ICD-10 certification prior to implementation (there weren't many) were demanding higher salaries from new and current employers. The coders who were certified to train ICD-10 were even more in demand. A wise coder (and that's you, of course) will always be current on trends and predicted transitions.

REMEMBER

"ICD-10 Certified" is not a thing! Do not put it on your resume and do not use it as a credential on your email signature. A working knowledge of ICD-10, as the diagnosis coding system currently in use, is an integral and required component of your general coding certification — and you are either a certified coder or you are not.

5 Working with Stakeholders

IN THIS PART . . .

Determine who the stakeholders are and how to do all the tasks your job requires while maintaining your integrity.

Get the skinny on working with commercial and government payers as well as working with patients and helping them understand their benefits.

Find out just how important documentation is and what happens when a claim needs to be made.

» Navigating networks and TPAs

» Getting your provider paid

Chapter 16

Dealing with Commercial Insurance Claims

You're going to connect with all sorts of people and organizations in your journey as a medical biller and coder, from individual patients and providers to big, all-encompassing organizations like Medicare. And smack in the middle of all these stakeholders are the Big Boys themselves — the commercial insurance companies. How you work with those insurance companies greatly affects your provider's bottom line. After all, they are the ones writing the checks, so it pays to know how to make the most of your relationship with them. This chapter has the details.

Meeting Commercial Insurance

As I explain in Chapter 6, most commercial payers, or insurance companies, offer several different levels of coverage to their members, ranging from health maintenance organizations (HMOs) to preferred provider organizations (PPOs) and point-of-service (POS) groups. You'll also run into exclusive provider option plans, high-deductible plans, discount plans, and ultra-specific plans that provide only prescription coverage, vision coverage, or other specialized coverage. All of these various flavors of commercial insurance come into play as your claims process.

THE BENEFITS OF HAVING A CONTRACT

The providers for whom you work already know the importance of a strong relationship with commercial insurance payers. In fact, being a contracted provider/member of the commercial insurance company's network offers many benefits: When a provider participates with an insurance company, the provider's name appears on materials and websites that the company produces, which serves as an advertisement of sorts for the individual provider. For physicians who are opening practices, the payer network directs patients to them. Another advantage to contracting with an individual insurance company is that the company defines payment schedules (that is, it clearly outlines the reimbursement amount for each procedure); this information assists the provider in financial planning — and assists you with keeping sane. Just remember: Make nice with the Big Boys, and your provider gets paid. It's a win-win!

The commercial insurance world revolves on an axis of variety. From PPO to HMO and in-between, a commercial insurance plan exists for just about every situation. Some of these plans are even combinations or iterations of other existing plans. No matter what plans you work with, though, the bottom line is that your provider's bottom line is your ultimate priority. For that reason, one of your top priorities should be to know which commercial insurance products are included in the provider contract, the reimbursement level associated with each product, and the eccentricities of each commercial insurance plan you encounter.

Noting big names in commercial insurance

You probably already know the names of some of the most common insurance companies. How can you not? Healthcare and the insurance industry are constantly popping up in the news, and many of them run huge PR campaigns that blanket everything from billboards to your TV. These commercial insurance companies usually underwrite the policies that patients and employers purchase (known as fully insured plans), or else administer plans for companies that choose to self-insure (known as administrative services only [ASO] plans). Some of the larger, more well-recognized players in the commercial insurance game are UnitedHealthcare, Aetna, Cigna, and Coventry (which is now owned by Aetna). These companies are nationwide and offer all types of healthcare plans for their membership.

Another big dog on the commercial insurance block is BlueCross BlueShield (BCBS). This commercial group may, in fact, be the largest of the bunch. The Blue Cross Blue Shield Association has 38 different companies that operate independently yet allow full reciprocity among plans. In other words — and in most cases — if a provider is contracted with a local Blue Cross association, the contract is honored by out-of-state BCBS plans.

TECHNICAL STUFF

This reciprocity makes life a bit easier for BCBS patients who may need care outside of their local zones. Specifically, a provider contracts with the local BCBS company, known as the *local plan*. Some companies that operate in different locations around the country get a plan that's local to the company but underwritten by BCBS affiliates that cover employees who live elsewhere. Claims are submitted to the BCBS in the state in which the provider practices, where they're priced based on the provider's contract. Then they're sent to the sponsoring BCBS company for payment. This way, patients get covered, no matter where in the country they are living or seeking medical care.

REMEMBER

Because commercial insurance companies are the bread and butter of the industry, providers contracted with the major commercial insurance companies have a solid patient base. As such, you can expect to spend a majority of your time working with these payers.

Working with the major players

As the coder, you and all members of the office staff who are part of the revenue cycle should be familiar with the provider's commercial payers. Specifically, you need to know the following:

- **Which commercial insurance payers are responsible for the majority of the practice's accounts receivable:** This information lets you know which insurances you'll need to understand best and where you will be focusing your efforts.
- **How much revenue is associated with each payer:** This information lets you know where the accounts receivable (outstanding payments) are to be found.
- **The eccentricities associated with each payer:** These include things such as timely filing requirements, timely payment obligations, and the other obligations outlined in each payer's contract.

TIP

Here's the best bit of advice I can give you when you work with several commercial insurance payers: Because each commercial payer is different, always, always follow the pertinent contract as you move claims through the coding process. The payer contract (which you can read more about in Chapter 11) is the final word on what you can and cannot code, so stick to it like glue.

REMEMBER

Although you must bill each carrier as obligated by the individual contract, varying the charge schedule for different payers is unethical. Suppose, for example, that the fee for a certain procedure is $5,000, and most payers have a reimbursement allowance based on the Current Procedural Terminology (CPT) procedural code, but one contract pays a percentage of the billed amount. In this situation, changing the fee when you're billing the carrier that pays a percentage in order to get a higher reimbursement from that payer isn't an ethical business practice and is likely also a breach of the terms of the contract.

Cashing In with Commercial Payers

Commercial insurance pays providers in its own way. Thankfully, that way is not in barter. Rest assured, it's real money. But how you go about getting that cash for your provider can vary, depending on the insurance company. Sometimes, a commercial payer bases how it doles out cash on what Uncle Sam does; more often, procedures are priced based on the amount of work involved by the physician plus a whole host of other factors. In the following sections, I discuss a few of those factors, both standard and rare, beginning with the basics of how reimbursement is determined.

Determining reimbursement

Here's a quick breakdown of how the docs get paid. The amount of work associated with each procedure is represented by the RVU, or relative value unit (you can read about RVUs in Chapter 13). The Centers for Medicare & Medicaid Services (CMS) assigns an RVU to each CPT code, and the amount is reviewed at least every five years. Medicare fee schedules are based on RVUs. Commercial insurance company payer contracts are often based on either Medicare fee schedules or RVUs; some are based on both (the payment allowance for a particular CPT code may be based on the Medicare fee schedule, for example, while the multiple procedural discount clause is based on RVUs for prioritization).

The other factor that determines reimbursement is the geographical location of the provider. Commercial payers all understand that operating a practice in a major metropolitan area, where the cost of living is higher, takes more money than operating the same kind of practice in a less populated, rural area, where the cost of living is lower. For this reason, actual reimbursement includes the cost of maintaining an office and other overhead expenses, like the malpractice expense associated with particular procedures.

Commercial payment is also based on contract allowances if a contract is in effect on the date of service. When no contract exists to dictate reimbursement, the service provider has the right to demand payment in full for services provided. That's why fees are often based on the same Medicare fee schedule that contracts are based on. Providers usually bill a multiple of the Medicare allowances.

As I note in the earlier section "Working with the major players," regardless of how you compute the billed charges, you should bill every payer the same: If a procedure costs $2,000, then the cost is $2,000 for every claim. Keep in mind, however, that although all insurance companies are billed the same, expectations regarding reimbursement are payer-specific and include things like procedures that may or may not be covered and how long the payer has to send payment.

Weaving through the ins and outs of pricing networks

Here's a point that confuses many people: They think that insurance companies and pricing networks (which are often referred to as "insurance networks" by laypeople) are the same thing. They're not. Commercial insurance companies and pricing networks are two different things. A pricing network is not necessarily the payer of claims; instead, the network prices the claims. The plan administrator or payer issues the payment. Some commercial payers participate in pricing networks rather than do the contracting themselves. In fact, they may participate in several networks simultaneously.

Because pricing networks work on the behalf of commercial payers, you need to know a bit about them. I explain pricing networks in detail in Chapter 6, but in the following sections, I highlight the things you need to keep in mind as you work with them.

Serving as middlemen

Network pricing companies are essentially the middlemen between the provider and the payer. Like individual insurance company payer contracts, pricing network contracts obligate a significant discount of the provider's fees. Most providers contract with the pricing networks that serve the patients in their geographic area so that they can be in-network with the commercial payers who participate in the pricing network.

Some pricing networks price claims for commercial payers but don't actually have a contract with the service provider. In this case, the provider is not obligated to accept the network's discounted fee and can demand that the unauthorized discount be removed, thus allowing full billed charges. For this reason, the provider must be vigilant about identifying which payers are included in the network when contracting with a network. You can read more about that topic in the following section.

REMEMBER

So that everyone knows what to expect, providers should identify the plans and networks they participate in, and patients (or the patients' payers) should identify the network(s) to which they belong. As the coder (and person who gets to navigate all this contract madness), you want to stay in close touch with your provider so that you know whenever a contract with a new payer has been entered into so that you can stay on top of the network details.

TIP

To know which pricing contract to apply to any particular claim, you must see the patient's insurance card.

Avoiding network pitfalls: The silent PPO

When contracting with a network, providers must demand that all plans that access the network are identified upfront and that the provider be notified when new payers are added to the network.

The downfall of some network contracts is that, sometimes, payers can get in the network through the back door. That is, these payers are allowed to access the network contract without being identified initially as a network member. This is known as a *silent PPO,* and it's not a good thing for your provider.

Here's how a silent PPO works: Sometimes a PPO network contract contains language that essentially allows the network to enter into a contract with any "individual, organization, firm, or governmental entity" on a case-by-case basis, which means that any payer who is willing to pay the commission can access the PPO contract — and its negotiated discount pricing — *unknown to the provider.* See the problem?

With a silent PPO, a payer can apply a discount rate for services from a healthcare provider without actually having a contract with the provider. This scenario is unfair to providers who sign a contract with the network and its members, which, at the time of signing, did not include the silent PPO. As a result, when the silent PPO pays the discounted rate, it cheats the provider out of a fair payment.

Here are some ways to identify and avoid falling victim to a silent PPO:

- **Pay attention to the remittance advice (RA).** You can spot when a payer accesses a silent PPO if you look at the RA (explained in Chapter 13). If it reflects a PPO discount for a patient who is actually out-of-network, a silent PPO alarm should sound for you.
- **Avoid networks that allow reimbursement that is much higher than what other commercial insurance companies allow.** Payers are in business to make money. If a network is willing to pay more than the going rate, you can bet that it's getting money on the other side — from the

organization that is actually responsible for the payment. For example, if a billed service of $1,500 is normally paid $500 but a certain network is willing to pay $750, then that other $250 is coming from somewhere. Chances are, it's coming from the non-network payer who is willing to pay $1,000 to the network rather than $1,500 to the service provider.

- **Verify network benefits as part of your provider's normal pre-encounter work.** Either you (or the front office staff) should check the network affiliations on each patient's card.

If you or your provider learns that a network PPO is allowing access to out-of-network payers, then the provider should notify the PPO network that the contract has been violated and terminate the agreement. The provider may also dispute any silent PPO payments in writing with demand for payment in full for services provided.

REMEMBER

Being vigilant is the hallmark of a good coder, and that's even more true when you find yourself working with commercial insurance payer networks, whether you patients are in- or out-of-network. Think of yourself as the sheriff of Payertown and keep a watchful eye on shady networks and payers.

Getting paid in- and out-of-network

One big benefit of working within a network is that the contract may allow the provider to secure a percentage of billed charges. The payer typically offers a standardized fee structure, and the two parties can (hopefully) reach an agreement that benefits both, which means less work for you and more reliable payments for your provider. Hooray for being in-network!

When a provider is not a participating member of a network, payment can be delayed for a variety of reasons. Often, a payer uses a third-party negotiator to get a discounted reimbursement agreement (you can read about third-party agreements in "Finessing third-party administrators" later in this chapter). Other times, the payer may simply pay a claim based on the reimbursement allowances of other network providers in the area.

REMEMBER

If a discount is applied to a claim without a prior agreement, the provider may be able to demand additional payment (refer to the earlier section "Avoiding network pitfalls: The silent PPO" for details). The exception is when the payment is based on the provisions of the patient's individual plan. What this means is that commercial insurance companies offer various levels of coverage, and these plans specify out-of-network benefits and define how much the insurance company pays versus what the patient is responsible for paying.

When a patient is being seen out-of-network, make sure you verify benefits before the encounter. Do the following:

1. **Verify that the patient has out-of-network coverage.**

   Some plans specify an out-of-network payment cap that may be much less than billed charges. The plan then may assign responsibility for the remainder of the balance to the patient. Sometimes this balance is quite large, and most people have difficulty paying it. Occasionally an out-of-network claim processes to allow full-billed charges and then pays according to the plan, usually 60 or 70 percent after the deductible has been met.

2. **Ask what, if any, language is contained in the plan benefit that defines exactly how out-of-network claims are processed.**
3. **If possible, verify what methods may be used to price out-of-network claims, which lets you know how much payment can be expected.**

   The payer representative will always provide the out-of-network deductible and coinsurance responsibility, but that's usually the extent of the information you'll receive. Although getting the payer to divulge the provisions of the plan in question is very difficult, it's worth a try.

REMEMBER

Regardless of whether the claim is in- or out-of-network, always treat the payer with respect and give each one equal consideration. The claim should be billed in good faith and be a truthful representation of the work done by the provider.

Working your way around workers' comp carriers

Just when you thought it was safe to code, along comes workers' compensation. Workers' compensation carriers underwrite policies that employers carry to cover treatment for work-related injuries or illnesses that occur as a result of employment. Processing workers' compensation claims adds yet another layer to the already teetering tower of things you need to know as a coder.

REMEMBER

When you're dealing with workers' compensation services, keep in mind the following points:

- **Workers' compensation claims are normally specific regarding which diagnosis code and body part are authorized for treatment.** In fact, workers may have multiple claims, with a different claim number for each body part.

TIP

When verifying a workers' compensation claim prior to an encounter, always check the approved diagnosis and body part connected to the claim number.

- **Follow-up treatments may be part of the claim.** For this reason, ask for documentation of the history of a particular illness or injury.

  Here's an example: A patient who broke her arm had pins put in to reinforce a fracture repair. Now she comes back in complaining of pain because of the hardware. If the fracture was part of a workers' compensation claim, then removing the hardware is part of the original claim. Similarly, if a patient returns for a hardware removal, and it's scheduled as a workers' compensation claim but you see that the original treatment was billed and paid by private insurance, you can contact the workers' compensation carrier to verify that the claim should have been billed to them. Then you can voluntarily refund the dollars paid to the commercial carrier.

WARNING

- **Sometimes, a workers' compensation carrier subrogates a claim with the patient's commercial insurance and simply reimburses the commercial insurance for a claim paid in error.** This action is unfair to the provider because the workers' compensation carrier benefits from a contracted discount that shouldn't have been used to price the claim. Make sure you catch errors of this nature before any outside negotiation occurs between the carriers.

  Subrogation is the process where one insurance company determines that another payer was responsible for claim payment. In this case, the insurance company that paid the claim can demand restitution from the company that was actually responsible. You can read more about subrogation in Chapter 13.

- **Some workers' compensation carriers are part of a PPO network (or several networks).** For your sanity, make sure that your PPO network contracts do not allow silent PPO access (refer to the earlier section "Avoiding network pitfalls: The silent PPO"). Figuring out how to handle workers' compensation claims is challenging enough; a silent PPO situation only slows the process.

TECHNICAL STUFF

Some states have workers' compensation laws that serve as contracts for any provider who offers services under claims filed in that state. This is another factor to consider when negotiating a PPO network contract. Verbiage that states a discount is applied to the fee schedule rather than to the billed charges prevents double discounting.

Finessing third-party administrators

A third-party administrator (TPA) is an entity hired to handle the administration of another company's insurance plan. The TPA is usually responsible for collecting premiums and issuing reimbursements, which includes paying medical claims.

Companies who use TPAs are required to notify plan participants in writing what the responsibilities of the TPA are. Typically, companies that use TPAs self-insure, which means that they function as insurance companies themselves. As such, they normally join a PPO network as a way to get the advantage of discounted claim pricing while retaining the right to determine deductibles, coinsurance amounts, copay obligations, and other plan provisions.

The company plans are funded by payments made by both the employer and participating employees (in the form of premiums). These payments go into a fund that the company owns and that is dedicated to paying claims made against the company's health plan. Here are things to keep in mind about these plans:

- **They allow employers to customize what the plan covers to best serve the needs of the company's employees.** In some of these plans, injuries or conditions that are common results of work-related duties are excluded from the plan benefit for the employee and delegated as workers' compensation claims. For example, a condition such as carpal tunnel syndrome may be identified as a work-related condition, in which case, all carpal tunnel claims are automatically denied upon submission. If, however, the patient is a plan dependent (an individual, such as a spouse or child, who is covered by another person's insurance) rather than an employee, the provider needs to contact the payer and ask that the denial be reconsidered.
- **The employer or insurance company pays for the TPA's services, not the member directly.** A third-party administrator can only collect payments for plan premiums from plan members.
- **The payer is responsible for determining the coverage benefit as it applies to each claim.** The TPA only issues the payment. Therefore, if payment is not correct, you need to contact the payer, not the TPA, because the payer is the one who determines whether the claim is payable under the conditions of the patient's insurance plan.
- **You have to determine where to send the claim.** The payer pays a fee to participate in a network, and the arrangement the payer has with the network determines where you send the claim. Here are the standard options:
  - If the network collects fees from both the provider and the payer, you usually submit the claim directly to the network, which prices everything and then requests that the payer present the RA and a check to the provider.
  - If only the payer pays the network, you send the claim to the payer, the payer sends it to the network for pricing, and the network returns the claim to the payer for payment to be issued.

  And you, oh lucky coder, get to monitor and follow up on the whole big process, sort of like a big-time TV producer watching all the magic from a secure location.

Knowing What's What: Verifying the Patient's Plan and Coverage

Perhaps it goes without saying, but to do your job well, you need to know not only the difference between the types of commercial providers (which the earlier sections in this chapter explain), but also their network affiliations, kinds of coverage, and more. Why? Because submitting a claim to the wrong entity delays correct processing. The few minutes it takes to verify benefits and claim-submission requirements can save days in accounts receivable and hours of follow-up chasing the claim.

Luckily, gathering the information you need is a fairly straightforward task, as I explain in the next sections.

Looking at the insurance card

How do you tell what kind of plan — a PPO network, a TPA, or a commercial payer — a patient has? Fortunately, a commercial insurance company that underwrites plans and administers those plans for the membership is usually easy to identify. Just look at the patient's insurance card.

The card provides phone numbers for members and providers to call. By calling the appropriate number, you can get a summary of plan benefits. Most commercial payers also have websites that enrolled providers can use to verify benefits and eligibility.

A company that is self-funded but part of a larger network (or networks) has a benefit and eligibility number on the patient's card, along with the address to which claims are to be sent. It also has the logos for the networks to which it belongs. When you verify these patient benefits, you may need to call both the payer and the network.

Plans that are part of the Patient Protection and Affordable Care Act (ACA) may issue cards that resemble cards from commercial insurance plans. However, that's where the resemblance ends. In most cases, these plans require provider enrollment specific to the ACA plan; if the provider isn't enrolled, the patient is out-of-network. Depending upon the specifics of the plan, either the patient is saddled with full financial responsibility or the provider is obligated to adjust the charges off without billing the patient (similar to Medicaid in many states).

REMEMBER

A patient is your first line of defense with verifying payer information. Treat each patient with respect and assure him that you're trying to do your job, which is to help his claim get processed in a timely and accurate fashion.

Contacting the payer and/or network

When you (or the front office staff) call to verify coverage, your first call is probably to the payer, who can verify plan benefits with regard to in-network coverage and out-of-network coverage. The payer can also advise you about any remaining deductibles, coinsurance responsibilities, and applicable copays. If the provider participates only in certain levels of the network (say, if the provider is a PPO-provider only), then you want to verify the patient's PPO benefits.

If you have any doubt about coverage, the next step is to contact the network and verify that the payer does actually participate in the network with which the provider has a contract. If the provider is PPO only, verify that the plan is enrolled in the network PPO. If you don't fully verify eligibility and benefits when a network is the pricing intermediary, you can't be certain that the claim will process as expected.

REMEMBER

Always call the benefit number on the patient's card. If the patient is part of an ASO plan, then specific benefits may differ from the commercial plan that is administering the plan.

» **Working with contractors and private Medicare Part C plans**

» **Understanding who makes decisions about coverage**

» **Checking in on Medicare and Medicaid plan requirements**

Chapter 17

Caring about Medicare and Medicaid

If you haven't spent much time with your uncle lately, prepare yourself because you're going to get to know him very, very well. I'm talking about Uncle Sam, of course, also known as the United States government, also known — for your purposes — as Medicare and Medicaid. These government payers, along with a few others, make up a huge portion of the payers with whom you'll work to secure payment for your provider. Medicare and Medicaid are a big deal because they pay out boatloads of cash to providers each and every day. In addition, these government payers also set the standard for many coding and billing procedures that you use for commercial payers.

TECHNICAL STUFF

Medicare was signed into law by President Lyndon B. Johnson in 1965 as part of the Social Security Act. It was designed to provide healthcare insurance for citizens 65 and over and individuals with certain disabilities. What started as a way to protect the country's most vulnerable populations continues today as one of the country's most widely recognized social programs — and one that you'll work with a lot as a medical biller and coder.

Brushing Up on Medicare Basics

At the top of the government heap is the biggest government payer of them all: good old Medicare. Medicare is funded by payroll taxes deducted from every employed American. (You've probably seen the acronym FICA, which stands for Federal Insurance Contributions Act, on your pay stub. This FICA deduction is what helps fund Medicare.)

Everyone who gets a paycheck gets FICA withheld, but you don't see the dividends of that investment until you actually qualify for Medicare. Here's how you can tell whether you (or any patients in your office) fall into that category. Generally those eligible for Medicare are

- Legal U.S. residents who are 65 or older who paid FICA for at least ten years
- Individuals who are suffering end-stage renal disease who are receiving dialysis treatments or are on a kidney transplant list
- Individuals who are eligible for Social Security Disability Insurance and are suffering from a permanent disability

Medicare has different levels of coverage, referred to as *Parts.* The coverage a patient gets is determined by how that patient paid (or continues to pay) into the plan. Here's a brief overview:

- **Part A** has already been paid for through the patient's payroll taxes.
- **Part B** is paid for through deductions, usually from the patient's Social Security dividends.
- **Part C,** added to the program in 1997, allows individuals who are eligible for Medicare to enroll in Medicare replacement plans offered by private health insurance plans.
- **Part D,** adopted in 2006, is the drug plan. Part D covers prescription drug coverage.

You can read all about these Parts and more in Chapter 6.

Working with Medicare Claims

Think of Medicare like a nice, distant relative who sends you a check for $7 each year for your birthday. It's not flashy, but it's reliable. In other words, Medicare should be your most predictable payer. How so? Well, the fine folks at Medicare provide you with as much information as possible so that you can do your job effectively (and they can do theirs).

Medicare policies and procedures are available on both the Centers for Medicare & Medicaid Services (CMS) website (`www.cms.gov`), as well as on all the local contractor websites. Medicare also reliably follows the National Correct Coding Initiative (NCCI) edits, and it recognizes modifiers and the payments that link to them. Medicare, for the most part, lets providers know upfront what to expect.

Here's how your provider gets paid with Medicare: Medicare Parts A and B (what's considered "original" Medicare) is administered through regional contractors that accept and process Medicare claims in accordance with Medicare policy. Professional providers, including most physician practices, are paid under Part B per fee schedules, which are available on your local contractor's website. Fee allowances are based on relative value unit (RVU) equations (I discuss RVUs in Chapter 13).

Getting Medicare-approved

Before a provider can receive payment for treating a Medicare patient, the provider must apply for Medicare's approval. The registration process to become a Medicare provider takes several weeks to complete. The enrollment forms are available on the CMS website, and you can complete most of the enrollment online. To enroll with Medicare, providers must be licensed professionals and have both a National Provider Identifier (NPI) number and a tax identification number (TIN). After completing registration, Medicare assigns a Provider Transaction Access Number (PTAN), which allows providers to submit claims and have access to check the status of claims that are in process.

REMEMBER

Providers who are not registered with Medicare cannot submit claims to Medicare, period. Large organizations often have employees who specialize in payer enrollment, but if you work for a small physician practice, you may be responsible for leading the effort to fill out all the necessary paperwork to get your provider Medicare-ready.

WARNING

Registering with Medicare does not automatically mean that a provider is a participating provider. A provider can be registered with Medicare and be what the pros call *non-par* (non-participating). If a patient visits a non-par registered provider, the provider is not obligated to accept fee schedule allowance as payment in full. Instead the provider can charge up to a higher level called a *limiting charge*, and the provider would then need to bill and collect payment from the patient. Medicare reimburses the patient for 80 percent of the fee schedule allowance, but the patient must pay the remaining 20 percent out of his own pocket. Sometimes collecting from patients is difficult, to say the least, so a provider must decide whether to participate with Medicare and receive a lower fee directly from the carrier or risk collecting his fee from the patient at a slightly higher rate.

Processing Medicare claims

After your provider is good to go as a Medicare provider, you can start processing claims. You submit all claims to the local Medicare contractor, which processes them according to Medicare processing guidelines and policies.

When no national policy applies to a particular service, the decision whether to cover the service may fall to the local Medicare contractor or something called a *fiscal intermediary*, a private insurance company that serves as an agent for the federal government in the administration of Medicare.

The lack of a national policy sometimes happens when a modification has been made with regard to a procedure. Procedural modifications are often the result of advancements in medicine. The development of new tools or equipment that may be used by physicians can result in new procedural codes, for example. Initially, these items are represented by unspecified codes, which are not reimbursable by Medicare. Subsequently, new codes are added to represent these services or items.

Similarly, when a claim is processed incorrectly, the initial appeal process goes through the local contractor, although the process is uniform for all regions.

Deciding What Gets Paid

Wouldn't it be nice if, as the coder, you got to make the final call on what gets paid? That certainly would make life easier! But you're not the one writing the checks. Uncle Sam is. For that reason, the government has set up a hierarchy of who gets to make the final decision on some of those tough call situations. In the following sections, I walk you through the more common steps in the decision-making hierarchy and explain how to keep track of them all.

Going from local to national decision-making: LCDs and NCDs

When a contractor or fiscal intermediary makes a ruling as to whether a service or item can be reimbursed, it is known as a *local coverage determination* (LCD). This determination is always based on medical necessity (which you can read more about in Chapter 5).

REMEMBER

LCDs apply only to the area served by the contractor who made the decision. Procedural codes that are LCD-dependent are noted as such in some editions of the CPT codebook, but all published LCDs can be found on the CMS and Medicare contractor websites. If the provider is planning on submitting a procedural code or a HCPCS code that's noted to be subject to an LCD determination, you need to verify the guidelines for the item in question prior to submission.

Sometimes, however, requests are made directly to CMS for a ruling as to whether a service or item may be covered. When CMS makes a decision in response to one of these requests, it's known as a *national coverage determination* (NCD). These rulings specify the Medicare coverage of specific services on a national level. All Medicare contractors are obligated to follow NCDs.

If an item or service is new, or not defined by an NCD, the local contractor is responsible for the decision for coverage. When neither an NCD or LCD exists and it's uncertain whether a service or item will be covered, but the patient desires the treatment or item, the provider must secure an advance beneficiary notice (ABN) prior to the service if he intends to bill the patient. I cover ABNs in the next section.

REMEMBER

Both NCDs and LCDs establish policies that are specific to an item or service. They also define the specific diagnosis (illness or injury) for which the item or service is covered. LCDs may vary from region to region. For example, SERVICE 12345 may be covered in Region A to treat diagnosis ABC. But the same service may be covered in Region B only to treat diagnosis XYZ. So when an item or service is in question, always check beforehand (see the later section "Tracking the guidelines: The Medicare Coverage Database"). If a Medicare beneficiary receives an item or service that is not a covered benefit and has not signed an ABN, the provider usually has to absorb the cost.

Using an advance beneficiary notice (ABN)

As the coder, you're responsible for abstracting reimbursable procedures from the medical record. When the provider performs services or provides items that are not reimbursable and for which there is no LCD, then you can bring the matter to the attention of the office management or the provider to discuss the need for something called an *advance beneficiary notice* (ABN).

The ABN is basically a waiver of liability that providers use when they plan to perform a service that Medicare most likely will determine is not medically necessary. The provider gives the ABN to the patient to sign. After the ABN has been obtained, the provider can hold the Medicare patient liable for the charges. This advanced warning is Medicare's way of insisting that providers inform their patients when Medicare may not reimburse them and alerting the patients to the fact that they will owe the entire amount billed.

PROCEDURES THAT ARE UNNECESSARY . . . EXCEPT WHEN THEY AREN'T

In certain circumstances, items or services are not covered by Medicare, but in other circumstances, they may be covered. For example, Medicare doesn't cover any cosmetic procedures, but when a normally cosmetic procedure is medically necessary, Medicare may cover it. Consider these examples:

- Blepharoplasty is surgery to remove excess tissue from the eyelid and surrounding tissue. Normally, Medicare doesn't cover this procedure. But if the tissue prevents the patient from seeing, Medicare may cover the surgery.
- Medicare won't pay to have skin lesions removed (even from the face) just because the patient doesn't like the way the lesion makes him or her look. But if the lesion is painful, impairs vision, or may be malignant, then Medicare covers its removal.

These "sometimes they're covered; sometimes they're not" scenarios are not limited solely to Medicare. You can also find examples in private insurance plans. The need for verification of coverage extends to all healthcare providers. The provider is the professional and is in the best position to be aware of medical necessity and national or local coverage determinations.

Currently, providers can customize their own ABN forms within the very limited allowance for customization according to the form instructions. Generally, the ABN must be easy to read; use a large font size; and identify the provider, the patient, the service or item in question, and the reason that payment is expected to be denied. In addition, the patient must sign the ABN every time the service or item is provided. (You can't have patients sign a blanket form that obligates them to pay for a service not deemed necessary by Medicare.) CMS requirements regarding correct notifications are available on the CMS website.

Tracking the guidelines: The Medicare Coverage Database

Making coverage decisions is a big deal, and the government doesn't take these decisions lightly. The Social Security Act grants Medicare contractors and fiscal intermediaries the authority to make these decisions, which must follow NCD guidelines. In addition, the decision is always in writing.

Thankfully, you can keep track of all these decisions and determinations so that you can use them for future reference. The CMS maintains a Medicare Coverage Database (`www.cms.gov/medicare-coverage-database`) that contains all NCDs and LCDs. Medicare updates this database regularly to keep it as current as possible.

Working with Medicare Contractors

When you think of Medicare, you probably (or will soon) immediately think of the umbrella organization, the Centers for Medicare & Medicaid Services (CMS). Who you *should* be thinking about are the local Medicare contractors or fiscal intermediaries, because these are the people providers deal directly with.

Submitting your claims

You submit your claims to the local carrier, who processes them. Each carrier is required to follow Medicare processing guidelines, which help contractors provide the same Medicare level of service to all providers. Each Medicare contractor must do the following:

- Accept electronic claim submissions
- Maintain an interactive voice response (IVR) provider phone line
- Follow the same timely filing requirements set by Medicare
- Make payment according to Medicare fee schedules and timely payment rules
- Operate the same way when it comes to the Health Insurance Portability and Accountability Act (HIPAA) communications and observe all HIPAA regulations

Regardless of which contractor you call, you can always expect the process to follow these steps:

1. At the contract's request, you supply the provider's PTAN (Provider Transaction Access Number), the provider's NPI (National Provider Identifier), and the last five digits of the TIN (tax identification number).

   For more information on these numbers, refer to the earlier section "Getting Medicare-approved."
2. You will be asked for the patient's Medicare number, name, and date of birth before any privileged information will be shared.
3. You may then make claim or member-specific inquiries.

By following the same protocols for every single phone call, the contractors allow Medicare to operate with more expedience and efficiency for the large number of claims that are submitted daily.

REMEMBER

Regardless of which government program you're dealing with, you work with a regional, or possibly a local, company. Each of these administrators has its own contact information (phone number, electronic payer identification number, and physical address).

Getting along with your Medicare rep

Each Medicare contractor has provider representatives available for assistance when you're not sure what is wrong with a submitted claim, but these representatives can't advise you how to code or how to bill. They can only direct you to the correct resources that will assist in getting your claim paid.

When calling Medicare, make sure you have the following info handy:

- The PTAN, the number assigned by Medicare to the individual provider
- The provider's NPI, the 10-digit provider number issued by CMS
- The last five digits of the provider's TIN, which is similar to an individual's Social Security number
- The patient's Medicare number
- The patient's name and date of birth
- The date of service and billed amount of the claim in question

Doing Business with Medicare Part C Plans

As I mention earlier, in addition to the Medicare contractors, commercial insurance companies also sponsor Medicare-approved plans. These plans are referred to as Medicare Part C plans (and are also known as Medicare Advantage plans or Medicare replacement plans), and they sometimes pay differently than standard Medicare plans.

Paying attention to plan differences

For Part B professional services, standard Medicare pays 80 percent of the allowed amount after the patient meets the annual deductible. The other 20 percent is the responsibility of the patient, who can enroll in a Medicare-approved supplemental plan to cover the other 20 percent. Other services are covered at different levels of coverage.

Patients who have chosen a replacement Medicare plan, however, must follow the provisions of that policy. Many of these plans cover 100 percent of the allowed amount after a deductible and/or copay has been met. If your provider is contracted with the parent company that sponsors the replacement plan, the contract dictates how much the claim pays (within the plan provisions).

Your front office needs to know the difference between a commercial insurance plan and a Medicare Part C replacement plan sponsored by the same commercial payer because the distinctions between the two can impact which codes you use. If the provider has a specific Part C contract with the carrier, you follow the carrier's claim process. If the provider doesn't have a specific Part C contract with the carrier, you follow the claim process specified by Medicare's reimbursement policy. The differences between these policies determine which codes you submit.

Turning to Uncle Sam for a helping hand

If the provider has a disagreement with a commercial Medicare payer, you must follow the dispute process defined by that company's policy for the original level-one reconsideration request. Higher level appeals, however, follow the dispute process defined by Medicare. (Head to Chapter 14 for detailed information on requests for reconsideration.)

When a dispute with a private Medicare plan fails to get resolved through the sponsoring company's appeals process, the provider (or beneficiary) may request a review by the Part C independent Review Entity.

Each Medicare Part C sponsoring company must give the provider information regarding which organization to contact if the provider feels that the appeal should be elevated to the next level. This information must be included with the response to the initial request for reconsideration.

In addition, for the non-par providers dealing with Medicare Part C payers, the appeals may follow a different path so make sure to know where to send any and all inquiries.

If you work in a small office or for a larger company with a focus on accounts receivable follow-up, expect this appeals process to be a daily part of your job. The request for reconsideration is the initial level of appeal, when a provider feels that the claim has not processed correctly. If the reconsideration is denied, then the second-level appeal goes through an independent review. If the provider is still unsatisfied with the outcome of the request, the same appeals process that standard Medicare requests follow applies. I discuss this process in Chapter 14.

Verifying Coverage and Plan Requirements

Both Medicare and Medicaid plans must follow federal guidelines, but each policy can have other specified requirements as well. These requirements are similar to those of most HMO plans, restricting patients to contracted providers, for example, or requiring prior authorization for treatment beyond the primary care provider services.

REMEMBER

Although Medicare and Medicaid fall under the jurisdiction of the U.S. Department of Health & Human Services (HHS), there is no national Medicaid program. Instead, each state voluntarily sponsors its own program, often through commercial carriers. Medicaid must work within the guidelines (such as meeting eligibility requirements for members), but beyond that, each state can do its own thing. Medicare, on the other hand, is a national program, and it must be administered as dictated by CMS.

Confirming plan specifics

REMEMBER

You absolutely must know the specific coverage requirements for the plans that sponsor your patients. Prior to any patient encounter, look on each patient's insurance card for the provider inquiry phone number to call to verify benefits and payer-specific policies.

Checking the insurance card or payer website

Most of these plans assign responsibility for denied services to the provider. Patients who qualify for Medicaid assistance (the insurance program designed for the poor), for example, are unlikely to personally have the resources to pay out of pocket for denied medical services. Even if the payer denies coverage and indicates that the patient is responsible for the charges, the provider still isn't going to get paid if the patient doesn't have the money.

Medicaid policies that are sponsored by private payers are sometimes difficult to locate. Because each state is responsible for Medicaid program administration and the states often rely on commercial carriers to facilitate these programs, you need to be familiar with these payer guidelines. Ideally, the payer is one that maintains a website that lets the providers and the coders view the payer policies.

Looking in the plan's provider contract

In some cases, commercial payers who underwrite Medicare and/or Medicaid plans include these plans with their other commercial products in the provider contracts. Having this information in the contract can be beneficial to providers, but you need to make sure that the payer intended for all products to be included. Most payer contracts, however, clearly identify which products are included; any product not listed is excluded.

REMEMBER

Make sure you don't assume that just because your provider has a contract with Payer ABC that Payer ABC's Medicare and Medicaid plans have the same requirements as its standard plan. Don't assume, for example, that the provider can see Medicaid patients without the required referral or prior authorization. Similarly, don't assume that, just because a referral or authorization was not necessary six months ago, it's not needed next week.

When verifying coverage for all patients, regardless of their plans, make sure you verify all possible scenarios that may occur in the course of the patient's treatment plan. If a particular procedure is a possibility, call the carrier, give the representative the corresponding code to make sure that that service is covered, and secure any necessary authorization.

Obtaining referrals and prior authorizations

As I mention previously, the provider is responsible for securing the necessary referrals and authorizations.

Make sure you're familiar with the difference between a referral and prior authorization. A *referral* is issued by the primary care physician, who sends the patient to another healthcare provider for treatment or tests. A *prior authorization* is issued by the payer, giving the provider the go-ahead to perform the necessary service.

Here are some things to keep in mind about referrals and prior authorization for Medicare and Medicaid services:

- **Standard Medicare does not require referrals or prior authorization for visits or procedures that meet medical necessity.** Fortunately, these represent the majority of treatment options.
- **A Medicare HMO or Medicaid patient who needs prior authorization before being treated by a specialist or to receive services provided by a facility may also need a separate referral or authorization for *each* provider and possibly for each visit.**

  If you get an authorization over the phone, always make note of the name of the representative with whom you spoke, along with the date and time of the call. If authorization was obtained via a payer web portal, print the screen for proof, just in case you need it later.

- **Some authorizations cover a period of time and/or a specified number of treatments or visits.** Consider this example: A Medicaid or Medicare HMO patient may come to the primary care physician with a broken arm. The physician will probably authorize the patient to see an orthopedic surgeon for fracture care. The referral may authorize the specialist to diagnose and treat the patient for up to three visits over a two-month period of time. If the specialist determines that the patient needs surgery, another referral or authorization is needed. The surgeon needs two things: authorization to perform surgery and a referral or authorization to treat the patient (perform the surgery) in the specified facility.

» **Authorizations normally are active over a specific date range and may expire if not used during that time.** If the authorization date has passed, you need to contact the payer again and request another authorization.

» **The initial referral or authorization doesn't cover additional services.** In my earlier example of the patient with the broken arm, if the services of a physical or occupational therapist are needed, another referral is necessary.

WARNING

» **Obtaining prior authorization is still not a guarantee of payment.** The submitted claim must still be 1) supported by medical necessity, 2) filed within the timely filing requirements, and 3) filed by the provider mentioned in the referral or authorization.

Oops! Getting referrals and authorizations after the fact

Somebody has to do the paperwork for referrals or prior authorizations, and that somebody is unlikely to be the physician. So whose job is it? Everybody's. The scheduler, the coder, and the biller should all know when a referral or prior authorization is needed. Of course, by the time the case reaches you, the biller/coder, the encounter has already taken place. So what do you do if the necessary referral or authorization wasn't secured before the fact? You play nice.

If you haven't sent the claim yet, it may not be too late to call the payer and secure the necessary referral or authorization. Or you may be able to contact the primary care physician and explain the situation. Often she will issue the necessary number or form that allows the claim to be submitted within the provision of the patient's plan.

If the need for referral or prior authorization goes unnoticed until after the claim has been denied, the job falls to the person responsible for accounts receivable follow-up to try to get the retroactive authorization or referral. Sometimes you can obtain this by submitting an appeal along with the medical records to support medical necessity.

TIP

Getting hostile with the payer if the claim has been denied because your office didn't do the necessary work upfront doesn't benefit anyone. Instead, explain that a miscommunication occurred and that you're sorry for the confusion; then very nicely ask, "What can I do to straighten this out and get the claim paid?" Afterward, to avoid a recurrence, use the denial as a teachable moment for other members of the staff. You also may want to post a list of known payers who require prior authorizations or referrals for services performed in your office.

» Adhering to accepted coding practices in all situations

» Guarding against charges of fraud

Chapter 18

Coding Ethics: Being an Advocate for Your Employer

The medical billing and coding job market offers so many kinds of opportunities that you may feel like you're at a job buffet! Just think of it: You can work in a larger office for a hospital. Or maybe you can set up shop with a billing company that specializes in specific provider types like physician practice management companies, ambulatory surgery center management companies, anesthesia practice management companies, or numerous other specialty services. Maybe you want to focus on one client and work for a physician where you are not only in charge of coding but also responsible for accounts receivable follow-up.

Whatever position you find, your fiduciary responsibility is always to your employer. You should always have the best interest of your employer in mind when dealing with payers and patients alike. You are the first and last line of defense when it comes to protecting your client's interests. The best way to protect your client's interests is to comport yourself professionally and follow accepted coding practices. This chapter has the details.

Playing the Part of the Professional Medical Biller/Coder

To secure timely payment for the provider (that is, your employer or client), you'll find yourself working and communicating with many different people. As a representative of the office, being friendly and approachable to patients and payers alike is fine. After all, the professional demeanor you exhibit toward patients, fellow office staff, your superiors, and the payers with whom you work goes a long way in helping you establish your role as advocate-in-chief. But you must respect professional boundaries and behave in a professional way at all times.

Whether you are discussing missing patient intake information with the front office staff or making your case to a payer representative after being on hold for an hour, you must temper your frustrations with some level of kindness and understanding. Claims processing is business, and you've got to view it and communicate about it objectively, especially when you're doing the detective work of following up on unpaid claims. No matter who you're dealing with — your friends in the front office or your new best buddy George from the Medicare help line — stay focused on the facts. Leave your emotions at the door and stick to what's on the paper or computer screen.

In the following sections, I tell you how to keep your employer/client at the top of your priority list as you interact with patients, payers, and others.

Dealing with patients

Although you'll spend the lion's share of your time cozied up to your coding books and software, you occasionally need to interface with patients. In these interactions, your diplomacy chops come in handy. Navigating the sometimes choppy waters of patient relations isn't always easy, especially when the patient with whom you're working may be visibly emotional.

In this kind of situation — or in any situation involving a patient — your best bet is to be courteous, maintain your professional demeanor, and focus on the facts. In the following sections, I explain how to handle some of the more challenging interactions you may have with patients.

Patients are the physician's clients (not yours), so always treat them with respect and empathy. Without patients, healthcare providers would have no revenue, and if they don't get paid, you don't get paid.

When the patient can't pay the bill

In a way, patients are payers of sorts because, in many cases, they're responsible for at least some portion of the bill you code. For example, a patient may be responsible for a 20 percent coinsurance, meaning she has to pay 20 percent of what you code and bill. (Chapter 6 goes into more detail on insurance plans and the kinds of patient contributions that are commonly expected.)

In a small office setting, you may be the same person who receives a call from the patient who can't pay her bill, and these issues can be very difficult to address. In this situation, remain professional but be sympathetic to the patient's dilemma. Here are some suggestions:

- **Follow your employer's rules about contacting patients.** Providers let you know when contacting a patient is okay and what method they prefer for this communication.
- **Identify yourself upfront.** When you call patients, always let them know that you are with Dr. Smith's billing office or the billing office at Smith's Clinic.
- **Be a listener, not a talker.** You don't need to impart too much information about the inner workings of your client or employer's office to a patient, if any at all. For example, providers don't necessarily want their patients to know when the billing company or representative (you) is off-site.
- **Explain any available payment plan options.** If your office accepts credit cards, installment payments, or financing options, explain those to the patient.

When the patient doesn't understand how his insurance works

Patients with whom you interact may not fully understand how insurance works, so you may be called upon to explain some insurance basics. This situation often arises when the insurance company sends a payment to the patient instead of the provider by mistake, when a patient receives an explanation of benefits (EOB) statement he doesn't understand, or when the patient receives a bill from the provider that he wasn't expecting.

Many such situations arise when patients are out-of-network and, as a result, are often responsible for a large portion of the bill themselves. In these situations, the following suggestions can help you resolve the issue:

- **Before making any calls, make sure you know what the provider's policy is regarding out-of-network patients.** If the provider is knowingly treating patients outside of the network, a policy should be in place to address how these claims will be handled.

- **If the patient receives a check from the insurance company by mistake, it may be your responsibility to call the patient and explain that they need to surrender the check to the provider.** An alternative is to inform the patient of the situation and then bill them for the full charges, explaining that they can use the insurance check to pay the bill. Unfortunately, some patients refuse to surrender the check. In that case, collection agencies get involved or lawsuits are filed.
- **Inform patients of payment plan options.** When additional payment is expected of the patient, explain any payment plans that are available, including credit cards or financing options accepted by the provider.
- **Always be cordial, even when patients may get angry and direct their anger toward you.** Don't allow yourself to be drawn into an argument. Try to remember that the patient's frustration isn't personal. Keep your comments friendly and professional, and you'll do right by your employer or client.

Working with payers

Your primary goal when interacting with payers is simple: Make sure payers show your client the money! Ideally, your billing software and clearinghouse will keep you apprised of the status of claims (where they are and when they were received) through reports they can generate. The clearinghouse (the agency that relays the claim from the provider to the payer) also generates a batch report that identifies the claims transmitted in each batch. As a result, you should know where every claim is in the process.

Occasionally, however, a claim doesn't process. In that case, you need to talk to a real, live human being to find out why. When calling a payer to follow up on a claim, you are the voice of the healthcare provider, so always act in a professional manner. Remember, being nice gets you better service.

TIP

Make note of the representative's first name (and the first initial of her last name) when you call to follow up on a claim, and then use her first name as you talk. People like to hear their own names, so repeat the representative's name back to her. After the rep says, "My name is Sue," you can introduce yourself with, "Hi, Sue. This is John from Provider Smith's office. How are you doing today?" Keep the tone friendly rather than confrontational (at least in the beginning). It doesn't hurt to note the phone number and time of your call either. That way, during subsequent calls, you can use this information to prove that you spoke to someone in the payer's office; this information comes in especially handy if the payer's system doesn't have a record of your call.

Remaining patient

Normally, the payer representative is required to get three pieces of identification for both the provider and the patient. In most cases, the representative asks you for the provider's name and specific information such as tax identification number (TIN) or National Provider Identifier (NPI) number. You also need to provide the patient name, member identification number, and date of birth. Only after providing this information can the provider representative discuss the specific claim information with you.

Asking for this information isn't a stall tactic on the part of the payer representative. It's required by the Health Insurance Portability and Accountability Act (HIPAA). HIPAA guarantees that a patient's privacy is protected, and only those with a need to know are privy to this protected information.

Getting the resolution you want

Only after getting through the initial step (proving you have a need to know the patient's confidential information) are you able to inquire about the specific claim in question. Here are some pointers:

- **If the person with whom you are speaking is unable to assist with your inquiry, ask to be transferred.** When you are transferred to a supervisor, don't cast blame. Simply describe the issue and the reason you feel that the other person was not providing the resolution you need. Let the supervisor know that you have every confidence that he or she can resolve the issue.
- **If you are still unable to resolve the issue, submit a written request and identify the issue in addition to your expectations.** Make sure you also define the contractual obligation that supports your position. After you submit this written request, follow up with a call to make sure that the request was received and forwarded to the correct department for appropriate action.

- **Don't threaten or accuse.** Instead, stand behind the claim in question and your expectations as defined by any contract or state laws with regard to claim processing and payment. You don't gain anything by accusing the provider relations representative of failing to process a claim. Instead, ask the representative to help you identify the reason(s) the claim processed incorrectly or was rejected. Make that person your ally, not your adversary.

Any information the representative gives you on the call is *not* a guarantee of payment (in fact, early in your conversation, the representative should tell you that directly). As always, payment depends on the benefits outlined in the patient's individual plan.

Providing positive feedback to colleagues

Part of being a professional is being able to provide positive feedback to coworkers. Let's face it: Office politics are often (okay, always) at play, so getting along with your coworkers is important. From the receptionist at the front desk to the intake nurse, you have multiple opportunities to keep things positive around the office (even if someone's driving you nuts).

The success of your job as a biller/coder depends largely on the accuracy of the information gleaned when each patient checks in. Here are some tips on how to get (or continue to get) the info you need from the front desk:

- Make sure that the people at the front desk who are facilitating this process understand its importance, and let them know how much you appreciate the effort they put into getting cooperation from the patients.
- If necessary information is often missing or incorrect, examine the form and see whether you can identify a particular area that makes gathering the necessary information difficult. Discuss the issue with the office manager and diplomatically remind the staff that mistakes on the front end of the claim delay payment.
- If the office uses electronic medical records that employ electronic patient registration, make sure that the necessary information is programmed to the required field.

TIP

Most offices that use electronic medical records are contracted with or have their own software support (the Information Technology department). Work with the IT department to make sure that the necessary information is entered.

When discussing deficiencies in an office process or a coworker's performance, try to use constructive suggestions. The following examples illustrate how to phrase feedback in a positive way. Notice how each identifies the issue and opens the door to a possible solution without accusation or blame:

- "Do you think that we need to revise the demographic form since we're not always capturing the necessary information up front?"
- "Do we have a contact at XYZ insurance that we (or I) can reach out to for assistance with this issue?"
- "I've identified a pattern that shows we're not differentiating between the AEIOU insurance plans when we enter them into the billing software. Please make sure to check the address on the each patient's insurance card when entering demographic and billing information."

- "Dr. Smith usually does not dictate until being reminded. Can we set up a remote dictation system to make it easier for him?"
- "It would make claim submission faster if we had the necessary invoices without requesting them. Can we set up a process to have the invoices copied to the billing office upon receipt?"
- "We can't submit claims that are waiting for pathology reports. Is there a way for us to access these reports directly through the lab?"
- "If Joe needs help with payer matching, I'd be happy to do it with him." (as opposed to telling Joe you will do it yourself).
- "Thanks!" The most important sentence of all.

Protecting Yourself and Your Integrity

Whether you realize it or not, your position as the person who codes every patient interaction and procedure makes you the most trusted person in the office. Clients and employers trust you not only with their patients' personal and private information, but they also trust you to code accurately, fairly, and legally. To be worthy of this trust, you must maintain your integrity as a medical biller/coder.

From time to time, however, you may find yourself faced with a client, patient, fellow employee, or payer representative who asks you to ignore your own professional standards. In these cases, your integrity must take priority over getting your client paid. By protecting your professional integrity and coding in a way that upholds professional coding standards, you can rest assured that you are doing the best job you can.

Surviving a sticky situation

When you become a certified coder and biller, you receive instruction in correct coding and claim submission procedures and rules. From that point on and throughout your coding career, you're responsible for observing and promoting those rules.

"But, I have a boss!" you say. Yep, you sure do — probably a coding manager, an office manager, or perhaps the healthcare provider. This person may sign your paychecks, but the onus for correct coding is on *you*, especially when your boss is unaware of or unconcerned about correct coding rules. Even some managers, despite being aware of coding rules, may ignore them. In the following sections, I offer advice on how to deal with both situations.

Superiors asking you to fudge the coding

Having an office manager challenge the coding of claims when reimbursement is low isn't uncommon, and it puts you in a tough situation. For example, some office managers may want you to use modifiers as a tool to increase reimbursement rather than as a tool to increase specificity when reporting services (Chapter 12 covers modifiers).

In cases where a superior wants you to fudge the coding, rely on your coding books for backup. The National Correct Coding Initiative (NCCI) edits are a good place to start. If you stick to your correct coding guidelines, you have the facts you need to make coding decisions that maintain your professional integrity.

Physicians asking you to submit codes the record doesn't support

Some physicians may want to submit procedural codes that the record doesn't support. In this case, you may need to review the code description with the physician and ask for clarification as to why he feels the code is justified. You may discover that he failed to fully document the procedure that was performed.

If, however, you are certain that you correctly abstracted the codes from the record, you can request an independent audit, in which another coder reviews the record and notes which codes he feels are supported by the documentation. If the audit supports your position, you've secured the necessary documentation and you can submit the claim as you coded it originally. If the audit indicates that you are under-billing the claims, you must be willing to alter the way you code. The good news here is that you get the opportunity to make the record right — and you now know how to code more accurately in the future.

WARNING

If you find yourself in an office that demands coding that is contrary to correct coding standards, despite the results of an independent audit, then it's time to find another job. You should always code and bill ethically. If the employer's business philosophy contradicts those ethics and your integrity, then leave. Acquiescing to unethical standards can get you into big trouble. When (or if) your employer is subject to a request for payment refund, an audit, or accusations of fraudulent billing, not only will those events not look good on your resume but you may also be considered an accomplice.

Coding resources you can use as support

When you're asked to do something unethical or contrary to accepting coding practices, base your discussions on the guidelines of coding ethics. Resources are available to support correct coding positions and help you know what to say when. These resources include the following:

- ***Healthcare Business Monthly*:** The monthly publication of the AAPC, this magazine is sent to all AAPC members, and back issues are available on the organization's website (www.aapc.com).
- ***CPT Assistant* newsletter:** This is an official guide for interpretation of the CPT code set by the American Medical Association and is available by subscription.
- **The Coding Institute:** The Coding Institute offers specialty newsletters that require subscriptions but keep readers abreast of coding developments. Find them at www.codinginstitute.com.
- ***Journal of AHIMA:*** This journal is available through the AHIMA website (www.ahima.org). AHIMA membership also entitles members to access the organization's newsletters.
- **Medicare and Medicare contractor websites:** You can find volumes of current coding information here.
- ***The Coder's Desk Reference* (Ingenix/Optum):** This coding book contains detailed descriptions of each CPT code. Ingenix also publishes coding companion books for various specialties that provide more in-depth descriptions of the procedures.
- **Coding software programs:** Look for those that offer access to expert resources for coding questions or challenging coding scenarios.
- ***Coder's Pink Sheet,* by DecisionHealth:** A favorite publication written by many seasoned coders, these newsletters are specific to various specialties. You can purchase a subscription through www.decisionhealth.com.

REMEMBER

When involved in any type of coding controversy or any interaction that involves a specific claim or account, keep your cool and document all conversations in the record, whether conversations are with payer representatives or patients. Remember that errors and differences of opinions are not fraud. Just because a provider thinks the work warrants a different code does not mean the coder is being asked to commit fraud. There are a number of grey areas in coding. It's important to keep an open mind and work through differences of opinion without jumping to conclusions or making accusations. As long as you stay positive and professional, the record will reflect that you truly have your client's best interests at heart.

Documenting your day

A great way to keep all your coding activities on the up and up is to spend some time each day writing down (or typing up) what you work on each day. I like to keep a time log for each project, making special note of any claims that have trouble getting through the claims process.

Not only does such a record keep you up-to-date on deadlines and how things are going with your claims, but it also provides a history should anyone question why certain decisions were made. In your documentation, record any special circumstances that affect a claim, such as the following:

- The date on which you must submit a corrected claim
- When a patient calls to make special payment arrangements
- Whether a claim was initially rejected and what action was taken
- If a claim paid incorrectly, the date the payment was received and the reason it was incorrect
- Any action taken as a result of incorrect claims processing, calls, letters, and so on
- All circumstances concerning a medical record and the reason the services were necessary (medical necessity)
- The patient's consent to services and agreement to be responsible for payment
- The date a payment was received and from whom
- The date the claim was submitted to the secondary payer and any communication that resulted from that submission

With all claim documentation, make sure that you include the names of the people you spoke to, the date and time that the conversation took place (most software records this automatically), and all details of the conversation.

Mum's the word: Keeping patient info private

Earning and keeping patient trust starts the moment you sign on for your new billing and coding job. Most healthcare providers require employees and vendors to sign confidentiality agreements. These agreements serve as your acknowledgment that you will keep any patient information confidential.

Keeping patient info confidential isn't just the right thing to do; it's the law as outlined by HIPAA. So when you sign your confidentiality agreement, be sure you mean it. Patient confidentiality is serious business, and violating this confidence may result in a fine or, in serious circumstances, imprisonment. For more information on HIPAA, refer to Chapter 4.

HIPAA AND CRIMINAL LIABILITY

In June 2005, the United States Justice Department issued a clarification regarding who can be held criminally liable under HIPAA. They are the big boys of healthcare: health plans, healthcare clearinghouses, healthcare providers who transmit claims in electronic form, and Medicare prescription drug card sponsors. Individuals such as directors, employees, or officers of the covered entity may also be directly criminally liable.

Any of these entities and individuals who disclose protected health information may face a fine of up to $50,000 and up to one year in prison. Offenses committed under false pretenses can result in fines of up to $100,000 and five years of prison. Offenses that involve intention to sell or use individually identifiable health information for personal gain, commercial advantage, or malice can result in fines of $250,000 and ten years of prison.

Taking steps to protect confidentiality within the office

Patients trust the provider and the provider's staff to protect their personal information. Providers ask for patient Social Security numbers, birth dates, addresses, and other information that opens the door for identity theft. A lot is at stake for your patients when they release this highly personal information to you, and you owe it to them, to the provider, and to yourself to treat it with the utmost care.

Protecting the patient's personal information begins in the reception area or waiting room. Gone are the days when the nurse or other employee would call a patient by first *and* last name (it gives away a patient's identity to everyone in the waiting room), or when the admitting personnel would ask the patient to explain the reason for the visit in front of other patients (no one wants fellow patients to find out about that unfortunately placed rash).

Today, because of HIPAA, providers have taken great steps to protect patient identity and privacy: Patient records are kept in locked files out of the view of the public. Patient registration information is kept in computers that are password protected and that time out within a few minutes of inactivity. Passwords for clearinghouse access, software access, and insurance website access must be changed at specified intervals. All employees must have their own usernames and passwords, and sharing their access information with others is a HIPAA violation. These are just a few of the changes.

You can help keep your client's circle of trust intact by working with fellow office colleagues to stay abreast of HIPAA rules and regulations. You can also offer to be the office HIPAA liaison with outside entities, checking in from time to time to find out about their efforts to maintain patient privacy and following up with your client or employer if you suspect any discrepancies.

Protecting confidentiality when working with others

You're not the only person who has access to a patient's personal information. The healthcare provider obtains permission from the patient to share this personal information with other stakeholders as necessary to receive reimbursement for the services provided. These other stakeholders include the insurance company (which needs to know the reason treatment was provided) and the clearinghouse (which is privy to the patient's personal health information during transmission of the claim). Both clearinghouses and payers must follow the same privacy standards mandated by HIPAA.

ACCOUNTS RECEIVABLE: YOUR SECRET ETHICAL WEAPON

When patients have trouble meeting their financial responsibilities or physicians fail to document, you may be asked to let payments slide or to go ahead and code an encounter that has no documentation. Fortunately, you have a secret weapon you can rely on to drive home the point that fudging just won't work: accounts receivable (AR).

Outstanding revenue needs to be collected (no one knows that better than your boss) before it can be used. Allowing patients to make installment payments is an option, but it increases the AR line on the balance sheet, and the provider can't invest money that hasn't been received, nor can he make payroll until the money is in the bank. The way to avoid this problem is to encourage the provider to collect all known deductibles, anticipated coinsurance amounts, and copayments before the patient encounter and to make patients aware of this practice prior to the date of service. That way, they're prepared to make payment when they arrive.

On the other end of your process is the provider who fails to document. Sure, he may see 75 patients a day with an average of $100 payment per encounter, but if he doesn't dictate until he's faced with the threat of privilege revocation, he can't get the money he obviously wants. Providers like this need to be reminded that they can't get paid until the claim is submitted, and the claim can't be submitted without the documentation. If pressured to fudge your coding process, remind such docs that you won't be able to pursue unpaid claims in AR without the proper provider documentation anyway, so getting paid won't even be an option. That tends to get their pens moving!

Keeping yourself honest when you make a mistake

As a biller and coder, you must be self-reliant, because you perform most of your daily office functions independently of others. The same is true of maintaining your ethical standards. You need to police yourself. After all, your job and reputation are on the line if something goes wrong in the coding and claims process, and claims aren't being paid in a timely fashion.

Your first charge is to make sure that you're submitting the claims correctly (refer to Chapters 11 through 13). Then follow them up and, if the claims aren't being paid, identify the reason for the delay and try to have the issue corrected (Chapter 14). Easier said than done, especially when the mistake that delays payment is yours.

Just keep in mind that you're human, and you'll make mistakes. By admitting that you screwed up a claim, you're not only keeping yourself honest, but you're also helping the issue get resolved faster. (Think of the time you'd waste — or the trouble you'd be in — trying to cover up your mistake or deflect blame.)

Getting the Most Bang for Your Client's Buck — Honestly

Your job as a biller/coder is, in plain terms, to get the provider paid for services rendered. Part of that payment comes from the payers, whether they're commercial (health insurance) or governmental (Medicare, Medicaid, and others). The other part of payment often comes from the patients themselves.

Collecting payments from patients

Yes, your most important job is to fully abstract all billable services and supporting medical necessity from the physician's documentation. But the other part of your job is to follow provider-payer contracts that stipulate that the provider is obligated to collect patient balances. Failure to do so may result in the contracts being canceled.

REMEMBER

The contract defines the conditions for submitting claims, the procedures to be submitted for payment and the medical necessity that supports the procedures, and reimbursement obligations of both the payer and the patient. When you try to collect payment from patients, you must follow the same principles of honesty and integrity that you follow when you code.

When you follow up on outstanding patient payments, be sure to do the following:

- **Treat all patients the same, regardless of what kind of insurance they have.** Most offices implement a policy to address patient billing. Follow this policy consistently for all patients.
- **Document, document, document.** Good documentation practices provide a paper trail that verifies your consistency. Most providers, for example, follow the "three billing cycle statements" rule: They bill patients at least three times before forgiving an outstanding balance. You should document each patient statement in the patient record along with any conversations with the patient or payer.
- **Know what the contract says.** Payer contracts generally indicate how patient balances are to be handled. Medicare, for example, requires a collection effort for all Medicare patient balances, regardless of the amount. Others usually have similar expectations. If the provider fails to make collection efforts for patient balances, the insurance company may view this as breach of contract and terminate the agreement or deny renegotiation.
- **Be aware of the False Claims Act, which makes defrauding government programs a crime.** You can run afoul of this act if you knowingly submit a false claim, cause a false claim to be submitted, or create a false record that results in a fraudulent claim. Billing 30 claims for a day that only shows 20 patients, for example, is a violation of the act. (Refer to the earlier section "Surviving a sticky situation" for advice on how to deal with employers who try to pressure you into doing things that are unethical or illegal.)
- **Know the boundaries of your claim.** You can't ask for money that isn't coded. Pretty simple. Knowing what procedure you can code on any given claim is a vital part of doing your job ethically and accurately. You can find this information in the payer contracts, in the CPT codebook, and in other coding resources, such as professional publications. You can also ask more experienced coders in your office. (Refer to Chapters 11 through 13 for detailed information on preparing and submitting a claim.)

TIP

The cardinal rule of ethical coding is "When in doubt, ask." If you find any ambiguity in the patient record, query the provider to get clarification. As I say throughout this book, any claim must be fully supported by the record.

Avoiding accusations of fraudulent billing

Attempting to collect balances of less than $25 can become costly, so having a write-off policy can save a practice both time and money. In your collection efforts, focus on larger outstanding balances. When balances are forgiven, note the account and, if the patient tries to return, collect all outstanding debts and copays prior to another encounter.

WARNING

Providers who routinely forgive patient debt run the risk of prosecution under anti-kickback statutes and possibly the False Claims Act. The reasoning is that, by not collecting coinsurance amounts from patients, providers are billing Medicare for excessive charges. Say Medicare pays $80 of a $100 bill, with the expectation that the patient will pay the remaining $20. By not going after the $20 patient contribution, the provider is essentially saying that he really only expected to receive $80, not the $100 he actually billed. And if he was expecting only $80 for the service, he shouldn't have billed $100.

To avoid accusations of fraudulent billing, do the following:

- Consistently apply the office hardship policy to all patients.
- Keep proof of financial hardship, which should consist of an application for financial assistance that documents the patient's financial stability. Also document all attempts to collect patient debts.
- Verify the wording in payer contracts with regard to patient balances.

Bottom line: You can forgive patients — but not too much!

6
The Part of Tens

IN THIS PART . . .

Check out ten common mistakes to avoid to keep your nose, and your coding, clean.

CDI, EHR, HIPAA, oh my! Find out the top need-to-know acronyms you'll hear, see, or use every day.

Get advice from the pros. Gather pointers and information from those who've been in the medical billing and coding trenches.

» Protecting your patients and provider

» Maintaining your integrity

Chapter 19

Ten Common Billing and Coding Mistakes and How to Avoid Them

Repeat after me: Ethical violations are bad. As a coder, you must consistently do the right thing at work, especially when related to providers, payers, and patients. By virtue of your position, you are privy to sensitive information and have an impact on the financial well-being of all the people who rely on you to do your job. In this chapter, I outline the most egregious of the ethical and legal violations that can land you in hot water if you ever stray from the straight and narrow.

Being Dishonest

Certified medical coders are trained to abstract billable procedures from the medical record. A true-blue coder respects the rules of coding. The biggest rule is that all the procedures you submit must be documented in the record, not just mentioned in the heading. Therefore, resist the temptation to submit codes that are only implied or that are not documented by medical necessity. Don't unbundle codes for the sake of additional reimbursement, and don't choose a procedural code that is "like" the actual service performed. Code honestly, code accurately, and you'll do just fine.

Shifting the Blame

You have nothing to gain by shifting the blame of inaccurate coding on to others. If you work in an environment with a department for each step of the coding cycle, ask for clarification as to how much leeway you have to facilitate. If you notice that claims are not being submitted in a timely manner, for example, and nothing in the documentation explains the reason for the delay, bring the matter to the attention of the appropriate party. If the entire revenue cycle is your job, then take responsibility to ensure that the claims are moving as they should through the cycle. To maintain your integrity and the respect of your superiors and coworkers, be a team player and stay focused on the bottom line: revenue for your provider or client.

Billing More than Is Documented

Physicians often dictate every step of a procedure, but that does not mean that each step is actually billable. To be eligible for separate reimbursement, the procedure must have required additional work and skill by the physician. Stick to the provider's documentation to bill exactly what you need to, no more and no less. If the documentation is ambiguous, take the time to clarify what occurred with the physician. Chapter 12 tells you how to conduct a physician query.

Unbundling Incorrectly

Codes that are bundled are considered incidental to another billable procedure. For example, a surgeon must make an incision before a surgery can be performed. The incision is incidental, and the surgeon must then close the incision. Again, a normal closure is incidental because it is necessary to complete the primary procedure. The physician usually fully documents the approach (the incision) and the closure, but that doesn't mean that you should bill for them. Similarly, a procedure that is a result of the surgeon "being in the area anyway" is not necessarily billable. The key is to know which procedures are bundled and which ones aren't. You can find this information by checking the National Correct Coding Initiative (NCCI) edits. If the procedures are considered incidental, they will be included in the bundling edits. Chapters 4 and 12 have the details of bundling.

Some practice management associations advise members to "bill everything and let the payer sort it out." This is terrible advice! Make it a point to educate staff with regard to unbundling guidelines and correct coding.

Ignoring an Error

Occasionally, the documentation has an error. Perhaps it's a transcription error or an omission by the provider. Either way, as the biller/coder, you're responsible for bringing the error to the attention of the physician and making sure that it is corrected. Sometimes resolving the error is as simple as correcting a patient name or a spelling error. Other times, the error may be in the coding — you (or someone else) abstracted the wrong code, for example.

In all cases, after you find and correct the error, you must submit the corrected claim. Failure to do so can result in the provider receiving an undeserved payment or being underpaid. Bottom line: Find the problem and follow up on it immediately to avoid bigger problems later. Go to Chapter 18 for details on what to do when you make an error on a claim.

Mishandling an Overpayment

Occasionally, a payer fails to process a claim correctly, either paying too much or too little. If a claim has been underpaid, the provider is quick to ask that the error be rectified. When a claim has been overpaid, the same policy should be implemented. If a payer has failed to follow the contract and allowed more than the contract obligates, the provider should notify the payer and prepare to return the erroneous payment. Often this is obligated by the payer contract. Doing so reinforces your integrity with the payer and also averts potential interest payments that may be obligated when the payer finds the error and asks for reimbursement. For information on how to deal with under- and overpayments and other reimbursement problems, head to Chapter 14.

Failing to Protect Patients from Out-of-Network Penalties

Most patients are not experts on insurance plans or the medical claim processes. If a provider treats patients out-of-network, the patient usually faces penalties in the form of high deductibles or higher coinsurance liability. Some plans don't cover out-of-network services at all, and the patient is responsible for the entire costs.

To protect patients from this scenario, providers should have office policies that define how out-of-network patients are to be billed. In addition, and whenever possible, you should verify patient benefits prior to any encounter and explain to the patient the provider's expectations regarding to copayments, deductibles, and coinsurance responsibilities. (You can generally find liability information on the patient's insurance card.) For a quick refresher on the different kinds of insurance plans, head to Chapter 6.

Failing to Verify Prior Authorization

Before they can be performed, some procedures require that the provider receive prior authorization, which is permission from the payer for the patient to be treated. Failure to obtain necessary authorizations or referrals (when a primary care physician sends a patient to another provider for treatment or tests) may result in the claim being denied. Depending upon the provisions of the patient's plan, liability for billed charges then falls on either the provider or the patient.

For this reason, checking whether planned procedures need prior authorization is a vital part of ensuring that the provider adheres to the contract he has with a payer and receives the negotiated reimbursement for the service he provides. Always ask the physician to note any and all procedures that may be performed and check for authorization requirements for each one. Obtaining an authorization that is not needed is better than finding out after the claim is submitted that one was required. For more on referrals and prior authorizations, head to Chapter 11.

Breaking Patient Confidentiality

As the coder, you have access to both the patient's clinical information and his or her personal demographic information, such as Social Security number, date of birth, address, and so on. It goes without saying that you need to guard this information as you would your own, not only because of the threat of identity theft but also because of ramifications of violating the Health Insurance Portability and Accountability Act (HIPAA). HIPAA governs to whom, under what circumstances, and what kind of information you can share about a patient, and violators may be subject to steep fines and the possibility of imprisonment. For more information about HIPAA and strategies for protecting patient confidentiality, go to Chapter 4.

Following the Lead of an Unscrupulous Manager

Most coding managers know about and adhere to correct coding processes and expect you to follow those processes as well. Unfortunately, you may encounter a manager who is less aware of correct coding rules or who, if cognizant of the rules, tends to bend or overlook them. These coding managers may see modifiers as a tool to increase reimbursement rather than as a tool to increase specificity when reporting services, for example, and may challenge the coding of claims when reimbursement is low.

If your manager or other superior encourages you to code out of bounds, don't acquiesce. Instead, do what you think is right and report the incident to an office leader who can follow up on the matter. You may get on the shady manager's bad side, but you'll be able to sleep much better at night! Chapter 18 offers strategies you can use when you're under pressure to code in questionable or unethical ways.

» Memorizing the big government names to know

Chapter 20
Ten Acronyms to Burn into Your Brain

The world of medical billing and coding is like one big bowl of alphabet soup. Just about any term that comes up in your daily dealings has a corresponding acronym. Every office becomes familiar with the abbreviations specific to that particular practice, but some acronyms are known industry-wide and are familiar to everyone who works in the healthcare business. In this chapter, I explain a few of the most common abbreviations and acronyms that all medical offices use.

TECHNICAL STUFF

Some states regulate the clinical abbreviations and acronyms used in medical records. These state regulations usually require that each abbreviation has only one meaning and that that meaning is documented on a list available to all clinical staff. For administrative staff, however, the acronyms and abbreviations aren't usually regulated, so you may find even more in-house acronyms floating through the office — which isn't necessarily a bad thing. After all, do you really want to walk around saying "Health Insurance Portability and Accountability Act" all day when you can just say "HIPAA"?

ACA: Patient Protection and Affordable Care Act

The Patient Protection and Affordable Care Act (often shorted to "Affordable Care Act" or ACA) refers to the federal statute signed into law by President Barack Obama on March 23, 2010 (for this reason, the slang term is *Obamacare*). This statute represents one of the most significant revisions of the U.S. healthcare system since the passage of the Social Security Amendments in 1965, which resulted in Medicare and Medicaid. The ACA is intended to provide access to healthcare coverage for all, with a goal of lowering the number of uninsured citizens and thus reducing overall healthcare costs. This law also requires insurance companies to cover all applicants within mandated standards regardless of preexisting conditions. The policies are marketed through the government website `www.healthcare.gov`.

ACO: Accountable Care Organization

An Accountable Care Organization (ACO) is intended to tie provider reimbursements to quality metrics that are tracked for patients. In other words, providers coordinate care of patients by using a strong base of primary care services complimented by specialists and hospitals who work together. Part of the ACA (discussed earlier in this chapter) includes a provision that allows ACOs to be rewarded for demonstrating savings when caring for Medicare populations. Some commercial payers are also supporting this concept by offering similar incentives or by purchasing providers in an attempt to improve patient care and control cost.

CDI: Clinical Documentation Improvement

Clinical documentation improvement (CDI) programs are dedicated to improving provider documentation in order to be able to capture a more accurate and complete picture of a patient's clinical status when it's translated into coded data. This data is then used to track physician performance, reimbursements, public health, disease tracking, and so on. As a coder, accurate and thorough documentation are essential to maintain correct coding. The implementation of the International Classification of Diseases, Tenth Revision (ICD-10) has been a driving force for improvement of clinical documentation due to the specificity of individual codes.

CMS: Centers for Medicare & Medicaid Services

The Centers for Medicare & Medicaid Services (CMS) is a division of the U.S. Department of Health & Human Services (HHS). CMS administers Medicare, Medicaid, and the Children's Health Insurance Program — programs that serve the most vulnerable segments of the population. In addition to serving these populations, CMS also sets the standard for healthcare, and many commercial payers follow CMS payment guidelines. You can read more about CMS's Medicare and Medicaid programs in Chapters 6 and 17.

EHR: Electronic Health Record

The electronic health record (EHR) is a digital record that may be shared by providers from more than one practice or entity such as a hospital. It is a key provision of the American Recovery and Reinvestment Act of 2009, which went into effect January 1, 2014, and required all public and private healthcare providers to adopt the use of electronic health records in order to avoid penalties that affect reimbursement. Financial incentives were also created for healthcare providers who demonstrate proof of "meaningful use," which is industry-speak for improving patient care. EHR implementation is the foundation of meaningful use; without EHR adoption, it is not possible to progress through the stages of meaningful use. The EHR differs from the EMR (electronic medical record), which is simply a digital version of a paper chart and is not shared outside the practice.

EOB: Explanation of Benefits

An explanation of benefits (EOB) is the document that the insurance company issues to the patient in response to a claim submission. The EOB reflects how the claim was processed and shows the billed charges, any reductions applied (either by contract, fee schedule, negotiation, or arbitrarily assigned), the allowed amount, and, finally, any remaining patient liability. Patients are billed as indicated by the EOB, meaning that providers can't bill them any additional amount to make up for any discounts applied to the claim. Chapter 13 has information on the EOB and what you, as a biller/coder, need to do with it. (The provider version is the remittance advice, or RA.)

HIPAA: Health Insurance Portability and Accountability Act

The Health Insurance Portability and Accountability Act (HIPAA) was approved by Congress to protect the privacy of patients and ensure that patients have access to their medical files. All patients must sign a notice stating that the provider made them aware of the practice's privacy policies, and all healthcare organizations must develop and enforce policies and procedures and ensure that their employees are trained to understand and comply with the requirements in place to protect patient confidentiality.

In addition, HIPAA requires patients to identify others (such as a spouse or parent) who can have access to their healthcare information. Under HIPAA, any conversation between a physician and patient that contains protected health information (PHI) is confidential, and information regarding that interaction cannot be left in a voice mail or on an answering machine unless specifically instructed to do so by the patient in writing.

INN: In-Network

An in-network (INN) provider is one who has a contract with either the insurance company or the network with whom the payer participates. Patients who go to in-network providers usually have to pay less in coinsurance and deductibles. In addition, INN office visits may require that the patient make a copayment at the time of the visit.

NCCI: National Correct Coding Initiative

The National Correct Coding Initiative (NCCI) is the CMS development intended to promote national correct coding methodologies and discourage improper medical coding that may lead to incorrect payment for Medicare Part B claims. It involves two categories of edits: Physician Edits, which apply to physician and non-physician providers in addition to ambulatory surgery centers; and Hospital Outpatient Prospective Payment System Edits (Outpatient Edits), which apply to other providers such as hospitals. Both sets of edits are maintained to identify codes that bundle together and indicate when unbundling may be permissible with the proper use of a particular modifier. They also indicate when unbundling is never appropriate. NCCI edits are maintained and revised, if necessary, on a quarterly basis.

OON: Out-of-Network

Out-of-network (OON) refers to insurance plan benefits. An out-of-network provider is one who does not have a contract with the patient's insurance company and, therefore, is not obligated to accept whatever discounted reimbursement the insurance company was able to negotiate with its in-network providers. Every commercial insurance plan outlines the benefit level for members. Usually when a non-contracted provider treats the patient, the benefits are lower. Your patient may have a fairly inexpensive copay for an in-network provider and a much larger copay for an out-of-network provider. Some carriers may not cover out-of-network providers at all!

» Ways to verify stakeholder information

» Best strategies for following up with payers

Chapter 21
Ten (Plus One) Tips from Billing and Coding Pros

You've now arrived at the unsolicited advice portion of the book. Usually, that sort of advice is unwelcome, like when your in-laws offer child-rearing advice without asking. But I'm betting you'll find this particular brand of off-the-cuff advice helpful because it comes from seasoned professionals who have walked the same path you're embarking on right now. Think of the pointers in this chapter as your own little coffee klatch, minus the coffee. Here I give you 11 tips that will help keep you sane when you're knee-deep in coding.

Insist on Proper Documentation

The revenue cycle begins when the patient completes the demographic form prior to admission and the provider verifies the patient's coverage. The cycle continues when the physician completes his or her documentation of the patient encounter. Your job ultimately depends on all involved parties recording the right kind of info at the right time. This preparation, if done correctly, sets the stage for correct claims processing and payment. To get the information you need, you must make sure that everyone involved is aware of the necessary documentation and works as a team to achieve that goal.

Verify Patient Benefits

When it comes to paying medical bills (the payers and patients) or receiving reimbursement (the providers), you don't want any surprises. To avoid unpleasant "Gotcha!" moments, call the payer to check for remaining deductibles, coinsurance responsibilities, and any applicable copayments, and collect them from the patient prior to admission. Also verify the need for a prior authorization for any planned procedures. Your goal should be to collect all this information before the patient even walks through the door of the provider's office.

Get Vital Patient Info at Check-In

Collect patient demographics (name, address, date of birth, phone number, marital status, employer, Social Security number, and so on), and get a copy of the insurance card upon patient arrival. You need this information when the time comes to code and submit the claim.

Also verify patient identification. Institute a policy, if your office doesn't have one already, that all patients must present a government-issued form of ID upon arrival; then make a copy of that ID and place it in the record.

Review the Documentation ASAP

As a biller/coder, you rely on the documentation. It has the physician's notes regarding diagnosis and treatment, as well as the demographic information you need. Although you technically have a few days before you must code and send the claim off, don't delay. Your goal should be to have the claim out the door within 72 hours. Review the medical documentation as soon as possible after the encounter or procedure to see whether it is as complete as you need it to be. And if you find any omissions or ambiguities to clarify, query the physician as soon as possible.

Set Up a System to Ensure Accuracy

From coding to reimbursement, the biller/coder has to perform several tasks: abstracting all billable codes and supporting diagnosis codes from the record; entering the claim into the billing software in preparation for claim submission and then submitting it; checking the clearinghouse submission reports; and following up on any problems or denials. To do this job well, you must be both accurate and efficient. Therefore, offices should have a system of checks and balances in place to audit and ensure the quality and completeness of these tasks.

Play Nice with Others

On its way to generating reimbursement, your claim will go either directly to the payer or first to a clearinghouse and then to the payer. In either place, it can get hung up. If claims are rejecting at the clearinghouse, work with the people there to identify the underlying reason.

If the payer is unable to accept your electronic claims (which may happen when the payer implements a new processing system or transitions from one platform to another), send your claims on paper until the problem is resolved. If your billing software is the problem (for example, claim forms not populating correctly), work with the software vendor to resolve the issue.

Follow Up on Accounts Receivable Daily

Putting claims through the process may be the main focus of your job, but making sure the money comes through is just as important. Set time aside each day to review the accounts receivable reports (making sure that you're always working with the latest report). Be sure to pay attention to whether the claims have been received; then watch the accounts receivable aging reports (which are generated by your billing software and show all the outstanding claims and the dollar amounts associated with each) to monitor all outstanding accounts. If you see that some are stalled, get on the horn with the payer to resolve the issue.

Be a Bulldog on the Phone

Persistence pays off. So does being clear on what you need and expect. So for every claim over 60 days old, call the payer. Verify that the claim is in process and make note of the claim number and when payment can be expected. If the representative tells you that the payment has been issued, get the date, check number, and the amount of the check (note whether it was a bulk check or single check). You can also verify the address the check was sent to and ask whether it was presented for payment or cashed.

Know Your Payer Contracts by Heart

The more familiar you are with all payer contracts, the more quickly and accurately you can process claims. Payer contracts stipulate things like what procedures are covered and whether prior authorization or referrals are needed. They also outline billing requirements, such as how long you have to submit the claim (called timely filing), how long the payer has to make payment before interest is earned, and other payer specific quirks, such as revenue code requirements or value codes that are expected.

As you become an expert on the details of the payer contracts, be sure to note any updates and changes (policies and benefit levels change regularly). Most payers post policy revisions and additions on their websites, but with regard to individual contracts, you need to know where your employer keeps these documents.

Create a File System That Lets You Find What You Need

If you or anybody else ever has a question about the status of a claim, the last thing you want to have to do is root around your office space looking for the relevant documentation. By creating a system that tells you instantly when things are received and where you can find them, you can more easily keep track of your claims and retrieve the necessary info whenever you need to.

For example, use a date stamp to document when you receive payments and remittance advice (RA), and keep a daily file of all received payments and non-payment claim documents. For most small- to intermediate-size offices, this can be as simple as keeping each day's RAs in a file folder. Then for each document that is claim related, note the account, what was received, the date it was received, and how it relates to the account. Link the payment for each claim to the date the RA was received and note each account of non-payment documents, including when they were received. That way if you need to refer to one of these documents, you know where to find it.

Make Payers Show You the Money!

Your primary objective as a biller and coder is to make sure that your employer is reimbursed appropriately for the services he provides. That means you can't let him be underpaid. To guard against the provider being underpaid, make sure you follow up and appeal any claim that does not pay as expected. If your provider has a contract with a payer and the claim didn't pay according to the contract, you can base your argument solely on the contract. If no contract exists between the provider and payer, call the payer and ask what method was used to price the claim. Claims that were paid "usual and customary" should be challenged. If a silent preferred provider organization (PPO) was accessed (you can find out more about these in Chapter 16), ask for the contract to be identified and then notify the network in writing that you want to terminate the relationship.

Glossary

AAPC (American Academy of Professional Coders): The nation's largest training and credentialing organization for medical coders.

accounts receivable (AR): The industry name for outstanding payments. For most companies, 90 days in AR is acceptable, although most contracts contain language that obligates payment within a certain time.

acute injury: Damage to the body incurred by accident.

adjudication: Payment obligation according to the patient's insurance benefits with regard to a claim.

advanced beneficiary notice (ABN): A notice the provider may ask a Medicare beneficiary to sign for a service or item that will probably not be covered. By signing an ABN, the patient agrees to be financially responsible in the event that Medicare denies payment. If the patient is not notified or doesn't sign the notice before services are rendered, then he or she does not have to pay for it.

American Health Information Management Association (AHIMA): The official association of health information management professionals.

anatomy: The study of the human body structure.

arthroscopic surgery: A surgical technique, using tiny cameras, employed by orthopedic surgeons, that allows them to visualize, diagnose, and possibly treat injury or disease inside a joint.

body system: A group of organs that performs a specific task.

bundling: The grouping together of one or more CPT codes that are considered incidental or inclusive to another and that should not be reimbursed individually. For these additional codes to be considered for separate payment, the physician must describe the extra work performed, including the extra time involved and why it was necessary.

Centers for Medicare & Medicaid Services (CMS): A branch of the United States Department of Health & Human Services that administers Medicare and Medicaid.

Certified Coding Associate (CCA): An AHIMA certification that shows the recipient has demonstrated the ability to abstract the correct procedural and diagnosis codes in hospitals and physician practices.

Certified Coding Specialist (CCS): An AHIMA certification that indicates competency in hospital coding and requires a higher level of expertise in diagnosis and procedural coding. CCS-certified coders also possess a strong knowledge of medical terminology and human anatomy.

Certified Professional Coder (CPC): AAPC certification that indicates proficiency in reading medical charts and abstracting the correct diagnosis codes, procedural codes, and supply codes. CPC-certified coders also have at least two years of experience in the coding profession.

Certified Professional Coder Apprentice (CPC-A): The initial AAPC certification indicating that the coder is an apprentice. After completing a two-year apprenticeship in coding or billing in a medical office, the CPC-A coder can request that the *A* be removed.

chronic injury: Damage that is a result of overuse or aging.

claims matching: The process that occurs when specific services are performed by several providers who submit claims for the same patient.

claims processing: The overall work of receiving a claim from the provider and determining eligibility for payment.

claims scrubbing: The process by which the editing system checks the claim for errors and verifies that it is compatible with the payer software before sending the claim to the payer.

claims submission: The process of sending to the payer the procedural codes that represent the work performed by the healthcare provider.

commercial insurance carrier: The company that writes the reimbursement check to the provider.

compliance: When an office or individual has set up a program to run the practice under the regulations set forth by the United States Office of Inspector General (OIG).

consultation: A visit with a physician specialist that has specific requirements that must be met (the visit must be requested from an authorized source, must be accompanied by an opinion from your provider, and must include a response to the requesting physician) before the claim can be billed.

contract payers: Payers with whom a provider has a contract or payers that are part of a network with whom the provider has a contract.

contracted carve-out: A special clause in the contract that allows certain procedures to be reimbursed at a different rate from the rate specified by the procedural code.

Current Procedural Terminology (CPT): The CPT code set is a medical code set maintained by the American Medical Association (AMA) through the CPT Editorial Panel that is used to report medical, surgical, and diagnostic procedures and services for reimbursement. The AMA publishes the codes annually in the CPT codebook.

critical care codes: Time-based codes used when a patient is critically ill and that support a high level of reimbursement. Per CPT guidelines, these codes include specific care that must be completed in order to bill.

definitive diagnosis: A diagnosis made after the body cavity becomes visible (that is, after the surgeon has either opened up the patient or inserted a scope to see the patient's inner workings).

Department of Health & Human Services (HHS): The primary U.S. government agency responsible for protecting the health of Americans. Medicare and Medicaid, part of the Centers for Medicare & Medicaid Services, are two of this agency's programs.

diagnosis terms: Terms that determine medical necessity as defined by the payers.

diagnosis-related groups (DRGs): The way in which an admitting diagnosis is linked to the severity of the patient's illness. Hospitals are reimbursed based on DRGs.

diagnostic laparoscopy: A diagnostic procedure using a scope.

disease process: A deviation of the normal structure or function of a body part that is represented by symptoms.

EDI (Electronic Data Interchange): The electronic systems that carry claims to a central clearinghouse for distribution to individual carriers.

electronic data interchange (EDI) number: An electronic number that serves as the payer's "address" or identifier. This number tells the clearinghouse which payer to send the claim to.

electronic health record (EHR): An electronic record of a patient's health history. EHRs are intended to do away with paper charts, thus making protecting and sharing health information easier.

evaluation and management (E&M) codes: The codes representing noninvasive physician services that are used for every office visit or encounter a physician has with a patient. Typically these encounters involve taking a history, an examination, and decision-making on the part of the provider. These are the most commonly billed codes.

evaluation and management encounter: A doctor's visit, also known as an E&M visit. E&M visits may take place in a physician's office, nursing home, hospital, emergency room, or clinic.

fibrosis: A condition resulting from excess fibrous connective tissue that is trying to heal itself.

first-level appeal: A friendly reminder to a payer that the contract was not followed or that a discount was applied without a contract.

Health Insurance Portability and Accountability Act (HIPAA): The law, sometimes called the privacy rule, outlining how certain entities like health plans or clearinghouses can use or disclose personal health information. Under HIPAA, patients must be allowed access to their medical records.

health maintenance organization (HMO): A health management plan that requires the patient to use a primary care physician who acts as a gatekeeper to other health services. In HMOs, patients much seek treatment from the primary physician first, who, if she feels the situation warrants it, can refer the patient to a specialist within the network.

Healthcare Common Procedure Coding System (HCPCS): HCPCS is a standardized code set used to report various services, drugs, and other medical equipment not found in the CPT code set.

Healthcare Financing Administration (HCFA) form: The paper form, also known as the CMS-1500 form, that physicians and clinical practitioners use to submit claims for professional services.

healthcare reimbursement account (HRA): An account funded by the employer that reimburses patients for money spent on out-of-pocket healthcare costs.

health savings account (HSA): A spending account funded pre-tax by the insured party.

illness: A feeling or condition of not being healthy.

implied procedure: A procedure that is listed in the heading of a record but is not documented in the body of the record.

inpatient: A person who has been officially admitted to the hospital under a physician's order. The patient remains an inpatient until the day before the day of discharge.

intermediary: The network that priced the claim for the payer.

International Classification of Diseases (ICD): Maintained by the World Health Organization (WHO), ICD is the common system of diagnosis codes that classifies every disease or health problem reported. These diagnosis codes represent a generalized description of the disease or injury that was the catalyst for the patient/physician encounter.

laparoscopy: A procedure in which the physician views or performs surgery in the abdominal cavity via a tiny camera.

manual processing: The act of processing claims that must be reviewed by a human, not just a computer system.

Medicaid: The federal program created by the 1965 Social Security Act that helps low-income people pay for part or all of their medical bills. The U.S. Department of Health & Human Services regulates the Medicaid program, but each state is responsible for its own program administration. These programs are completely voluntary, but each state has some form of Medicaid program available to eligible residents.

medical biller: The person responsible for correctly billing insurance companies and patients.

medical coder: The person responsible for deciphering the documentation and determining the appropriate CPT and diagnosis code(s) that represent(s) the services provided.

medical necessity: The reason for the visit or surgery that defines the disease process or injury.

medical terminology: Terms that describe illness, injury, conditions, and procedures.

Medicare: The federal health insurance program for people 65 years or older, under age 65 with certain disabilities, and any age with end-stage renal disease or Lou Gehrig's disease. Medicare has four parts: Part A (hospital insurance), Part B (medical insurance), Part C (known as Medicare Advantage Plans), and Part D (prescription drug coverage).

Medicare Administrative Contractor (MAC): The area contractor with the fiduciary contract with CMS to administer payments and denials to providers for Medicare Part A and Medicare Part B claims. MACs encompass several states, and their areas are listed on the CMS website.

Medicare Appeals Council: Part of the Departmental Appeals Board of the U.S. Department of Health & Human Services that provides the final administrative review of claims filed by beneficiaries or healthcare providers and suppliers relating to Medicare entitlements, coverage, and payment.

missing procedure: A procedure for which a diagnosis is listed but no treatment is noted.

modifiers: Alphanumeric symbols used to indicate that the published description of a service or supply has been altered.

multiple procedure discount: The discount applied to the second, third, or any additional procedures when multiple procedures are paid.

multiple procedure reduction: A pay-rate scale in which the first procedure is paid at 100 percent of contractual allowance, while the second may be paid at a reduced rate (often 50 percent), and the third at whatever percentage is deemed appropriate per the contract.

mutually exclusive procedure: A procedure that can't be performed or coded in combination with another. An example would be coding for a fracture repair on the left forearm and then coding for an amputation of the left forearm.

National Correct Coding Initiative (NCCI) edits: Edits established by CMS to help ensure correct coding and eliminate inappropriate coding and reporting. NCCI edits indicate which procedures are incidental to (or included with) another specific CPT code.

National Provider Identifier (NPI): A unique identification number assigned to covered healthcare providers that must be used by health plans and healthcare clearinghouses. HIPAA laws require the use of this number.

network: Essentially a middleman that functions as an agent for commercial payers. Payers may participate with a network that contracts healthcare providers, and the network will price the claims for the payer according to the contract.

non-contracted payers: Payers with whom the provider does not have a contract. Payment for these claims is considered out-of-network and needs to be carefully investigated prior to any patient encounter.

Office of Inspector General (OIG): The federal office that provides oversight for the U.S. Department of Health & Human Services and programs under other HHS institutions, including the Centers for Disease Control and Prevention, the National Institutes of Health, and the Food and Drug Administration.

Office of Medicare Hearings and Appeals (OMHA): The federal office, created by the Medicare Modernization Act of 2003, whose purpose is to streamline and make the appeals process more efficient. OMHA is responsible for the level-three Medicare appeals process.

open procedure: A procedure in which a patient's body is cut open.

open surgery: The term used to refer to traditional procedures involving an incision made by a surgeon.

operative report: The information that the physician dictates, which is then transcribed into a written document that details exactly what was done during the surgery.

outpatient: A patient who comes to a hospital or other facility but has not been admitted as a patient, even if spending the night. Outpatients may come through the emergency room or may be undergoing tests or minor surgery.

payer: The entity that reimburses the provider for services. Insurance companies, government programs like Medicare and Medicaid, and third-party administrators are all payers in the healthcare industry.

payment floor: A set length of time the payer has to complete and process claims.

physician query: The process of asking a physician for clarification about documentation.

portal: An incision made either for visualization or used to insert instruments or a camera.

preauthorization: The process of getting an agreement from the payer to cover specific services before the service is performed; also known as *prior authorization*.

preferred provider organization (PPO): Health management plan that allows patients to visit any providers contracted with their insurance companies. If the patient visits a non-contracted provider, the claim is considered out-of-network.

prefix: The beginning segment of the word. In medical terminology, the prefix is the first indication of the area where the procedures may be located.

preoperative diagnosis A diagnosis made prior to an operation, based on test findings and examination.

Professional Medical Coding Curriculum (PMCC) instructor: The AAPC certification indicating that an individual has received additional instruction above and beyond a coding certification and has passed the certification tests and is, therefore, qualified to teach coding courses.

relative value unit (RVU): A monetary value assigned to every CPT code that represents the amount of work necessary to perform the procedure.

retired modifiers: Modifiers that were removed from the Medicare list and are no longer valid for Medicare. Commercial payers that use older processing software may still use retired modifiers.

revenue cycle: The process, from beginning to end, of translating the work performed by the doctor and his staff into payment. The cycle begins with the appointment and ends with payment from the carrier or patient.

scope families: Procedures that go together. This designation is used when performing an additional, related procedure that does not require additional time or skill by the surgeon and, therefore, is not eligible for additional reimbursement.

scope procedure: A procedure in which a minimally invasive scope (or tiny camera) is used to perform a procedure inside the body.

second-level appeal: A more formal appeal, sent after a first-level appeal has failed to resolve an issue. Any information not previously given should be submitted with this appeal.

suffix: The ending section of the word that, in medical terminology, describes the condition of the area being treated or action that was taken.

super-bill: A billing form created specifically for an individual office or provider that is generally pre-populated with the patient's information and contains the most common diagnosis and procedural codes used by the office.

surgical field: The area being operated on.

tax ID number: An identifying number for a business. (Think of it as a business's Social Security number.)

third-party administrator (TPA): Intermediaries who either operate as a network or access networks to price claims. TPAs often handle claims processing for employers who self-insure their employees rather than use a traditional group health plans.

transmission format: Uniform format in which claim information is sent and received. The template indicates the service received, the reason for the service, the cost of the service, and information identifying the patient and the provider.

Tricare: The healthcare system, funded by the U.S. Department of Defense, that active and retired military and their dependents use.

unbundling: Coding procedure in which the coder includes additional codes on the claim that represent procedures that were incidental to the primary procedure.

underwriting: When a commercial carrier uses the health history and age of employees to price healthcare policies for small companies providing healthcare for their employees. The company then accepts liability for costs incurred under the policy.

Uniform Bill 04 (UB-04) form: The claim form used by facilities, rather than physicians, for their health insurance billing. The UB-O4 form is also called the CMS-1450.

up-coding: Billing for a higher level of service than was performed. Up-coding may be considered fraud if it's done over time with intention.

write-off: The part of the claim not paid by the payer or the patient and that is forgiven. A write-off can also be referred to as a discount.

Index

Numbers

A

B

C

D

E

F

G

H

I

J

L

M

N

O

P

Q

R

S

T

U

V

W

About the Author

Karen Smiley studied human anatomy in addition to Latin and Greek before settling down to raise a family. After several years working around the clock as a stay-at-home mom, she decided to enter the world of medical coding. After earning her certification, she found work at a nationally known practice management company.

She continued to advance her career through working at an ambulatory surgery center, followed by a large billing company where she used her coding and billing skills to identify revenue cycle issues for various clients. She went on to work as an auditor/consultant for different companies and as an independent consultant serving physician practices to maximize their revenue. Along the way, she earned recognition at the local level and assisted in teaching coding. She currently is employed by a large payer organization.

Dedication

I dedicate this book to my family and to the countless physicians who have mentored me along the way. Without the support of these individuals, completion of this book would not have been possible.

Author's Acknowledgments

I wish to express my sincere gratitude to the physicians, nurses, and seasoned coders who have shared their expertise throughout the years. The technical component of this book is a compilation of my own knowledge and experience, much of which was learned working alongside these professionals.

Publisher's Acknowledgments

Executive Editor: Lindsay Lefevere
Project Editor: Katharine Dvorak
Technical Editor: Thomas B. Field, CPC, CEMC
Illustrator: Kathryn Born, MA

Editorial Assistant: Matthew Lowe
Production Editor: Siddique Shaik
Cover Image:
© Nora Carol Photography/Getty Images